Previous Books by David Wanetick

Solution Nation: One Nation is Disproportionately Responding to the World's Most Intractable Problems

The Strategic Negotiator: A Manual for Negotiating at the Elite Level

Business Model Validation: What Makes Business Models Work?

The Power of Incremental Advantage: How Incremental Improvements Produce Dramatically Disproportionate Results

Hot Sector Investing: Profit from Over 100 Emerging Opportunities

Bound for Growth: How to Pick Winning Stocks Using Industry Analysis

PLIGHT OF THE PATENTEE

The Case for Restoring Inventors' Rights

DAVID WANETICK

Chief Executive Officer
Certified Patent Valuation Analyst

ISBN: 978-0-578-60771-9 (sc)
ISBN: 978-0-578-60772-6 (hc)
ISBN: 978-1-684-71298-4 (e)

Library of Congress Control Number: 2019917796

Lulu Publishing Services rev. date: 12/19/2019

Dedication

Plight of the Patentee is dedicated to the inventors who challenge the laws of science and physics...and are crushed by the laws that prevail over the current patent regime.

Table of Contents

Author's Note ix
Introduction xi

Part 1: The Battle Before the Battle 1

Part 2: Gearing Up for Patent Battle 41

Part 3: Inventors Engage in Battle 113

The HairZings Story: A Hair-Raising Patent Ordeal 114
Costs of Litigating Against Infringers Balloon Out of Control 128
    Difficulty of Licensing 138
Inventor Promotion Company Fouls Inventor 143
The Rainbow Loom Story 148
Patent Prosecution Purgatory 156
Retroactive Application of Patent Rules Decimates Patent Portfolio 160
    Challenges in Retaining Contingency Counsel 163
The Patent Trial and Appeal Board Plays Musical Chairs 168
Do Companies Really License Invalid Patents? 177
Crimes Against Patentee Declared in Nuremberg 181
Duplicitous Delaying Tactics Damage Patentees 189
No Way to Treat a Veteran 195
Much Will Be Taken From Those Who Have Given So Much 201
Despite Rampant Infringement, The Mighty (Mugs) Have Not Fallen 205
How Pervasive is Infringement on Amazon? 211
Patentee Busts Infringers But Comes Up Flat 215
Patenting Money Goes Down the Drain 223
Inventor Builds A Better Raccoon Trap 227
Shoot First, Rationalize Later 236
An Unbelievably High Price to Pay for A Million Dollars 243

Examiner to Garage Door Inventor: Don't Let the Door Hit Your Ass on the Way Out ... 260
Patent Prosecution and Litigation Tricks from Netflix ... 267
Transformative Invention Deemed to be Non-Inventive ... 276
The Plight of an Incandescent Inventor ... 283
    A Luminary in Holography ... 284
    The Father of LCD Projectors ... 290
Early-Stage Company Becomes a Victim of Economic Espionage ... 300
The Risks of Patent Reissuance ... 304
Character Assassination and Patent Invalidation ... 308
Waterboarded by the Patent System ... 324
Infringer Walks Away with Disproportionate Share of the Market ... 335
Intimidating Inventors with Fraudulent Cease-and-Desist Letters ... 339
Licensee Seeks to Destroy Licensor ... 343
Inventor Encounters a Gut-Wrenching Ordeal with Sears ... 347
GoPro Delivers a Body Blow to Small Inventor ... 357

Acknowledgments ... 371
About the Author ... 373

Author's Note

Browse the business section of any bookstore or search Amazon. The vast majority of business books focus on wildly successful businesspeople and highly successful innovators. Fair enough. Powerful lessons can be learned from the most successful among us. Reading about the amazing accomplishments of industry luminaries is highly inspirational.

But the vast majority of businesspeople and innovators are not remotely as successful as the people profiled in business books. By definition, ninety percent of innovators cannot be in the top ten percent. Most members of the small business and independent inventor communities merely struggle to survive. In the pages that follow, I try to articulate their plight.

In writing this book, I made absolutely no effort to adhere to the doctrines of political correctness. If we live in a country that cherishes freedom of expression, authors should feel free to express themselves. Authors should neither self-censure nor grovel at the feet of those who voyeuristically strum their sensitivities. Books should be more than processions of pirouettes designed to avoid offending anyone. Authors should not be reduced to feelings fondlers. While most of us are appalled at the censorship that takes place in faraway countries such as China, North Korea and Iran, we have too often come to kneel before the fascistic enforcers of politically correct censorship in our own communities.

There are no safe spaces in these pages. However, I did put some of the social commentary in the first section of this book in indented, grey insets. If you want to avoid reading such commentary, simply skip the insets that appear in Part 1 of this book.

If science and technology are to progress more rapidly, some degree of equity will have to be restored to the patent system. As you read Plight of the Patentee, I hope you will agree that inventors and patentees are deserving of relief.

Without apology,

David Wanetick

Introduction

Generations of Americans have been raised to believe that if they work hard enough for years on end, they may be able to achieve the American Dream. If we work assiduously, persevere, spend our money frugally, invest our savings wisely, behave ethically, and take calculated risks, we just might be able to create and grow a successful business or enjoy a lucrative career.

If our business throws off enough cash or if we are sufficiently remunerated, we may be able to go a step further. If we can accumulate the means or raise the capital necessary for investing in research, we might be able to produce an invention.

If we play by the rules of the patent system, we might be able to protect our invention with patents. Our patented invention—whether it be a life-saving medicine or a recreational product that brings joy to its users—may lead to a one-time cash infusion from a patent buyer or become the source of recurring royalties from a licensee.

That is one example of how the American Dream is supposed to work. In reality, at least when it comes to independent inventors making money from their inventions, achieving financial success as a patentee has become increasingly rare. A great number of American Dreams harbored by individual inventors come to a screeching halt at the research stage. Many independent researchers crash against insurmountable technical hurdles or deplete their funds before they generate commercial interest in their projects.

But let's suppose that after many years of toil, we are among the fortunate ones. A promising invention eventually arises out of our countless failed research initiatives. We wish to own the invention we so diligently and tenaciously created, so we go about seeking patent protection. Since the patent world is foreign to us, we retain a capable patent lawyer. We soon realize that the process of receiving patents is arcane, confusing, expensive, time consuming and indefinite. We accept that we will likely have to address our examiner's concerns in multiple rounds of rejections, participate in interviews with our examiner, obtain declarations from industry authorities attesting to the "non-obviousness" of our invention, narrow or amend the scope of our invention as described in the patent application, and pay sizable fees. We realize that—no matter how much time or money we invest or how many concessions we are willing to make in our quest to obtain patent protection—there is no guarantee that we will be granted a patent. We decide to proceed; we abide by all of the prevailing procedures for obtaining a patent.

Several years later our patent application is granted. We think we are on the road to riches. Six months go by. Then twelve months pass. It is now eighteen months later and nothing happens. Our company is too small to commercialize the invention alone. We can't entice any potential buyers or licensees to take an interest in our patent. None of the candidate partners that we approached are willing to speak with us, let alone make an offer to purchase or license our patent. Such a cold reception could be judicious; we cannot detect any interest on the part of consumers in our intended market. There doesn't appear to be any prospect of our being able to monetize our patent.

We accept our fate as fair. We knew we took enormous risks in investing our hard-earned savings in a research project that was unlikely to succeed. When our research bore fruit, we knew that if we were granted a patent, such issuance would come at a high price in terms of fees paid, efforts expended and patent scope surrendered. Starting from the time we earned the money that we invested in our research, our patenting initiative began well over a decade ago. Precious years of our lives were dedicated to producing a patented invention that no one cares about. We really can't bear to think about all of the sacrifices that we forced our families to make over so many years. The near-necessities that we hoped to provide our families but have been beyond our financial reach—the travel, the educational opportunities, the after-school activities—will haunt us until our last breath. The years we devoted to seeking protection for our inventions will never be returned.

We are devastated but there is no one to blame. We lodge no complaint. We file no claim. We seek no damages. We knew the challenges. We knew the risks. We knew how capitalism works. We realize that, if the rules of the game are adhered to, failure is a fair outcome. Failure is inherent in inventing. We lick our wounds and carry on. Our inventive fire still flickers. We realize that setbacks are an intrinsic factor in making progress.

However, the laws that currently govern intellectual property rights in the United States are far from fair. It is not fair when patent examiners take a decade or more to review patent applications, thereby burning years off the life of the presumptive patent. It is not fair when others misappropriate our trade secrets. It is not fair when others infringe our patents. It is not fair when a government tribunal that acts like a kangaroo court wantonly invalidates patents on a wholesale basis. It is not fair when corrupt judges in foreign countries pressure patentees to accept minimal lump-sum royalties for perpetual licenses. It is not fair that the Court of Appeals for the Federal Circuit regularly extinguishes decades of excruciating sacrifice and millions of dollars of investment with one-word verdicts. It is not fair that rightful inventors are held liable when infringers introduce cancer-causing agents into their knock-offs. It is not fair that patentees are forced to pay to settle meritless, tortious interference suits brought against them by infringers. It is not fair that infringers fabricate prior art and then force legitimate patent applicants to present such forgeries to patent examiners under the fear of being subject to inequitable conduct charges based on failing to disclose prior art. It is not fair that product-producing patentees must compete against infringers who subcontract out the manufacturing of their infringing items to Chinese-prison laborers. It is not fair that infringers continue to produce infringing products for years and years after they agree to settlements that call for them to only sell their remaining inventories.

In the pages that follow, we will meet Inocencia Erfinder, a fictionalized character who portrays the plight of countless self-funded inventors. Part I of this book discusses the never-ending challenges of establishing and running a business. Through Inocencia we have a window on some of the obstacles independent business owners must navigate. We catch a glimpse of a few of the unspoken but inescapable difficulties that proprietors must contend with on a daily basis. We will witness several of the sacrifices and abuses that the small business community constantly confronts through the eyes of Inocencia Erfinder. We will get a taste of the enormous hurdles that small business owners must overcome to eke out any earnings.

Part II of *Plight of the Patentee* begins by alluding to some of the challenges that independent inventors face in funding and performing their research initiatives. But the thrust of Part II of this book focuses on the inequities that plague the American patent system. I try to accomplish this by providing a dialogue between Inocencia and her patent lawyer. While the participants in this interview are fictionalized, the substance of this dialogue is accurate, to the best of my understanding at the time the pages were written. (Of course, that interview does not constitute legal advice and must not be relied upon as such.) Part III of *Plight of the Patentee* provides real-life stories of how dozens of inventors' lives have been shredded by the American patent regime.

Let's get started on our journey together.

Part I
The Battle Before the Battle

Inocencia Erfinder began her career in the restaurant industry as a teenager. Her first job was custodial; she cleaned the toilets and emptied the garbage before she was promoted to busing tables and then dishwasher. Over the years, she performed just about every job a restaurant has to offer—server, hostess, food preparation, cook, catering and delivery. She also gained a wealth of experience in a variety of managerial capacities such as menu development, food procurement, marketing, interviewing candidates and scheduling shifts.

Inocencia was a loyal and dedicated employee. Some might say she harbored old-fashioned values as a young lady—she did what she was told without complaining. But everyone who knew Inocencia for at least a few months knew that she was no automaton. She had a darn good head on her shoulders. Inocencia liked resolving problems whether they involved disappointed customers, conflicts among employees or disputes with vendors. She was a natural tinkerer who enjoyed disassembling equipment, diagnosing problems and testing her repair efforts. Over the years, Inocencia made scores of suggestions that enhanced the profitability of her employers. She loved researching issues ranging from the best kitchen equipment on the market to new techniques for preserving food. She was invigorated by creating low-calorie menus and orchestrating innovative marketing campaigns. She conceived ideas that had the potential to become promising inventions but never had the time or money to turn her ideas into products. Inocencia dreamed of owning her own diner; this would give her the opportunity to make the money and carve out the time she would need to pursue some of her inventions.

By the time she decided to open up a diner of her own in Concord, California, this thirty-eight-year-old restaurateur had two decades of experience in the food service industry. This mother of three young children had no illusions about the difficulties that would await her as the sole proprietor of Concordia Diner. Inocencia was not deterred by the fact that approximately 90% of new businesses fail by their third year. This resolute entrepreneur stared down the statistics of defeat. Inocencia steeled herself to invest most of her life savings and to devote 16-hour days to the diner.

What Inocencia did not know when she decided to open her restaurant is that many surviving business owners find themselves in perpetual struggle. Their existence is that of the living dead. Their businesses are alive, but they never seem to stop circling the drain. On the other hand, small business owners cannot easily shut down their nearly flatlining enterprises. What would be the business cessation costs? Can they really bring themselves to fire so many employees? Could they stand to be marked as failures in their communities? What would the owners do? Who would employ them? Many small business owners are trapped in a slow motion and inescapable nightmare with no end in sight.

Those that have never founded or managed their own business will not appreciate the risks, investments, dedication and sacrifices that starting a business entails. Like most business owners, Inocencia will find herself fighting one fire after another in keeping her business afloat. (Actually, I am being too optimistic. The reality is she will have to fight multiple fires concurrently.) She has to attract customers but has little budget for marketing. Inocencia must purchase high quality food at reasonable prices and then quickly sell her perishable inventory. She must recruit, train and retain staff in an industry notorious for its high-turnover. She has to obtain and maintain equipment. Inocencia is responsible for keeping the books, depositing cash, scrutinizing vendors' invoices, paying the rent, remitting tax payments and making sure adequate insurance coverage is in place at all times.

Before Concordia Diner opens its doors, Inocencia can expect to wait at least six months to receive required permits. She won't be able to generate any revenues during this period but she will have to pay rent or a mortgage. (Permitting is so debilitating that successful restaurateurs decide not to expand their stores—the losses related to multi-month shutdowns are prohibitive.) As the owner of Concordia Diner, Inocencia must comply with a bewildering and ever-changing quilt of regulations—environmental mandates, fire codes, building inspections, food preparation ordinances, payment processing contracts, employment law, advertising law, zoning issues, liquor licensing, and even privacy preservation practices. Some of the regulations that Inocencia is required to comply with are not codified. Upon learning of small businesses being sued for having websites that are not compliant with the Americans with Disabilities Act, Inocencia instructed her web developer to make sure Concordia Diner's website can accommodate the needs of the blind. She was shortly thereafter informed that there are no ADA-standards to comply with.[1]

[1] https://www.forbes.com/sites/legalnewsline/2016/03/29/judges-handling-ada-lawsuits-over-websites-not-waiting-on-doj-regulations/#365ecceb5e0f

Let's consider a few of the work-related regulations that Inocencia faces:

- As Inocencia understands it, she can get in trouble if she hires additional workers before offering her existing employees overtime.

- California law requires employers to provide certain information to employees with their paychecks. Such mandatory notices must include the employee's employment status, terms of employment, their hourly rates, hours worked, total pay and deductions. The notices must include a statement, in multiple languages, that informs employees that they may require their employer to provide them with the same notice in another language.

- If Inocencia fails to post the required Cal/OSHA notice "Safety and Health Protection on the Job" in a conspicuous location frequented by employees, she could face a $12,471 penalty.[2] (There are no requirements for posting employers' rights, probably because employers have so few rights.)

- When Inocencia processes the final paycheck for a departing employee, that check must include not only compensation for all hours worked (including the overtime premium, if applicable), but also payment for all accrued, unused vacation time. If that paycheck is late or does not include all of the wages or vacation pay the employee is owed, the employee may be entitled to waiting time penalties. For every day Concordia Diner is late in remitting the final, correct paycheck to the departing employee, the diner would be liable to pay waiting time penalties equal to a full day of wages at the employee's regular rate, up to a maximum of 30 days. If it takes Concordia Diner ten days to correctly

---

[2] https://calchamberalert.com/2017/09/01/california-dramatically-increases-penalties-for-violations/
Allow me to provide another frame of reference regarding how disproportionate the penalties can be that government authorities impose on businesses. In *Super Pumped: The Battle for Uber* by Mike Isaac, it was revealed that back in 2010, when Uber was a poorly-funded start-up, the San Francisco Municipal Transportation Agency said that Uber faced fines of $5,000 per trip and its senior executives faced as much as 90 days in jail for each day Uber remained in operation beyond October 20, 2010.

process an employee's final check and that employee typically earns $100 per day, Concordia Diner would have to pay $1,000 in waiting time penalties. Under many state laws, the threat of such penalties is compounded by employees having the right to collect attorneys' fees and court costs. The laws of some states hold that violations of wage laws are subject to criminal penalties, including up to 100 days in jail. Worse yet, Inocencia's exposure is aggravated by labor lawyers perpetually on the prowl to instigate class action complaints against employers. Some states have extended the statute of limitations for minimum wage and overtime claims from two years to six years—substantially increasing the exposure for noncompliant employers.

It's not as if it's easy for employers to correct innocent mistakes relating to the likes of payroll calculations, state franchise taxes or federal tax remittances. From time to time, Inocencia fears that she has made an innocent mistake in terms of paying a tax, fee or penalty of one kind or another. So, she calls the appropriate government office to determine the payment that is needed to correct the miscalculation. She waits on hold for at least twenty minutes, often only to have her call dropped. This sequence of events is frequently repeated two or three times. When she finally reaches a person, she finds that the demeanor these bureaucrats exhibit to the businesspeople they are supposed to serve is downright contemptible. They evade answering questions, give incomplete or misleading information, and snicker at the hardships entrepreneurs experience. They do not tell Inocencia how much money she owes. Instead, she is dismissively told to complete and send in other forms. She complies but, in many cases, the government workers claim that these recently-completed forms were not received by the appropriate department. These circuitous procedures waste Inocencia's time and end up costing her more in penalties.

No matter how convoluted, constrictive or contradictory regulations become, Inocencia and her staff must produce results from the time Concordia Diner opens in the morning until it closes at night. Deliveries must be inspected, weighed and unpacked. Shelves and refrigerators must be stocked. Food must be prepped and preserved. Meals must be prepared to the satisfaction of every customer. Hostesses must be cheerful and polite. Servers must be knowledgeable about the menus. The diner must be clean—trash must be timely removed, the floors swept and the toilets scrubbed.

The imperative for Inocencia to perform across a wide spectrum of activities, all day and every day, is in stark contrast to the politicians who promulgate the regulations that suffocate small businesses. These politicians are garlanded for the length of time they hold office rather than what they accomplish. U.S. Representatives such as Elijah Cummings boast about "serving" their communities for thirty years even though their communities have decayed under the yoke of such service. Liberal politicians are celebrated for their failed stewardships of their communities whereas independent business professionals are made to feel embarrassment for whatever success they are ultimately able to produce.

No business owner has the luxury of allowing his business to deteriorate for thirty years, let alone boast about its sorry state. If one mouse were ever to streak across the floor of Inocencia's restaurant, negative reviews would be posted on social media, Concordia Diner's reputation would be destroyed, traffic to the restaurant would decline, fines would be issued and her business would be at risk of shutting down. The same consequences would await Inocencia if more than a spec of feces were ever to be found in Concordia Diner's bathrooms. Not so for liberal politicians. The swarms of rats running around Los Angeles are causing outbreaks of typhus and maybe even Bubonic plague. There is so much human feces on the streets of San Francisco that apps such as Snapcrap have arisen to enable pedestrians to notify clean-up crews as to where human excrement lies. Profitable businesses are pinatatized for their success while liberal leaders are feted despite their gross mismanagement of their cities. Small businesses can't get away with a fraction of the crap that liberal leaders get away with. Business professionals must deliver while politicians dither. Proprietors must produce results but politicians are placed on pedestals based on their pontifications.

Achieving results day in and day out requires hard work. It also requires making sound decisions. The business decisions that Inocencia must make have long feedback loops and are difficult to reverse. The consequences of making suboptimal decisions relative to the countless issues associated with running a small business can be severe. Wrong decisions repel customers, deprive businesses of revenue, increase the costs of equipment and supplies, fray relationships with vendors, cause a loss of morale on the part of employees, shake the confidence of investors, attract regulatory scrutiny and generate unwelcome attention from the media.

Don't pity Inocencia too much, you might say; she can always seek advice from knowledgeable outside advisors. But identifying and retaining quality advisors can be an arduous pursuit. Research must be conducted, referrals solicited, introductory discussions need to be scheduled and consummated, and references reviewed. The best advisors might be out of reach for Inocencia as they are either too busy to take on small clients, have conflicts with existing clients or are just too expensive. Once a suitable advisor has been identified, the scope and duration of the engagement must be negotiated. So too must his fees.

This laborious process of seeking and retaining advisors must be repeated for every advisor that Inocencia wishes to retain. She can retain legal counsel to advise her on the legal quandaries she faces. But this advice is often prohibitively expensive and riddled with disclaimers, exclusions and scope limitations. Five thousand dollars after seeking advice from a lawyer, Inocencia's questions remain unanswered. Essentially all of the consequences of making bad decisions or falling outside of the boundaries of laws and regulations remain with Inocencia.

> Concordia Diner can be fatally blindsided even before it opens its doors. Consider what happened to Innovative Higher Ed Consulting, a two-woman startup in New York. When it was in the process of setting up its website, cyber thieves ran some 100,000 stolen credit card numbers through that burgeoning site's payment system. The fraudsters paid $1 each time they ran a stolen credit card number through the site to test if the card numbers were still valid. Shortly after the rightful cardholders complained about these charges, Innovative Higher Ed's bank charged the nascent business $25 for each chargeback. The $27,000 collection notice that Innovative Higher Ed received was enough to cause its founders to abort their startup enterprise. With everything else Inocencia would

have to worry about when establishing Concordia Diner, it would be very easy for her to overlook activating the payment processor's security features when the diner's website is in an embryonic state. But, as we have seen, such an innocent oversight could be catastrophic.

Even if Inocencia's decisions are largely sound, she cannot possibly allow for every contingency. Years of hard work can be destroyed by any number of contingencies over which Inocencia has no control. Inocencia must contend with the nearly unbounded risks inherent in running a restaurant; a worksite boiling with stress, fire, knives of every kind, alcohol and a tendency to attract employees who have histories of substance abuse. Concordia Diner's payroll processing provider might declare bankruptcy, leaving in limbo the question of whether the diner's federal, state and local taxes have been delivered to the appropriate authorities. A customer might choke on his food. Concordia Diner's reputation can be damaged by fake reviews posted on social media by cutthroat competitors, disgruntled employees, employees' jilted lovers, jealous neighbors, or duplicitous customers such as those who place a strand of their own hair on their plates after eating their meals so as to connive the diner out of free dinners. As we will see, Concordia Diner will be targeted by left-wing activists. (We will meet the key left-wing antagonist in later pages when I introduce the allegorical Hans-Manuel Cherkoff, a fictionalized professor of Animal Humanities at the University of California at Berkeley. Professor Cherkoff is a frequent customer at Concordia Diner but harbors a venomous vendetta against the diner.)

Let's traverse a few of the innumerable challenges and inequities that entrepreneurs constantly confront. We will begin with a discussion of some of the financing issues that arise when establishing small businesses.

For Inocencia, the financing of her emerging business could be relatively easy or completely ruinous. She may be able to borrow money or raise capital from friends and family. She may be able to obtain a Small Business Administration loan. She may be able to obtain credit quickly by margining her securities. If she owns a home or the real estate on which her restaurant is located, she may be able to obtain a line of credit. However, no matter how well Inocencia complies with the terms her bank sets, her line of credit can be pulled without warning. She may have to load up on high-interest credit card debt. If she later becomes desperate, she may have to dip into her (payroll) tax withholdings accounts, a measure that is fraught with risk.

When she opens Concordia Diner, Inocencia must preserve capital, which is a nice way of saying that she is capital deficient. So Inocencia decides to lease computers, point-of-sale terminals and a variety of kitchen equipment. She has no idea how many ways she can get in trouble entering seemingly innocuous equipment lease agreements. If she fails to notify a lessor of her intention to terminate a lease at least 180 days before the contract expires, she will be forced into a (one-year) renewal. Of course, many proprietors of small businesses will fail to appropriately calendarize all relevant renewal dates for the equipment lease agreements they enter into.

Entering into lease agreements is just one of dozens of issues that demand Inocencia's attention. But the lessors that she negotiates with are real sharks; equipment leasing is their primary business. Their contracts are prepared by lawyers who have developed an expertise in negotiating and structuring equipment leases over many years. Entrepreneurs like Inocencia are invariably outgunned when it comes to negotiating equipment lease contracts. How many entrepreneurs are aware that the enhancements or upgrades they make to leased equipment belong to the lessor? How well can Inocencia be expected to understand the tax implications of leasing? Even if she takes the time to become familiar with a potpourri of leasing terms—such as end-of-term purchase price provisions, restocking fees, refurbishing fees, and shipping fees—she still will not have any leverage to negotiate a more favorable agreement. She may be able to ask a few intelligent questions of her prospective lessors, but Inocencia will not have time to negotiate with a multitude of equipment leasing companies.

If Concordia Diner hits a rough patch, Inocencia may have to pursue a small business loan offered by an aggressive capital provider. She must be careful because there are financial scammers that prey on struggling entrepreneurs like herself. Inocencia could agree to accept a "merchant cash advance" which is really a loan that can carry an interest rate in excess of 400% per year. Because these loans are called "merchant cash advances" they skirt lending regulations. With such high interest rates, Inocencia's interest payments could very well end up exceeding the principal she initially borrows.

Inocencia's fate could become far worse if she gets entangled with an unscrupulous provider of merchant cash advances. A shady lender is likely to require that Inocencia sign a "confession of judgment" governed under the laws of New York. When signing a confession of judgment, borrowers give up their right to defend themselves in the event their lenders file suit against them. Should a lender obtain a confession of judgment from Inocencia, the lender can accuse her of having a hiccup in her loan repayment plan and seize her assets held at other institutions. The lender need not present proof of Inocencia failing to meet her repayment obligations; many times, when proof is presented it is forged by the lender. Such asset seizures could be triggered quickly and with no notification to Inocencia. Due to lenders receiving their principal, interest and additional fees so quickly, lenders are often better off enforcing confessions of judgment than managing performing loans. The combination of having her cash balances depleted and the confession of judgment in place will almost certainly result in Inocencia being unable to obtain legal representation. Succumbing to pernicious merchant cash advance outfits could doom both Concordia Diner and Inocencia.

It is said that in real estate, the only three things that matter are location, location and location. Inocencia will have to find a site for her restaurant that is traversed by significant flows of traffic during much of the day. A building located on a corner is especially desirable as its signage will be seen by traffic flowing from different directions. Access to public transit could be crucial for many of Inocencia's employees. But locating her diner too close to throngs of competing restaurants could be problematic. Since she is interested in entering into a long-term lease, Inocencia will need to determine the safety of the neighborhood and project the vibrancy of the site many years into the future. Finding a suitable site on reasonable leasing terms will not be easy. Inocencia needs a real estate broker. But will she really be well-served by a real estate agent given that real estate agents are paid by landlords?

> Maybe Inocencia should not locate her diner too close to a government building such as a post office or the Concord BART station. Since the penalties for assaulting government workers are more severe than those meted out for assaulting private sector employees, criminals are better off battering small business owners than government workers. In the eyes

of many left-leaning legislators, the lives of entrepreneurs don't matter as much as those of government employees.

And it's not as if the BART police care about the safety of BART passengers. Panhandlers pervade BART platforms and terror reins on the trains. Throughout the BART system you will find panhandling, pickpocketing, menacing behavior, death stares, grotesque gestures, physical taunts, shouting, break dancing, blaring music, belching, spitting, farting, vandalizing, spraying graffiti, urinating, defecating, vomiting, undressing, gambling, groping, copulating in every conceivable position, masturbating, consuming a wide range of alcoholic drinks, smoking, vaping, snorting and injecting a kaleidoscopic variety of drugs, beatings, rapes, starting fires, stabbings and, sometimes, even murder.[3] But the spineless BART police are nowhere to be found during the commission of any of these crimes, which occur every hour in which BART purports that its trains are in operation. Some official BART apologist will claim that jurisdictional issues are responsible for rendering the BART police impotent. (Inocencia is shocked at the irony of the situation; criminals are granted carte blanche to move about while the movement of BART police is severely restricted.) However, such official statements are contradicted when eight BART police officers converge, from every direction, on a frail octogenarian who struggles to lift a bottle of water to his lips so that he can take his heart medication. Four police officers could easily have made the arrest—drinking is nominally prohibited on BART—but Bay Area liberals value bloating government sector payrolls over efficient use of taxpayer remittances.

The real estate lease is no less important than the diner's location. If Inocencia cannot lease a building that provides sufficient square footage

[3] The incident that most disgusted Inocencia began when a well-dressed, successful-looking man who would exit at the Walnut Creek BART station held his little dog close to his chest. At first, he kissed his dog on its head. Then the dog licked its owner. Twenty seconds later, the two were full-on French kissing. The other passengers looked on approvingly. Inocencia felt sick to her stomach.

and parking for a reasonable rate, her diner will most likely be doomed from the outset. She needs to determine if she will be permitted to provide outdoor seating as well as project the likelihood of obtaining a liquor license. In addition to the rent, she will have to budget for property taxes, insurance premiums and common area expenses. Each of these considerations requires research. Take common area expenses, for instance. Common area expenses typically include maintenance and repairs of the common walkways and parking lots, security, property management and utilities for common areas. These common area expenses can be tricky; Inocencia will have to determine how likely it is that other neighboring storefronts will remain occupied. As other associated lessees vacate their premises, Inocencia will have to shoulder a greater proportion of the common area charges. If all of the associated tenants depart, Inocencia will have to pay 100% of the common area expenses.

Inocencia will have to become acquainted with restaurant-specific issues such as whether the building includes a hood system, fire suppression system and a grease interceptor.[4] Will she have to install her own electric panel or can electricity be transmitted from a central hub owned by the landlord? What are the economics of each scenario? Is the building compliant with the Americans with Disabilities Act? If not, how expensive will it be to bring the building into compliance? Who is responsible for repairing the roof, or replacing it? Is Concordia Diner expected to maintain the waterlines inside and outside of the building?

Inocencia should understand a bit about the agreements the landlord has with other tenants. She would want to know if other restaurants have exclusive-use clauses in their lease agreements that might bar Concordia Diner from serving certain dishes (such as Mexican fare or sushi). On the other hand, Inocencia should insist on her lease agreement containing restrictions on which neighboring tenants the landlord is allowed to accept. Politically correct drivel aside, neither Inocencia nor any other bootstrapping restaurateur would want a pet shop or drug counseling center located within a few doors of their business.

Inocencia must be prepared to negotiate other terms typically found

---

[4] A kitchen hood system is a device that contains a mechanical fan. This fan hangs above the stove and removes airborne grease, combustion products, fumes, smoke, heat and steam from the air. Restaurants can easily spend $12,000 having hood systems professionally installed.

in commercial real estate leases such as landlord delivery condition, tenant improvement allowances, rent abatement, relocation clauses, options to extend and assignment rights. Inocencia may not be completely content with each clause in her lease agreement but she may have to provide a personal guarantee to the landlord to secure the structure.

Even something as mundane as collecting payment requires careful consideration on Inocencia's part. She must accept cash payments. What does she need to do to make sure there is no skimming? Should there be a dedicated cashier or should each server check out their own customers? Are the security cameras configured to catch a cashier pocketing cash? How frequently will cash deposits have to be made? How can these deposits be made in a safe manner? Is it better to make these deposits at random times during the day? Will making deposits at random times interrupt the diner's workflow? Who will make these deposits? What are the diner's liabilities if an employee is injured while making deposits?

Of course, Concordia Diner will accept the major credit cards and debit cards. But how much of Concordia's revenues will be consumed by related fees? Comparing fees charged by each credit card company is difficult since there are so many fees, and credit card processors quote their fees differently. Inocencia will have to try to determine who offers the most compelling combination of processing fees, intercharge fees, monthly minimums and chargeback fees. Other crucial issues such as security will have to be considered. There seems to be a constant stream of new payment methods hitting the market. Should Concordia Diner accept ApplePay? GooglePay? Stripe? Facebook's Libra? Will newer payment methods be reliable, blindingly fast and widely popular? How much complexity is involved in accepting the proliferating payment methods? Can the cashiers keep up with the advances in payment technologies? Do the new payment methods require hardware that taxes limited counterspace?

Like every other business, Concordia Diner needs to bring customers in the door. But how should Inocencia grow her clientele? Should she hire someone to hand out flyers in front of her diner? Maybe. But are there local ordinances stipulating where and when such fliers can be disseminated? Will Inocencia have to police the appropriate discarding of fliers? Will Concordia Diner face fines if the marketing materials end up littering the sidewalk? Whoever she finds to distribute such material must have a pleasing and non-overbearing appearance. But how many well-put-together people would want such a gig and for how long? What exposure would the diner have if an altercation arose between the flyer-hander-outers and pedestrians? What if Concordia Diner is located just a few doors down from a liquor store, which is frequented by all kinds of characters? Does Inocencia really want just anyone off the street as a customer? If the flyer distributors apply discretion as to whom they offer flyers, will Inocencia be liable for discrimination or accused of profiling?

Should Concordia Diner undertake a mass mailing campaign? Inocencia might be able to target such mailings to more desirable clientele based on zip code, income or the recipient subscribing to food-related magazines. There is merit in sending out mailings but doing so is extremely time consuming and expensive. Inocencia would have to sketch out the copy of the marketing piece. A graphics artist would need to put the brochure in InDesign to make the piece look appealing. Lists of recipients would have to be obtained. This is a crucial step. No matter how attractive the brochure may be, it will be a complete waste of money if the wrong audience receives it. As Inocencia researches the issue, she realizes that one problem with obtaining a good list of targets is that the more relevant an available list is, the less likely the list provider (often a publication, trade association, or conference organizer) will approve Inocencia's request to rent the list. Once she purchases a list, the list provider will send it directly to the printer, due to the list provider's fear that list renters will make unauthorized use of their data. How will Inocencia know what she is getting? How many redundant or bogus addresses will be included in the list? For all Inocencia knows, the list provider could send the printer a list of fictitious recipients.

Inocencia could place an ad in a local newspaper but in the age of electronic media who reads newspapers? Can she trust the paper's audited circulation statistics, assuming such verified data exists? And how many times would she have to run the ad to attract any customers? The same questions could be asked relative to running ads on the radio. Concordia Diner could sponsor local sports teams as a means of increasing its visibility in the community. But which teams should the diner sponsor? How much will it cost? How much visibility will her business get for its sponsorship? Will other teams in the area be less inclined to frequent the diner if it sponsors rival teams? In the meantime, Inocencia hopes that word-of-mouth will bring customers in the door. But she really can't control word-of-mouth referrals and, in any event, it takes a long time for word-of-mouth to bring in steady streams of customers.

Inocencia could ramp up Concordia's digital marketing efforts, but she would be out of her element. Concordia's website functions but doesn't have any bells or whistles. Should Inocencia bother with upgrading Concordia's website? How would she determine if her investments in the website are effective?

Should Inocencia reconfigure Concordia Diner's website for mobile users? Or should she have an app developed? Will creating an app mean that Concordia Diner will be able to avoid working with meal-delivery services such as DoorDash? Inocencia would be happy to be relieved of paying delivery services their steep commissions but does she really want the diner to be responsible for managing its own delivery service? What will the switch from relying on external delivery services to managing delivery internally mean in terms of customer service, reputation, legal liabilities and insurance rates? Inocencia is learning that there are few easy decisions: Every decision that confronts Inocencia impacts other, often seemingly remote, parts of her business.

Everyone seems to rave about the power of Google's AdWords. AdWords campaigns supposedly deliver potential customers to advertisers' sites when consumers are most likely to make purchases. Concordia Diner would be able to control its AdWords budget and track results. However, Inocencia has heard from her friends that it takes many months and thousands of dollars in investments until AdWords campaigns begin delivering any real traffic to advertisers' sites.

Should Inocencia give it a shot? She doesn't know much about search engine optimization, page authority, relevancy scores, lookalike audiences, lead nurturing, quality scores or hard bounces versus soft bounces. She has heard enough about click fraud to be skeptical of reported click-through rates, costs per impression, engagement rates and costs per acquisition. What will happen to Concordia Diner's page rankings if she stops using AdWords? If Inocencia suspends the AdWords campaign, will Concordia Diner's website be banished to the hinterlands when people search for diners in Concord? It is reasonable to believe that this may be the case; when anyone stops paying any vendor, the quality of their service deteriorates dramatically. Maybe it is better for Inocencia to never begin marketing through Google's AdWords.

There is another reason that Inocencia wishes to keep her profile under Google's radar. As is her right, from time-to-time, Inocencia has made lawful financial contributions to campaigns of politicians whose views are to the right of Leon Trotsky. These contributions can easily be discovered by searching public records. No one can search such records more efficiently than Google and Google detests conservatives. Googlers openly and proudly hound their peers that have right-of-center views. Google directors have taken to calling Googlers with such views "repulsive" in mass emails. Google awards "peer bonuses"—cash bonuses awarded by fellow Googlers when one's work is recognized as exemplary—to Googlers that disparage their fellow employees whose views are inconsistent with the vast majority of Googlers.[5]

Google—which removed the "Don't be evil" mantra from the preface of its corporate code of conduct in 2018—maintains vast personal data on hundreds of millions of people. Inocencia knows that it wouldn't take long for Google to figure out that she is the owner of Concordia Diner. Inocencia fears that if Google's management encourages destroying the careers of its own employees that have right-of-center views, it will have no compunction about destroying a business owned by a stranger with similar views.

Recruiting, managing and retaining good employees is Inocencia's biggest challenge. Finding reliable help in the restaurant industry is never easy. For many candidates, employment with Concordia Diner will be their first job. Few interviewees have extensive employment histories to review or references to check. Some job-seekers have pasts that intersect with the criminal justice system. People who work behind the scenes at restaurants are not always terribly articulate; some candidates do not speak English as their first language.

Maybe having a strong command of English no longer matters given that employers are so restricted in the questions they are allowed to ask

[5] https://clashdaily.com/2018/01/tucker-carlson-google-hates-white-male-conservatives-heres-proof/

job candidates. The inability to understand English is no excuse to deny a candidate a job—or to terminate an employee.[6] Any question that Inocencia poses during an interview can be deemed to be evidence of discrimination, an invasion of privacy or otherwise outside of legal bounds.

Every hire represents a risk. Every candidate that Inocencia interviews, every person that she employs, and every employee that she terminates is simply one more person that can sue her. Inocencia can't discriminate against former convicts but is liable if a recent convict assaults his co-workers or customers. It doesn't matter who she hires or doesn't hire; some liberal activist like Hans-Manuel Cherkoff will accuse Inocencia of some type of discrimination. It seems to Inocencia that the only way she can avoid being sued for employment discrimination is to hire whoever the hell walks through the door. But even this isn't enough; proving that there was never a trace of discrimination in her hiring practices doesn't matter. Inocencia could still be hit with a catchall "impact disparity suit" which means that some protected classes of people are not adequately represented on Concordia's employee roster. Concordia Diner could be exposed if employment lawyers determine that "intersectionality" exists at Concordia Diner. This means that if Inocencia has a history of promoting a high proportion of Hispanics and Asians, her diner could still be exposed if she has not promoted enough people that are both Asians and Hispanics.

On top of all of this, Inocencia is expected to eradicate whatever pay disparities that may exist between male and female workers. Professor Cherkoff may think that "gender equality" has a nice ring to it but to Inocencia it is an encroachment on her ability to manage her business. A host of factors collectively determine the wages that various staff members earn at Concordia Diner. Some jobs are harder to perform while other positions are more difficult to fill. No two jobs are exactly the same and no two employees perform all facets of the same job equally well. An employee's versatility, skills, attitude towards work, length of employment, reliability and customer service ratings are just some of the considerations that account for one's wages. Besides, in the restaurant business, much of the compensation earned by Concordia's wait staff is a function of tips,

---

[6] As a reference point, New York City's Commission on Human Rights announced that calling people "illegal alien," commenting about someone's "limited English proficiency," or using gender pronouns other than those preferred by employees and tenants carry fines of $250,000.
https://www.foxnews.com/us/new-york-city-250g-illegal-alien-immigration

which customers determine. Should the diner be liable if customers tip one gender more than the other?

Gender equality laws threaten to dramatically inflate payrolls. Guess which direction wages will move when it is determined that a woman is making less than a man of equal skill and contribution? The man's pay won't be reduced, rather the woman's pay will be enhanced. Wage adjustments will always hurt Inocencia in the pocketbook.

But how can one know which jobs should offer comparable pay? And how should comparable pay scales be modulated to take into account the quality of work being performed by the various employees in those positions? Should a hostess earn the same wages as a busboy? Hostesses can add a sense of decorum to the dining experience but busboys lift heavy trays of dirty dishes. Should an assistant chef be paid the same as a cashier? Which is more important, collecting money or preparing food? Which position requires more training? Which position can be covered more easily if the designated employee misses a shift? Which individual performs his job better? What metrics are in place to make such a determination?

These largely unanswerable questions are compounded by gender fluidity. If employees don't know their genders, do not identify with any particular gender, or wish to be gender fluid, how can Inocencia produce statistics relating to the compensation paid to men versus women? If she tries to answer this question based on what she observes, is she more likely to be sued because certain employees resent being classified according to their birth genders? Wouldn't Inocencia have to ask her employees highly personal questions to ascertain their gender identities? Wouldn't such questions be invasions of privacy?

Labor lawyers have caused the employer-employee relationship to become completely skewed. First, a small detour. Did you watch the movie *Goodfellas*? If so, do you remember the scene where the mobster Henry Hill beats his mistress's (Janice's) boss to a bloody pulp? After Henry and his fellow thugs bloody Janice's boss's face, Henry menacingly warns, "Janice can do whatever she wants." Employment lawyers are modern-day thugs; by strangling business owners with inequitable labor laws, they allow employees to do whatever they want.

Thanks to the ever-present risk of existential litigation as well as draconian fines from the Equal Employment Opportunity Commission and similar state agencies, employees have become largely unmanageable. Employees can arrive late. They can take days off when they wish. They can text throughout their shifts. They can be rude to their bosses, colleagues and customers. They can choose not to do what they are told. They can sabotage their place of business. They are forgiven for failing to sign out, which is contrary to company policy. Inocencia struggles to maintain a dress code but as long as employees can allude to some religious or cultural reference, they can dress however they wish even if such appearances are extremely off-putting to the vast majority of Concordia's customers.

While employees can do just about whatever they like, employers are restricted not only in their actions, but also in their right to speak freely. Every utterance that Inocencia makes to an employee can be held against her. She is afraid to commend her employees when they do their jobs well because such praise could be used against her in a wrongful termination suit. Anything Inocencia says can be cast as racist, sexist, ageist or otherwise discriminatory or demeaning to one's ethnicity, gender, gender identity or sexual preference. Simply saying, "you need to serve the customers their food faster" can be classified as a micro-aggression. Such statements are considered harassment and many businesses operate under a one-strike-and-the-employer-is-out regime. The ever-metastasizing restrictions on free speech render it increasingly difficult for proprietors to manage their businesses.

In many ways, Inocencia's employees receive better terms working at the diner than she does. Founders of businesses often expect to lose money for several years when starting up their enterprises. Further losses might be sustained as a function of seasonality, cyclicality, operating challenges, competition or as a result of other exogenous shocks. Any economic shock could result in an unavoidable delinquent tax remittance. Inocencia is petrified that the IRS will seize Concordia Diner if she gets behind on her tax payments; she has overheard armed IRS agents boasting about their seizures of businesses more than once at the diner. Inocencia's employees will never have to absorb losses or invest their capital in the diner. Nor will they tolerate even slight delays in receiving their paychecks. Employees stand at the front of the line in terms of receiving their wages while proprietors can take money out of their businesses only after all of the bills have been paid. Inocencia can't give herself a pension without providing her employees with pension coverage. Employers must administer their employees' unemployment insurance payments but can seldom collect unemployment benefits when their businesses fold.

Inocencia often feels that she is working for her employees—not the other way around. These thoughts are especially pronounced when she knows that some of her employees occasionally cheat on their timecards. She knows that food and tableware are occasionally smuggled out the back door. For the most part, Inocencia considers such acts of minor theft as costs of doing business; better to overlook a little stealing than to have to recruit and train a new employee. It is better for employee retention if she can demonstrate to other employees that Concordia Diner is a stable employer, as evidenced by low staff turnover. Inocencia prefers to avoid taking unnecessary risks of being sued for firing someone. Sometimes there are no great courses of action to take when running a business; there are only less bad alternatives.

Inocencia isn't running a charity but she does what she can to help her employees earn a living and to work their way up at Concordia Diner. When she can afford to do so, Inocencia allows employees to work additional hours and to earn overtime, even when the workload does not warrant the extra hours. She allows Veronica, Concordia Diner's catering manager, to book events that Inocencia has essentially closed so that Veronica can collect healthy commissions. A few years ago, several of Concordia's employees requested that the diner arrange for them to receive payroll advances. Inocencia knew that Concordia Diner would be squeezed—the restaurant wouldn't be able to offset the accelerated payroll disbursements by stretching out its remittances to vendors. Nevertheless, Inocencia accommodated this request and facilitated payroll advance services several years ago.

Employees don't appreciate all that employers do for them. The bonuses that Inocencia stretches to give to her better employees when the diner is profitable become a floor for their expectations a year later. When employees clamor for a better "work-life balance" they mean they want more time off for the same pay. A better "work-life balance" for her employees means that Inocencia will have to work longer hours and see her family less. Employees do not take rejections of their requests for additional benefits well; they label employers as "haters." Employees denied additional benefits magically and immediately become toxicologists; they designate their workplaces as toxic environments, bereft of any redeeming qualities. There is a whole genre of books that bash business owners and bosses—some of the titles include, *How to Work for a Jerk: Your Success is the Best Revenge*; *A Survival Guide for Working With Bad Bosses: Dealing With Bullies, Idiots, Back-stabbers, And Other Managers from Hell*; *The Toxic*

Boss Survival Guide: Tactics for Navigating the Wilderness at Work; *The Asshole Survival Guide: How to Deal with People Who Treat You Like Dirt*; *My Boss is a Jerk: How to Survive & Thrive in a Difficult Work Environment under the Control of a Bad Boss*; and, *Bad Bosses, Crazy Coworkers & Other Office Idiots: 201 Smart Ways to Handle the Toughest People Issues.* Within two years of arranging for her staff to receive payroll advances, Inocencia's concern for her employees was reciprocated with a class action lawsuit based on the allegedly usurious interest rates that the selected intermediaries charged.

During her 16-hour work-days, Inocencia often deprives herself of the breaks that she is legally required to give her employees every few hours. Inocencia gives her two-top managers and two chefs two-weeks of paid time-off each year even though she must work doubly hard when these employees are away from the diner. There is no paid time-off for Inocencia and when she takes time away from the diner, she is still connected to its operations through phone calls, emails and texts. Inocencia has fielded calls when attending weddings, graduation ceremonies, anniversary celebrations, her children's birthday parties, and while visiting hospitalized relatives. She rarely stays away from the diner for more than three days because she can't afford the inevitable slowdown that will result from her absence. Small business owners like Inocencia don't have time to be sick; they are the first to recover from illnesses and the last to file (let alone fraudulently file) disability claims.

Inocencia will be maligned if her employees are not paid ever-escalating livable wages. But there is no notion of livable wages or livable returns-on-investment for entrepreneurs. Radical redistributionists such as Hans-Manuel Cherkoff never worry about income inequality when founders of small businesses are losing money or earning less than their lowest-paid employees. Liberals are so full of contempt for business owners like Inocencia that they do not include them in their definition of "the working class" even though proprietors of small businesses work far harder than their employees. Liberals don't even count small business owners among "the people."

Even if Inocencia turns Concordia Diner into a success, her employees are likely to make better profit margins than she will. Every check presented to customers suggests gratuities of 18%, 20% and 25%. Tips at the lowest end of this range far exceed the pre-tax margins that Concordia Diner can hope to earn. (As an aside, the tips that servers collect are in addition to their hourly wages due to California law prohibiting tip income from counting towards required hourly wages.)

> Listening to liberals address social issues such as minimum wages is like witnessing a politicized auction. The mayor of Seattle bids $14.75 an hour for minimum wages. Two days later, the mayor of San Francisco counters with $15.25. The next day, the mayor of New York tops that with $16.05. The following morning, the mayor of Los Angeles cries out for $16.65. Later that afternoon, the governor of California bests that with $17.95. Over the next few hours, the mayor of Portland ups the ante at $18.35. And the bidding with other peoples' money continues. Unions, workers' rights groups, the media and academics add their two cents to the discussion. Everyone has a voice in the wages employees should receive except for the people that pay them.

Despite all of the difficulties and uncertainties that Inocencia faces, there are few avenues for her to seek advice. Formal advisors are expensive. She doesn't have the luxury of intimating concerns about running her diner to her employees, for fear of shaking their confidence in her managerial ability. She can't afford for good employees to mutiny. Inocencia must constantly project confidence, no matter how many battles she is fighting or how much trepidation she feels about the future. Inocencia is learning that being a CEO is lonely.

The one thing worse than contending with all of the challenges of running a busy business is silence. Inocencia would trade a hectic day for a quiet one any day. When customers don't patronize the diner, revenues freeze up and the losses mount. Rent and employees have to be paid. Inventory spoils. Employees begin to look for the exits. Customers begin to believe that something is wrong with the diner if they don't see other patrons. Slippage can quickly snowball into a vicious cycle.

Just like most small business owners, Inocencia's struggles are not confined to her place of business. She strives to be a good mother. Inocencia doesn't have much time to take her three kids to their activities—her husband and mother help out and babysitters are relied upon for backup logistical support. But she does make a priority of helping her kids with their studies, especially as she has become increasingly disappointed with their teachers. In order to ensure that her children progress academically, Inocencia spends a large part of her few discretionary hours working through lessons contained in the workbooks she purchases at the after-school centers where her kids are enrolled.

Many of the assignments her youngest child receives from his teacher are really projects that parents are supposed to complete; for example, baking the child's favorite dessert or preparing mini family albums. "Who do these teachers think they are, giving parents homework?" Inocencia thinks to herself. "Not only do I have to work about five times as hard as teachers, they are giving me assignments. What gall!" Protesting such assignments with teachers, principals or school boards is impossible without Inocencia risking being labeled as an uncaring parent. (Who knows where such a tarnished reputation might lead. Maybe Inocencia's kids will be taken away from her on account of her being a bad parent.) No parent wants to get on teachers' bad sides as they have asymmetric power over their captive students for at least six hours every day school is in session. If Inocencia ruffles one of the teachers, will her child be deemed to have "trouble channeling his energy" and be placed on a heavy Ritalin regimen?

The more Inocencia intersects with her children's teachers, the more frustrated she becomes. She knows that any deviation from Lehrerverehrung—unconditional and unmitigated praise of all teachers—is sacrilegious and a serious violation of politically correct permissible thought. Inocencia will be the first to admit that there are many wonderful educators; these teachers not only teach their students a great deal but instill in them a hunger for life-long learning. Fair enough. But WTF? No one in their right mind can honestly say that all teachers are wonderful. Some are downright terrible and most fall in between these extremes. Even Inocencia's teacher-friends estimate in private conversations that about 30% of teachers are excellent, 10% are terrible and 60% are mediocre.

If the vast majority of teachers were wonderful, American students wouldn't consistently rank so poorly in one academic test after another compared to their peers from around the world. If the overwhelming majority of teachers were fantastic, public schools would not be a de facto line of last resort. Parents who have the time homeschool their kids. Parents who have the budget send them to private schools. Millions of other parents yearn to send their kids to charter schools but are blocked by politicians intimidated by teachers' unions. And make no mistake about it, due to the power of the teachers' unions, school days and curriculum are designed to benefit the teachers, not the students.

American kids spend less time in school than in just about any other developed country. The number of "no-school" days always seems to creep up, forcing business-owner parents like Inocencia to work doubly hard. Inocencia's children have a solid two weeks of early dismissal running up to the Christmas break. Many school districts have one early-dismissal each week, which is supplemented by about a dozen other random early-dismissals during the already truncated school year. And as a gratuitous F*&K YOU to parents, school authorities don't coordinate these random early dismissals. This means that parents with kids attending two different schools in the same school district have to make arrangements for the care of their kids on the twenty additional days that random early dismissals are in effect.

Nonetheless, teachers demand more and more time off, despite the fact that kids are deprived of millions of lunches when school is not in session. In fact, one of the touted benefits of the four-day school week, which appeals to many teachers, is that money will be saved by not serving kids their lunches.[7] It's not like public-school teachers have it so bad now. They are no longer poorly paid. The excellent medical benefits teachers receive are largely unobtainable for small business owners. No matter how good or bad they are, teachers receive benefits that Inocencia can only dream about; she can't think of a profession that receives more time off than teachers. Inocencia isn't sure she will ever be able to afford to retire, certainly not with retirement benefits comparable to what teachers receive.

As if this wasn't enough, teachers do everything they can to automate their jobs; for instance, spelling quizzes are administered via computers so that teachers are relieved of having to grade those tests. Parents just can't ask teachers what their children are learning. No. Before parents can speak with their kids' teachers they have to navigate three websites for each child to get a glimpse of the projects they are working on. And since not all teachers are helpful in providing log-in credentials, Inocencia has spent many nights wracking her brain about how to access these websites.

To lessen their workload, teachers give students less homework. Some teachers don't believe in homework at all. Inocencia's children aren't

---

[7] https://education.seattlepi.com/advantages-four-day-school-week-1548.html

learning as much as they should. She witnesses pedagogical meltdowns despite sending her children to very good public schools for which she pays a fortune in property taxes. Like other parents who can afford to do so, Inocencia ponies up another $850 per child every year in "suggested donations." But monetary donations are not enough. Parents are pressured to "volunteer" with teaching activities in their children's classes. Failure to volunteer can lead to ostracization by the PTA Cosa Nostra à la the movie *Bad Moms*. Well, the ostracization is not complete: Parents placed in PTA penalty boxes are still solicited for what seems to be monthly "teacher appreciation" collections. It could be worse for Inocencia. At least there is a nice gift shop in the same strip mall where her children's Kumon tutoring service is located. Now when she makes her $1,825 monthly payment to Kumon, she can just walk a few doors down to pick out gifts for the teachers that are supposedly deserving of all of the credit that her children are making academically.

Inocencia is frustrated that public-school teachers are failing her children. She is frustrated that there is little she can do about it without putting her kids in potentially vulnerable situations. She is frustrated that she has to work so hard to pay her property taxes while even the worst teachers have cushy jobs from which they cannot be removed. She is also frustrated with the economic distortions that such cushy public service jobs cause private enterprise. Inocencia has to pay consistently higher taxes so that teachers receive their annual raises. Then she has to pay her managers more money as they are tempted to become public sector employees in view of ever-escalating public sector compensation.

Inocencia feels that there is some consolation to all of the difficulties that she is forced to contend with—at least she is not a man. Inocencia laments that men face not only unrestrained ridicule and disparagement but government mandated discrimination.

It has been politically acceptable to call men "male chauvinist pigs" for decades. It is so commonplace to more endearingly call men "jerks" that the book *All Men Are Jerks – Until Proven Otherwise* released its 15th Anniversary edition. Any man can be accused of demonstrating *toxic masculinity* at any time—no one knows what that means, but it doesn't matter because that derogatory term serves its mission by degrading all men. As per the MeToo movement, all men are guilty of a crime that any one man is accused of committing. (No proof or due process is needed to substantiate even the initial accusation.)

On the other hand, any man who utters one uncomplimentary word about women will quickly be fired, forced to resign or hauled off to a reeducation camp. Consider what happened when Uber announced that it was adding a woman, Wan-Ling Martello, to its Board of Directors. David Bonderman, a fellow board member and one of the most successful businessmen in the country, said of Ms. Martello joining the board, "...it's much likelier to be more talking on the board." That one comment cost Mr. Bonderman his board seat at Uber, which at the time was one of the most promising companies in the world.

Women are encouraged to take pride in being women. Fair enough. Everyone has the right to take pride in who they are.[8] There is International Women's Day, Women's History Month and there is constant banter about every year being the "Year of the Woman." There are more women's organizations than anyone can count. A few of these organizations include: the Ms. Foundation for Women, the International Alliance of Women, the International Alliance for Women, the International Association of Women Police, the National Association of Women in Construction, Every Woman Foundation, International Federation of Business and Professional Women, LeanIn.Org and the National Organization for Women. Every professional organization—from licensing organizations to hedge funds associations and from medical associations to aerospace groups—have subgroups that promote the careers of their women members.

But which groups represent men's interests? Who would take the risk of trying to form such a group? The momentum is going in the other direction; men's groups are being tossed into the dustbin of history. Women-only colleges abound but men-only colleges are almost a complete historical relic. Almost every university has a women's studies program but Inocencia has never heard of any university offering a men's studies program. Even young boys are being deprived of their rights to assemble together; the Boy Scouts buckled to political correctness and now admits girls. Opportunities reserved exclusively for women are promoted and praised not only nationally and across the globe but also throughout the

[8] Well, not everyone has the right to take pride in who they are without being pilloried. Among those deprived of this right are men, police officers, Caucasians and Southerners.

universe—the all-women spacewalk in October of 2019 being an example. Every time positions are reserved for women, there are men whose candidacy is rejected even before it is submitted. The male astronauts who were discriminated against could very well have carried a half-million dollars of student debt and have worked tenaciously for far more than a decade. For many male astronauts, another opportunity for participating in spacewalks will never reemerge. And yet, it is men who are constantly accused of being misogynistic. Inocencia doesn't know the corollary for "misogynist" to denote hatred of men, but if there is such a word it must be the most underused word in the dictionary.

> Inocencia has had disappointing experiences attending professional conferences. In recent years, she attended one conference on franchising and another on licensing. (Inocencia wanted to explore franchising Concordia Diner and to learn how to go about licensing her inventions.) Both events were conducted in well-appointed hotels and each conference cost Inocencia more than $4,000 in registration fees, airfare, hotels and the like. Both of these conference organizations pulled bait-and-switches. The agendas were completely hijacked by the political correctness police. Instead of running the sessions that were marketed before the events, the conferences focused on issues such as "Empowering Women," "Disempowering White Male Managers," "Don't Listen to Your Male Boss, He Doesn't Know What He's Talking About," "How to Blow the Whistle on Your Sexist Boss," "How to Overcome the Racism that Lies in All of Us," "Ending Racism in Licensing," and "Halting Discrimination in Franchising." (Some panels at the conferences were deceptions within deceptions. For instance, all-female panels of eight glowed about the diversity on the panel.) Inocencia has no problem with conferences focusing on these issues as long as their organizers are honest about the topics that will be covered. But Inocencia feels as though she was robbed; she lost more than $8,000 and a week of running her diner when she attended these two events from which she learned absolutely nothing.

Women are free to ascribe their success as a function of their gender. For instance, International Monetary Fund Chairwoman Christine Lagarde has gone on television and said that being a woman enabled her to solve some monumental problem confronting the IMF. What man can say that his success is a function of being a man? In the olden days, such a man would only be called a "male chauvinist pig." Today, such a fellow would be fired and have difficulty finding another job in light of the ensuing social media uproar.

Discrimination against men in the workplace is not only accepted—it is aggressively promoted and enforced. It is forbidden for employers to say that any particular position is reserved for men but lawmakers in states such as California promulgate legislation requiring companies to appoint women to their boards. Companies can boast that the majority of their executives are women or that, on average, their female employees earn more than their male employees. But no company can say the same thing about men without risking governmental retribution, boycotts, negative press or at least public disapproval. These lessons are now being taught from an early age. Hasbro stated that its Ms. Monopoly was designed so that "women make more than men." In the 2019 release of the timeless board-game, female players receive $240 when they pass "Go," while the male players receive $200.

It feels to Inocencia as if the enforcers of political correctness are trying to make society Männerrein. Professional organizations like upper-tier law firms banish their menfolk from pictures on their homepages with about as much sentimentality as North Korea's Kim Jong-un airbrushes his cashiered uncles out of official photos.[9] References to the male gender in any form of writing or speech, such as he/his/him, are being deracinated from the English language. Use of such terms is quickly approaching the level of "hate speech."

Inocencia thinks that the glorification and victimization of women and the degradation of men is pervasive and unrelenting. She reckons that if liberals believed in G-d, they would push to have Ariana Grande's hit song, *G-d is a Woman* become the new national anthem. She also offers a story to illustrate how ridiculous the one-sided battle of the sexes has become. Suppose there was a national farting contest and one of the two final contestants was a man and the other was a woman. If the man won the farting contest, the

[9] For instance, Fisher Investments ran a full-page ad in the *Wall Street Journal* on November 1, 2019 (page A4A). This ad contained five pictures with hundreds of women in them, but no men. The whole ad boasted about their female employees. One statement towards the top of the page read: "Over 800 women strong, with women leading 63% of employees."

media would be appalled. Claims would ring out that the contest was rigged. Consensus would quickly declare that the judges must have failed to develop an appreciation for the charms of women's farts. They need to be reeducated. Or maybe men are so deficient in their ability to judge farting contests that they should be banned from such duties. Liberal commentators would hold that society is at fault for not encouraging girls to fart frequently enough or loudly enough. It would be said that tremendous work, maybe a Marshall Plan-type effort, is needed in the field of flatology to achieve equality in flatulence release. However, if the woman won this contest, statues would be erected in her honor and the media would write glowing pieces hailing how much progress women have made in the art of farting.

Not everything can be predicted when opening a business. When Inocencia was preparing to open Concordia Diner, she was concerned about competing with local restaurateurs. It turned out that competition is the least of Inocencia's worries. Sure, there are other restaurants in the neighborhood. But those owners and managers are too busy running their own businesses to engage in underhanded competitive tactics. By serving high quality meals at reasonable prices in a comfortable setting, Concordia Diner has been able to compete with the local eateries.

As she went about opening the diner, Inocencia was concerned that Concordia could be shaken down by mafia figures. She feared that she would have to pay for protection or fork over exorbitant fees to shady characters for garbage collection. The diner's garbage removal is far too expensive, but that's because Concordia relies on the municipal sanitation service. The effort that Concordia Diner is compelled to make to sort and present its refuse is overbearing; at least organized crime families didn't require businesses to go through religious refuse removal rituals. Inocencia has been shaken down by her employees, municipal service providers, government regulators and tax authorities but not by the mafia.

Whenever someone opens a business, there are unknown unknowns. One of Inocencia's biggest unexpected concerns is Berkeley professor Hans-Manuel Cherkoff, a frequent customer who regularly agitates against Concordia Diner's interests. Inocencia never imagined that one of her customers would prove to be a serious source of angst and lost business, especially not a man of letters such as Professor Cherkoff.

Professor Cherkoff and his posse show their contempt to Inocencia by purposely degrading the customer experience at Concordia Diner.

Their body odor and demeanor repel customers. They never close the doors behind them when they exit the restrooms. They emerge from the bathrooms with wet hands, which they vigorously shake, drizzling customers and their meals with bathroom water as they walk by. These intellectual hoodlums loudly play videos on their phones, remove their shoes or put their dirty shoes on chairs. They react abrasively when various team members and customers ask them to silence their phones and to stop extending their bare feet so close to other customers' tables. These animal humanists don't just bring their pets into the diner, they put them on chairs and allow them to eat off of tables and tableware. Professor Cherkoff and his associates cause Concordia Diner to lose revenue and are the source of several acidic Yelp reviews. Inocencia is afraid she might be fined for the pets the Cherkoff gang bring into the restaurant. She feels that she is at the mercy of intellectual gangsters.

Inocencia googled Berkeley Professor Hans-Manuel Cherkoff and she didn't like what she read. Professor Cherkoff is a Holocaust denier despite having been largely raised by his Holocaust survivor grandparents whose arms bore tattoos of their concentration camp numbers. His career as an academician and agitator cranked into high gear when he published his paper *The Mendacity of Microaggressions and the Morality of Murdering Republicans.* This paper won Professor Cherkoff well-paid speaking engagements and appearances on national news programs and talk shows. Professor Cherkoff's paper has been credited as the genesis of the storyline in *The Hunt,* a movie in which liberals hunt and kill pro-life advocates and conservatives for sport.[10] Liberal politicians vie for Professor Cherkoff's endorsement and an investor has expressed an interest in funding a lobbying group to be headed by Professor Cherkoff, tentatively called "The Cherkoff Circle."

Professor Cherkoff is Chairman of Animal Humanities Studies at Berkeley. Sounds innocent enough, you might think. But his ideas are radical. Bringing pets to restaurants, hotels and on airplanes is just the start for his Animal Humanities Project. Professor Cherkoff wants pets to have seats at the table in restaurants. He insists that eating establishments prepare menus for pets and that wait staff be required to inquire about

---

[10] Universal Pictures produced but has not released *The Hunt* as of the time of my writing these pages. https://www.lifenews.com/2019/08/08/new-film-the-hunt-has-liberals-hunting-killing-pro-lifers-for-sport/

orders for pets. He petitions hotels to place animal relief areas in each guest room and foments pressure on airlines to do the same on their entire fleets. His Animal Humanities Project demands that pets have their own seats on airplanes with specially designed protective restraints. He wants it to be obligatory for airlines to send their flight attendants to courses that teach them how to reduce the stress and fears that pets feel when flying. Professor Cherkoff has written favorably about the government paying reparations to pets for the mistreatment that some animals have suffered at the hands of humans over the last several centuries. He has proposed that some of these reparations be funded from fines imposed on pet owners and others that speak to animals in manners that are "commanding, insulting, demeaning or smack of human superiority over animals."

Professor Cherkoff has radical ideas regarding the health care, financial and happiness rights that governments owe pets. He wants pet owners to have disproportionate voting rights, as they represent the rights and interests of their animals. He seeks to make it mandatory for estate planners to inquire about naming pets as beneficiaries in their owners' wills. Professor Cherkoff insists that pets be deemed "persons" for purposes of being granted intellectual property rights.[11] He has even spoken about breaking down the "taboos against intimate human-pet relations." In speaking out against people eating meat, Professor Cherkoff has stated, "it is better to make love to animals than to kill them." (The Animal Humanities Project attracted loads of attention and significant donations when footage of one of its members wildly fornicating with a frisky American Eskimo Dog—on whose back the organization's web address was written in lipstick—was released all over social media.)

Professor Cherkoff has an effective and canned retort to anyone who

---

[11] In 2015, PETA filed a lawsuit on behalf of a male Sulawesi crested macaque named Naruto, arguing that the monkey owns a copyright in the famous "monkey selfies." This case was dismissed but David Slater, the photographer whose camera Naruto used, agreed to donate 25% of any future gross revenue that he derives from using or selling any or all of the monkey selfies to registered charities dedicated to protecting the welfare or habitat of Naruto and other crested macaques in Indonesia. PETA declared, "PETA and David Slater agree that this case raises important, cutting-edge issues about expanding legal rights for non-human animals."
https://www.peta.org/media/news-releases/peta-statement-monkey-selfie-case-settled/

suggests that pets are subsidiary to people. He will quickly spout out something like, "Are you saying that pets are *untermenschen*?" Then this Holocaust denier goes on a twenty-minute tirade about ominous historical parallels between Nazi programs and those who have the audacity to suggest that animals are undeserving of the rights humans have. (However, Professor Cherkoff is left speechless when asked about similar historical parallels in justifying partial and post-birth abortions on the basis of deeming that some life is unworthy of living.)

Professor Cherkoff makes no bones about his despising businesses of all kinds. His articles are filled with diatribes against businesspeople becoming rich by exploiting workers and destroying the environment. He fulminates against all forms of private property, including patents which he openly admits he knows nothing about. His students have reported that his anti-business views bleed into anti-Semitic diatribes. (However, when Professor Cherkoff was deathly ill a year ago, he insisted on being treated by a Jewish doctor at a for-profit hospital.)

Hans-Manuel Cherkoff's views are one thing. His remarks to Inocencia and her staff are another thing. Professor Cherkoff frequently conveys some smartass remark to Inocencia but at a volume meant for others to hear; these remarks are designed not only to insult Inocencia but to create wedges between Inocencia and her employees. One day he will say, "You must have been a slave driver in a previous life." Another day, he will sarcastically ask, "How many millions [of dollars] have you made so far this year? How does it feel to be part of the top one percent?" One afternoon he even quipped to Inocencia, "Why haven't I ever seen you eat at the diner? I guess the food here isn't high-class enough for rich people like you!"

Whenever Inocencia brings new technology or a new device into the diner in anticipation of achieving greater efficiency, Professor Cherkoff and his fellow academicians complain about the inequity of ever expecting anyone (e.g., Concordia's employees) to learn anything new. Professor Cherkoff's questioning employees about their breaks and overtime seems more sinister than idle chatter. Is he trying to document Concordia's violations of labor laws? Maybe Professor Cherkoff is trying to pave the way for Concordia's workers to unionize.

On one occasion Professor Cherkoff asked Inocencia to consider the merits of allowing her employees to unionize. She told him that she already thought about how unions affect the customer experience a few weeks ago when she missed her return international connecting flight at Philadelphia

International Airport. Why did Inocencia miss her flight at Philadelphia's largest airport? The unionized baggage handlers took over two hours to drop the suitcases from her British Airways flight onto the carousel. Without claiming and rechecking her luggage, she couldn't proceed with the check-in process for her next flight. Inocencia had nearly six hours to speak with other passengers who also missed their connecting flights due to the unionized baggage handlers' sloth. Some of these people were deprived of their last chance to wish moribund loved ones farewell. Other passengers merely missed funerals, weddings, graduation ceremonies, Bar Mitzvah's, christenings, job interviews and critical business meetings. Inocencia just can't understand how unionized workers can remorselessly inflict so much harm on so many innocent people on a daily basis. In any event, paying higher wages for a more calcified workforce that would produce worse customer service just hasn't appealed to Inocencia.

> Let's look at one example of Professor Cherkoff causing a scene at Concordia Diner. Professor Cherkoff was in a particularly jovial mood one fine winter morning; he was elated that Starbucks changed "Merry Christmas" on its cups to "Merry Coffee." On this morning, a group of dentists were eating their breakfasts at a table across from where Professor Cherkoff was sitting. There was an international dental convention nearby and its delegates were busy carrying on multiple conversations, straining to keep up with a variety of languages being spoken.
>
> Professor Cherkoff was looking to spread his good cheer. He waved to the dentists in a friendly manner and asked, "Where are you from?"
>
> No one in the group knew who Professor Cherkoff was addressing, so several voices simultaneously asked, "Who are you asking?"
>
> Professor Cherkoff responded, "The handsome African-American gentleman."
>
> So, Hugo, a well-dressed white man said, "South Africa."
>
> Professor Cherkoff retorted in a slightly scolding voice, "You're not African-American." Then he pointed to a young black man and said, "I meant to ask you. 'Where are you from?'"

This man, Alain, said, "I'm French. I live in the St. Germain neighborhood in Paris."

Before Professor Cherkoff could respond, Hugo said, "Actually, I am an African-American. I have South African and American citizenship. Would you like to see my passports?"

Alain piped up before Professor Cherkoff could say anything. "I'm not African and I'm not American. Actually, this is my first trip to the United States."

Professor Cherkoff engaged Hugo and Alain. "Hugo, you have no right to represent yourself as an African-American. You make for a bad imposter." He continued, "Alain, what's wrong with you? You should be proud of your heritage.[12] You should be proud to be African-American."

Alain looked at Professor Cherkoff like he was crazy. "Actually, I am proud to be a Frenchman. I was born and raised in France and make my dentistry (sic) in France. I studied French literature during my university days. My parents and my children were born in France and I have family only in France. The only language that I speak well is French." Then Hugo set his record straight. "I was born in South Africa, raised in South Africa and spent the first thirty years of my life in South Africa. But after living and working in Maryland for eleven years, I recently became an American citizen."

The entire delegation of dentists was becoming annoyed with Professor Cherkoff. The discussion became heated and went downhill from there. Within a minute or two, Professor Cherkoff was calling every one of the nine dentists seated at the table "racist." He labeled Alain a race-traitor and an Uncle Tom. Professor Cherkoff then told Hugo that he hoped the South African government would seize the homes of white people without compensation and that it is not unjust for white people in South Africa to be mutilated or murdered. Fortunately, the ugly situation was put to rest when two former marines who

[12] It may be interesting to note that Professor Cherkoff changed the spelling of his family name from Cherkov to Cherkoff, so that "it would appear less Jewish and more Americanized."

were sitting at the other end of the diner approached Professor Cherkoff and suggested that he would be more comfortable sitting down. "Enough is enough with your race baiting," they said. Professor Cherkoff muttered one of his usual offensive remarks about military service but complied with the marines' suggestion.

"Isn't it twisted," Inocencia thinks to herself, "that people who only view others as a function of their race call everyone else a racist. If you are a doctor that only diagnoses patients based on their x-rays, then you are a radiologist. If you believe you can forecast someone's future simply by looking at their palms, then you are a palm reader. If you are an investor who restricts your analysis of the investment merits of stocks to reviewing the charts of past trading activity, then you are a chartist. So those liberals who define people by their race are racists. For liberal racists to call everyone else a racist and to exclude themselves from that label is jaw-droppingly ironic."

Inocencia's concerns are warranted. The Cherkoff gang are no idle theoreticians. They are activists who seek to intimidate anyone whose political views run counter to theirs. They have organized book burnings of the works of conservative authors. They create such uproar and security threats that the most powerful people in the world cancel their invitations to speak at Berkeley's campus. The ulterior motive for stamping out free speech is more mendacious than may be readily realized—the Cherkoff gang's bigger motivation is to silence the few conservative voices on campus. The message that the Cherkoff clan sends when they orchestrate to have world leaders disinvited to speak on campus is, "if we can control the itinerary of the most important people in the world, we can certainly control your rights of freedom of expression."

The Cherkoff group goes further; they openly discuss inflicting harm on Concordia Diner. They talk about placing notices on windshields of cars in Concordia's parking lot; these flyers will be laced with accusations of the diner contributing to global warming (when it prepares food) and environmental degradation (when it disposes of its trash). Sometimes the Cherkoff cabal discuss shaming Concordia into donating significant amounts of food to the homeless. Other times, they chat about protesting against the diner for serving meat. Professor Cherkoff plots to organize an Earth Day rally at a park near Concordia Diner, knowing that the environmentalists will trample everything in their midst, including the greenery surrounding the diner. The environmental activists can also be counted on to blanket Inocencia's parking lot with discarded placards.

Professor Cherkoff talks about making lists of Republicans who patronize Concordia Diner and how they will harangue such customers until they leave.[13] What if the Cherkoff gang finds out that Inocencia has made political contributions to Republican candidates? Will they attempt to organize a boycott of the diner? Will these promoters of safe spaces show up on Inocencia's doorstep and harass Inocencia and her family? Will these preachers of tolerance throw rocks through the windows of the Erfinder home? Inocencia can't help overhearing the Berkeley professors bantering on about baiting members of minorities to dine-and-dash and then launch an all-out media campaign accusing Inocencia of being a racist if she presses charges.[14] They plot to ensnare Inocencia in a variety of

---

[13] United States Representative Maxine Waters said cabinet members and highly visible Trump enablers should expect harassment at restaurants, gas stations, shopping places, and even their homes.
(https://www.realclearpolitics.com/video/2018/06/25/maxine_waters_god_is_on_our_side.html)

Liberals have chased so many conservatives out of restaurants that comedian Bill Maher has implored them to stop. https://www.realclearpolitics.com/video/2018/10/06/bill_maher_liberals_must_stop_chasing_conservatives_out_of_restaurants.html

[14] Chipotle rehired one of its managers in Minnesota who refused to serve questionable customers who happened to be members of minorities unless they paid first. It turns out that the manager made a prudent decision because these schemers boasted of their frequent dine-and-dash exploits on Twitter. Similarly, Oberlin College in Ohio was required to pay nearby Gibson's Bakery more than $11 million in damages because it libeled the store as being racist and interfered with its business. What precipitated Oberlin College's attack on Gibson's Bakery? Allyn Gibson and three black shoplifters got into a physical altercation. Oberlin reflexively called Gibson's efforts to obstruct shoplifters as racial profiling.

https://www.yahoo.com/gma/chipotle-rehires-minnesota-manager-fired-over-racial-discrimination-211504879--abc-news-topstories.html

https://nypost.com/2019/06/07/oberlin-college-fined-11m-in-bakery-racial-profiling-case/

similar Catch-22 situations while sitting in her diner. (Professor Cherkoff, an ardent open borders advocate, never invites anyone to his house even though hosting visitors is within the rules of his gated community.)

Inocencia fears that she will be forced to work for causes that she doesn't support. For instance, Professor Cherkoff has been scheming to pressure Concordia Diner into catering Drag Queen Story Hours at local libraries; these events consist of drag queens in full get-up reading stories to toddlers. (Ostensibly these events are marketed as exercises in combating discrimination against transgenders. But how many toddlers discriminate against anyone? All disingenuous politically correct doublespeak aside, Professor Cherkoff has admitted that Drag Queen Story Hours are really about mainstreaming the transgender lifestyle and attracting more adherents.) Inocencia is concerned that her fate will be similar to that of Jack Phillips if she refuses to cater Drag Queen Story Hours. Mr. Phillips, the owner of the Masterpiece Cakeshop in Denver, politely refused to make a wedding cake for a same-sex couple in 2012.[15]

Powerful companies such as Apple and Amazon joined the Colorado Civil Rights Commission in seeking to force Mr. Phillips to produce such a cake. Eventually, the United States Supreme Court threw out Colorado's case against Mr. Phillips. But Inocencia has no time or budget to argue a similar case before state regulators, let alone all the way up to the Supreme Court. She feels as though she is on the receiving end of a threat. If she doesn't serve the Drag Queen Story Hour troupes, Concordia Diner might be subject to the same kinds of protests and boycotts that Chick-fil-A experiences. Worse yet, Professor Cherkoff is scheming to time Concordia's coerced catering of

[15] A somewhat similar conflict arose in 2018 when a transgender woman wanted to get a Brazilian wax in Ontario, Canada. The Muslim woman working at the hair-removal spa refused on account of it being against her religion to touch male genitals. A human rights complaint was filed and the spa was hit with a demand for $50,000.
https://www.lifesitenews.com/news/trans-woman-sues-spa-after-muslim-woman-waxer-refused-to-touch-his-pubic-ha

an upcoming Drag Queen Story Hour with a sick-out by the diner's employees so that Inocencia will have to prepare the catering for this group herself. Inocencia thinks to herself, "Why must I be compelled to perform work that I don't wish to take on? Isn't slavery over?" Even if Inocencia provides the catering, who is to say that Professor Cherkoff won't instigate having the drag queens demand a refund based on trumped up charges of Concordia being a discriminating diner that intentionally delivered poor quality food to the Drag Queen Story Hour event?

When it comes to citizens' abilities to think freely, Inocencia feels that she is living in something resembling the Stalinist era or contemporary North Korea. There is no room to think beyond the boundaries of government-sanctioned political correctness. Mentioning a protected group without endlessly proclaiming love, support and respect for that group is now deemed to be the equivalent of hate speech. And you better make sure you take a deep breath right before you begin extolling a protected group because if you need to catch your breath midway through idolizing such a group, their advocates will get in your face and start screaming about your intolerance. (Inocencia has heard that the politically correct police are now advising us to hermetically seal our lips to the sippy cups that Starbucks now uses so that no politically incorrect statements will leak out.) When in the presence of a protected group, failing to prostrate one's self at their feet is close to becoming a hate crime. It may even be dangerous to be the first one to stop clapping at a politically correct applause line.

Whatever ideas lie outside of politically correct guardrails are automatically deemed to be hateful, reprehensible and invalid. When organizers wanted to run a Straight Pride parade in Boston in the late summer of 2019, Boston mayor Marty Walsh immediately, but without evidence, began characterizing the proposed Straight Pride event as an abominable effort run by hate-mongers. Lee Pelton, president of Emerson College, called the event a "perversion." Counter-protesters at the event shouted “Nazi scum” at the passing Straight Pride participants. Inocencia never knew that being straight proved that one was a Nazi. How do Mayor Walsh, Emerson College President Pelton, and the counter-protesters believe they came into this world? Perhaps they believe that they descended from apes. But Inocencia bets their births resulted from their mothers and fathers making love.

[16] https://www.theguardian.com/world/2019/sep/01/boston-straight-pride-parade-arrests

Part II
Gearing Up for Patent Battle

Let's fast forward twelve years. Inocencia's decades of struggle in the restaurant business have begun to bear fruit. Concordia Diner has been generating healthy cash flows over the past five years.

Inocencia is immensely proud that Concordia Diner has finally become financially successful. Over the past few years, she has been able to work slightly fewer hours and to worry a little less about the diner. She hopes that she will be able to leave the business to her children or sell it for their benefit sometime over the next decade.

Except for her family, no one cheered Inocencia when Concordia Diner finally became profitable. Not that she seeks recognition for her accomplishments. On the contrary, Inocencia tries to keep her moderate financial success as quiet as possible. She doesn't want to dampen the ambition that she has instilled in her children by projecting wealth. She doesn't want her employees to hit her up for raises all the time. Nor does she want stock-brokers and financial advisers scratching at her windows. She contributes what she can to political campaigns and charities but doesn't want to attract swarms of locked-on fund-raisers pestering her for contributions and donations.

Inocencia can't help but think about how skewed the public's empathy is. When the federal government shut down for 35 days at the end of 2018 through January of 2019, hundreds of thousands of government workers were furloughed. As a result, and by no fault of their own, their pay was delayed. (This ephemeral situation is par for the course for most businesses who have to chase down their receivables.) The delay in the federal workers receiving their paychecks was unfortunate. But they did get paid for not working. They also received enormous public support. For instance, food banks distributed tons of free food to these furloughed workers.

Inocencia thinks to herself, "Give me a break. If the shutdown would have lasted seven months, should non-working federal employees be paid for sitting on their asses for the majority of a year? Don't we live in the gig economy? College students and employed septuagenarians find room in their schedules to drive for Uber. At most, furloughs only occur a few times during a civil servant's entire career. Why can't federal workers take some responsibility for themselves and make a little effort to generate income when their checks are delayed? Government workers experienced a rough 35 days but business owners would be lucky if their difficult runs only last 35 months. Many small businesses struggle to stay afloat for 35 years.

And what about the businesses that depend on these furloughed workers? Where is the concern for them? When government workers don't come to work, the restaurants that cater to them don't experience a delay in their receipts—forgone sales are lost forever. The local businesses still have to pay their vendors, employees, rents and electric utilities. And speaking about electric utilities, when California's PG&E ran its premeditated power outages in October of 2019, I lost at least $5,000 in spoiled inventory. The furloughs cause local businesses to hemorrhage losses, but no one gives a damn. Those food banks that provide boxes of food to any government worker who wants help don't give suffering business owners one bloody grain of rice."

A few months after this government furlough ended, U.S. Representative Katie Porter grilled Jaime Diamond, CEO of JPMorganChase, in his appearance before Congress. What was Ms. Porter haranguing Mr. Diamond about? She was hyperventilating about the imbalance of a hypothetical employee's high living costs relative to this non-existent employee's salary. The liberal establishment, including national media outlets, cheered on Ms. Porter's inquisition of Mr. Diamond. In doing so, it was demonstrated that more sympathy is accorded to hypothetical workers than real-life business owners.[17]

With her success, Inocencia has become a target for liberal politicians. She is not in the top one percent of income earners, but is ridiculed as such by Professor Cherkoff and his minions. Instead of showing respect to self-made businesspeople like Inocencia, people like Professor Cherkoff claim that the decades entrepreneurs dedicate to their businesses are irrelevant to their success. Voices from academia and the media echo President Obama's sentiments when he said, "If you've got a business, you didn't build that. Somebody else made that happen."[18]

Inocencia doesn't understand why self-made business professionals should feel embarrassed by their success. She found the remarks that Snoop Dogg made when he placed his star on the Hollywood Walk of Fame refreshing: "…I want to thank me for believing in me. I want to thank me for doing all this hard work. I want to thank me for having no days off. I

[17] https://www.youtube.com/watch?v=8X4A_EefxnM

[18] https://www.washingtonpost.com/blogs/the-fix/post/obamas-you-didnt-build-that-problem/2012/07/18/gJQAJxyotW_blog.html

want to thank me for never quitting…"[19] Inocencia is much more in line with Mr. Dogg than Mr. Obama.

The Professor Cherkoffs of the world vilify Inocencia for supposedly not paying her fair share of taxes, even though at least fifty cents of every dollar she earns goes to pay one tax or another. Professor Cherkoff would castigate Inocencia if she paid eighty cents of every dollar she earned in taxes. Of course, she has a view different from that of Professor Cherkoff. She believes she pays more than her fair share of taxes. Inocencia also strongly believes that she disproportionately contributes to the local economy; Concordia Diner has expended millions of dollars on payroll over the years and Inocencia is proud of the fact that she has helped hundreds of unskilled workers become more employable.

Inocencia thinks to herself, "If Professor Cherkoff and his ilk want to accuse people of not paying their fair share, why not look at the Europeans? Why can't they pay for their own defense, or at least most of it? For crying out loud, their citizens receive free health care and free education. They take pretty much the whole damn summer off of work. Yes, why can't the Europeans pay their fair share of their own defense costs? Why should hard-working Americans like me have to pay higher taxes so that Europeans can enjoy so many comforts that elude Americans?" She knows if she would express these thoughts out loud, people like Professor Cherkoff would accuse her of being racist and xenophobic even though almost all European leaders are white and are not seeking to emigrate to the United States.

Over the last half of a decade, Inocencia has allocated $50,000 of Concordia's annual profits to a "special account." When Concordia Diner turned its financial corner, and after decades of self-deprivation, Inocencia decided it was time to spoil herself a bit. Did she splurge on clothes? Jewelry? Travel? A Tesla? Remodeling her house? None of the above. Inocencia decided to take as many robotics courses at the local colleges as time would permit. Inocencia didn't care about earning a degree. Why would she need it? This self-made woman had no intention of ever working for anyone else.

Approximately three years into her studies, Inocencia thought she knew enough about robotics and the restaurant business to program robots to handle a variety of tasks related to food preparation. She decided to

---

[19] https://www.huffpost.com/entry/snoop-dogg-hollywood-walk-of-fame_n_5bf40c0be4b0d9e7283d2b15

invest the entire $250,000 reserved in the "special account" in her research efforts. As she embarked on her research project, she knew the odds were extremely low of developing a robot that could complete food preparation tasks quickly, repeatedly, unfailingly and safely. She was well aware that the chances of commercializing fully-debugged robots would be even more remote.

Despite the miniscule chances of realizing commercial success, Inocencia was unflagging in her research efforts. She read everything she could get her hands on and taught herself more about robots than she learned in all of her courses. She learned about software, electronics, artificial intelligence, information processing, haptics, gyroscopes, microcontrollers and visual sensors. She hired specialists when they were needed and when she had the budget. She conducted volley after volley of experiments, which produced an endless stream of failures and dashed expectations. She blew through the $250,000 long before any promising invention appeared on the horizon. Inocencia was left with little choice but to put a second mortgage on her house, raid her pension account, liquidate a chuck of her investment portfolio and borrow money from friends and family. More experiments and discouraging results were encountered.

And then...one day...every feature of what may have been experiment number 918 worked. The electronics, the software, the sensors and the artificial intelligence all seemed to perform to expectations. Could it be? Could Inocencia really have invented a versatile robot that could play important roles in preparing food? Maybe all that she needs to do now is obtain patent protection and license such patents to large food processing equipment manufacturers. She thinks to herself, "Surely, darn near every restaurant owner in his right mind would want to buy my robots. Given how much money restaurateurs stand to save from deploying my robots, they should be indifferent to price." But then again, Inocencia's road to riches may not be nearly as unobstructed as she believes.

She is ready to take the next step, patenting her invention. As she is new to the world of patenting, Inocencia begins teaching herself about patents, just as she taught herself robotics. After a few months of immersing herself in the world of patents, she decides to confer with a patent attorney. Below is a transcript of the interview that Inocencia conducted with a patent lawyer.[20]

[20] Nothing in this book should be construed as legal advice.

Inocencia: What could stop me from patenting my invention?

Patent Lawyer: Your invention must be eligible for patent protection.

Inocencia: What inventions are eligible to receive patent protection?

Patent Lawyer: That used to be an easy question to answer. The 1952 Patent Act clearly and unambiguously holds that anything made by man is patent eligible. (Thus, that which occurs naturally is not patent eligible.) However, since around 2010 (with the Bilski v. Kappos decision) and 2012 (with the Mayo v. Prometheus decision), the Supreme Court began supplanting the clarity of the 1952 Patent Act with a Rorschach-like test for patent eligibility.

Inocencia: Wait. Isn't Congress supposed to write the laws governing patents, including what is patentable?

Patent Lawyer: Yes. The Supreme Court effectively writing laws governing which inventions are eligible to receive patent protection is a usurpation of its authority. (Admittedly, inaction by Congress has left a vacuum on patent eligibility issues.) In rewriting patent eligibility laws through a series of what has become an unintelligible morass of decisions, the Supreme Court did not bother to hold any public hearings or listen to testimony.

Inocencia: I can understand why the Supreme Court's intervention in determining what is eligible for patent protection is outside of its authority. But what are the ramifications of the Supreme Court's decisions?

Patent Lawyer: There are two deleterious ramifications of the Supreme Court's decisions. First, wide swaths of innovative solutions to technological problems have been disqualified from receiving patent protection. The Supreme Court has taken the position that many new inventions are abstract or nothing more than laws of nature, and therefore ineligible to receive patent protection. This has caused inventors to be on the receiving end of some pretty silly decisions about patent eligibility. For instance, in *ex parte* Hiroyuki Itagaki, the Patent Trial and Appeal Board (PTAB) ruled that a magnetic resonance imaging machine is an abstract idea and thus patent ineligible.

Such wholesale declarations of patent ineligibility contravene premonitions from the Supreme Court's review of the Bilski case. Opinions from that case expressly stated that "categorical rule[s] denying patent protection for 'inventions in areas not contemplated by Congress . . . would frustrate the purposes of the patent law.'" Indiscriminately labeling patents as abstractions is in conflict with warnings from the Alice case, where the Supreme Court acknowledged that an overly expansive view of what constitutes an abstract idea would swallow all of patent law because every invention must necessarily begin with an idea.

Inocencia: MRI machines are far from abstract concepts; they house an amazing quilt of inventions. In deriding inventions as being abstract, it seems that the Supreme Court has indeed forgotten that most inventions begin as ideas. Also, I imagine that some cures for diseases would be most efficacious if they were accepted by the body. I suppose these innovations should embrace nature. Thus, not every invention that has a natural nexus should reflexively be deemed patent ineligible.

Patent Lawyer: Your analysis sounds logical to me. Thanks to the Supreme Court, the most exciting innovations, technological advances, and scientific discoveries of the twenty-first century are no longer patent eligible. Knowing that they cannot protect their technical and scientific breakthroughs must be a terribly discouraging development for pioneers in personalized medicine, machine-printed organs, artificial intelligence and medical diagnostics. The risk of their inventions being deemed patent ineligible will certainly handicap American inventors and companies pursuing the commercialization of related solutions.

Inocencia: What is the second problematic ramification of the Supreme Court's decisions on patent eligibility?

Patent Lawyer: No one can understand the existing body of case law because there is absolutely no consistency. Thus, no one—not examiners, not Administrative Patent Judges (APJs), not the district courts or the community of patent lawyers—knows how to determine if an invention is patent eligible. There is no single decision from the Federal Circuit that is not contradicted by another decision. For example, in Electric Power Group v. Alstom and SAP America v. Investpic, the Federal Circuit announced a categorical rule that a claim that did nothing more than gather data, process data and display data cannot be patent eligible. This rule cannot be reconciled with at least a half-dozen other decisions.

Further, in one very troubling case, Finnavations v. Payoneer, the U.S. District Court for the District of Delaware sanctioned Finnavations for filing a lawsuit gainst Payoneer for infringement of its U.S. Patent No. 9.569,755. Why did the Delaware district court sanction Finnavations? Because during prosecution of its '755 patent, Finnavations relied on the USPTO's determination of patent eligibility based on the examiner's analysis of §101 and the Alice decision. The court reasoned that '[p]atent examiners are non-lawyers, [thus] an examiner's opinion on the legal question of patent eligibility does not relieve a patent attorney from her obligation to make an independent assessment based on an evaluation of the relevant law." Translation: Patent examiners cannot be expected to know what they are doing (at least with respect to eligibility issues) and patentees that act as if patent examiners know what they are doing stand to be sanctioned by courts.

Inocencia: What else could stand in my way of being able to patent my invention?

Patent Lawyer: Even if your invention overcomes the eligibility issue, you would not be able to patent your idea if a patent was previously filed on the invention. Nor would you receive a patent if your invention was deemed to be lacking in novelty or was obvious.

Inocencia: I can certainly understand that I wouldn't deserve to receive a patent on an invention that has already been patented or disclosed in a publication. But I don't understand how my patent application could be rejected on obviousness grounds. If no one else ever came up with my idea, my invention could not have been obvious.

Patent Lawyer: For the most part, I don't like to see patent applications rejected on obviousness grounds. My sentiments on this issue are best reflected in the following inset entitled, "Could Have, Should Have, Would Have."

Could Have, Should Have, Would Have

Charles H. Duell was the Commissioner of the U.S. Patent Office in 1889. Commissioner Duell is widely quoted as having stated that the patent office would soon shrink in size, and eventually close, because…"Everything that can be invented has been invented."

Today, if anyone anywhere on our planet espoused the view that there is nothing left to invent, he would be unceremoniously laughed out of the room. The notion that innovation continues to change the world is nearly universally accepted. Even Karl Marx said, "The only constant is change." However, such troglodytic sentiments are fodder for endless reflection at the United States Patent and Trademark Office.

Patent examiners deem inventions to be "abstract" if they are too revolutionary or "obvious" if the invention is less than revolutionary. Those patent applications that survive such prosecutorial gauntlets are likely to be clipped if they become subject to *inter partes review* challenges. For example, in *Ex parte Hiroyuki Itagaki,* the PTAB ruled that a magnetic resonance imaging (MRI) machine is an abstract idea and thus patent ineligible.

I can largely understand the merits of rendering laws of nature and natural/physical phenomena ineligible for patent protection. (There is, however, tremendous room for clarity as to what exactly is patent eligible.) But I cannot understand the logic of rejecting patent applications because a series of people skilled in the art could have (should have, would have) sequenced their knowledge in a manner similar to the applicant but never did so.

Suppose Mrs. Johnson from San Diego, California assigned all of her third-graders with the task of writing an eight-page term-paper. Little Johnny worked diligently preparing his term paper on autonomous automobiles, the subject that consumed his imagination. Reading and writing were never easy for this dyslexic child. Nevertheless, he persevered. When the other little San Diegans were immersed in playing Fortnite and grazing on Doritos, little Johnny spent hours researching, composing, editing and proofreading his eight-page report.

His labors bore fruit: Little Johnny received an "A" on his report. The teacher was so impressed with his term paper that she praised little Johnny in front of his classmates. Mrs. Johnson seized the moment to motivate the 30 eight-year-olds under her care. She told the students, "With enough hard-work and focus, high hurdles can be overcome. To achieve goals, sacrifices are often required. Research leads to learning. While learning is its own reward, learning acts like compound interest; the more you know, the further you can go." While all of the eight-year-olds understood Mrs. Johnson and committed to work harder in school, a cabal of parents unsheathed their swords.

Just a few days before little Johnny's teacher issued her report cards the parents of some of his classmates protested little Johnny receiving an "A" on his paper to San Diego's School Board. Some parents expressed their beliefs that issuing different grades to different students is inherently unfair, elitist and even smacks of racism. One academic redistributionist made his case for depriving little Johnny of his "A" by arguing that his paper was obvious in view of:

> **Page 1** sharing similarities in terms of brakes with a report prepared in 1972 in Spanish by little Carlos in Chile;
>
> **Page 2** sharing similarities in terms of gas pedals with a report prepared in 1931 in Arabic by little Fatima in Jordan;
>
> **Page 3** sharing similarities in terms of seats with a report prepared in 1868 in Russian by little Svetlana in Russia;

Page 4 sharing similarities in terms of doors with a report prepared in 1903 in Japanese by little Hinata in Japan;

Page 5 sharing similarities in terms of mirrors with a report prepared in 1982 in Greek by little Konstantinos in Greece;

Page 6 sharing similarities in terms of a boomerang with a report prepared in 1957 in Swahili by little Barongo in Kenya;

Page 7 sharing similarities in terms of motion detection sensors with a report prepared in 1961 in Korean by little Seo-hyeon in South Korea; and,

Page 8 sharing similarities in terms of antennae with a report prepared in 1995 in Hebrew by little Nimrod in Israel.

The San Diego School Board acquiesced to the parents' ire. The board overlooked the fact that none of the children cited above produced a term-paper even faintly resembling little Johnny's in its entirety. They also skirted the issue that even if all of the other children wrote their papers in English, those papers still couldn't possibly flow together as seamlessly as little Johnny's paper. The narrative just wouldn't work. Nevertheless, the school board agreed with the parents and rescinded little Johnny's "A." Little Johnny's parents were forced to pay the costs of the hearing in which they were not invited and in which their son was unable to edit his term paper. Mrs. Johnson was threatened with removal from her position should she ever again dare to praise a sham creator.

This litany of events sapped little Johnny's creativity and motivation. The librarian became less helpful to little Johnny and his friends no longer agreed to review his writing. His writing abilities showed so much promise but were extinguished before his work saw the light of day.

It is irresponsible for adults to give children who fail to complete their work credit based on the excuse that the children could have, should have, or would have completed their assignments. It is much more inequitable for the U.S. Patent Office to deprive inventors of the credit they deserve (in the form of patent allowances) because some conjured up combination of disconnected individuals—who have little, if any, temporal or linguistic ability to communicate with one another—could have, should have, or would have eventually produced the claimed invention.

Postscript

Decisions from PTAB and the courts continue to become increasingly unhinged on the issue of obviousness. Celgene developed a system to safely distribute thalidomide to patients. (Thalidomide has a notorious history of disturbing the development of embryos and fetuses.) The Federal Circuit's July 2019 ruling in Celgene Corp. v. Peter basically accepted the argument that obviousness is demonstrated by motivation. (Four *inter partes review* petitions were filed against Celgene's patents, and the PTAB deemed all claims except one as obvious in view of multiple references.)

According to this decision, somehow the motivation of one inventor to avoid accidents is sufficient to block another inventor from receiving a patent when he develops an invention that actually provides greater safety. It seems to me that the warped patent system is actually endangering lives by demotivating inventors to produce patentable safety products.

Inocencia: I suppose all patent applications can be deemed ineligible. A disclosed invention can either be deemed to be abstract and therefore lacking eligibility, or the invention can reflect a combination of known elements and therefore be deemed to be obvious.

I wish the detractors of the inventor community had a little appreciation for the work that goes into coming up with inventions. Those who take to disparaging inventors and patents hold that there is no such thing as a new invention. According to them, every innovation is obvious. In the minds of the anti-patent community, everyone is a genius except for inventors. What is perhaps most ridiculous is that these sentiments are applied to pharmaceutical inventions. In that industry, maybe one drug candidate out of 10,000 will be successful. And the one drug candidate that ultimately proves to be successful usually surprises the researchers most intimately familiar with the given research project. Then, during litigation, infringers convince judges and juries that the invention was obvious.

It is important to realize that even seemingly banal inventions require more research than you would think. Take the frisbee, for example. You may think that frisbees are simply round pieces of plastic. But the inventor, Walter Frederick Morrison, spent years researching the development of an optimal frisbee. At first, he threw around tin cake pans and popcorn lids. Then, Walter began molding plastic into flat and round shapes and raised the central hub. Throwing instructions were molded into the underside. Later he added grooves to the top of the frisbee's surface and patented more aerodynamic improvements to the disc. Separately, Super Soakers (a line of toy water guns) hail from research that Lonnie Johnson was pursuing at NASA's Jet Propulsion Laboratory.

Back to the novelty issue, how would a patent examiner know if anyone else ever came up with my invention?

Patent Lawyer: The examiner would undertake a prior art search, basically a wide-ranging search for similar inventions. Patent applicants can also undertake prior art searches, either directly or by hiring third-parties. In any event, patent applicants must disclose the prior art that is known to them. (As far as I know, patent applications are the only documents submitted to the government in which the applicant is required to disclose every conceivable known reason that his application should be rejected.) Prior art searches are necessary to ensure that patent applications are not issued to applicants that do not deserve them.

However, it is important to note that as search technologies, including artificial intelligence, become more powerful, there is more risk that prior art will surface during searches. Google Patents makes it extremely easy to search for prior art; a "Find Prior Art" link appears right under each patent number on Google Patents. Some anti-patent entities have built large reservoirs of prior art, largely to render patent invalidation easier. For instance, Cisco and a few large tech companies have teamed up with MIT to build and make public an archive of prior art that will accept contributions from everyone.

Also, companies such as Article One Partners have basically deputized researchers all over the world to search for prior art. A scenario for how Article One Partners' services may be engaged follows: Omega Company files suit against Gamma Company for its infringement of Omega's '123 patent. Gamma responds by trying to invalidate the '123 patent. As an initial step, Gamma agrees to pay Article One Partners $50,000. Article One Partners turns around and offers $35,000 worth of bounties to its network of researchers all across the globe. The researcher that produces the most damaging piece of prior art receives a bounty of $20,000. The researchers that produce the second and third most damaging pieces of prior art receive bounties of $10,000 and $5,000, respectively. Article One Partners would retain the remaining $15,000.

Inocencia: Are there any other issues that could stop me from receiving a patent?

Patent Lawyer: There are. Many of the issues are quite procedural. I recommend that you let me handle the minutiae. I will just mention a few other factors for you to consider. There are some inventor scams out there that prey on uninitiated inventors. So be careful. Some of these charades entail a marketing company charging inventors increasingly large sums of money to perform market research, which is never delivered to the inventor.

Some patent examiners (and art units) have very low allowance rates. Competitors may file pre-grant oppositions through a strawman, disguising the competitor's identity.[21] Patent pendency can become quite extended. Some inventors run out of money midway through the examination process.

---

21 Some large companies make a practice of reading published patent applications and opposing those that they believe threaten their businesses, often by producing

Perhaps this is a bit off topic, but I would like to mention a risk associated with purchasing patents. It is possible that a patent buyer will purchase a patent from a seller who does not own title to that patent. Suppose Seller A, who is listed as the assignee at the USPTO, sells a patent to Buyer B. Because Buyer B has heard the persistent rumors that Unified Patents and RPX trawl the USPTO assignment records looking for newly assigned patents against which to file *inter partes review* petitions, Buyer B does not inform—at least not in a timely manner—the USPTO that it is the new owner of the patent. Later, a new buyer comes along and purchases the patent from Seller A, who produces a patent purchase agreement which the new buyer signs. The new buyer signs that agreement in good faith as he believes that Seller A still owns the patent. The problem for Buyer B is that the new buyer may own the patent, even though Seller A did not lawfully have ownership at the time of the sale to the new buyer. The reason is that the new buyer was a good faith purchaser and Buyer B failed to record the assignment with the USPTO; such assignment would have put the new buyer on notice of the change of lawful title to the patent.

---

prior art. But these situations are rare. According to statistics from the United States Patent and Trademark Office, in its 2018 fiscal year, there were only 141 third-party submissions of prior art for consideration by patent examiners, or about 0.02% of the patent applications filed in that year. The low incidence of potentially invalidating prior art being furnished to patent examiners should not be misconstrued as magnanimity on the part of patent challengers. A more likely explanation for the low incidence of potentially ruinous pre-grant prior art submissions is that companies that may be infringing wish to deprive the patent applicant the ability to work with the examiners in narrowing applications' claims scopes as doing so would make those patents stronger.

Engaging Patent Brokers

Suppose you wish to sell your house. Since you seek to sell your house "as-is," you want to minimize your investment in the selling process and elect not to spruce up your house for potential buyers. To avoid paying a real estate agent commissions, you independently put your house on the market. While some lookie-loos avail themselves of the wine and cheese you serve at your open houses, no serious buyers emerge. The months tick away and, before you know it, you miss the sizzling summer selling season. However, the buying community—consisting of local potential buyers and real estate agents as well as online real estate marketplaces such as Zillow—notices that you failed to attract a buyer: Your house is perceived as an increasingly stale damaged good.

You eventually realize that you have no choice but to retain a real estate agent. Since you are very busy, you do not want to waste your time conferring with a lowly real estate agent. You think, "Isn't it the job of a real estate agent to sell my house? Since I am prepared to pay a healthy commission at the closing, I simply can't justify investing time with agents. While I could have provided a lot of nuanced selling points about my house, my agent will just have to figure out the selling proposition herself." Unsurprisingly, not every real estate agent jumps at the opportunity to market your house.

A similar situation often occurs in the world of selling patents. But the plight of the patent broker is much bleaker.

Selling Patents Is More Difficult Than Selling Houses

When unprepared patentees prematurely market their patents, they tend to spoil markets sparsely populated by buyers. As everyone in sales and marketing knows, you don't get a second chance to make a first impression. Further, many patentees are of the mindset that it is the responsibility of the patent broker to invest tens of thousands of dollars preparing marketing documents, patent valuation reports and claims charts on their behalf. These out-of-pocket expenses are on top of the patent broker's time, travel and overhead allocable to clients.

The expenses borne by patent brokers pale in comparison to the efforts they make hustling patents. Selling patents is much more difficult than selling houses. The former is much more nuanced than the latter; much more work is required to understand patents. Patent brokers lose money in the first months of their engagements as they invest considerable time learning about specific patents, technologies, markets, and extent of infringement. Great effort is expended in surveying the landscape in order to identify potential buyers. (By the way, patent brokers are more effective when they tailor value propositions to each potential buyer's specific situation.) In a sense, patent brokers are more invested at the outset of seller-agent relationships than sellers since sellers can remain on the sidelines until buyers begin negotiating. Patent brokers are under ever increasing pressure to execute patent transactions because each day that passes brings the day that the patents will become worthless closer.

Patent Brokers Are Not Always Treated Fairly

In many cases, patents simply fail to attract sufficient interest among potential buyers for deals to close. In other situations, patents do attract interest from buyers but sellers get cold feet and withdraw their offers to sell. I am aware of a situation whereby a patentee's new Intellectual Property Manager simply decided that she did not want her company to use patent brokers anymore; the result was that the company's patent broker was left at the altar with a stranded buyer.

Unfortunately, sellers often fail to show their patent brokers the slightest courtesy. Some patentees fail to respond to their brokers' emails and phone calls even when the brokers are proffering up buyers. This can happen when sellers' business models pivot. In these and similar cases, patent brokers receive no commissions even though they deliver buyers willing to pay patentees the consideration initially sought. Patent brokers seldom receive consideration in any form for the value-added services they render—such as introducing the patentee to a buyer who ends up acquiring the patentee's company rather than just its patents, or by facilitating acquihires.

Even when a deal is concluded flawlessly, the patent broker has to wait a long time until he receives his commission. But when patent sales close and patentees receive their funds, patentees do not always fulfill their end of the bargains. In other words, some clients stiff their patent brokers. As one licensing executive at a large Silicon Valley-based electronics company told me, "the higher a patent broker's commission, the more reasons one can find for not paying."

Certainly, many patentees behave honorably with their patent brokers. And there is less risk that contingency litigators, compared to patent brokers, will be jilted. But how should patentees manage their relationships with patent brokers?

Managing the Patentee-Patent Broker Engagement

First, if a patentee is uncomfortable working with patent brokers, he should simply refrain from engaging these professionals. If a patentee can sell his patents by himself, then by all means he should do so. If a patentee can sell his patents quickly, at a high price and without paying a broker a commission, then he absolutely should manage the transaction by himself. The reality is most people cannot sell their houses by themselves. Neither can many patentees independently sell their patents.

Second, patentees that elect to work with patent brokers should treat them with respect. This is not necessarily a magnanimous gesture but a practical consideration. There are millions of issued patents and patent applications. Almost all patent owners would like to monetize their patents in some fashion. The problem is that there are very few patent brokers (roughly 30 throughout the world by my count) that have records of successfully monetizing patents. (Many who call themselves patent brokers are really seeking full-time employment elsewhere. One risk of engaging with these transitory patent brokers is that when they land their next positions, efforts to monetize your patents will come to a screeching halt. Other patent brokers believe they can just work their own limited networks without making necessary investments in things like databases.) The reality is that the volume of inquiries from patentees interested in selling their portfolios exceeds the successful brokers' bandwidth.

Whatever agreements patentees and patent brokers negotiate in good faith are legitimate. However, a few ideas for the two parties working in at least a semi-harmonious fashion include:

- Just as a homeowner is often well advised to apply a coat of paint and to plant flowers in his front yard before showing his home to prospective buyers, patentees should prepare (or have prepared at their expense) marketing documents, patent valuation reports, claims charts and the like.

- Patentees should be prepared to execute deals that meet predetermined targets. It is simply not fair to encourage a patent broker to shop a patent portfolio around the world for what turns out to be more than a year only to back out of deals that meet predetermined thresholds. If such deals must be avoided, the broker is entitled to some combination of retainer and success fee.

- In return for paying a lower commission on success, the patent broker should be offered some cash (or stock) retainer. When the patent broker stands to receive a very high commission at the close, patentees often take the attitude that they need not make any effort to educate or assist the patent broker. This stance repels cooperation, to the detriment of closing a transaction. Paying the patent broker during the course of his marketing efforts helps keep the agent focused on the assignment at hand: The absence of retainers often causes deal momentum to decelerate to the point where the deal is dead.

One equitable retainer arrangement calls for paying larger retainers at the beginning of engagements and towards the closings, when most effort is exerted. Lower retainers can be paid in the middle months, when the broker is waiting for responses from solicited potential buyers.

Further, buyers are often skeptical of acquiring patents from inventors. These buyers are concerned that the inventor / patentee is too emotionally wedded to his patents and will not relinquish them even if the buyer makes a generous offer. Patent buyers are too busy to risk spending months on a deal only for the patentee to withdraw his offer to sell. When buyers learn that the seller is paying a (monthly) retainer, they believe that sellers are becoming less emotionally attached to their patents and therefore more likely to agree to reasonable offers, if for no reason other than to end the pain of paying regular retainers.

Inocencia: Is inventorship based on a first-to-invent or a first-to-file basis?

Patent Lawyer: The United States now operates on a first-to-file (not a first-to-invent) basis. This means that the patent will go to the inventor who is slower in the laboratory but quicker to race to the patent office, not to the inventor who more quickly produces his invention but is slower to file his patent application. There are a few unfortunate developments related to the first-to-file patent regime. For instance, some large companies have flooded the USPTO with poorly drafted placeholder patent applications. They then wait until the technology is better understood before pursuing the patents they really desire. Such practices crowd out the ability of true innovators to secure patents.

Second, in industries such as toys and apparel, the product development cycles are long but the selling cycles are short. Inventors are under tremendous pressure to share prototypes of newly-invented products with retailers and licensees as soon as possible. If an inventor complies by sharing his invention with the licensee, he does so at the risk of the licensee beating the inventor to the patent office. But if the customer or licensee does not embrace the new invention, the invention may not warrant the expense of pursuing a patent.

Inocencia: You mentioned that some examiners allow very few patent applications to issue. Why would they reject patent applications? I understand that there can be tension between patent applicants and examiners. Such tension can arise when a patent applicant responds to an examiner's rejection—the applicant is basically saying that he thinks the examiner is wrong. Aren't patent examiners good people?

Patent Lawyer: Not all patent applications should be allowed. Since patents give rights to patentees, everyone else is necessarily deprived of such freedoms to operate. Thus, examiners absolutely should be judicious in their examinations and allowances.

As for the quality of patent examiners, I disagree with patent critics who claim that most examiners must be buffoons because the PTAB kills so many supposedly "bad patents" that the examiners grant. Most examiners are highly intelligent and behave honorably most of the time. But that doesn't mean patentees should be naïve. American patent examiners have much less experience than patent examiners in other parts of the world, such as Europe. (The standards for becoming an examiner are much more rigorous in Europe and European patent examiners are much better compensated than U.S. patent examiners.) Also, according to Professor Melissa Feeney Wasserman of the University of Texas at Austin School of Law, examiners spend an average of only 19 hours reviewing patent applications.

Of course, there are some bad patent examiners. You can't have 9,000 employees anywhere and expect all of them to be great at their jobs, especially if it's almost impossible to fire such employees. In the second half of the 2010s, more than 400 USPTO patent examiners were found to have cheated on their timecards, costing taxpayers about $18 million in potential excess wages.[22] The incentives placed on these unionized examiners do not always serve patentees well. The following are disappointments that patent lawyers have expressed with regards to patent examiners:

---

[22] Inventors Digest, November 2018, page 24.

- Patent examiners are required to locate and provide evidence to support their factual findings when examining claims in connection with eligible subject matter. However, some examiners have routinely dismissed claim elements as conventional or well-known for purposes of patent eligibility analysis without citing supporting evidence.

- Some patent examiners are only assigned to examine apparatus claims even though some of the patents cited as prior art by the applicant contain both apparatus and methods claims.

- USPTO examiners do not always consider 'secondary indicia' affidavits filed to overcome obviousness rejections. Under the Graham v. John Deere decision, such secondary evidence of non-obviousness may include evidence of commercial success, long-felt but unsolved needs, failure of others, copying by the industry and unexpected results. Examiners often fail to consider such factors, as they are required to do, when they summarily reject any and all evidence with a form paragraph.

  Judges have also been dismissive of such secondary indicia. For instance, in the Allergan-Saint Regis case, Judge William Curtis Bryson of the Court of Appeals for the Federal Circuit found that there was no doubt that Restasis was a commercial success, citing the medication's $1.2 billion in net sales during 2015 alone. However, Judge Bryson stated, "the problem with Allergan's evidence of both commercial success and long-felt need is that Allergan's patents have long blocked others from entering the space in the market that is now occupied by Restasis." Perhaps Judge Bryson forgot that patents are supposed to exclude others from entering markets. It appears that Judge Bryson failed to consider that $1.2 billion in net sales is strong evidence of need regardless of how many or how few competitors are in the field.

- Examiners have become promiscuous in terms of issuing restriction requirements, requiring patentees to separate and file multiple applications instead of one. Restriction requirements generate more patent issuance and maintenance fees for the USPTO but are more expensive for patentees. Restriction requirements help examiners score more points (related to their compensation) without working too hard since the examiner has already learned the art. For each successive divisional patent application, there is less art to examine and the prior art searches become easier to conduct.

- There is absolutely no patent quality review of unallowed patents, absent the applicant going through the trouble, time and expense of filing an appeal. Further, to my knowledge, overturning cases on appeal does not have any negative impact on examiners.

- There have been instances where patent examiners have refused to grant a patent application unless a particular word was inserted into the application. Years later, such patents were invalidated because of the inclusion of these examiner-mandated words. In the case of prolific inventor James Logan, the word was "determinant" and the patent application number was 08/634,618.

Inocencia: What could stop me from asserting my patents once they are issued?

Patent Lawyer: Patent litigation is exorbitantly expensive; not all patentees can afford to litigate to verdict, let alone through appeal. For instance, in 2015, the American Intellectual Property Law Association estimated that the median cost to pursue patent litigation when $1 million or less was at risk was $600,000, and $2 million when between $1 million and $10 million was at risk.[23] Most lawyers believe that these numbers were underestimates when they were published; certainly, they have become increasingly understated over the ensuing years.

Inocencia: Well, at least patentees get their day in court as long as they can afford it. Correct?

Patent Lawyer: Actually, subsequent to the Alice decision, many district courts have suffocated patent infringement cases before they even got started. They have done so by invalidating patents at the pleadings stage of litigation. Four years after the Alice decision, district courts addressed patent eligibility 810 times. Approximately 60% of these decisions, or 480

---

23 https://www.patentattorney.com/aipla-survey-of-costs-of-patent-litigation-and-inter-partes-review/

decisions, found that claims were unpatentable due to ineligibility. Roughly 74%, or 355, of these invalidations were handed down based on pleadings.[24] Invalidations at the pleadings stage are averse to long-standing procedural rules and patent doctrines, such as the presumption of patent validity.

Inocencia: If a patentee's case proceeds beyond the pleadings stage, would the patentee be able to assert all of the claims that he elects to assert?

Patent Lawyer: No. It is common for judges to limit the number of claims patentees may assert. For instance, Judge Sammartino in the Southern District of California narrowed a set of 112 asserted claims down to only 24.[25] A Court in the Central District of California narrowed 225 asserted claims spread over nine patents to only four claims per patent, and a Court in the District of Delaware reduced the number of asserted claims from 90 to only 10.

Inocencia: Such drastic limiting of the number of claims that are allowed to be asserted can really decimate patent value.

Patent Lawyer: There may be some truth in that statement. However, I believe the reality is that there are constraints on the time that courts, judges and juries can devote to patent litigation. The courts have an obligation to be fair to the defendants as well. Defendants should not have to defend themselves against the 225th claim if the patentee couldn't prove infringement of any of the 224 claims for which he believed he had a better case of demonstrating infringement.

In a similar vein, many judges prefer to dismiss patent disputes. Patent law is extremely nuanced and judges often do not understand the technical issues being discussed. Worse yet, patent infringement cases can tie up a judge's calendar for years. For reasons such as these, many judges despise patent cases and the patentees that initiate them.

Inocencia: Can you give me a specific citation of a judge articulating his disdain for patent cases or the patentees that file them?

Patent Lawyer: Judge William Curtis Bryson of the Court of Appeals for the Federal Circuit dedicated four pages of his 11-page opinion relating

[24] https://www.ipwatchdog.com/2018/09/18/alice-age-four-grow-up/id=101447/

[25] West View Research, LLC v. BMW of North America, LLC

to Allergan's patent arbitrage deal with the St. Regis Mohawk Tribe to excoriating Allergan. Judge Bryson was irate at Allergan for its attempt to use the tribe's sovereign immunity to escape invalidity challenges in *inter partes review* proceedings brought against it. The strange thing was that the issue of the tribe's sovereign immunity wasn't before the court; Judge Bryson ultimately found that Allergan's dealing with the Regis Mohawk Tribe in relation to the drug-maker attempting to escape invalidity challenges "do not bear on this Court's power to hear this case."

Separately, suppose a judge dislikes patent cases in general and shows no favoritism to plaintiffs or defendants. The advantage would still go to the defendants. If the two sides became exasperated in front of an indifferent judge, the case would likely be dropped which would benefit the alleged infringer. The advantage also goes to the infringer when the judge requires the two sides to negotiate a resolution to their dispute.

Inocencia: There are no patent police. If a patentee wants to enforce his patents, he (or his licensees) must police the market for infringers. If amiable discussions with alleged infringers do not proceed in a manner that is satisfactory to the patentee, then the patentee (or exclusive licensee) has little choice but to enforce his patents. Correct?

Patent Lawyer: That is largely true. In contrast to the FBI pursuing some cases of trade secret misappropriation, the FBI does not investigate patent infringement and there are no patent police. But remember that not all patentees can afford to assert their patents. Patent litigation requires an enormous commitment of time and causes entrepreneurs to lose focus in terms of running their businesses. It should not be forgotten that the more time inventors are tangled up in patent litigation, the less time they can spend on research. There are even more risks for patentees. Patent-holders find it almost impossible to license their patents-in-suit to others during litigation. They can have their patents invalidated and can even be countersued on the basis of defamation or tortious interference.

Inocencia: When patent infringement is determined, how are damages awards calculated?

Patent Lawyer: The calculation of patent damages is a very broad and intricate topic and largely beyond the scope of this discussion. However,

I will make a few comments. At a minimum, patentees are supposed to receive a reasonable royalty award for the use of their inventions. The formula for calculating royalty damages seems very simple; just multiply the reasonable royalty rate times the extent of the infringement.

What should we use for the base, against which the royalty rate is to be multiplied? Now, the issue becomes more complicated. One school of thought says that we should use the entire market value of the product that infringed. Detractors of the 'entire market value rule' rightfully point out that the governing code states that the patentee should be compensated for the use of the invention, not the entire market value of the underlying product that infringed. Also, detractors of the entire market value rule claim, with some legitimacy, that the application of this school of thought could overcompensate inventors.

However, another school of thought holds that the royalty base should be the smallest saleable unit upon which the infringing feature rests. This notion is fraught with even more problems than the entire market value rule. For starters, licensing professionals who negotiate licensing agreements have no idea what their procurement officers pay for components. Why not ask their finance people what components cost? Because the finance people don't know either. In some cases, the finance people may have a number but will not share it with their intellectual property managers. Even if the finance people produce a number that is supposed to reflect the cost of components, that number is more for accounting convenience (tax minimization) as opposed to a reflection of an arms-length price. Even if numbers are produced by the accounting departments of licensees, how are adjustments supposed to be made for volume discounts, return policies, stock-outs, special promotions, payment terms, delivery policies, rebates, insurance, penalties for late delivery or for delivery that does not meet the customer's specifications? Even if average prices could be fairly determined, the prices of components and the value of those components are not the same. Sometimes, small components have a big impact on end unit prices. For instance, a microprocessor may cost 0.7% of the retail price of a server but may be the reason that consumers are willing to pay a 20% premium for that end product.

Inocencia: It sounds like the smallest saleable unit mythology is just one more excuse to not pay patentees what they deserve. I don't see the problem with starting with what you know when calculating royalty bases; wholesale and retail prices of end products are much more available and credible than prices of obscure components. It seems to me that the Fermi method of determining addressable markets, which holds that you start with what you know, supports my position. I can understand that patentees should not be overcompensated for their inventions. (There is so much anti-patent sentiment that I wouldn't be surprised if Amber-type alerts are set to be activated whenever a patentee is overcompensated for his invention.) But where is the concern in jurisprudence to make sure that patentees are not *underpaid* for their inventions?

Patent Lawyer: That is a question that should be asked much more frequently. On a related note, even when large patent damages awards are handed down, they are almost invariably dramatically reduced when the case is appealed. Also, sometimes inventors can inadvertently shoot themselves in the foot. For instance, in the early stages of his research, an inventor might have sent out an email saying that he would be pleased to receive $1 million or $2 million for his patent portfolio. Years later, the invention proves to be incredibly valuable. Maybe it's worth several tens of millions of dollars. But in the midst of litigation, the inventor's email is presented to a jury. The defendant will argue, "Seven years ago, the inventor stated that he would have been satisfied with $1 million. A few hundred thousand dollars above that figure is more than fair compensation for past use of the subject patents."

Inocencia: Are patentees entitled to add interest to their damages awards during the time in which their cases are stayed due to PTAB proceedings?

Patent Lawyer: In many cases, patentees are allowed to add interest charges to their damages awards that accumulate during stays in their patent infringement suits. However, judges have tremendous discretion on this issue. So, patentees cannot count on interest enhancing their damages awards when their cases are stayed due to PTAB proceedings.

Inocencia: What is a patent troll? I often hear that term in the press and during campaign seasons.

Patent Lawyer: Wikipedia has defined a patent troll as a derogatory phrase coined by former Intel Assistant General Counsel Peter Detkin to impugn entities that hold patents but do not manufacture products. Thus, these entities do not sell products that incorporate the inventions claimed by the patents they hold. The only way they make money is by selling their patents or licensing them out to others. Some of these licensing agreements are friendly deals in which the licensor does not believe that his patents are being infringed. In other cases, the patentee believes that his patents are being infringed and the alleged infringer is under some pressure to reach a licensing agreement. These licensing agreements may be negotiated during, or in anticipation of, patent infringement litigation.

Inocencia: So, universities, teaching hospitals or national laboratories could be considered patent trolls since they do not manufacture anything. Right? If they detect that a company is infringing their patents and they seek compensation for such exploitation of their patents, they are considered trolls. Correct? It seems to me that a patent troll could be any inventor who does not self-impose a gag order, take a vow of poverty, and resign himself to the sidelines as others make money off of his inventions. I suppose vendors that pursue the collection of their account receivables could be labeled "account receivables trolls." Further, in Abraham Lincoln's day, patent trolls were called "patent sharks." Where would we be if we shut down the patent system in the 1860s?

Patent Lawyer: You are right that universities, teaching hospitals, and national laboratories are considered by some to be patent trolls. In fact, Professor Adam Mossoff, a Professor of Law at George Mason University, said that in 2015, "Congressman Darrell Issa condemned universities as patent trolls because they licensed their patents to companies that produced products."

Moreover, for-profit entities that acquire and enforce patents provide a valuable service to the inventor community. (There are a variety of names for such entities. Among them are patent trolls, non-practicing entities and patent assertion entities.) Small inventors face almost impossible odds in enforcing their patents. Large companies often see no reason to pay inventors royalties if they cannot enforce their patent rights. So, patent assertion entities that have the financial resources and legal skills to enforce patents provide a marketplace for small inventors to sell their patents. Due to the emergence of non-practicing entities, a small inventor who does not have the money, time or expertise to enforce his patents against a large infringer can sell his patents to an entity that can better enforce such rights.

Inocencia: It doesn't seem to me that so-called patent trolls are so bad. But they have a terrible rap. For instance, the *Denver Post* has written: "The latest predator to terrorize boardrooms is a creature called the "patent troll." This is a patent-holding company that collects licensing fees from users of its technology and sues those who won't pay."[26] *Fortune* magazine defines patents trolls as "shell companies that acquire old patents in order to shake down real businesses."[27] I bet the reporters who wrote those missives would sue their employers if their employers didn't pay them. Would that make them "salary trolls?"

Patent Lawyer: To be fair, there was once a legitimate concern that some patentees were abusing the system. Back in the 2013 timeframe, a patent holding company known as MPHJ sent out thousands of demand letters to businesses that used office scanners, which MPHJ hinted might be infringing its patents. These demand letters did not reflect actual investigations of specific acts of infringement. Neither did the letters specify which patents were alleged to have been infringed nor did they explain how MPHJ calculated the $1,000 to $1,200 per user licensing fees that MPHJ sought from businesses that operated scanning technology. Also, MPHJ concealed its identity in some of the demand letters that it dispatched.

In more recent years, the term "patent troll" has been broadened to such an extent that it includes just about every patentee who tries to monetize his patents. As Professor Mossoff explained in congressional testimony, the greatest innovators such as Thomas Edison, Charles Goodyear, Elias Howe, and Nikola Tesla would today be considered patent trolls. The patent troll epithet is defamatory, derisive, and demeaning. Casting a patent-holder as a patent troll depreciates their legitimacy in a court of law and in the court of public opinion. Real business losses can be inflicted on patentees as a result.

Inocencia: Can you give an example of how labeling a business a patent troll can cause it to lose money?

Patent Lawyer: Yes. In his defamation case against the American Bankers Association, David Barcelou and Automated Transactions (a company David founded), asserted that the ABA defamed them by referring to them

---

[26] Greg Griffin, "Trolling for patents," The Denver Post, March 12, 2006

[27] https://fortune.com/2015/05/26/scotus-cisco-patent-trolls/

as "patent trolls." The ABA made comments that Automated Transactions was a "patent troll" that "targets" banks. In at least one presentation to its members, the Credit Union National Association identified Automated Transactions as a "well known troll." Such name calling exposed David and Automated Transactions to hatred, ridicule and contempt. Worse yet, it caused them to be ostracized by the automated transaction machine (ATM) operators throughout the country, which was Automated Transactions's client base. Automated Transactions's royalties from its some 200 existing licensees in the financial services sector dried up after it was lambasted by the AMA. Needless to say, these royalties were not replaced by new licensees.

Chicago-Kent College of Law Professor, Edward Lee pointed out in the *Stanford Technology Law Review*, "some courts have even barred the use of the term [patent troll] altogether during patent trials on the grounds that the term is unfairly prejudicial." One such instance arose in litigation between Apple and Samsung on one side, and Smartflash on the other side. The defendants tried to cast Smartflash as a patent troll by writing in their brief, "Smartflash does not practice these patents or make any products." Fortunately, the district court granted a motion filed by Smartflash, which precluded Apple from making "any insinuation that any... aspects of Smartflash's corporate structure are suspicious or improper." Also, after conducting a study on patent assertion entities in 2016, the Federal Trade Commission called the term "patent troll" both unhelpful and prejudicial. (The same commission also specifically recognized that patent assertion entities can and do play a valuable role in the market.)

Also, the incidence of patent litigation initiated by non-practicing entities is vastly overstated. And to a large extent, the litigation initiated by such entities is a result of the America Invents Act. Under the AIA, suits filed against multiple defendants must be filed separately instead of on a consolidated basis. So, before the AIA, if a patentee believed that ten companies were infringing its patent, it could file one suit. After implementation of the AIA, ten lawsuits would have to be filed.

If pejorative terms like patent troll are to be used in contemporary times, they should be used to describe those who seek to invalidate patents they are practicing but for which they do not wish to pay royalties. Lots of large companies like Microsoft, Apple, and Google file unmeritorious cases and petitions at the PTAB, repeatedly relitigate decided issues (sometimes on the same or similar prior art), assert unnecessary motions and legal procedures, and burden targets with ruinous defense costs.[28] In some cases, such tactics are undertaken by hedge funds that short the shares of the pharmaceutical patentees they are attacking.

Inocencia: The intersection of patent trolls and short sellers sounds very interesting. I would like to learn more about that. But first, what precautions are in place to prevent frivolous patent infringement cases?

Patent Lawyer: There are major hurdles and disincentives to filing patent infringement lawsuits that lack merit. The Federal Trade Commission has cracked down on demand letters and federal rules have heightened pleading standards. Local rules now permit summary judgment early in cases. Judges can sanction lawyers who file meritless cases and they even have the power to throw them in jail. Also, Octane Fitness gave judges the discretion to award attorneys' fees for bad faith litigation tactics.

Inocencia: Are you saying that short sellers have tried to destroy patents covering pharmaceuticals just to make money on their investments? Are these short sellers considered patent trolls?

Patent Lawyer: Short sellers are not labeled as patent trolls. In the eyes of the anti-patent community, there is nothing wrong with trying to bankrupt pharmaceutical companies that are trying to produce medicines by wantonly moving to destroy their patents. Some short sellers throw rationality to the wind when trying to assail patents. For instance, Citron Research attacked PolarityTE, a commercial-stage biotechnology and regenerative biomaterials company located in Utah, for committing fraud in the first half of 2018. What was the basis of Citron's accusation? PolarityTE failed to notify shareholders that the patent examiner issued a non-final rejection, and a final rejection, during the prosecution of one of its patent applications. These accusations were ridiculous; they only highlighted Cirtron's complete lack of knowledge of how patents are reviewed. Almost all patent applications receive at least one non-final rejection and there are a multitude of steps to take to achieve patent issuance after one (or even multiple) final rejections are issued.

---

[28] According to a study conducted by the law firm Robins Kaplan LLP, the rate of duplicative *inter partes review* filings was 59% for Microsoft, 56% for Apple and 38% for both Samsung and Google.

In any event, the most prominent short seller dedicated to destroying the shares of pharmaceutical companies by attempting to invalidate their patent claims has been Kyle Bass of Hyman Capital. The chart below lays out which patent claims Mr. Bass has invalidated (or at least attempted to invalidate) as well as the drugs and patient groups exposed to his invalidity attempts.

Inter Partes Review Proceedings Initiated by Kyle Bass

IPR Case No.	Patent Owner	US Patent No.	Claims Invalidated	Drug	Targeted Indication
IPR2015-00988	Shire Inc. / Cosmo Technologies Ltd.	6,773,720	None	Lialda	Ulcerative Colitis
IPR2015-00990	NPS Pharmaceuticals, Inc.	7,056,886	46-52 and 61-75 of 75	Gattex	Short Bowel Syndrome
IPR2015-01092	Celgene Corporation	6,045,501	1-10 (all)	Pomalyst and Revlimid	Multiple Myeloma / Slows Tumor Growth
IPR2015-01093	NPS Pharmaceuticals, Inc.	7,056,886	1-27, 31-40, and 44-45	Gattex	Short Bowel Syndrome
IPR2015-01096	Celgene Corporation	6,315,720	1-32 (all)	Pomalyst and Revlimid	Multiple Myeloma / Slows Tumor Growth
IPR2015-01102	Celgene Corporation	6,315,720	1-32 (all)	Pomalyst and Revlimid	Multiple Myeloma / Slows Tumor Growth
IPR2015-01103	Celgene Corporation	6,315,720	1-32 (all)	Pomalyst and Revlimid	Multiple Myeloma / Slows Tumor Growth
IPR2015-01718	Horizon Pharma USA	8,945,621	None	Vimovo	Arthritis Pain Reliever
IPR2015-01776	Anacor Pharmaceuticals, Inc.	7,582,621	1-12 (all)	Kerydin	Antifungal Drug
IPR2015-01780	Anacor Pharmaceuticals, Inc.	7,767,657	1-24 (all)	Kerydin	Antifungal Drug
IPR2015-01785	Anacor Pharmaceuticals, Inc.	7,767,657	1-24 (all)	Kerydin	Antifungal Drug
IPR2015-01835	The Trustees of the University of Pennsylvania	8,618,135	None	Juxtapid	Cholesterol-Lowering Drug
IPR2015-01836	The Trustees of the University of Pennsylvania	7,932,268	None	Juxtapid	Cholesterol-Lowering Drug
IPR2015-01850	Acorda Therapeutics, Inc.	8,440,703	None	Ampyra	Multiple Sclerosis
IPR2015-01853	Acorda Therapeutics, Inc.	8,007,826	None	Ampyra	Multiple Sclerosis
IPR2015-01857	Acorda Therapeutics, Inc.	8,663,685	None	Ampyra	Multiple Sclerosis
IPR2015-01858	Acorda Therapeutics, Inc.	8,354,437	None	Ampyra	Multiple Sclerosis
IPR2015-01993	Biogen MA, Inc.	8,399,514	None	Tecfidera	Multiple Sclerosis
IPR2016-00245	Alpex Pharma	8,440,170	1-3, 5-6, and 8-9	Suprenza	Weight Loss
IPR2016-00694	Nissan Chemical Industries, Lt	8,796,464	1	Bravecto	Flea & Tick for Dogs

Data compiled in 2017.

Interestingly, Mr. Bass has taken to characterizing his policy of never settling with patentees in his efforts to invalidate their patents as a sign of his virtue. The reality is that settling such invalidation attempts would be counterproductive to his short selling investment strategy.

I don't know how Mr. Bass's investments are working out. But the disparity of the stock performances of publicly-traded licensing companies (also referred to as patent assertion entities) and the most prolific infringers couldn't be more profound. Shares of many of the licensing companies have been delisted or are at risk of becoming delisted. On the other hand, shares of the most unrepentant infringers like Apple and Alphabet (formerly known as Google) are Wall Street darlings.

I want to mention another group of patent antagonists, state attorneys general. In recent years well over 15 states—from Alabama to Wisconsin—have adopted anti-troll legislation. The vitriol spewing from state attorneys' general has truly been venomous. For example, New York's former Attorney General Eric Schneiderman said, "Patent trolls exploit loopholes in the patent system and have become a scourge on the business community."[29]

Inocencia: Isn't patent law a matter of federal law? Why are a variety of states interfering with something that is the remit of the federal government?

Patent Lawyer: You are right. Patents fall under the laws of the federal government. Patentees would find it very difficult if they had to adhere to a bewildering quilt of fifty state laws in terms of licensing, defending and enforcing their patents. Nevertheless, some states are preempting federal law by promulgating state laws that reduce the enforceability of patents. Many patent lawyers are concerned that state attorneys' general might take action against counselors representing patentees on the supposition that those counselors are practicing law in their states without proper licensure. The result is that patentees are increasingly intimidated to file patent infringement suits. To wit:

---

[29] https://www.ipwatchdog.com/2014/01/14/ny-attorney-general-settles-investigation-into-patent-troll/id=47411/
Mr. Schneiderman then went on to define patent trolls extremely broadly by holding that "patent trolls are those entities that buy patents owned by others and then try to turn a profit by aggressively pursuing businesses they claim infringe the acquired patents."

- In Wisconsin, demand letters that fail to contain required information or that contain false, misleading, or deceptive information are subject to a $50,000 fine for each violation. The required information is quite exacting in Wisconsin and includes the identification of each claim of each patent or pending patent being asserted as well as the target's product, service, process, or technology to which that claim relates.

- A variety of states—including Ohio, Vermont, Kansas, Maine and Oklahoma—have the ability to impose punitive damages on patentees that disseminate "bad-faith communications" to businesses in those states. As a result, patentees such as MPHJ have agreed to refrain from sending out demand letters in certain states (such as Minnesota) without permission of the state attorney general. Some state laws allow recipients of so-called bad-faith demands to bring their own enforcement actions independent of the state attorney general.

- States such as Vermont, Idaho, Indiana, Ohio and New Jersey have the authority to require patentees to post bonds when they assert their patents against alleged infringers in their states.

Some attorneys general have lost all semblance of equity in their war on patentees. For instance, New York's Eric Schneiderman excoriated MPHJ for threatening to sue hundreds of businesses and then failing to follow through with these suits when they did not respond to that patentee's letters within two weeks. Mr. Schneiderman seemed to be suggesting that he would have been more content if MPHJ actually did initiate litigation against businesses in the Empire State.

The Genesis of the Patent Troll Pejorative

What is the genesis of the term "Patent Troll"? The short answer is, "Peter Detkin." When Mr. Detkin coined this term in 2001, he was an Assistant General Counsel at Intel Corporation. (Interestingly, Mr. Detkin later became a Managing Director at Intellectual Ventures, a company that has been cited as the prototypical patent troll.) What follows is some etymological history of the term "patent troll."

In March of 1994, a company called International Meta Systems (IMS) filed a patent application titled RISC Architecture Computer Configured for Emulation of the Instruction Set of a Target Computer. The underlying invention was compatible with Intel's computing architecture; it could read Intel chip instructions but also included some enhanced features. This patent application issued as U.S. Patent No. 5,574,927 on November 12, 1996.

IMS's RISC invention was said to be poised to give Intel a run for its money. Despite the promise of the IMS chip, no major computer manufacturers wanted to transact business with IMS. As an early-stage company, IMS was in no position to supply them with high volumes of its chips. These chip buyers also feared retaliation from Intel. At the time, Intel had a reputation for halting chip sales to customers that supported competing technologies. In view of its dwindling resources, IMS sold its '927 patent to TechSearch in January of 1998. Shortly thereafter, IMS was forced to file for Chapter 11 bankruptcy protection.

At about the same time, TechSearch sought to license its newly-acquired patent to Intel as it was TechSearch's analysis that the chip giant was producing approximately $8 billion worth of infringing Pentium Pro and Pentium II chips annually. In June of 1998, after Intel refused to license the '927 patent, TechSearch initiated patent infringement litigation against Intel and sought $500 million in damages.

Intel quickly moved to invalidate what it labeled a "clearly invalid" patent. The silicon powerhouse also threatened TechSearch with sanctions if it did not abandon its lawsuit. Intel's first prong of attack on the '927 patent was to hire the inventor of the IMS patent and his attorney to testify that the patent at issue was invalid. Initially, the inventor testified in a deposition that he didn't know whether or not an allegedly critical piece of prior art was indeed prior art. However, the inventor soon changed his tune regarding the same piece of prior art by stating that, "I would consider it prior art."

Intel Moves to Invalidate and Acquire the Same Patent

While Intel was busy trying to invalidate the '927 patent, it was also conniving to acquire that patent. Intel tried to claw the patent out of the hands of TechSearch so that TechSearch would be forced to withdraw its patent suit against Intel.

Intel's strategy was to convince the federal bankruptcy court to approve an avoidance motion. Avoidance gives bankruptcy trustees the power to void a transfer if the debtor "received less than a reasonably equivalent value" in exchange for the transfer if the transfer occurred while the debtor was insolvent or if the debtor was rendered insolvent by the transfer. Intel was ready and motivated to put on a case in which it would try to prove that the transference of the '927 patent from IMS to TechSearch should be voided because TechSearch did not pay IMS sufficient money.

To put itself in position to seek an avoidance action, Intel secretly created a shell company called Maelen Limited in the Cayman Islands. This shell company was formed in August of 1998, shortly after TechSearch acquired the '927 patent from IMS. Intel tried to mask its ownership of Maelen Limited by having Bank of America put its fingerprints all over Maelen. All of Maelen's officers and directors were employees of Bank of America but Mr. Detkin called the shots. Intel, disguised as Maelen Limited, was so eager to pry the '927 patent away from TechSearch through the avoidance action that it offered to fund the costs of litigating against TechSearch and to pay the administrative costs of the trustee. Maelen also proposed that if IMS recovered its patent, an auction would be held and Maelen would tender a minimum bid of at least $325,000 for that patent.[30]

Intel's gambit did not work. Counsel for TechSearch said that Maelen's failure to disclose that it was a "front" for Intel was fundamentally improper. Judge Frank R. Monroe (and the trustee) agreed and denied Maelen's motion for avoidance and concluded that Intel was being deceptive. Judge Monroe also concluded that Intel and Maelen had adverse interests with respect to IMS. If the patent reverted back to IMS, IMS would likely want to pursue maximum recovery arising from Intel's alleged infringement of the '927 patent while Intel would certainly want to terminate such litigation.

When he spoke to the tech press a few years later, in 2002, an Intel spokesman by the name of Chuck Malloy called Ray Niro (who represented TechSearch) a "patent extortionist." This inflammatory charge prompted Mr. Niro to file a defamation suit against Intel. Mr. Detkin, an associate general counsel at Intel, needed to coin a term that would both demonize patentees that assert their patents and also deter further defamation charges. Thus, the term "patent troll" was born.

Postscript

The history behind Intel's defamation of patentees reflects a shallow attempt to mask its own duplicity. Intel lost in a federal bankruptcy courtroom but it scored points in the court of public opinion. By casting those who assert their patents against large companies as patent trolls, large companies have turned the tables. In many circles—such as in Congress, the Supreme Court and in the media—infringers have become subjects of sympathy while patentees are the targets of scorn.

Inocencia: How active have state attorneys' general been in enforcing their state laws against patentees? To what extent are these efforts political stunts pushed forward by state attorneys' general positioning themselves for higher office?

Patent Lawyer: That is a fair question. Honestly, I don't know to what extent these laws are being enforced. However, they are on the books and enforcing

---

[30] https://www.martindale.com/matter/asr-596486.pdf

[31] It didn't completely backfire either: A California judge ruled that Intel did not infringe on TechSearch's patents.

them plays into populist sentiment. I would advise you not to test these laws. It should be noted that state attorneys' general are not the only politicians to bad mouth so-called patent trolls. Former President Obama described trolls as companies that "essentially leverage and hijack somebody else's idea and see if they can extort some money out of them."[32] In his dissenting opinion in Commil USA v. Cisco Systems, Supreme Justice Antonin Scalia decried that the Court's ruling "increases the *in terrorem* power of patent trolls."

The Supreme Court expressed concerns about patent trolls in other cases brought before it —such as Halo Electronics and eBay v. MercExchange—despite no patent owner involved in those cases having ever been alleged to have been a patent troll. Also, the Supreme Court's decision in the TC Heartland case had the (intended) effect of making it much more arduous for patentees to sue alleged infringers in the Eastern District of Texas (considered to be one of the fairest courts to patentees), despite the patent-holder (Kraft Foods) in that case being far from anyone's definition of a patent troll.

Inocencia: Aside from these rulings, how would you describe the Supreme Court's decisions on other cases touching on patent-holders' rights?

Patent Lawyer: Terrible. Except for the Halo decision, the Supreme Court has consistently done everything in its power to eviscerate patentees' rights. The Supreme Court's 2006 eBay v. MercExchange decision largely revoked the right of a patent owner to obtain an injunction against infringers. Non-practicing patentees will almost invariably fail eBay's four-point test and will thus be deprived of injunctive relief.[33] According to 2017 data, over 75% of the requests for contested temporary injunctions are denied.[34] The difficulty of obtaining injunctive relief shifts leverage in negotiating reasonable royalty awards from the patentee to the infringer—resulting in below-market licensing rates.

The Supreme Court's Alice and Prometheus decisions created extreme

---

[32] https://www.usatoday.com/story/news/nation/2013/11/25/state-ag-patent-trolls/3696889/

[33] Under the four-point eBay test, to obtain a permanent injunction, a patentee must demonstrate (1) that it has suffered irreparable injury, (2) that monetary damages are inadequate, (3) that considering the balance of hardships, an injunction is warranted, and (4) that the public interest would not be disserved by a permanent injunction.

[34] https://anattorney.com/2018/03/06/3-things-the-2017-patent-litigation-statistics-show-us/

confusion and uncertainty as to which inventions are even eligible for patent protection. That court hasn't exactly rushed to clarify what constitutes a patentable invention. Since the Alice decision was rendered in June of 2014 until the beginning of June 2019, the Supreme Court has denied *writs of certiorari* dealing with patent eligibility issues 42 times.

Separately, the Octane Fitness decision can result in litigants deemed to demonstrate bad behavior to be required to pay their opponent's attorneys' fees. Some judges, such as those in the Southern District of New York, now seem to whimsically slap plaintiffs with Octane sanctions.[35] To a considerable extent, the Octane Fitness decision has destroyed the value of patents held by venture capital funded companies.

Let me provide you with a little background on concerns that venture capitalists have about patents. The venture capitalists that back emerging companies often veto their portfolio companies' plans to assert their patents. In some cases, venture capitalists' aversion to patent litigation is logical. The company allegedly infringing its portfolio companies' patents is often a potential acquirer of those companies. Suppose a venture capital firm invests in semiconductor companies. Companies like Intel could often be alleged infringers. But if the venture capital firm allows its portfolio companies to sue Intel for patent infringement, Intel may decide that it will never acquire another one of the investor's portfolio companies. (Another factor that limits smaller companies' abilities to file for patent infringement is that the expense of patent litigation often causes such patentees to violate the covenants surrounding their lines of credit.)

Even without considering the Octane Fitness decision, patent litigation is extremely expensive, time-consuming and distracting. There is always a good chance that the patentee will lose. Post-Octane Fitness, venture capitalists are even more wary of their portfolio companies asserting their patents. Losses in litigation can be ruinous. By the time patent litigation runs its course, the portfolio company is likely to have burned through its initial investments. Now, it not only has to pay its own legal fees but it may also have to pay its adversary's legal fees.

Inocencia: Why do you think the Supreme Court has made so many rulings adverse to the interests of the patent community? But first, in fairness to the Supreme Court, please tell me what you like about its Halo decision.

[35] https://www.ipwatchdog.com/2018/07/12/bittersweet-milestone-ten-million-patents/id=99132/

Patent Lawyer: On June 13, 2016, the United States Supreme Court unanimously ruled in favor of Halo Electronics in Halo Electronics, Inc. v. Pulse Electronics, Inc. This decision is rendering it less difficult for plaintiffs to demonstrate that defendants' infringement is willful and that patentees are deserving of enhanced (treble) damages.

The Halo decision corrected a travesty of justice known as the two-part Seagate test, which was used to determine willfulness. The now moot Seagate test basically permitted willful infringers to avoid being labeled as such as long as their lawyers could make up a good excuse as to why the infringers' known infringement (at the time of infringement) was not willful based on what was believed at the time of trial. Here is a scenario that would have been acceptable under Seagate:

> On June 12, 2018, the Chief Financial Officer of Bravo Company asks his sales director why sales of Bravo's Majugalie x104 are so light. Bravo's sales director responds that Tango Company placed a new gizmo on its competing device, which is causing Tango to take significant market share away from Bravo's Majugalie x104. Bravo's CFO tells the manufacturing director to put the same gizmo on the Majugalie x104. Bravo Company's chief counsel learns of these discussions and informs the CEO that putting Tango's new gizmo on the Majugalie x104 would infringe Tango Company's patents. The CEO and CFO of Bravo Company respond by saying, "We know that Tango Company has a valid patent that unquestionably covers its new gizmo. But we don't care. We knowingly and willfully authorize the infringement of that patent in order to try to restore revenues." Let's further suppose that this statement was witnessed and recorded.
>
> Nonetheless, under Seagate, the foregoing vignette would not have been sufficient to demonstrate willful infringement. At the time of the infringement trial, on January 15, 2019, Bravo Company could have hired a lawyer who claimed, "In light of the Alice decision, Tango's patents could be ruled invalid. I also found prior art that seems to invalidate the patent-in-suit. Further, I hired a technical expert who tells me that our gizmo does not infringe the patent-in-suit."

While the Halo decision does not make willful infringement easy to demonstrate, it does restore some rationality to the issue. The Halo decision yields a great deal of leverage to plaintiffs. Not only can damages awards be tripled but lawyers' fees can be added to the total damages awards. Typically, jurors find it difficult to grapple with arcane patent law, obtuse economics, and high-level engineering concepts. However, jurors do understand smoking guns such as CEOs caught on videotape ordering infringement. Halo renders such smoking guns admissible in trials while Seagate did not. Many defendants are now more willing to settle once they understand that plaintiffs possess smoking guns. Indisputable evidence of known infringement makes it more difficult to defeat willfulness charges with a summary judgment motion.

Inocencia: Thank you for giving me an insightful overview of the Halo decision. Now, please tell me why you think the Supreme Court may be biased against patents.

Patent Lawyer: I don't want to speculate on what the supreme justices think about patents other than what they have written on such issues. Maybe we can't expect the supreme justices to empathize with patentees because none of the nine supreme justices are patent-holders.

However, there is reason to believe that the Supreme Court is overly-influenced by amicus briefs; these briefs have turned into unsubstantiated position papers put forth by special interest groups. Let me back up a bit. Appellate courts (of which the Supreme Court is a part) are not supposed to be in the business of determining facts. That is the responsibility of the trial courts, where evidence is submitted and scrutinized. During the trial courts' adversarial process, opponents have the opportunity to take issue with data presented and to identify flaws in the methodologies of the studies that their adversaries put forward.

According to Allison Orr Larsen, a professor at William & Mary Law School, over the five terms from 2008 to 2013, the Supreme Court's opinions cited factual assertions from amicus briefs 124 times. Some of these so-called facts hailed from blog posts (in some cases from blogs which expired), emails or nothing at all. Other "studies" presented in amicus briefs were published solely on the Internet and were paid for, or conducted by, the group that submitted the brief.

Inocencia: Well, at least Google (Alphabet) is getting something for its money. I say this because Google spent $18 million on lobbyists the year the AIA was passed.[36] According to a *Wall Street Journal* article, Google financed hundreds of research papers—paying as much as $400,000 per piece—to combat challenges to its market dominance.[37] Further, it has been reported that Google has funded groups dedicated to lobbying against inventor rights such as the High Tech Inventors Alliance, Engine, and the Electronic Frontier Foundation.[38] Organizations such as these sponsor research papers, position papers and amicus curiae briefs.

Let's move on to another topic. I would like to ask you several questions about the PTAB. First, what is the PTAB?

Patent Lawyer: The Patent Trial and Appeal Board is an administrative law body of the USPTO which was designed to quickly decide issues of patentability. The PTAB was formed on September 16, 2012 as one part of the America Invents Act. Among the proceedings heard by Administrative Patent Judges serving on the PTAB are *inter partes reviews* and covered business methods cases.

Inocencia: Can a series of attackers file *inter partes review* petitions and, to the extent those petitions are instituted, stay patent litigation for years on end?

Patent Lawyer: Yes. That can happen. Let me tell you a true story.

On November 8, 2013, Applications in Internet Time sued Salesforce.com for alleged infringement of its patents (7,356,482 and 8,484,111). Salesforce.com tried to invalidate these patents by filing a petition for the PTAB to review the patents-in-suit under its Covered Business Methods program. The parties agreed to stay their litigation when the petition was filed but that stay was lifted after the PTAB denied the CBM petition.

A short while after the CBM petition was denied, RPX Corporation filed an *inter partes review* petition with the PTAB. Salesforce.com filed a new motion for a stay, which the district court judge granted after the

[36] https://www.opensecrets.org/lobby/top.php?showYear=2012&indexType=s

[37] https://www.wsj.com/articles/paying-professors-inside-googles-academic-influence-campaign-14997852

[38] https://campaignforaccountability.org/wp-content/uploads/2018/05/CfA-The-Lobbyist-in-the-Garage-5-30-18.pdf

PTAB granted RPX's *inter partes review* petition. The district court judge's reasoning for granting the stay was that Salesforce.com was not a party of interest in the RPX petition, which is unfathomable given the points discussed below.

Inocencia: Okay. I see how multiple players could elongate stays by filing consecutive *inter partes review* petitions. But, just for my education, did Applications in Internet Time also initiate patent infringement litigation against RPX?

Patent Lawyer: No. Applications in Internet Time never accused RPX of infringing its patents.

Inocencia: I'm confused. If RPX was not a defendant, why did that company move to invalidate Applications in Internet Time's patents?

Patent Lawyer: You may want to pose that question to RPX. But here is my take. RPX is in the business of extricating the companies that pay it large sums of money from paying damages relating to infringing activities. While Salesforce.com was busy with its CBM petition, it lost its one-year window (subsequent to the initiation of patent litigation) to file a petition for *inter partes review.* So, a few months later, RPX swooped in and filed its own *inter partes review* petition in an effort to invalidate the patents that were asserted against Salesforce.com.

Inocencia: Aren't there standing requirements to move to invalidate someone's patents via *inter partes review* proceedings? Can anyone at any time use *inter partes review* to seek to invalidate someone's patents?

Patent Lawyer: Let me answer your second question first. Anyone can attempt to invalidate any patent at any time for any motive, or for no motive. The only exception is that defendants in patent litigation who choose to go the *inter partes review* route must file a petition for *inter partes review* within one year of the beginning of the patent litigation. I suppose I inadvertently answered your first question; there are no standing requirements to file an IPR. However, Section §312 states that *inter partes review* petitioners must disclose all real parties in interest.

Inocencia: So, was it just coincidental that RPX's *inter partes review* petition dovetailed with Salesforce.com's efforts to invalidate the same patents?

Patent Lawyer: In its *inter partes review* petition, RPX stated that it was the only party of interest, the only party involved in preparing and presenting its *inter partes review* petition, and that RPX was not representing anyone else in its petition. Nonetheless, there is quite a bit of evidence that RPX was motivated to rescue Salesforce.com from its embroilment as an accused infringer. To wit:

- Salesforce.com was the only entity that Applications in Internet Time accused of infringing its patent in-suit; no other company had any immediate stakes in seeing the subject patents invalidated.

- Salesforce.com was an RPX client; Salesforce.com made substantial and increasingly large payments to RPX.

- RPX's advertising materials stated that its interests were "100% aligned" with those of its clients, that it provided patent infringement "insurance" services to its clients, and that it served as an adjunct to its clients' in-house legal departments.[39]

- RPX was aware of the Applications in Internet Time lawsuit and the denied CBM petitions as evidenced by numerous communications between RPX and Salesforce.com leading up to the filing of its *inter partes review* petition.

- The two companies had a mutual director on their boards.

- RPX and Salesforce.com were located in the same building.

Whatever the degree of coordination or water carrying on RPX's part for the benefit of Salesforce.com, Applications in Internet Time must have felt that it was at the epicenter of a full-on pincer movement. In the district

[39] https://www.schwabe.com/newsroom-publications-applications-in-internet-time-llc-v-rpx-corp-appeal-nos-2017-1698-et-al-fed-cir-july-9-2018-unsealed-july-24-2018

court, Salesforce.com argued that the claims it was accused of infringing should be construed very narrowly—so narrowly that Salesforce.com could not possibly be infringing them. When RPX took a whack at Applications in Internet Time's patents, that San Francisco-based company argued the claims of Applications in Internet Time's patents were extremely broad, making the mission of producing patent invalidating prior art much easier.[40]

Inocencia: So, what you're telling me is that anyone can move to invalidate any patent at any time for any reason through a government tribunal that former Federal Circuit Chief Judge Randall Rader depicted as "death squads killing property rights" as long as the attackers disclose who is really behind the invalidity attempt; but even if a patent attacker fails to meet that minimum requirement, the attack is still allowed to proceed?

Patent Lawyer: That is not how the system is supposed to work. Judges and Administrative Patent Judges have days where they make bad decisions. It can happen to the best of them.

Inocencia: For every day that a judge or APJ makes a bad decision, there is an inventor who realizes that he just had a bad decade in terms of investing in patent-worthy inventions. Just for clarity, as long as a person has money, he can attempt to invalidate any patent at any time?

Patent Lawyer: Yes. As mentioned, anyone (except the patent owner) can attempt to invalidate any patent at any time, with the caveat that defendants in patent litigation have one year from the time they are served with a complaint to file for *inter partes review*. Patents can be challenged under the PTAB even if that patent was granted before the America Invents Act (which gave birth to the PTAB) was implemented. Anyone can attempt to invalidate even a patent that has lapsed by filing an *inter partes review* petition within six years of a patent expiring given that this is the statute of limitations for bringing a patent infringement action. Further, according to the U.S. government's thinking, the petitioner doesn't even need to be

---

[40] To be fair to RPX, Unified Patents has also been accused of helping infringers circumvent the one-year statute of limitations that kicks in after an alleged infringer has been sued in district court.
https://www.law.com/therecorder/2018/07/16/federal-circuit-cracks-down-on-rpx-activity-at-ptab/

a person in the sense that you and I think of the term "person." In Return Mail Inc. v. United States Postal Service, a Supreme Court case, the federal government argued that it is a person who may petition the PTAB to institute patent validity review proceedings.[41]

Inocencia: Why in the world would the federal government want to be an active participant in invalidating patents that the USPTO grants? Does the federal government believe that an insufficient number of patents are challenged through *inter partes reviews*, that there is insufficient gang-tackling (which occurs when another petitioner requests joinder in a PTAB proceeding by using a near-photocopy of the original petition), or that there are insufficient serial attacks on the same patents? In other words, does the federal government really believe that nine attacks against some patents are needed? Anyway, at least there is still the requirement to pony up some money to launch an IPR.

Patent Lawyer: That is true but a bit of qualification might be in order. First, I don't know if agencies of the federal government pay fees to the PTAB when petitioning that body. Second, petitioners for *inter partes review* are eligible to receive a partial refund of their filing fees if they elect to halt their IPR proceedings before a decision is reached. Third, Unified Patents has supported the training of law students in "identifying prior art and properly making arguments which could be used at the PTAB to invalidate such patents." In supporting such training in conjunction with both the University of Detroit's Mercy School of Law and Berkeley Law, Unified Patents can reduce the cost of putting IPR petitions together.[42]

Inocencia: As to your second qualification, does the patent office refund patentees for any of the expenses they bear in defending their patents in IPR proceedings? Does the patent office refund patentees for the maintenance

[41] The Supreme Court, in a 6-3 decision issued on June 10, 2019, ruled that the government does not constitute a "person." However, less than two months later, in early August of 2019, the Federal Reserve attempted to invalidate patents at the Federal Circuit. The government's bringing such cases to the Supreme Court and then to the Federal Circuit indicates how adamant some government officials are when it comes to emasculating the patent system.

[42] https://www.unifiedpatents.com/news/2018/2/16/unified-works-with-detroit-mercy-law-school-to-stop-patent-abuse-against-small-businesses

fees they have paid when their patents are invalidated? Do patentees receive extended terms on their patents to compensate for the time their cases are stayed while going through IPR proceedings?

Patent Lawyer: The answer to your first two questions is, "of course not." On the contrary, the USPTO's position has been that patent applications must pay the expenses the patent office incurs when patent applicants appeal denial of patent applications before the Federal Circuit Court. Back in 2013, the USPTO unilaterally started including its attorney and support staff fees amongst the expenses it expected patentees to pay.[43] The answer to your third question is that patentees receive extended terms on their patents when prosecution is overly-extended. However, opportunities to license patents are often lost when patent applications experience extended pendency.

Let me say something before you ask me about Unified Patents supporting the training of law students in attempting to invalidate patents. Training law students is a good thing. Purging bad patents also has merit. So, I don't have a problem with Unified Patents supporting the training of new cadres in the methods of invalidating patents.

Inocencia: Then, there shouldn't be a problem with someone sponsoring scholarships directed to training aspiring real estate lawyers in the best ways of dispossessing people of their homes because chains of title problems exist or because of misrepresentations on mortgage applications. Maybe law students studying employment law should receive similar support in learning how to conduct rigorous employment law compliance audits. It would be incongruent for the principals of Unified Patents to object if such subsidized scrutiny were directed to their residences or business.

Patent Lawyer: I haven't thought about that. But I can't argue with the logic.

Inocencia: In view of all of these problems with the US patent system, I am tempted to file patent applications abroad where patent rights are stronger. It is much easier to receive injunctions in Mannheim than in Manhattan. But the costs are prohibitive for small inventors like me. Let's get back to

---

[43] In the summer of 2019, the Supreme Court agreed to hear whether or not the word "expenses" includes the government's attorneys' fees in Peter v. NantKwest.

the merits of the PTAB itself. Doesn't the PTAB play an important role in providing a relatively inexpensive forum for quickly determining the validity of patents?

Patent Lawyer: The public has always had the opportunity to challenge patents. Those opportunities still exist. But the underpinnings of the PTAB tribunals seem to be fundamentally flawed and biased towards petitioners. For starters, I have a problem with the structural decision-making process at the PTAB in terms of how it decides which petitions to institute. The same APJs that decide to listen to cases are the ones that decide those cases. This is like having the same policeman that tickets a driver serve as the presiding judge in traffic court. There is an inherent bias on the part of the APJs to find the instituted claims to be invalid so they can demonstrate that they were judicious in instituting the petition.

Second, the level of evidence required to invalidate claims at the PTAB has been much more lax than is the case in federal courts. In federal courts, it is presumed that a patent is valid until a challenger provides "clear and convincing" evidence to the contrary. At the PTAB, however, challengers are only required to show that it is more likely than not that a patent is invalid. Also, until 2018, the PTAB applied its broadest reasonable interpretation standard to evaluating patent claims. This approach necessarily resulted in the consideration of more pieces of potentially invalidating prior art. (In 2018, the PTAB adopted the Philips standard, which interprets claims in light of the related specifications and filing histories.)

Third, due to severe discovery limitations, patentees find it almost impossible to gain access to damning evidence that lies in the hands of accused infringers. Such evidence could include the alleged infringer having memos stating it believes that the plaintiff's patent is valid, that it is infringing, and that it has failed to design around the claims of the patent it is now seeking to invalidate.

Inocencia: Is there a limit as to how many times a patent can be attacked at PTAB proceedings?

Patent Lawyer: There is no limit to the number of times that petitioners can bring forth *inter partes review* petitions. Finjan, a developer of security-related apps, won more than 80 battles it fought at the PTAB. Thus, patent battles are asymmetric. Infringers can take as many swings at patents as they like. There is no point at which title to a patent quiets. The only time some battles to invalidate patents cease is when the patent is invalidated.

Let's take a look at Zond, a maker of plasma generators used in manufacturing semiconductors. On average, its patents have been challenged 12.5 times in *inter partes review* proceedings. One of Zond's patents was challenged 23 times. Challengers are free to coordinate their attacks against any patents they choose. In the case of Zond, coordinated attacks were waged by Fujitsu, Gillette, Toshiba, Advanced Micro Devices and Taiwan Semiconductor Manufacturing. This is another manifestation of asymmetry in patent invalidity attempts. Not only do small patentees find themselves battling much larger companies, they find themselves battling consortiums of much larger companies.

Inocencia: What you are telling me about Zond pretty much defeats the trope about PTAB serving a purpose of eliminating bad patents from the system. If Zond's patents were so bad, how could it possibly take the death-panel (PTAB) more than 12 tries on average to invalidate them? The fact that Zond's patents withstood so much intellectual and financial firepower lobbed against them indicates that the patents were not "lousy," but extremely strong patents. Further, I would imagine that Zond would have had a hell of a time trying to license those patents when they were confronted with so many invalidity challenges.

Patent Lawyer: Trying to license patents—or to raise capital—in the midst of invalidity challenges is almost impossible. And let's not forget that patents are wasting assets; there is no way to recapture the royalties lost during the days in which no licensing agreements are in place. I would like to get back to the inequity of the PTAB. There are many instances of the PTAB breaking its own rules in its quest to invalidate patents. I can give you two examples of the PTAB's malfeasance that were suffered by the same patentee.

Inocencia: Please do.

Patent Lawyer: Back in 2004 or 2005, Napster filed to have the USPTO reexamine all three of SightSound's patents relating to the delivery of digital media over the Internet. Based on data available at the time, Scott Sander of SightSound rightfully believed that this reexamination proceeding would take 18 months. It took nearly four times as long, almost six years. However, at the end of that tortuous process, in 2010, all of SightSound's patents emerged affirmed and upheld by the USPTO.

By that time, Apple was raking in a fortune from iTunes, but the Cupertino-based company refused to license SightSound's patents which Mr. Sander believed it was infringing. Instead, Apple requested that the USPTO examine SightSound's patents under the PTAB's new Covered Business Method review. The governing regulations limit patents eligible for CBM review to those having claims "used in the practice, administration, or management of a financial product or service."

The PTAB agreed that the patented inventions as a whole had no relation to a financial services business. However, through linguistic gymnastics, the PTAB found a rationale to subject SightSound's patents to CBM review. The financial step, unclaimed in the patent, but which the PTAB deemed to be implied, was that CBM scrutiny was appropriate because customers have to pay for the music transmitted through the Internet. In doing so, the PTAB expanded its jurisdiction by classifying anything commercial as financial.

With a greenlight from the PTAB, Apple brought eight grounds for invalidation of SightSound's patents in its petitions to the PTAB. But SightSound resoundingly prevailed—all eight grounds presented by Apple were rejected by the PTAB. Apparently, the PTAB just could not bear to see SightSound's patents survive. So, the PTAB shot them down on its own volition after the proceedings initiated by Apple concluded. The PTAB claimed it had discretion to raise new grounds entirely on its own. The PTAB put the final nail in SightSound's coffin when it invalidated that company's patents on October 7, 2014—based on prior art that Apple neither presented nor was raised by any of its testifying experts.

While on the topic of SightSound, I would like to take note of one tactic that Apple seemingly applied to create dissention within SightSound. Walt Disney Studios recruited Art Hair, Mr. Sander's co-founder at SightSound, as its Chief Technology Officer. Of course, Apple's Steve Jobs was Disney's largest individual shareholder and a member of Disney's Board of Directors. Due to onerous restrictions that Disney placed on Mr. Hair, Mr. Sander was no longer able to discuss SightSound's patent litigation with his fellow co-founder.

Inocencia: Raising new grounds to invalidate patents sure sounds like overreach on the PTAB's part.

Patent Lawyer: I concur. There is another issue that I would like to address with respect to the PTAB. The PTAB has proven to be a body that destroys not only patents but also the enterprises that hold them. Inventive companies that initiate patent infringement claims against large companies may find that large companies disproportionately retaliate. The alleged infringers may lob volley after volley of IPR petitions against the asserted patents. They may also file multiple attacks against all of the patents owned by those that accuse them of infringing.

Apple applied this tactic against Valencell. Valencell is a North Carolina-based developer of biometric sensors that determined that the Apple Watch infringed several of its patents. Apple filed more than half a dozen IPR petitions against the patents that Valencell asserted against Apple; it also filed IPR petitions against Valencell's patents that were never asserted against Apple. Despite the survival of its challenged claims, Apple's unrelenting efforts to burn much of Valencell's patent portfolio posed an existential threat to the emerging developer of biometric sensors. Thus, Valencell relinquished its litigation against Apple and settled, on undisclosed terms, with its antagonist in September of 2018.

I would like to make note of a few other issues associated with the Valencell-Apple dispute. As per Valencell's pleading in its complaint, Apple came to learn about Valencell's biometric technology when its employees downloaded whitepapers under fictitious names from the Valencell website; these whitepapers described Valencell's biosensor technology. Separately, Apple's efforts to invalidate Valencell's patents paralyzed the North Carolina company in one of its other assertion efforts. Valencell sued another direct competitor, Bragi, for allegedly infringing four patents. However, the district court stayed the entire Valencell-Bragi litigation, despite the fact that Apple was not seeking to invalidate two of the patents that Valencell sought to assert against Bragi.

Inocencia: It doesn't sound like Apple made any attempt to negotiate with Valencell.

Patent Lawyer: Once Apple begins infringing patents, negotiating with that company is usually futile. Let me tell you another story about Apple. A jury in the Southern District of California entered a $145.1 million award against Apple in the summer of 2018 for Apple's infringement of two of Wi-LAN's patents. But Wi-LAN did not instigate this litigation. Rather, the Canadian company engaged Apple in discussions about incorporating its patented technologies relating to Wi-Fi and 4G data speeds into Apple's mobile devices years prior to Apple's introduction of its own infringing 4G LTE devices. During the previous years of discussions, Wi-LAN claimed that it showed Apple blueprints detailing how its wireless technologies would enable computers and mobile devices to stream video and connect to the Internet.

Rather than negotiate in good faith, Apple tried to invalidate five Wi-LAN patents in June of 2014 when it filed a complaint seeking a declaratory judgment. Apple disparaged Wi-LAN by painting it as a patent troll in its complaint by holding that Wi-LAN "has been solely in the business of acquiring and asserting patents." That statement was patently false and misleading. The patents that Wi-LAN asserted in its countersuit against Apple were developed by a team led by Wi-LAN's Ken Stanwood, who was instrumental in helping Wi-LAN become the world's first company to build Wi-Fi and 4G data speeds into mobile devices. At around the time of Wi-LAN's counterclaim, Mr. Stanwood had been awarded 87 U.S. patents and had more than 100 patent applications pending at the USPTO.

Inocencia: I remember Steve Jobs's famous words praising innovators. To paraphrase the Apple co-founder, "You can't ignore inventors because they change things. They push the human race forward. The people who are crazy enough to think they can change the world, are the ones who do." It seems that Apple has changed its stance towards inventors.

Patent Lawyer: Actually, I am familiar with a situation involving a company called Pen-One. This company owned more than 25 patents covering a variety of biometric inventions, such as allowing users to replace styli with their fingers. In 2012, Pen-One tried to negotiate with Apple about having that company acquire or license such patents. These negotiations did not result in an agreement. Then in September of 2013, Apple introduced its iPhone 5S. After commissioning the preparation of extensive claims charts, Pen-One's founder and financial backer believed that Apple's iPhone 5S, and future versions of its iPhones, infringed at least one of Pen-One's patents.

Based on Pen-One's disclosures prior to the introduction of the iPhone 5, Pen-One believed that Apple was exposed to massive potential damages, given the popularity of iPhones and the risk of Apple incurring treble damages based on willful infringement. Pen-One once again attempted to open a dialogue with Apple regarding its unauthorized use of Pen-One's patents. Pen-One was stonewalled.

Pen-One then hired a patent broker to try to open negotiations with Apple. This patent broker took a very accommodating stance with Apple by intimating that Pen-One would rather not sue. He also hinted that the patent owners would likely accept a very reasonable price for their patents; maybe a sum approximating the $5 million invested in Pen-One. It was even conveyed to Apple that Pen-One's wealthy backer would invest his share of the proceeds from a patent sale in The Kynan Duke Company, another one of the backer's companies that is pursuing a cure for pancreatic cancer, the same cancer that ended Steve Jobs's life. These extremely accommodative (and humanitarian) overtures were not reciprocated. Pen-One ended up selling its patents to a patent assertion entity and this entity's efforts to enforce such patents failed.

Inocencia: There is a big difference in a company's public image and the reality of how it treats the innovators whose patented technology it infringes. Can you cite any examples of the PTAB's decisions conflicting with those of other judicial tribunals?

Patent Lawyer: Yes. In December of 2017, the U.S. International Trade Commission found that Comcast was infringing patents—numbers 8,006,263; 8,578,413; 8,046,801; 8,621,512; 8,768,147; 8,566,871; and, 6,418,556—owned by Rovi. Consequently, the ITC prohibited the importation of certain Comcast's digital video receivers as well as hardware and software components. A cease-and-desist order was also issued against Comcast.

Less than a year later, the PTAB went on a rampage against the same patents. On September 19, 2018, the PTAB ruled that all challenged claims associated with Rovi's '263 patent were invalid. All of the claims challenged relative to the '413 patent were declared to be invalid by the PTAB on October 16, 2018. The PTAB also ruled that all of the challenged claims in the '871 and the '801 patents were invalid.

Inocencia: To what extent are the PTAB's decisions consistent with those from the courts, particularly the Court of Appeals for the Federal Circuit?

Patent Lawyer: There is effectively no consistency in decisions relating to patent validity between the PTAB and the courts. Patentees are condemned to live in Schrödinger's Paradox: Their patents are simultaneously valid and invalid depending on the forum that reviews them. According to one study, only 63 of 263 patents that were found valid in full and fair trials in a court of law were also found to be valid at the PTAB. If the courts are correct then the PTAB's error rate is 76%.[44]

I will give you a few real-world examples of how patentees have been impacted by inconsistencies regarding the validity of their patents. Soultran is the assignee of U.S. Patent No. 8,311,945 which covers a method of processing paper checks. Over six years of expensive patent litigation, this patent survived the PTAB and district court. However, the Federal Circuit ruled that this patent was invalid based on it being abstract.

Let's take a look at U.S. Patent No. 6,158,011 which was assigned to SSL Services and titled Multi-Access Virtual Private Network. This patent generated approximately $22 million in licensing and infringement revenue over 16 years. The '011 patent sustained an unrelenting stream of attacks, which included three reexaminations, two PTO *de novo* reviews of those reexaminations, a district court jury verdict and judgment, and a 2014 precedential Federal Circuit decision. None of these attacks dented the '011 patent; each time the challenged claims were confirmed to be valid. However, in 2015, Cisco petitioned for *inter partes review* of the '011 patent. Cisco's petition was based on the same prior art that had been repeatedly argued in so many prior reviews; this fact should have resulted in the PTAB rejecting the petition to institute on grounds of it being duplicative and barred by the Multiple Proceedings rule. However, the PTAB instituted *inter partes review* proceedings which determined that the '011 patent was invalid as obvious in view of the same previously presented and rejected prior art.

Inocencia: Well, I would imagine that, at least, patentees can have inventors testify at the PTAB on their behalf.

Patent Lawyer: You would think so. But this is not always the case. For instance, Dr. Michael Masini was issued U.S. Patent No. 6,558,426 on his

---

[44] https://www.ipwatchdog.com/2017/10/30/ptab-patent-trolls-bad-patents-wakeup-aia-apologists/id=89609/

Posterior-Stabilized Knee Prosthesis but the PTAB prohibited him from testifying at the tribunal on behalf of his own patent. On January 23, 2019, in proceeding number IPR2018-00315 the PTAB stated, "A conference call was held between the parties and the Board on January 23, 2019, to discuss the Patent Owner's request to allow Dr. Michael Masini—the inventor of the subject patent in this proceeding—to address the panel at oral hearing. Patent Owner's request is denied."

Inocencia: Okay, maybe the PTAB has swerved off course a few times, but overall, isn't it a legitimate body that provides an important service as a forum to eliminate bad patents?

Patent Lawyer: I have already provided several examples of it taking many invalidity attempts at the PTAB to void patents. Lousy patents would be invalidated on the first (or at most, the second) challenge. I think that upon reviewing the PTAB's structure, statistics and decisions, any sane person would come to the conclusion that the PTAB is a fundamentally flawed institution. These contentions are supported throughout this interview as well as in the stories presented after this interview.

The PTAB has been so abusive to inventors that some have tried to assign their patents to Native American tribes; the sovereign immunity these tribes enjoy is supposed to shield them from being subject to federal tribunals such as the PTAB. However, the tribes' sovereign immunity protections from the PTAB were stripped away by the Federal Circuit.

Inocencia: Well at least the *inter partes review* procedures are quick, reducing the amount of time that both patentees and defendants must spend in litigation. Correct?

Patent Lawyer: Sometimes this is true but not always. *Inter partes reviews* were designed to accelerate the resolution of patent disputes. However, patent infringers have begun to institute proceedings attempting to invalidate patents by filing with both the PTAB and in federal court simultaneously. This two-pronged approach is directly contrary to the America Invents Act's goal of providing an alternative to resolving validity challenges in expensive district court litigation.

Also, when district court judges stay litigation and when decisions from the PTAB are appealed to the Federal Circuit, *inter partes reviews* delay patent litigation. There have even been times when district court judges stay patent litigation cases when patents other than those in-suit are being challenged via the *inter partes review* process. The judge in one such case took the position that it would be instructive to await the disposition of the patent scrutinized at the PTAB since the patents in-suit and the patent going through the *inter partes review* process were members of the same patent family. This stance was adapted despite the patents having different claims sets. Also, the judge did not explain how justice would be served by taking into account the lower invalidity threshold (preponderance of the evidence) of the non-litigated patent going through the *inter partes review* process when adjudicating the disposition of the in-suit patents that are subject to a higher invalidity threshold (clear and convincing evidence).

Inocencia: Perhaps the PTAB's structure is flawed. But wouldn't you say that its Administrative Patent Judges are good people who are honestly striving to run fair tribunals?

Patent Lawyer: If a judge mistakenly sends scores of innocent people to jail, would we reflexively assume that the judge must be a fundamentally honest man because he didn't send all innocent defendants to prison? Would we salute his efforts to implement justice? If a sheriff's department frequently dispossess rightful inhabitants of their homes, would we celebrate the virtues and work ethics of those law enforcement officers? If kangaroo courts in North Korea, Venezuela and Iran were abolished, would we bemoan the displacements of those judges? The PTAB is a warped government tribunal, which has more than occasionally taken the shape of a kangaroo court. True, APJs do not send defendants to their deaths, but they do strip patentees of their life's work; they do so regularly with enthusiasm and with reckless abandon.

Let's not fall into the politically correct intellectual swamp pit. Not all pursuits are equally noble. In my opinion, the pursuits of entrepreneurs and inventors are more noble than those of patent examiners. And patent examiners are much more honorable people than APJs. Of course, there are anti-patent zealots serving as APJs. But I wouldn't say that APJs are irredeemable. I bet that if the PTAB were to cease to exist, the vast majority of AJPs would find a means to demonstrate their integrity through honest work.

Let me add a little more specificity to my comments. The PTAB does not have any specific Code of Conduct that applies to APJs akin to the Judicial Code of Conduct that applies to federal judges. APJs have not always recused themselves when presented with conflicts. For instance, one APJ heard and decided at least 25 post grant challenges where his former litigation client was the petitioner.

There are nominally three APJs assigned to listen to each case but the reality is that cases are nearly uniformly decided by a single APJ. The other two APJs merely rubber stamp the decision of the APJ responsible for writing the opinion. What is worse is that the PTAB actually discourages dissenting and concurring opinions. Unless the APJ can justify to the Vice Chief Judge why a dissent or concurring opinion should count toward production goals, the work necessary to prepare such opinions will not count towards the APJ's production goals. Thus, the diversity of opinions is squelched because preparing dissent or concurring opinions must typically be done on the APJ's personal time.

Further, research and logic indicate that the incentives placed on APJs not only fail to result in deep deliberations (a deficiency shared with other kangaroo courts), but they encourage assaults on patent owners. To stay in business, the PTAB has to receive its fees. Petitioners will be less likely to use the PTAB and remit related fees if that Board fails to demonstrate its value to the community of infringers.

The reality is even worse. APJs are motivated to allow multiple attacks on the same patents. Instituting multiple *inter partes review* petitions against the same patent allows APJs to more quickly reach their work production quotas—they are reviewing more challenges. At the same time, APJs exert less effort on such reviews because much of the prior art presented by multiple challengers is the same.[45]

Inocencia: It is disheartening to learn that APJs are motivated to invalidate patents. They are even incentivized to facilitate gang-tackling.

Patent Lawyer: I would like to address the USPTO's history of producing misleading statistics regarding gang-tackling. In 2018, Chief Administrative Patent Judge David Ruschke addressed the issue of

[45] https://www.ipwatchdog.com/2019/08/14/honeymoon-time-iancu-take-action-ptab-harassment-patent-owners/id=112191/

patents being the subject of multiple IPR petitions, otherwise known as gang-tackling. In presenting data about the incidence of gang-tackling, Mr. Ruschke downplayed and misled the public on the severity of the issue. Looking at the table below makes it appear as if 87.2% (67.0% + 20.2%) of challenged patents have only one or two petitions filed against them. One would also be inclined to think that only 1.3% (55/4,376) of such patents have been the subject of seven or more IPR petitions. But the real incidence of gang-tackling is much worse.

The slight-of-hand is that if a patent has already been invalidated by the first IPR proceeding, no further IPR proceedings are necessary to invalidate it. The real question is, "How many patents could survive the IPR gauntlet multiple times?" Suppose that a patentee has 1,000 patents in his portfolio and that the IPR survival rate is 50%. If all 1,000 patents were required to traverse the IPR process, only 500 would remain valid after the first round. However, by the end of the seventh round, only eight patents would survive.

Multiple Petition Study

Petitions Per Patent

No. of Petitions per Patent	**Patents**	**% of Total**
1	2932	67.0%
2	885	20.2%
3	256	5.9%
4	142	3.2%
5	54	1.2%
6	52	1.2%
7 or more	55	1.3%
Total	**4,376**	**100.0%**

Inocencia: Are there any other instances of the USPTO manipulating statistics?

Patent Lawyer: Unfortunately, there are. Statistics regarding invalidity rates at the PTAB understate institution and invalidity rates. Suppose five petitioners seek to invalidate four claims listed in a particular patent.

If the PTAB only institutes one petition, the institution rate is just 20%. However, if all of the challenged claims are invalidated in that *inter partes review* proceeding, then the invalidity rate sustained by the patentee is 100%. Worse yet, the patentee would have to expend huge sums of money to respond to five separate petitions on the same patent, even though only one petition was ultimately instituted. (On the other hand, infringers can collaborate and share the costs of their gang-tackling.) Furthermore, petitions can be repeatedly filed against the non-instituted claims until they ultimately are instituted.

Separately, USPTO statistics state that only a small percent—16% according to one report—of challenged patents are fully invalidated. Such figures include settlements, which occur about 25% of the time, as victories for the patent owner. But a settlement where the patentee surrenders by giving a royalty free license does not feel like a victory for the patent-holder.

Inocencia: Patentees can appeal unfavorable decisions from the PTAB and district courts. Correct?

Patent Lawyer: That is correct. However, the Federal Circuit can affirm the PTAB's or district court's decisions to invalidate patent claims without providing any analysis or reasoning. They can issue a Rule 36 affirmation of the trial court's or the PTAB tribunal's decisions in favor of the alleged infringer. In January of 2019, 24 of the 44 decisions rendered by the Federal Circuit were Rule 36 affirmations. Those affirmations are limited to one word: "Affirmed." Thus, to a large extent, the PTAB has become the final arbiter as decisions from district courts and even the Federal Circuit have become perfunctory rubber stamps.

Inocencia: If no explanation is provided, how can the patentee know if the one-word affirmation issued by the Federal Circuit reflects that court's understanding of the technology?

Patent Lawyer: There is no way to know that. The Federal Circuit's affirmations may be made for sound reasons, expediency in disposing of cases, improper interpretations of the law, as a device to avoid contending with difficult technical subject matters, or as a result of misunderstanding underlining technologies.

Such rubber-stamping of previous decisions really does mask the fact that circuit judges struggle with disputed technologies. For instance, during oral arguments in Parallel Networks v. IBM, Circuit Judge Jimmie Reyna struggled to tell the difference between a web page and a web server. He asked: "You're saying that those web pages are web servers?" Then he continued by saying, "So a web page and a page server are the same thing?"

Also, during oral arguments in Cascades Projection v. Epson, Judge Todd Hughes told an attorney, "I mean, you may be wrong for all I know, you may be right, I have no idea without expert testimony to distinguish between the two [technical terms at issue]." Nonetheless, a Rule 36 affirmation was issued.

Inocencia: Rule 36 affirmations seem to deprive inventors of due process.

Patent Lawyer: That is true. Adjudicators are supposed to give cases proper disposition. Unfortunately, it is quite common for Rule 36 decisions to be issued the day after oral arguments, or at least within a few days of oral arguments. In giving their one-word affirmations, the Federal Circuit is failing to meet its requirement to issue opinions pursuant to 35 U.S.C. §144.

The Federal Court's tendency to render one-word affirmations also systematically and unfairly biases outcomes in favor of affirmance. When cases do not receive deliberation, the opportunity for "vote fluidity" is curtailed. Vote fluidity occurs when a justice changes a vote between the initial conference vote and the publication of the opinion. The act of codifying one's thoughts challenges writers' beliefs, assumptions and conclusions. Statistics from a study of Supreme Court cases decided between 1969 and 1985 demonstrated that at least one Justice exhibited vote fluidity in 36.6% of cases. Such fluidity cannot take place when the Federal Circuit issues a Rule 36 affirmance. As I alluded to a few moments ago, another unfortunate result of the Federal Court's one-word affirmances is that the PTAB can make decisions with impunity since there is little likelihood of meaningful appeal.

Inocencia: It seems that the Federal Circuit's use of one-word affirmances can be an expedient measure to dispose of cases. But does the Federal Circuit have a corresponding one-word (or few word) summary judgment to reverse a district court's decision (or a decision from the PTAB) to invalidate patent claims?

Patent Lawyer: No. Rule 36 does not offer a succinct and definitive "Reversal." Another travesty of Rule 36 affirmances is that these affirmances are only supposed to be invoked when the decision is of no precedential value. But Rule 36 affirmances are invoked when the decisions are precedential.

Inocencia: It seems unfair to patent owners that the Federal Circuit is so quick to set precedent of upholding decisions to invalidate patent claims without explanation, but has nothing resembling a quick way to reverse decisions whereby patent claims have been unfairly invalidated.

> In 2012, St. Georgen, Germany-based Papst Licensing acquired two patents from Rambus Incorporated for a purchase price in the high six figures. These patents were subject to a few encumbrances as Rambus had already entered into broad licensing agreements with several companies.
>
> The acquired patents related to a Method for Verifying And Improving Run-Time of a Memory Test in the semiconductor manufacturing process; those patents claimed inventions that enabled engineers to simulate tests on computer chips before being hardwired into hardware. The underlying technology provided insight into how highly condensed circuitry would function under scenarios such as when clock cycles were shortened by pre-set amounts or when voltage was reduced.
>
> Shortly after Papst Licensing concluded the purchase of these patents, suspicions of infringement on the part of several field-programmable gate array (FPGA) industry players arose. Papst Licensing reached out to these alleged infringers for purposes of achieving amiable resolution of unauthorized use of its recently acquired patents. The response by one infringer, Lattice Semiconductor, was indeed constructive. Pursuant to an open exchange of arguments on infringement and validity as well as multiple rounds of negotiations, Lattice remitted a lump-sum payment for a license to the subject patents in the fall of 2015.

The other alleged infringers reacted differently. After several meetings relating to technical and business issues, one prospective FPGA licensee, Xilinx, filed a declaratory judgment action with the District Court of Northern California. However, Papst Licensing was able to thwart this gambit by filing a patent infringement complaint with the Delaware courts (where Xilinx was incorporated) just a few hours earlier. Nonetheless, the Delaware case was transferred to the Northern District of California based on the convenience of the forum; most witnesses resided there.

Litigation against Altera, another alleged infringer, commenced in Northern California in the fall of 2014 with Judge Lucy Koh presiding. During this proceeding, the alleged infringer filed an *inter partes review* petition with the PTAB in early 2016. Prior to the time of the *inter partes review* proceedings, in June of 2014, the Alice Corp. vs. CLS Bank decision was rendered by the Supreme Court, forcing Papst Licensing to argue that its patents were indeed patent eligible subject matter under §101 of the patent code. Shortly before the PTAB issued its decision that all of the petitioned claims were valid, Judge Koh held the patents-in-suit invalid based on her belief that they covered non-patentable subject matter (or merely abstract ideas under the Alice decision). Papst Licensing appealed the district court's decision but it was rubber-stamped with a Rule 36 affirmation from the Court of Appeals for the Federal Circuit in July of 2016.

The result of a district court judge rushing to declare that the patents-in-suit were invalid—before the PTAB rendered its decision on the matter—was that the infringers ended up paying nothing for the use of the patents acquired by Papst Licensing. Had Papst Licensing entered into a running royalty licensing agreement with Lattice Semiconductor (the infringer that amiably settled), its royalty receipts would have come to a screeching halt once Judge Koh took it upon herself to invalidate the Papst patents.

Inocencia: Maybe we are overreacting to the dismemberment of the patent system. Does it really matter that the patent system has been mutilated? Innovation will still take place. There will just be more reliance on trade secrets.

Patent Lawyer: The dismantling of the patent system has already begun to discourage innovation. According to the Alliance for U.S. Startups & Inventors for Jobs, venture capital investments in the industries that aim to preserve and extend life have plunged from 20.95% of total venture capital funding in 2004 to 3.22% of total venture capital funding in 2017.[46] Among the industries included in these statistics are pharmaceuticals, drug discovery, surgical devices, and medical supplies. Also, research conducted by Professors Richard Florida and Ian Hathaway found that more than half of the 12 cities that received the most investment in startups from 2015 through 2017 were outside of the United States.

The USPTO predicts that the average annual growth of patent applications will rise at an anemic 0.8% rate from its fiscal year 2020 through 2024.[47] Such lackluster interest in patents results in a vicious cycle. The languid growth rate in patent applications was cited as one of the reasons that the USPTO planned to raise its fees across the board in 2019. Higher patent fees will discourage yet more patent filings.

Inocencia: Sorry for interrupting you. But at least all of the fees collected by the USPTO accrue to the benefit of the USPTO. Correct?

Patent Lawyer: I wish that were the case. Unfortunately, much of the fees collected by the USPTO are diverted to the federal government for other purposes. Sometimes, these diverted fees are simply squandered.

Inocencia: That's really disheartening. Please continue where we left off—about the differences between patents and trade secrets.

---

46 https://static1.squarespace.com/static/5746149f86db43995675b6bb/t/5b43e8706d2a73cc9b2dab2f/1531177082005/USIJ+U.S.+Startup+Formation+Trends+--+2014-2017+--+Final.pdf

47 https://www.ipwatchdog.com/2019/08/04/submit-comments-uspto-proposal-raise-ipr-fees/id=111869/

Patent Lawyer: Certainly. The weaker the patent system becomes, the more compelling trade secrets become. Trade secrets are certainly a legitimate form of intellectual property and can be very valuable. However, patents spur improvements to innovations since they disclose inventions to the public. This is not the case with trade secrets. Since trade secrets conceal inventions, the public cannot improve upon them.

Further, while fully realizing that both trade secrets and patents are forms of intangible assets, patents are perceived to be more tangible than trade secrets. Why is this important? Because it is much easier to license patents than trade secrets. Many commercializers refuse to talk to inventors unless they have secured patents. It is also at least a little bit easier to raise capital when a company has obtained some patents.

Inocencia: Why is it easier for companies to raise capital when they have patents versus trade secrets?

Patent Lawyer: Let me give you four scenarios. First scenario: A company pursues research into a promising area but runs out of money. The company will have to abandon its research project. But it can keep its patents alive and license them to another company that produces products for the targeted markets. Second scenario: A startup changes course from its initial business plan. In such an event, the sale of now irrelevant patents can help recoup earlier sunk costs and the related proceeds can be used to fund more promising lines of research. Third scenario: Simply having strong patents helps companies raise debt, which can be collateralized by patents. If the borrower honors its repayment schedule, everything is fine. The patentee company suffers no dilution since it has taken on debt rather than equity. Also, the borrower benefits from paying lower fees to its intermediary; investment bankers charge lower fees on debt raises compared to equity raises. However, if the borrower defaults, the patents can be assigned to the lender, who may assert them against infringers.

Fourth scenario: When the patent system is functioning, investors in a failed company can reclaim the patents and assert them against infringers. The Papst story is instructive. Papst Motoren, based in Germany, was a leader in electric drive technology for tape recorders, hard disk drives and electronic cooling applications. Faced with massive infringement in the 1980s, predominantly from Asian companies, the company's lenders forced the sale of the business in 1992. However, the creditors did not value the IP portfolio, which included more than 600 patents and patent applications. Georg Papst bought back the patent portfolio. The company he founded, Papst Licensing, concluded more than 160 licensing agreements with many well-known IT and electrical engineering companies, including all of the current hard disk drive manufacturers.

Inocencia: USPTO Director Andrei Iancu is effecting wonderful reforms at the Patent Office, even at the PTAB. Do we really have to worry so much about the patent system when we have such a capable director?

Patent Lawyer: Directors of the USPTO are political appointees who serve at the pleasure of the sitting president. There could be five serving USPTO directors by the time a patent runs its course. Such volatility in the directorship of the USPTO is contrary to the stability that inventors, and their investors, seek. I agree that Mr. Iancu is an excellent Director of the USPTO. Other directors have been, and may again be, far worse. However, as of July of 2019, more than 18 months after Mr. Iancu became the Director of the USPTO, the PTAB was still invalidating more than 80% of the claims embedded in patents challenged by that panel. The reforms that Mr. Iancu is bringing to the USPTO lack the force of law. We really need legislation to fix our broken patent system.

Administrative fixes unaccompanied by the force of legislation simply do not stick for long. Let me give you an example. Supposedly, gang-tackling was addressed. However, in reality, it may not have been addressed. For instance, in early August of 2019, Apple petitioned for an *inter partes review* of U.S. Patent No. 5,796, 183. This expired patent is titled Capacitive Response Electronic Switching Circuit and is owned by UUSI, which does business as Nartron. The following week the PTAB instituted two IPRs on this patent.

Inocencia: How much power does the patent community have to remedy existing patent problems?

Patent Lawyer: Not nearly as much power as the efficient infringer community. The most unabashed infringers—such as Google and Apple—are revered by the public. Google and Apple produce top-of-the-line products that are used by at least tens of millions of Americans every day.

Google enjoys immense public support as its products are ubiquitous and free. Apple users interact with their Apple devices many hours every day.

On the other hand, the community of inventors is only a tiny fraction of the number of people who use products from the large infringers. Many inventors may not feel comfortable advocating for reforms to the patent system as they are not American citizens. The community of American inventors do not make for the most charismatic lobbying group. They are typically reserved introverts. Few could be mistaken to come out of central casting. To put it mildly, I doubt that many contemporary inventors are as attractive as Hedy Lamarr. Organizations that one would normally expect to stand up for inventors have been eerily silent as inventor rights have been trampled upon for more than ten years. On top of that, some of the senior-most lawmakers are downright hostile to patentees. Paul Morinville, founder of US Inventor, reported [to your author] that House Speaker Nancy Pelosi threatened to challenge his patents by way of *inter partes review* proceedings unless he exited the House of Representatives, where he was trying to solicit support for inventors.

Unfortunately, we can't expect all patent lawyers to fully embrace needed reforms as they benefit from some of the injustices the current patent regime inflicts on patentees. The PTAB certainly creates a lot of work for patent lawyers. By making it extremely difficult for patentees to win injunctive relief, the eBay decision ensures continued litigation over patents and damages awards. Also, the legislation that prevented patent owners from suing groups of infringers in one suit creates more work for patent lawyers.

Sadly, even if the inventor community were able to convince Congress to pass reasonable legislation, the courts and the executive branch still appear to be hell-bent on damaging patentee rights. In Celgene Corp. v. Peter, the Federal Circuit decided that *inter partes review* may be applied to invalidate pre-AIA patents without running afoul of the Fifth Amendment's prohibition of taking property without just compensation. In Christy, Inc. v. The United States, both the Department of Justice and the USPTO argued that when the PTAB cancelled a patent it meant that the inventor never had a patent so nothing was taken.

Inocencia: So, an inventor can play by the rules. An inventor can do everything right. And at the end of the day, the inventor often gets screwed.

Patent Lawyer: What do you mean?

Inocencia: After decades of working in the restaurant industry, I was somehow able to scrape together sufficient funds to invest in research. Then, I defied all odds and came up with an invention that has real market potential. Suppose I then hire a qualified patent lawyer such as yourself, and at great expense, go through the trouble of securing a patent. And then an infringer wreaks havoc. Once I broach the subject of that party's unauthorized use of my patent, the infringer moves to invalidate my patent. The odds are definitely against my being able to sustain the validity of my patent once an *inter partes review* proceeding commences. The PTAB is far from a fair forum to rule on the subject of patent validity. When I lose at the PTAB, I can appeal but the Federal Circuit is likely to affirm the PTAB's decision.

It seems like the whole country is adverse to patentees. I watched the movie, *Flash of Genius*, about Robert Kearns, the inventor of the intermittent windshield wiper. His battles with automotive infringers lasted years on end. He was placed in a mental hospital. His wife divorced him. He became estranged from his children. Eventually he prevailed. But Mr. Kearns "only" had to battle infringers. Today, an inventor's battles to uphold and enforce his patent would include skirmishes with infringers. The PTAB. District courts. The Federal Circuit. The Supreme Court. State attorneys general. Congress. The executive branch. Even if a resilient patentee recovers damages, the media will cast him as a patent troll, a scourge on society.

Patent Lawyer: I can certainly understand your frustration with the patent system. Don't be too discouraged; some inventors still make considerable money from their inventions. The patent system may return to some semblance of rationality in the years ahead. Maybe we can end our discussion with words of wisdom from Hedy Lamarr. The brilliant bombshell from yesteryear said, "Give the world the best you have, and you'll be kicked into *(sic)* the teeth. Give the world the best you've got, anyway."

Background on the Christy Case

David McCutchen founded CDC Larue Industries in 2003. This Oklahoma-based company (now known as Pulse-Bac Vacuum Systems) remains a provider of industrial vacuums that capture the hazardous silica that are liberated when cement floors are grinded; such grinding is necessary to smooth floors and to render them receptive to epoxies placed on them. Without effective industrial vacuums, those laborers operating floor-grinding equipment would breathe cancer-causing silica.

In 2003, David had a eureka moment for taking industrial vacuums to the next level: David figured out how to get a vacuum's filters to self-clean with only the vacuum motor pulling ambient air through the valves and through the filters. David's invention made additional blower motors unnecessary. With his invention, filters operate while adjacent filters self-clean, enabling the vacuum to operate without interruption. David applied for a patent for his ambient air backflushed filter vacuum on July 18, 2003. This patent application issued almost exactly three years later, on August 1, 2006, as U.S. Patent No. 7,082,640. David placed this patent, and seven others that CDC Larue Industries created, into Christy, Inc., a patent holding company named after his daughter.

Within a few years, large industrial companies began taking an interest in CDC Larue's patented vacuum technologies. The progression of potential licensees included Emerson Electric, Bosch, Milwaukee Tools and Black & Decker. An NDA was executed between Black & Decker and CDC Larue Industries in December of 2008. Negotiations for a licensing agreement got underway and continued for some 18 months, but no deal was ever consummated.

Chris McCutchen, who took over the reins of CDC Larue from his father (David), had plenty of reasons to believe that Black & Decker used the prolonged and inconclusive negotiations as a ruse to abscond with his company's intellectual property. (Black & Decker was consumed with negotiating to acquire Stanley Tools at the same time that it was conducting due diligence on CDC Larue's vacuums; Black & Decker had virtually no bandwidth to negotiate any other transactions during this time.) CDC Larue's new CEO also had gathered a great deal of evidence that Black & Decker was infringing the '640 patent. Chris wanted to have his day in court so he filed a patent infringement suit against Black & Decker in the United States District Court for the Northern District of Oklahoma on June 2, 2014. Chris expected that his legal team would have the chance to call witnesses and to cross-examine the alleged infringers. He wanted to dispel any notions that CDC Larue was a patent troll—by the time of this court filing, CDC Larue had been generating revenue from selling products that incorporated the claims of the '640 patent for at least nine years.

Chris never had a chance to tell his story of Black & Decker's alleged misbehavior to jurors. His case was stayed shortly after Black & Decker filed two *inter partes review* petitions against the '640 patent on December 19, 2014. How much deliberation did the PTAB invest in the proceedings relating to the '640 patent? Chris's legal team was given twenty minutes to make its case before three APJs, only one of which bothered to show up in person. The other two APJs Skyped in. As evidenced by their questions, the APJs, at least two of which were former Googlers, had no understanding of elementary fluid mechanics, which underlie the '640 patent. On June 17, 2016, the PTAB decided that the petitioner met its burden of proof by a preponderance of the evidence and invalidated claims 1-18 of the '640 patent.

Chris appealed the PTAB's decisions to the Federal Circuit. That court gave CDC Larue's counsel twenty minutes to make its arguments and then affirmed one of the PTABs decisions and dismissed the other. The federal district court followed shortly thereafter by dismissing the case that Chris filed in June of 2014. On August 14, 2018, the USPTO issued and published a certificate officially cancelling claims 1-18 of the '640 patent.

Postscript

When I spoke with Chris in the summer of 2019, he wasn't at all dismayed with the quality of the more than eight patent examiners that played a part in examining the eight patent applications that eventually issued and were assigned to Christy, Inc. On the contrary, he sung their praises: Chris said that all of the patent examiners that he and his father interacted with were intelligent, well-versed in the technologies at hand, professional and responsive. Chris told me that he supports examiners taking years to review all relevant prior art before granting patent applications so that only meritorious patent applications will issue.

He wasn't terribly upset at Black & Decker allegedly conducting espionage, stringing his father along in what may have been disingenuous negotiations, misappropriating proprietary information from CDC Larue, or infringing the '640 patent. All of those things happen in business and Chris acknowledges that perhaps he and his late father should have applied more discretion in their dealings with Black & Decker. Chris didn't bemoan the more than $500,000 that his family's business spent in litigation costs; fortunately, CDC Larue's ever-expanding operations provided the McCutchen family with the wherewithal to support its litigation against Black & Decker.

What infuriates Chris is the PTAB. That body's uninformed and, at best, disinterested pseudo-judges invalidated 18 patent claims after listening to the assignee's arguments for no more than twenty minutes. How could Chris, or any other rational observer (let alone impassioned inventor) feel otherwise? How could three APJs issue an equitable verdict if they didn't understand the basic technology resident in the patent before them? With so little attention paid to the *inter partes review* proceedings—two APJs didn't even attend the hearing in person—how could those APJs so quickly come to the conclusion that 18 claims were invalid when those same claims and related prior art spent three years under intense examination by skilled examiners?

The issue of the PTAB invalidating patents that were granted before that tribunal was created is the subject of a class action lawsuit filed by Timothy C. Davis of Heninger, Garrison Davis in Birmingham, Alabama. This suit, which references the plight of Christy's '640 patent, argues that the PTAB invalidating patents that were issued before that body went into operation is a violation of the Fifth Amendment's takings clause.

Part III
Inventors Engage in Battle

The HairZings Story: A Hair-Raising Patent Ordeal

Francesca Kuglen is a thrice-successful inventor and entrepreneur; each of the companies she founded has prospered for at least eleven years. All of them have been self-funded. Only a few months after completing her college studies she founded her first company, Jontee Accessories, in August of 1985 with just $250.

Jontee Accessories was a purveyor of women's accessories (such as scarves, bridal accoutrements, hair accessories, veils, and hats) that were sold through just about all of the large department stores. Jontee was acquired in 1996 by what is now publicly-traded Newell Brands. Francesca not only made a small fortune when she sold Jontee but was paid an earn-out during a transition period and received running royalties for Newell's use of her patents.

Clever Results, Francesca's second company, was a business-to-business design and product development company. Its expertise was designing, producing and marketing glassware to retailers. This company, founded in 1997, sold its wares though channels ranging from QVC to Walmart, and was profitable in its first year of operations. Clever Results is now a holding company for real estate.

Francesca's third company is called Sennits LLC and is the purveyor of the HairZing line of double-stretch elastic combs. It is here that Francesca's harrowing ordeal with contentious patent prosecution, duplicitous service providers, and cutthroat copycats begins. Her story will take you through a labyrinth of litigation, punctuated by an uncannily concurrent IRS audit, and a mountain of circumstantial evidence pointing to knockoffs being produced by Chinese prisoners. You will see how copycats can drive a profitable inventor to penury.

The HairZing Hair Accessory

Before reading about Francesca's traumas with HairZing, allow me to discuss the product. Most hair accessories designed to hold women's hair in place—such as bows, hair-comb pins, and headbands—put pressure on the hair. Extended use of these common hair restraints typically causes headaches and hair damage. Traditional hair pieces cause creases in women's hair, which strips the cuticles and breaks the follicles. Repeated adjusting of most hair pieces is often required, especially when the woman is active. Removing hair accessories, like scrunchies, can be painful when hair becomes entangled in them.

Francesca's patented double-stretch elastic combs hold hair in place without putting pressure, or clamping down, on hair. HairZings expand and contract to comfortably hold however much hair needs to be put in place. These combs have no open edges to catch hair. Instead of holding the combs in place by jamming the teeth together, HairZing works by maintaining the tension between the combs. HairZing's woven wire-combs feature a patented resin that is ten times stronger than elastic and resists tangling and attaching to hair. Despite the sophistication of Francesca's invention, placing HairZings in one's hair is a breeze. The user places two hair combs in her hair, turns them backwards and joins them together with elastic.

Each HairZing is handcrafted by women artisans in collectives in remote outposts in China and Kenya. These women receive fair wages and participate in profit-sharing programs. Sennits is a benefactor to the communities from which its workers hail; the Company pays for the tuition of a group of Maasi (Kenyan) girls to ensure they complete their schooling. Great pains are made to ensure that the artisans perform their work in respectable settings. For instance, in China, the workers' children are allowed to do their homework at their mothers' sides and then walk home together when their mothers' shifts end.

Francesca's Story: Scene 1

I am about to tell you Francesca's travails and tribulations as an entrepreneur and inventor. However, as a successful and resilient businesswoman, Francesca does not want to be labeled a victim. But she was brutally victimized by a legal system gone haywire: A system where an inventor could only evade penury by paying the company knocking off her product and by submitting to other grotesquely unfair terms in a settlement agreement. Here is Francesca's story as she related it to me.

Shortly after inventing the HairZing in 2006, Francesca placed HairZing on QVC. The product resonated with QVC's customers; sales reached nearly $2 million the first year. Francesca was not complacent about her success with QVC. She wanted to sell many more HairZing packages through multiple new channels. In order to do this, she needed to understand her (potential) customers better. As great a partner as QVC was for Sennits, one shortcoming that QVC had was that product creators like Francesca had no access to QVC's buyers.

New products benefit from educational campaigns aimed at potential customers. Intended customers must be made aware of new products and trained how to use them. Commercializers must learn who their customers will likely be and what triggers their buying decisions.

So, in 2007, Francesca went on a crusade to understand how customers could best use HairZing. Francesca conducted market research with missionary zeal. She spent an entire year traveling around the country meeting with women who could benefit from HairZing. She attended state fairs, motorcycle festivals, hot-air balloon events, high-tech art shows, and many similar events. She was so impassioned that she was only home for three days from April 2007 to November 2007.

After amassing such a treasure trove of consumer insights, Francesca was determined to begin marketing HairZing through infomercials. Armed with a year's worth of customer research, Francesca believed she could help create compelling infomercials. Francesca was aware that some players in the infomercial world were ethically challenged. Nevertheless, in February 2008, Francesca entered into an agreement for the production of an infomercial for HairZing with Concepts TV Productions, which had a reputation as being a relatively above-board infomercial producer. The deal was that Concepts TV Productions would produce the infomercial and Francesca would make arrangements for airing it. Not leaving anything to chance, Francesca presented Collette Liantonio, CEO of Concepts TV Productions, a non-disclosure agreement. Leading up to presenting Ms. Liantonio with the non-disclosure agreement, Francesca expressed her fears that Telebrands, a New Jersey-based direct response marketing company, might try to purloin her idea. Ms. Liantonio assured Francesca that there was nothing to worry about as all of the research results that Francesca garnered would remain safe with Concepts TV Productions.

Once the non-disclosure agreement was in place, Francesca released a torrent of data and insights to Concepts TV Productions. All she had learned about selling HairZing to women during the year she crisscrossed the country gushed out. Francesca told Concepts TV Productions which HairZing combs were most appropriate for women with different kinds of hair, how to apply the product, how to detect the moment at which a prospective customer would most likely decide to make a purchase, the best way to take headshots and much more. Francesca intimated to Concepts TV Productions all of the valuable marketing nuggets—those seemingly anecdotal insights that are crucial for success—that she gleaned from her unflagging customer research.

After arming Concepts TV Productions with so much consumer insight and paying that firm approximately $30,000, Francesca was expecting to receive her infomercial. That didn't happen. According to my discussions with Francesca, here is what happened: While waiting for her infomercial, Francesca was approached by Telebrands, a commercially successful retailer that generates tremendous revenues from the infomercials it runs. During a face-to-face meeting, Telebrands indicated that it would like to sell the HairZing line. Francesca politely rejected such overtures, largely based on her seeing no way the ladies involved in manufacturing HairZing could earn fair wages at the price points Telebrands was contemplating. She did make mention that she had a patent application pending with the United States Patent and Trademark Office. A short time after this meeting, Francesca stumbled upon an infomercial featuring something resembling double-stretch elastic combs. However, these infomercials were not advertising HairZing, but rather a knockoff from Telebrands called EZ Combs. Kernels of Francesca's insights were sprinkled into the Telebrands infomercial.

There is no verdict that holds that Concepts TV Productions conveyed to Telebrands the confidential information that Francesca shared with the infomercial producer. But Francesca never sued Concepts TV Productions either. Francesca told me it was her understanding that Ms. Liantonio had a partnership with Poonam Khubani, wife of A.J. Khubani, who founded and is the CEO of Telebrands. And, as we will see at the end of this story, Telebrands conditioned a settlement with Francesca on her agreeing not to retaliate against Concepts TV Productions.

Francesca took a rival infringing her patent application, coopting her product and hijacking her marketing campaign in stride. Her outlook was along the lines of, “You have to roll with the punches. This is capitalism. In the long-run, the best product will win the day.” Instead of suing Telebrands or Concepts TV Productions, Francesca focused on developing the HairZing line. She flew to China and Kenya to prime production. She produced another infomercial, albeit with a different production company. She met with distributors and invested in Sennits’ relationships with QVC and the Home Shopping Network. In the beginning of 2009, she met with a buyer at Walmart with whom she had conducted business for many years, for purposes of selling HairZing through that mass merchant. That’s when the real fireworks started.

Let me rewind a few frames. When Francesca called her long-time Walmart buyer to request a meeting, the buyer was confused; he said that he had already seen the related commercial and had been pitched the product. Of course, he was inadvertently alluding to Telebrands’ EZ Combs and infomercial.[48] Nevertheless, the Walmart buyer agreed to meet with Francesca. During this meeting, the buyer indicated that he wanted to buy the original double stretch elastic combs but that Walmart was already purchasing EZ Combs from Telebrands. When the discussion turned to the integrity, reliability and redundancy of the two vendors’ supply chains, Francesca suggested that Walmart audit both Sennits’ and Telebrands’ supply chains so that Walmart could form its own conclusions. This sounded logical to the Walmart buyer who promptly triggered the dual supply chain audits. In what seems to be a policy at Walmart, the commencement of the audit into Telebrands’ supply chain resulted in the big-box retailer freezing hundreds of thousands of dollars in orders to that company. Also, since these audits were conducted by third parties, they could not be halted once they got underway.

Francesca’s Story: Scene 2

Telebrands’ reaction to the initiation of its supply chain audit was visceral, violent, and venomous. Telebrands promptly sued Oakland,

[48] Oftentimes, inventors that are not immediately warmly received by Walmart buyers must lobby these buyers by securing item submission forms from store managers that believe the product would succeed in their stores.

California-based Sennits in a district court in New York on grounds of tortious interference and slander. The Walmart buyer with whom Francesca met disappeared within a few days of Francesca having been served with a subpoena. It is unclear as to whether he was fired or demoted.

Francesca believes that Telebrands' true mission was not to win the case or even to have its day in court but rather to use litigation as a means of destroying Sennits. Telebrands delayed and complicated the case as much as it could, causing Francesca's legal fees to skyrocket. Francesca was required to travel from California to New York as many as ten times. Telebrands obtained all of Sennits' files when it copied that company's hard drives. But whenever Sennits wanted to obtain a document from Telebrands, the plaintiff refused to hand it over. Sennits was compelled to file motions for just about every document that it wanted to review, often at a cost in the neighborhood of $30,000.

To demonstrate that its supply chain predated that of Telebrands, Sennits flew in two of its craftswomen from the Maasi tribe in Kenya. Sennits filed a motion for these women to testify well before their arrival in the courtroom. However, on the day of the trial, Telebrands objected. A closed-door session among the opposing counsels and the judge ensued in the judge's chambers. The result was that the women were prohibited from testifying.

During the course of her litigation with Telebrands, Francesca received a number of calls from her channel partners and business associates. These people related to Francesca that they had received calls from investigators seeking dirt on Francesca. These inquiries produced no damaging information that was used against Francesca during the trial. The sponsor of these investigative efforts has not been identified. However, in a similar vein, Telebrands found a woman who claimed she was the rightful inventor of HairZing. Without Sennits having the opportunity to depose this woman beforehand, this woman appeared in court. However, after a few questions from the judge, she was seen to be unfit to testify.

Another petulant litigation tactic unfolded. Prior to the trial, Francesca wrote a blog called *Hair We Go Again*. In one of her first posts, she wrote a satirical piece in which a fictional customer asks a hypothetical infringer how one goes about making knockoffs of HairZing. One hypothetical character asked, "How can you sell your counterfeit products for such low prices?" Carrying on with this fictitious dialog, in the voice of the allegorical infringer, Francesca typed, "We make the crappiest products possible. And we lie to our customers." I paraphrased the posts. But never did Francesca use Telebrands' name in this imagined exchange. However, in the courtroom, Telebrands' counselors placed these blog posts on a huge flat-panel display screen. Without providing any context or mentioning the playfulness of the posts, the opposing litigators pointed out that Francesca was the author of statements such as, "We lie to our customers."

The ridiculousness of these litigation gambits did not lessen the real costs that Francesca was required to bear. Francesca was paying the senior partners on her case roughly $750 an hour, associates $600 an hour, and paralegals $350 an hour.

Francesca's Story: Scene 3

In the midst of her excruciating litigation, Francesca found herself beset by a "leave-no-stone-unturned" Internal Revenue Service audit. This line-by-line audit, triggered by an anonymous caller, required Francesca to document every dollar of revenue and expense to hit her business over as many as seven years. (I leave it to the reader's imagination as to who could have baited the anonymous caller.) This audit was a highly distracting time sink that lasted about seven months. Francesca found herself spending inordinate amounts of time with her accountant. All of the related aggravation proved to be unnecessary as Sennits passed its audit with flying colors.

On top of her travails with the litigation and IRS audit, Francesca found no easy sailing with the prosecution of her patent application. (Francesca filed a patent application for a Stretch Comb Hair Retainer on January 22, 2004. This patent application became U.S. Patent No. 7,748,390 on July 6, 2010.) In the early stages of the examiner's review of her patent application, the examiner rejected 28 of the 31 claims presented. It should be noted that such broad-brushed initial claims rejections are not unusual in initial office actions. However, what followed was unusual. The examiner reviewing the patent application preceding the '390 patent told Francesca that a third-party contacted the Patent Office. This unidentified third-party alleged that Francesca was trying to perpetrate fraud on the Patent Office by falsely claiming that she was the real inventor.

As a result, a tremendous onus was placed on Francesca's shoulders to prove that she was the real inventor behind the '390 patent. She complied and obtained declarations from around the world, including from producers of kabuki theaters in Japan. (What is the connection between HairZing and Japanese kabuki theaters? The female performers in these theaters spend hundreds of hours and thousands of dollars putting fine, decorated, easily removable, wire-combs in their bouffant hairdos.) The declarations vouched that she was the conceiver of a novel and unique invention, now known as HairZing, from QVC's Director of Accessories, a professor of Textile Development and Marketing at the Fashion Institute of Technology in New York, plastics producers, wire-comb manufacturers, professionals in the hair industry, and from representatives of Dorfman Pacific Hats (the largest hat manufacturer in the United States). To obtain each one of the declarations, Francesca had to pay her attorneys and the attorneys representing the individuals that submitted declarations on Francesca's behalf. In the case of the Japanese producer of kabuki theaters, she had to retain the services of professional translators and pay for the producer's transportation.

The submission of all of these declarations was not persuasive enough to cause the patent examiner to immediately allow Francesca's patent application. Rather, Francesca felt it necessary to travel to Washington D.C. herself (she could no longer afford to have her patent lawyer accompany her) to ask what else she could possibly do to demonstrate that she was the rightful inventor of a patent-eligible invention. This cross-country flight paid off as the '390 patent was quickly granted after the live examiner interview.

The '390 patent had a pendency of 6.5 years. The examiner, Robyn Doan, held up Francesca's patent application 62% longer than the 2.5 years that she has taken, on average throughout her career, to review patent applications.[49] Prior to filing the application which became the '390 patent, Francesca filed several other patent applications and never experienced anything resembling the resistance she received relative to the '390 patent application. The lawyers at the patent boutique that Francesca retained also reported that the review of the '390 patent application was abnormally extended and contentious.

Let's assume that (some of) the extended pendency of the '390 patent application was a function of an anonymous caller alleging that Francesca was an impostor inventor. One legitimate question then becomes, "What level of credibility must an accuser reach?" Second, "What level of proof does

49 https://examiner.ninja/examiners/DOAN-ROBYN-KIEU#timings-tab

an applicant need to present to demonstrate that he is the true inventor?" Another legitimate question is, "In deciding the merits of allegations and contentions of innocence, at what point does the reputation of both parties come into the picture?" As Francesca relates her experience with patent review, it seems that the answers to the preceding questions, in respective order are, "Accusers need no level of proof to claim that an applicant is an imposter." "Named inventors on patent applications must comb the ends of the earth to demonstrate that they are indeed the rightful inventors." "Character and reputation have no bearing as to the standards of proof required relative to the two proceeding questions."

Francesca's Story: Scene 4

In addition to contending with a harrowing litigation, an invasive IRS audit, and contentious patent prosecution, Francesca's business was being destroyed by Telebrands. Telebrands was confusing customers with its EZ Combs as well as dramatically underpricing HairZing. To wit: Telebrands was selling its EZ Combs for $10 (for a pack of three) while Sennits was selling packs of two of its HairZings for $18. As a result, QVC ended its marketing and selling of HairZing. To add insult to injury, Francesca's tab for buying back QVC's inventory of HairZing ran into the hundreds of thousands of dollars; she was contractually required to take back her inventory because QVC works on consignment.

QVC was not the only retail channel that could no longer compete with Telebrands' aggressive pricing. All of Francesca's 18 mom-and-pop distributors were driven out of business by EZ Comb's scorched-earth prices. Unlike with QVC, Francesca had no contractual obligation to repurchase residual HairZing inventory from the 18 distributors who relied on that product for 100% of their sales. But, at a cost of several hundreds of thousands of dollars, she made each one of her distributors whole.

Despite these tremendous setbacks, and like most entrepreneurs, Francesca was an optimist. She thought that sales of HairZing would immediately snap back once the litigation was settled in her favor and her patent granted. So, for about 18 months, Sennits continued to employ some 1,000 women workers from rural China and Kenya's hinterlands. Their output was stored in the dedicated warehouse that Sennits owned in Lynchburg, Tennessee. When the market for HairZings failed to rebound, Francesca donated this inventory, valued at hundreds of thousands of dollars at cost, to organizations serving the likes of battered and impoverished women.

Considering that she was fighting a four-front war (litigation, IRS audit, contentious patent pendency, and destruction of her business), how was Francesca holding up in 2009 and 2010? Not well at all. Her husband suffered a heart attack and she fell into a state of clinical depression. (Remember this was the 2009 time period; there wasn't much to be upbeat about.) Even the IRS auditor, at the conclusion of the audit, expressed his amazement that Francesca was able to keep her company afloat during a time in which expenses were mounting and revenues were plunging. On top of the destruction of her business, the cost of litigation alone reached approximately $3 million. Francesca and her husband were forced to liquidate 25 years of life savings. They depleted their retirement accounts, re-mortgaged their house, and would soon find themselves drowning in $1 million of debt.

Francesca was trapped; not only economically but also strategically. She couldn't file a patent infringement suit against Telebrands because her patent application had not yet issued. She would have had more leverage in the litigation lodged against her had she filed a countersuit. But that would have cost significant money which Francesca simply did not have.

How did Telebrands make out during the trauma Francesca was going through? Like a bandit. According to customs reports that surfaced during discovery, Telebrands reported importing roughly one million packages of its EZ Combs (each consisting of three hair pieces) every week for approximately nine months. (Of course, Telebrands made healthy sales during the remaining 15 months in which its EZ Combs infringed Francesca's patent application.) These units were selling at retail for $10 each. Since Telebrands is a private company, its financials are not available to the public. But it can be assumed that Telebrands sells much of its products directly to customers; Wikipedia describes Telebrands as a "direct response marketing company." Nevertheless, let's assume that Telebrands sold all of its EZ Combs through retailers who demanded 50% markups. If Telebrands earned a 10% margin at wholesale, it would have made a *profit* of $19.5 million just during the nine months of its peak sales. Even if Telebrands' legal expenses were three times those of Francesca's, Telebrands would still have cleared $10.5 million while Francesca was sweating blood.

There is reason to believe that Telebrands' costs of producing its EZ Combs could have been Chinese-prison-labor cheap. There is no conclusive evidence that Telebrands was sourcing its EZ Combs from laborers in Chinese prisons and I am not declaring that to have been the case. However, at a cost of many tens of thousands of dollars, Francesca hired CIA agents turned private investigators to glean insight into Telebrands' supply chain. These American investigators, in turn, collaborated with Chinese investigators to try to ascertain the veracity of Telebrands' representations that its EZ Combs were manufactured from three specific factories in mainland China.

What did the U.S.-Sino investigatory effort reveal? There was simply no factory or any building at one address submitted by Telebrands. There was a building at the second address, but it was really a roofless ramshackle. There was some production occurring at the third address disclosed by Telebrands. When the Chinese investigators chatted with some of the workers exiting this far-from-state-of-the-art facility at the end of their shifts, it was learned that some EZ Combs were produced at this site. However, it also surfaced that less than ten workers were employed at this facility. There is some inherent degree of hand work required to produce EZ Combs; even a slapdash copycatter cannot automate the entire process. In other words, there is no f*&king way that fewer than ten workers can produce three million EZ Combs each week.

The investigators also surveyed other hair product manufacturing facilities in China to see if they were producing EZ Combs for Telebrands. These surveys came up dry. The investigators also traced the origins of some of the trucks that were delivering EZ Combs to the ports for shipment to the United States. Some of the trucks appeared to have commenced their journeys from the vicinity of Chinese prisons. (Even Chinese investigators were not able to get too close to the prisons.) So, the question becomes, "If the EZ Combs were not (to any notable extent) produced where Telebrands said they were being produced and if the other hair accessories producers were not making them, where else in China could so many EZ Combs have been produced so cheaply? Would a captive labor force have been needed?"[50]

[50] Separately, I have heard from multiple sources who are well versed in China's legal system that prison labor is used to produce copyright infringing books.

Francesca's Story: Scene 5

After two years of torment, the tide was finally beginning to change for Francesca. End customers and big-box retailers were growing increasingly disenchanted with EZ Combs' poor quality. Much of EZ Combs' shoddiness was due to Telebrands using a low-grade resin while HairZings uses a high-quality resin that looks like a regular resin. Also, in the first half of 2010, it was becoming increasingly clear that Francesca's patent application would soon issue. (It did with 29 of the 31 claims sought, on July 6, 2010.) Telebrands became concerned that if Francesca's patent issued, the direct-to-consumer marketing company would be on the hook for millions of dollars in patent damages.

In 2010, Telebrands thought it best to reach a settlement. Francesca came to the same conclusion even though her patent issued on July 6, 2010. It seemed that she had a good chance of winning a patent infringement case against Telebrands because the three factors enabling a patentee to sue an infringer for infringing a patent application were met. (Those conditions are: (1) the infringer must have known that it was infringing a patent application, and Francesca notified Telebrands about her patent application at the outset of this story; (2) the patent application has to issue, which it did; and, (3) the patent application must be almost identical to the issued patent, and 29 of the original 31 claims were granted.)

Nevertheless, Francesca had no money to continue her battle against Telebrands. She tried to enlist a patent litigation firm to assert her newly granted '390 patent against Telebrands on a contingency basis but found no takers. The potential damages were too small for a large law firm and Telebrands was too vicious of an opponent for smaller law firms. Additionally, the law firms feared that even if they won a judgment against Telebrands, they would not be able to collect it.

Telebrands never proved that Francesca slandered or interfered with Telebrands' business as it originally alleged. It seems to me that it would have been difficult for Telebrands to claim that its business was suffering when it was importing a million units of its EZ Combs every week for nine months. And Telebrands wanted to keep the issue as to whether or not it purloined Francesca's initial infomercial sealed, which is why Telebrands conditioned a settlement with Francesca on her agreeing not to retaliate against Concepts TV Productions. Long story short, an agreement was reached in 2011.

What did Telebrands demand from Francesca? Between $1.0 million and $1.5 million. Fortunately for Francesca, The Hartford, her general liability insurance carrier, stepped in and threatened to defend Francesca to the tune of as much as $2 million unless the New Jersey marketing company assumed something resembling a reasonable negotiating posture. The Hartford's intervention helped. Instead of Francesca having to pay Telebrands as much as $1.5 million, The Hartford agreed to pay Telebrands $350,000 on Francesca's behalf. When informed of this settlement condition, Francesca understandably became inconsolable. The only time she cried during the many hours that I interviewed her was when she told me that it would be Telebrands that would receive money from her side.

The other pillar of the settlement held that Telebrands would refrain from manufacturing products competitive with HairZing. Francesca agreed to allow Telebrands to sell its existing inventory of EZ Combs through 2012 because she was led to believe that Telebrands was going to have its affiliated companies sell outside of the United States. She wanted the customer-confusing EZ Combs to be dumped as far away from the U.S. market as possible.

But what really happened was that most of Telebrands' excess inventory was sold in the United States. Telebrands claimed that most of its sales are conducted through its affiliates and that those affiliates are not bound by the settlement. The inventory that sold outside of the United States enticed more copycats, further destroying foreign markets for HairZing. As I write these pages, EZ Combs are being sold on Amazon. There was one element of the agreement that was positive and that has held up for Francesca—neither Telebrands nor its affiliates sold EZ Combs through mass merchants.

Rather than bemoaning a grossly unfair settlement, Francesca dusted off her bruises and reasserted herself in growing her business. Once again, she proved to be a resilient entrepreneur and inventor. But getting back on her feet was no easy feat. Her first objective was to secure financing. So, she turned to the bank she had done business with for 30 years. Despite an impeccable payment history with the institution, her loan application was rejected as she was deemed to be an unacceptable risk. Online small business lenders pounced on her desperation for funds and extended lines of credit amounting to $60,000 in return for requiring her to pay $13,000 in fees in addition to the repayment of the underlying loans.

Francesca's big break came in her discussions with Conair, the largest manufacturer of women's hair accessories. Actually, Conair was not interested in representing HairZing before her ordeal with Telebrands. But after she reached a settlement with Telebrands, Francesca insisted on meeting with a senior Conair executive. This executive was still reluctant to represent HairZing. But, in the 2012 meeting, Francesca indicated to him that the product was proven to be wildly commercially successful; Telebrands sold many tens of millions of dollars' worth of an inferior version of HairZing. The Conair executive partially relented. He said, and I am paraphrasing, "Conair is the largest hair accessories company in the world. I have been in this business for 40 years. We know everything there is to know about hair accessories. Your product will never sell more than 765,000 units on a worldwide basis. We will neither license the patent nor manufacture the product, but we will sell it through mass merchants." Between the time of that discussion and the time of my writing these pages, Francesca sold more than five million HairZing units. Not one HairZing product has ever been returned to Conair.

Postscript

Francesca places much of the leverage she had in bringing Telebrands to settlement discussions on her (impending) patent. Back in 2010 and 2011—a safe temporal distance from the America Invents Act taking effect on September 16, 2012—that credit may have been appropriately placed. However, as we will see in our next story about Josh Malone and Bunch O' Balloons, Telebrands would certainly have used the Patent Trial and Appeal Board to, at least attempt to, invalidate Francesca's patent. Even the threat of petitioning the PTAB would have shifted tremendous leverage to Telebrands.

Costs of Litigating Against Infringers Balloon Out of Control

In 2006, Josh Malone was a 34-year old process engineer with Texas Instruments. He enjoyed the intellectual challenges his job provided and appreciated the comforts of corporate life. But he couldn't control the entrepreneurial and inventive flames that were raging from within. So, Josh resigned from Texas Instruments and began his quest as an inventor.

Josh's Ventures Hit and Missed

Josh's first venture was inspired by his wife and mother-in-law, both of whom were active in scrapbooking and card-making. In the mid-2000s scrapbooking enthusiasts had to use multiple industrial paper cutters, each designed to cut out specific shapes and letters that were then placed in albums and featured on greeting cards. Scrapbookers had closets full of cutting machines; they had to lug around suitcases of heavy paper cutting equipment when they met at one another's homes and at conventions.

Josh thought there must be a way to produce one machine that would replace the variety of scrapbooking machinery. But producing a compact and versatile machine was rife with engineering challenges. Josh had to shift the power source from electrical cord to battery technology, make the user interface friendlier and transition the orthogonal platform to a rotary platform. Eventually, Josh overcame these engineering hurdles when he developed a motorized, software-controlled device that cut shapes out of paper with a small swivel knife.

When he first demonstrated the Shape Cutter, as he called his digital paper cutter, at a Memory Trends trade show in Las Vegas in 2007, it generated quite a bit of interest. But Josh soon learned that there is a big difference between creating buzz at a trade show and generating revenue. The twelve months or so post trade show proved to be a slog. Scrapbooking companies were low-tech businesses; the industry leaders were risk-averse and in no hurry to introduce a machine that could cannibalize their existing revenue streams. And at the time, there were no crowdfunding platforms upon which innovators could test the appeal of their inventions. Undeterred, Josh persevered. How could he not? He ended up pouring his life savings and draining his retirement accounts in the venture. Josh supplemented his seed investment when he recruited angel investors that approximately matched the $200,000 that he invested in the Shape Cutter. Through his hard work over four years, Josh made this venture a relative success. He entered into a licensing arrangement with a company called Making Memories which sold as many as 150,000 units of the Shape Cutter. By the time demand for the Shape Cutter fizzled out, Josh more or less made as much money as he would have made had he remained with Texas Instruments.

Josh's next entrepreneurial inspiration came from his children who were wading in the fad of trading silly bands. These liquid silicone molded rubber-like bracelets were produced in a variety of shapes; animal shapes were among the most popular genre. These silly bracelets were so popular in the 2010 timeframe that many schools banned them. In another of his inventive moments, Josh asked himself and his children why they couldn't make bracelets into shapes of their choosing. It didn't take long for Josh to figure out how to achieve such ends. Within eight weeks, he developed a way to use thermoplastic elastomers and pegboards to create and bake Shapelets—a line of bracelets in a variety of shapes. The problem was that Josh latched onto the tail end of the silly band hysteria. (Such ill-timing is a recurring phenomenon for entrepreneurs who live in the interior of the country: By the time fads that originate on the coasts reach Texans like the Malone family, the fads often have already begun their decent.) To cut to the chase, it didn't take long for Josh to lose roughly $100,000 of the money he made from his Shape Cutter invention on the Shapelet venture. Josh had to find another source of income.

Throughout his wilderness years, Josh maintained a roster of clients that hired him for consultations on engineering challenges. After the Shapelets venture fizzled out circa late 2012, Josh dedicated more time to his consulting business. The income he earned from his intermittent consulting practice never amounted to a fortune but it did smooth out the ups and downs of his entrepreneurial ventures.

Resolving the Water Balloon Fight Bottleneck

In addition to his striving as an engineer and then as an entrepreneur, Josh made time to play with his eight children. Having enjoyed water balloon fights since his childhood, Josh was no slouch when it came to throwing water balloons with his kids. However, there was one part of water balloon fights that vexed Josh and his children: It just took too long to fill up the balloons with water and to tie them. This sounds like a minor inconvenience but children lose their interest in the activity when they have to spend upwards of 90 minutes to prepare for a water balloon fight. Josh calculated that by the early 2010s he must have filled 10,000 water balloons. Despite such extensive experience, Josh never became more adroit or faster when it came to filling balloons with water.

Again, Josh thought there must be a more efficient way to fill up water balloons. Josh had been tinkering with possible solutions off and on for quite a few years. He experimented with sealing balloons with floating balls, a variety of biodegradable materials as well as by pressurizing and steaming an array of foams. Josh even tried to engineer an efficient means to seal balloons with marshmallows. By the time 2014 rolled around, the impatience that Josh's children felt while filling up water balloons was not the only factor that motivated Josh to devise a means to more expeditiously fill up water balloons. After seven years on his own, the Malone family's finances were strained. Josh couldn't postpone sending some of his children to the orthodontist any longer and he was way behind on saving for his children's education. And then his wife became partially paralyzed. Josh was unsure whether, or how fast, he could come up with a hit. To hedge his bets Josh began to prepare to search for a full-time engineering position.

Just before he was about to send out his first resume, Josh was struck by a flash of genius. In a breakthrough experiment, Josh placed small o-rings around the necks of empty balloons. Then he shoved tubing down the necks of these balloons. He then drilled holes in caps that cover water hoses. Finally, he placed a connecting pipe from the holes in the caps to the tubes inserted into the balloons. Walla! When he turned on his garden hose, tens of balloons were filled simultaneously. Not bad for a quick experiment. But Josh realized that it would take about 30 minutes of labor to produce a pack of what was soon to be called "Bunch O' Balloons."

Josh was determined to keep the end product simple for customers. After all, the idea was for kids to be able to quickly engage in water balloon fights. Today, when you buy a package of Bunch O'Balloons, you will only see four components—a connector, tubes made out of recyclable plastics, elastic rings made out of latex rubber and 105 semi-biodegradable latex balloons.

This simplicity—which infringers later derided as evidence of obviousness—required clever engineering. Josh had to figure out how to automate the insertion of tubes into fragile balloons without piercing them. He had to devise a means of expanding the o-rings just enough to slip over the plastic tubes to which they were attached without expanding them so much that they would no longer seal the balloons. He had to determine the optimum numbers of holes, and their positioning, on the caps that were connected to hoses. Josh also had to develop the best practice for welding and melting the tubes to the holes in the caps. Today, with the engineering kinks resolved, consumers can enjoy Bunch O' Balloons simply by inserting the connector to the end of a hose. When the water is turned on, 105 pre-attached balloons are filled in just one minute. Shaking Bunch O' Balloons causes the balloons to fall off of the device.

Josh Kicks Ass on Kickstarter

Josh didn't waste any time filing for patent protection or raising capital for Bunch O' Balloons. In February of 2014, within a week of developing a prototype, Josh filed a provisional patent application. A related non-provisional patent application issued as U.S. Patent No. 9,051,066 about 16 months after the provisional application was filed.

Josh also launched a Kickstarter campaign in February of 2014. He hired a consultant to help him position the crowdfunding campaign and with copyediting. But he didn't go out of his way to gin up demand on Kickstarter; no professional videos were shot. His invention's elegance, in terms of filling so many balloons so quickly, spoke for itself. Josh absolutely obliterated his official goal of raising $10,000 in 30 days. The first $10,000 was pledged within the campaign's first few hours and by the end of the 30-day campaign some 22,000 people pledged roughly $920,000. The demand for Bunch O' Balloons was genuine. The math indicates that most of the supporters pledged amounts sufficient to ensure that they would receive multiple packs of Bunch O' Balloons.

Within the first few days of launching the Kickstarter campaign, Josh was also hit with an avalanche of inquiries from retailers, distributors, licensees and manufacturers who were interested in partnering with Bunch O' Balloons. Several of these roughly 40 potential partners highlighted their ability to have the product manufactured very inexpensively by Chinese labor. However, Josh already had experience working with Chinese manufacturers and didn't see the value-add that these companies could bring to the table. He was also concerned that low cost manufacturing would result in workers being subjected to unsafe conditions and exploitive wages.

One of the parties interested in partnering with Bunch O' Balloons was Zuru. (Josh was so flooded with interest stemming from his Kickstarter campaign that it took Zuru three emails to capture his attention.) Zuru, owned by a family from New Zealand, relieved Josh's concerns about exploiting workers when its executives explained that Zuru's fully automated manufacturing facility in China would minimize labor intensity. With mutual respect flowing, an agreement was forged between Josh and Zuru on August 19, 2014, about 27 days into Josh's Kickstarter campaign.

> There are tremendous advantages associated with licensing a patent to reputable and capable companies such as Zuru. However, small inventors should be aware that doing so comes at the expense of their losing their small entity status, which results in higher patent filing and patent maintenance fees.

Josh didn't wait for Zuru to scale up its manufacturing lines. He immediately put the Kickstarter funds to use as he had many tens of thousands of orders to fill from his highly successful Kickstarter campaign. Production equipment was purchased but production snafus naturally arose, resulting in the disposal of units whose quality was below standards. Also, problems arose with getting packages of Bunch O' Balloons to customers on a cost-effective basis. Initially, Josh was spending $4 or $5 shipping out Bunch O' Balloon packages that were only generating $15 in revenues. Josh assiduously worked through a variety of manufacturing and fulfillment problems. By the spring of 2015, Josh produced and delivered about 200,000 units to his Kickstarter patrons.

Infringers Were Fast Out of the Gate

Once Zuru hit its stride in early 2015, packages of Bunch O' Balloons flew out the door. By mid-2019, more than 40 million units were sold. That's more than four billion water balloons sold in four years. Disconcertingly, Josh and Zuru were not the only ones that quickly began selling large volumes of Josh's patented invention. Initially, infringers from as far away as China saturated websites such as Amazon and eBay with knockoffs. But these relatively small-time infringers were just the warm-up act for the grandmaster of infringement.

By December of 2014, Josh detected that Telebrands was infringing his patents covering Bunch O' Balloons. Due to its more robust resources, Telebrands began delivering its infringing products to the market roughly five months before Zuru, the authorized licensee, was able to do so. (Interestingly, I have been told that Telebrands doesn't even bother to initially produce knockoffs. Rather, Josh told me that the New Jersey-based telemarketer is known to simply paint genuine products different colors when it runs its consumer trials.[51] It has also been stated that unscrupulous infringers troll crowdfunding platforms like Kickstarter and have standing policies that if anyone raises a certain amount of money, they will immediately start working on the same thing in order to beat the start-up to market.[52])

Mega-retailers such as Walmart, Walgreens, Bed Bath & Beyond, Home Depot, and Kroger happily sold such knockoffs. In fact, many retailers did not agree to be bound by later injunctions against Telebrands as it is common for retailers to have indemnification agreements with their suppliers. (Many retailers apparently believe that they have immunity from patent litigation. To some extent, they are right: Patentees who initiate patent assertion efforts against retailers run the risk of being sued by the infringer for tortious interference.)

[51] This contention is supported by the Final Judgment from the District Court for the Eastern District of Texas in the Tinnus v. Telebrands litigation, rendered on March 27, 2019.

[52] http://www.ipwatchdog.com/2019/02/16/patenting-delicate-dance-between-confidentiality-investment/id=106405/

Patent Litigation Heats Up

As you may have surmised after reading Francesca Kuglen's story, Telebrands neither agreed to cease its infringement nor to remit royalties to Josh or Zuru. Rather, Telebrands proved to be a relentless and rapacious litigation foe. Perhaps this is not surprising for a company sued at least 70 times for infringement.

Telebrands hired the most aggressive lawyers, including David Boies, the famed litigator. At the time of my writing these pages, Josh was contending with four massive cases in the Eastern District of Texas, one in New Jersey, eight at the Patent Trial and Appeal Board, and thirteen cases before the Court of Appeals for the Federal Circuit. Hundreds of motions running into many tens of thousands of pages have been filed in these proceedings. Telebrands' lawyers filed a countersuit against Josh and served him with a temporary restraining order on Christmas Eve of 2015. Josh estimates that he and Zuru spent as much as $3 million arguing about the meaning of "substantially filled" as in filling balloons up with water. (According to the PTAB, "*... the Specification does not supply an objective standard for measuring the scope of the term 'filled' or 'substantially filled.*'") Josh directed more time and treasure to dispelling the notion that his Bunch O' Balloons invention was obvious in light of surgeons using balloons in endoscopic procedures.

Further indicia of Telebrands' vexatious litigation practices were described in the Final Judgment issued by the District Court of the Eastern District of Texas on March 27, 2019. Here are excerpts from that Judgment: "Rather than offering new arguments or evidence, Defendants found creative ways to reassert their rejected positions...Defendants repeatedly attempted to circumvent the Court's orders and drive up the expense of litigation, this factor favors enhanced damages...Telebrands' discovery conduct weighs in favor of enhanced damages....these types of tactics waste resources and necessarily prolong the resolution of discovery disputes. Defendants' counsel violated their own objection...in light of this conduct and the previous conduct that we've repeatedly discussed throughout this trial, I am on the verge of reducing your closing arguments by 20 minutes...At nearly every stage of this litigation, Defendants took untenable positions and created unnecessary and wasteful work for the parties and the Court. This type of behavior is sanctionable and, indeed, did result in sanctions by the Court."

The PTAB Shreds Josh's Patents

In Josh's case, the PTAB has lived up to former Federal Circuit Chief Judge Randall Rader's depiction of it as a "death squad killing property rights." The PTAB initially deemed all the claims on Josh's first patent unpatentable. Josh appealed and the PTAB reinstated these claims but Telebrands again tried to get the patent invalidated. The PTAB instituted *inter partes reviews* on all of the claims in Josh's second, third and fourth patents. The first three of Josh's patents sustained invalidity attacks in district courts but succumbed to them at the PTAB. In other words, the PTAB canceled everything that the courts awarded. Thus, we see how the PTAB frequently sides with infringers and against both examiners and inventors.

Josh's patents were not the so-called "bad patents" that the America Invents Act was purportedly designed to cull out. The USPTO issued six patents that read on Josh's Bunch O' Balloons. The primary examiner uncovered over 100 pieces of prior art through his own search efforts and reviewed more than 150 prior art references in total. And the review of Josh's patents was not confined to one examiner. His patent applications were reviewed by two different primary examiners, three different supervisory examiners, one or more training quality assurance specialist(s), and a Technology Center Director. (Interestingly, one of Josh's subsequent patent applications was granted despite it having been pointed out to the patent examiner that the PTAB invalided one of its patent family forebearers.) At least 20 examinations were performed on Josh's patent applications by foreign patent offices. Nevertheless, a procession of PTAB panels, each consisting of three administrative patent judges, thought they knew more than everyone else and hastily invalidated Josh's patent portfolio.

Victories are Nominal, Pyric and Fleeting

After spending large sums of money over long periods of time, Josh achieved some victories in his litigation against Telebrands. The District Court for the Eastern District of Texas issued some preliminary injunctions against the infringing products. But one of the four preliminary injunctions that Josh was granted cost $1 million in legal fees, took nine months to obtain and required Josh and Zuru to lay out $4 million for a bond.

These hard-fought victories were short-lived for Josh because Telebrands simply made a few tweaks to its rebranded knockoffs. To wit, the New Jersey marketing company called its infringing products Balloon Bonanza in 2015,

Battle Balloons in 2016, and Easy Einstein Balloons in 2017. The inveterate infringer's cash registers continued to ring. Less than five years after putting Telebrands on notice of its infringement, Josh and Zuru have spent more than $20 million combatting Telebrands. When I spoke to Josh in the first quarter of 2019, he told me that this figure was increasing by $50,000 every week.

At long last, Josh won a $12.4 million jury award in March of 2019, which the judge doubled in light of Telebrands' willful infringement. Adding in some of the plaintiff's attorneys' fees resulted in Josh collecting $31 million. He stands to collect even more damages awards based on other actions brought against Telebrands. Josh's perseverance paid off. But patentees who win damages awards typically must wait a while to collect their money; it can take a good 18 months for a final order to issue post-verdict. Further, the Supreme Court's TC Heartland decision provides infringers with a ready-made cause for appealing damages awarded to patentees—even when such decisions are rendered by the District Court for the Eastern District of Texas to patentees like Josh who lived, worked, conducted research and paid taxes in that jurisdiction.[53]

Postscript

At the very most, Josh spent $2 million inventing and developing Bunch O' Balloons. Thus, the $20 million in legal fees that he has spent (through mid-2019) protecting his patents is at least ten times (but probably closer to 20 times) his investments in bringing this invention to the market. This warped invention-to-litigation ratio is emblematic of the disproportionate damage that infringers inflict on the community of inventors. Where is the justice in any patentee having to spend anything in the vicinity of $20 million to derive utility from his patents?

There are at least three further tragedies associated with litigation expenses dwarfing investments in research. One is that inventors tied up in litigation are deprived of the resources they need to produce new inventions; many inventors fund future research initiatives from the proceeds that they receive from earlier inventions. The second is that such enormous legal exposure could very well discourage inventors like Josh. Few innovators will go to bat multiple times in terms of trying to develop

[53] Interestingly, Apple announced in early 2019 that it was closing its stores in Frisco and Plano, Texas. It seems that Apple's motivation was to deprive patentees of a needed nexus to the Eastern District of Texas.

new products if they contemplate having to pay such exorbitant legal fees while protecting their patents. They might rightfully expect their patents to protect their products, rather than the inventor having to spend money to protect their patents. Similarly, such intense expenditure on legal fees could repel licensees such as Zuru from licensing promising new inventions, thereby depriving inventors of crucial commercialization channels.

Despite his misfortune of colliding with feral infringers, Josh is the first to admit that he has been blessed more than most inventors. How many inventors can afford to write a $10,000 check for litigation every working day after having already invested $20 million in patent assertion efforts? Josh can afford to expend such funds because Bunch O' Balloons is a smash hit that shows no sign of becoming obsolete.

For just about every other patentee (aside from Josh) whose products are experiencing infringement, the decision to assert patents is a harrowing one. Patentees are often unfamiliar with litigation, the patent invalidation tactics that may be perpetrated against them, and damages calculations. Many must scramble to retain legal representation. Even for those patentees that are familiar with patent litigation and have representation, sufficient information about their particular case is almost always lacking. Also, there is so much angst and uncertainty surrounding patent litigation that related deliberations can fracture the partnerships to which patents are assigned. One reason is that patent litigation may very well outlive the partnership and the partners seek definitiveness when determining their final distributions. On the other hand, filing a patent infringement suit can detract investors as the act often appears to be a desperation play to keep key players onboard in hopes of winning a large award.

The only certainty that patentees have relative to pursuing litigation lies on two planes. One certainty is that their legal fees will be astronomical. Lawyers fill up time vacuums and run up legal bills; they can always file motions and petitions while patentees wait months and months for judges to make simple decisions on previous motions. An inventor's lawyer can get everything wrong and still get paid. Some inventors with whom I have spoken lament that their lawyers become wealthier even when they become poorer. Patentees are caught in a Catch-22 situation. If a patent owner lacks deep pockets or good lawyers, his patent will not survive invalidity attacks. But having deep pockets and capable counsel does not guarantee that justice will prevail.

The second certainty that patentees can be assured of is that they will effectively subsidize the infringer's defense. Infringers are relieved of costs related to research and consumer testing. They save fortunes by limiting their commercialization efforts to promoting products that have already generated significant consumer interest. They lurk in the shadows of the halos created by legitimate manufacturers. When infringers enter the market, they typically sabotage the prevailing pricing structure, steal market share from patentees and cause patentees to expend huge sums of money on patent assertion. As such, inventing companies most often have to sue infringers when their rapidly deteriorating economics coincide with the infringers' rising prosperity.

Difficulty of Licensing

Entering into licensing agreements is the primary path for small inventors to monetize their patents. They simply do not have the financial or human resources necessary to commercialize their inventions independently. But as far as I can tell, probably no more than two percent of patents have attracted licensees.

Let's consider all of the difficulties that inventors face when they try to license their patents. At the outset, inventors do not have issued patents. Rather, they have non-provisional patent applications, or even provisional patent applications.[1] A patent application may never issue due to the inventor running out of money. Competitors may destroy a patent application by filing pre-grant oppositions. I am aware of a situation where a very large medical device company opposed all of the patents that its rival was seeking to register throughout Europe. (Pre-grant oppositions can be particularly lethal to patent applications because a business adversary may provide the most relevant prior art to the examiner, or provide a combination of references that did not occur to the examiner.) If the patent application does issue, there is a good chance its claims will be narrowed.Of course, if the patent issues, it could be subjected to post-grant challenges, such as *inter partes review* at the PTAB.

[1] It is true that inventors can sell or license these patent filings pre-issuance. I know of an inventor who sold a provisional patent application for $1.5 million. However, such monetization events are extremely rare.

Few issued patents attract any interest from licensees. Potential licensee organizations often prove to be impenetrable. Calls and emails go unanswered. You would be surprised how few licensing professionals even the largest companies employ. Researchers are resistant to bringing in outside innovations as they feel this demeans their work. Patent lawyers are reluctant to license in patents as they are concerned that they may have to correct the oversights that arose during the preparation and prosecution of such patents.

Few patentees that enter into licensing negotiations end up executing licensing agreements. Requests for NDAs often do not result in the receipt of executed NDAs. In some cases, potential licensees simply use the veneer of licensing negotiations to conduct competitive intelligence. Worse yet, patentees that seek to secure licensing partners—perhaps by sending out teasers—run the risk of those intended licensees moving to invalidate their patents. Potential licensees may initiate Declaratory Judgment actions in forums and at times of their choosing, or simply try to invalidate the subject patents in post-grant opposition proceedings.

The best-case scenario for a patentee is that a company is genuinely interested in licensing his patent. But even well-intentioned licensees are motivated to delay the execution of licensing agreements. The longer they wait to consummate a licensing agreement, the longer they can continue to practice the patents at no cost. When negotiations seem to be moving at a respectable clip, patentees do not want to derail those discussions by alluding to past or current infringement with their presumptive partners. Licensees are aware of patentees' reluctance to discuss infringement and thus see no adverse consequences to delaying negotiations as long as possible.

Not All Licensing Agreements Yield Royalties

Even when a patentee enters into a licensing agreement with a licensee, its receipt of royalty revenues is not assured. The licensee may have no intention of commercializing products that read on the patent; the licensee may be inclined to sabotage the patentee to ensure that competing technologies do not enter the market and compete against one of its cash cows.

Let's assume that the licensee is dedicated to making a concerted effort to practicing the patent in terms of developing and promoting products that read on the patent. A multitude of factors could impede the licensee's ability to execute. Problems may arise with refining the research. Manufacturing setbacks may surface. Financing might not be available. There may be supply chain impediments. Regulatory approvals and import/export licenses may be denied. Marketing and sales complications could derail go-to-market initiatives. Unions may not want to handle or install the inventive device.

The invention may be leapfrogged by a superior technology. The executive who championed bringing in the patented technology may have been reassigned, demoted, retired, or may have passed away. The licensee company could have filed for bankruptcy, reorganized, been acquired, spun off the division charged with commercializing the subject invention, or made an acquisition of a company that has a technology competitive with the in-licensed patent. I had a client who built a stellar portfolio of patents directed to the plastics and chemicals industries. We felt like the kings of the world when we found ourselves negotiating with both DuPont and Dow Chemical. When they announced their plans to merge, both of those prospects went radio silent.

Any one of these hurdles is sufficient to foreclose the licensor receiving royalties. Even if all such hurdles are overcome, it is common that years separate the executing of licensing agreements and the disbursement of royalty payments. After all, the product has to be designed, manufactured, marketed, distributed, and sold. The licensee must collect and account for its revenue before the first royalty check is prepared. Interestingly, even the licensee's efforts to promptly remit royalties to its licensor may not result in the receipt of those royalties. I know of situations where currency control officers in the licensor's country blocked such payments.

Difficulties of Enforcing Licensing Agreements

Even when licensees make a concerted effort to remit the royalties that licensors are owed, innocent mistakes can be made which end up shortchanging patentees. Large companies manufacture thousands of products that read on thousands of patents. They also have high levels of employee turnover. It is easy for these companies to fail to properly mark or report all of the products that use a patented technology. Or the licensing agreement may have been overly complicated, causing the accounting professionals at the licensee company to incorrectly calculate royalty remittances. Other complications arise when the licensee changes its accounting systems or accounting personnel.

Of course, not all licensee lapses in royalty remittances are inadvertent. Some licensees simply, and unabashedly, steal from their licensors. They know that it is very difficult for a small licensor to sue (one of) its primary licensees.

In some cases, the licensor-licensee relationship starts out well enough. But at some point, the licensee infringes one of its licensor's patent. The inventor is afraid that the licensee will stop remitting royalties on all of the other patents that the licensee is licensing if the inventor tries to assert his infringed patent.

In other cases, licensors effectively become trapped with their initial licensee. Suppose an inventor has a long-term relationship with a licensee. Things go well and the licensee remits royalties. Then the licensor produces another patented invention. In light of the positive, long-term relationship, the inventor faithfully offers the new patent-protected product to his long-time licensee. For what may be very legitimate reasons, the licensee declines to license the second patented invention. Now, the licensor is afraid that the licensee will retaliate if he shops the second patented product to another licensee: The initial licensee does not want its competitors to receive a license because the new licensee may take valuable shelf-space away from the initial licensee.

Finally, licensors are deprived of their rightful royalties when their licensees overlook infringement. Sometimes large companies find it more expedient to give passes to their peers than to litigate. This look-the-other-way thinking often arises when there are mutual transgressions.

Inventor Promotion Company Fouls Inventor

In early 2009, Barbara Jefferson's father, Melvin, was dying of leukemia.[54] One visible sign of leukemia ravaging Melvin's body was his extremely delicate skin. His sensitive skin made the bandages the nurses applied after transfusions extremely difficult to remove. In fact, Melvin died in June of 2009 with a bandage firmly affixed to his shoulder; the nurses simply could not remove the bandage without the risk of tearing a large portion of his skin.

Despite her distress in witnessing her father's suffering, in April of 2009 Barbara believed she spotted a solution to the difficulty of removing bandages from delicate skin. She tried rubbing small alcohol swabs on top of her father's bandages. Her thesis worked! The bandages became less adhesive and removal became possible. Thus, the idea for embedding slow-release ointments such as alcohol into the bandages themselves was conceived. Specifically, Barbara's invention features gauze in between the top part of the strap and the bottom layer of the punctured adhesive surrounded by a breakable tubing filled with alcohol or other liquid.

Inventor Gets Burned by Promotion Company

Despite being a successful businesswoman, Barbara was a neophyte when it came to inventions and patents. She sought assistance in patenting and commercializing her invention—which she called First Aid Pain Free BandAid—from Invention Resources International (IRI) in December of 2010. Soon after contacting IRI and remitting an initial payment, Barbara was looped into IRI's Houston office. That firm seemed to be sufficiently

[54] Barbara Jefferson is not the real name of the inventor in this story. I had a lengthy interview with the real inventor but she got cold feet in terms of my revealing her true identity.

pro-active in helping Barbara meet her business goals. Through IRI, a contract patent agent conducted a prior art search and drafted a provisional patent application. IRI also moved with alacrity on the commercialization front: In collaboration with Barbara, IRI's Phoenix office promptly produced a snazzy brochure and website. The company also sent out the brochures and a draft of the provisional patent application to companies in the medical field.

IRI's rapidity in pursuing commercialization opportunities did not match its pace of patent prosecution. Barbara's provisional patent application was filed on April 25, 2012, and her non-provisional patent application was filed a year later, on April 25, 2013. While there were a few Office Actions, the prosecution process was relatively uncontentious, at least until 2016. According to my discussions with Barbara, in March of 2016 the examiner stated that he intended to issue a Notice of Allowance for Barbara's patent application (number 13/870,651) in short order as long as Barbara made a couple of picayune amendments. But then there was silence from the USPTO.

To IRI's credit, the patent agent it retained and who was tasked with prosecuting Barbara's patent application made follow-up calls to the examiner from April of 2016 through November of 2016. The agent received no responses despite a verbal understanding in March of 2016 that a Notice of Allowance was forthcoming.

The reason for the eerie silence was explained in November of 2016 when Barbara learned that her examiner was replaced. The new examiner rejected all of the claims in the '651 patent application, largely in light of the 13/603,803 patent application which listed Ryan Michael Rea as the inventor and has a September 6, 2011 priority date. Barbara demonstrated to the new examiner that she conceived the same idea at least as early as May 25, 2011 by producing appropriately dated marketing material created in cooperation with IRI. Barbara could have sent the new examiner a December 2011 postmarked envelope containing a notarized Invention Disclosure but did not want to take a chance on this critical evidence of early inventorship becoming lost. Barbara's submission of a Declaration of Prior Invention was quickly rejected. Barbara reached out to both the primary examiner and the supervisory examiner; messages were left but not returned. She received her Final Rejection in July of 2017.

Based on her account, Barbara was ill-served by Invention Resources International. That company promoted Barbara's invention before protecting it. Filing a provisional patent application before promoting Barbara's medical product would have gone a long way in protecting Barbara's interest in her invention. Barbara tried to get in touch with IRI since her patenting efforts came to a halt but that company has been completely uncommunicative. Calls to the main phone number are routinely dropped once the caller hits "0" to be transferred to an operator. Barbara already invested $20,000 in pursuing her patent, and when I spoke with her, she was willing to invest more money if there was a possibility of reviving her patent application. Barbara sustained another misfortune in the midst of this saga. When she got divorced, she retained rights to her patent application but received less than 50% of the couple's assets because—at that time—her patent application was perceived to hold significant value.

Postscript

Barbara is deserving of sympathy. And to the extent that patients with highly sensitive skin are deprived of bandages like the ones Barbara invented, they too are deserving of sympathy. Society is worse off because we are unlikely to benefit from the other ideas that Barbara would like to patent—she is simply too discouraged to try to develop her envisioned products.

However, the patent system cannot be blamed for Barbara's misfortunes as described above. I have no idea how or when Ryan Michael Rea conceived of his claimed invention. For all I know, he could have been researching the removability of bandages from hyper-sensitive skin for 20 years. Or, he could have cut-and-pasted material from the provisional patent application and marketing materials that IRI prematurely disseminated.[55]

> Let's review a few of the lessons to be learned from Barbara's story.
>
> **Beware of Inventor Promotion Companies** Inventor Resources International is not the only company to have preyed on inventors who are by nature susceptible to scams due to their

[55] Related inventions do tend to cluster. For instance, two patent applications for the telephone were filed on the same day.

hopefulness and optimism. Gene Dolgoff (whose stories appear later in this book) told me that such a company connived him into paying a fee and then sold his idea (for a mask that would help cold sufferers breathe in steam) to another promoter.

The Federal Trade Commission banned World Patent Marketing from the invention promotion business and ordered payment of $25,987,192 as that company was deemed to be nothing more than a scam, bilking millions of dollars from inventors. Specifically, the FTC charged World Patent Marketing with deceiving consumers by charging them thousands of dollars to patent and market their inventions based on bogus "success stories" and testimonials promoted by the defendants.

According to the FTC, many customers ended up in debt or lost their life savings with nothing to show for it. Then, when customers complained, World Patent Marketing suppressed complaints directed towards the company by using threats of criminal prosecution against dissatisfied customers. In one case, after a dissatisfied customer filed a complaint with the Better Business Bureau, he received a letter from World Patent Marketing's lawyer which stated that seeking a refund was extortion under Florida law and, "since you used email to make your threats, you would be subject to a federal extortion charge, which carries a term of imprisonment of up to two years and potential criminal fines."

Patent Lawyers In general, inventors are in good hands with their patent lawyers. The vast majority of patent lawyers are highly capable professionals who serve their clients with integrity. However, inventors can get hurt when capable patent lawyers make mistakes. For instance, I was once called upon to calculate the value of a claim that a world-class chemist was in the process of filing against her lawyer. The patent attorney neglected to file the chemist's non-provisional patent application within one year of filing the corresponding provisional patent application. As a result, this Ivy League professor was deprived of the possibility of patenting her discovery. Recovery was limited to the lawyer's malpractice insurance coverage.

A few patent lawyers may succumb to the temptations of large budgets and little supervision. I once valued a large patent portfolio that consisted of patent applications filed in countries ranging from Serbia to Nigeria and from Saudi Arabia to Turkey. I asked the patent lawyer what the logic was of filing for patent protection in countries that offered neither markets nor patent protection for the inventions at issue. The response I received from the patent lawyer was, "Oh, that's an easy question. The client is a billionaire."

Like every other segment of society, there are a few duplicitous characters among the ranks of patent lawyers. During a Certified Patent Valuation Analyst training session in London, one candidate told me a story of how a South African inventor retained a South African lawyer to draft and file a patent application relating to television technology. After disclosing the invention to the lawyer, the inventor did not hear from the lawyer for a few weeks. The lawyer maintained his silence for another few weeks. After a few months passed, the inventor learned that the South African lawyer moved to the United States where he filed a patent application for the same invention under his own name.

As a further aside, I am aware of a situation relating to a Chinese graduate student at a university in one of the southern states. This Chinese student copied verbatim a patent issued to the university and filed it as a patent application in China. The Chinese patent examiners did not uncover the U.S.-issued patent and issued the copied application. The American university did not protest as its funds were limited and it did not plan to pursue the Chinese market.

The Rainbow Loom Story

Entrepreneurs see things others don't. This was definitely the case with Choon Ng, a former engineer with Nissan Motors and an ethnic Chinese emigre from Malaysia.

In 2010, Choon observed his two daughters making bracelets and other accessories with colored rubber bands. While many parents would consider rubber band weaving as nothing more than a cute pastime, Choon saw the seeds of a commercial opportunity. But before the roots of any such opportunity could take hold, Choon would have to make it easier for children to design more sophisticated bracelets and accessories with rubber bands. An obvious constraint to making such accessories was that children have a limited number of fingers to hold and manipulate the colored rubber bands. Choon put on his engineering hat and designed a loom with multiple rows of pins that would hold rubber bands. These pins enabled users to loop and crisscross rubber bands to make thicker bracelets as well as a variety of patterns such as squares, triangles, rectangles, rhombuses and honeycombs. The resulting product was christened the Rainbow Loom.

With the help of a patent attorney friend, Choon filed a provisional patent application in November of 2010. A non-provisional patent application was filed in September of 2011 and issued as U.S. Patent No. 8,485,565 in July of 2013. The examination of this patent application went smoothly. In my opinion, a patent pendency of less than two years is perfectly reasonable. However, Choon pointed out that the toy industry is a hits business where few products are relevant for more than a year. Thus, he would have liked to have seen a more rapid examination of his patent application. In fairness to the United States Patent and Trademark Office, Choon could have also filed a patent application for accelerated examination, where pendency is usually a matter of mere months.

In any event, subsequent to the issuance of his '565 patent, Choon grew his patent portfolio dramatically. At the time of my writing these pages,

Choon maintained 23 patents issued by the USPTO as well as patents issued in the United Kingdom, Germany, France, Japan and China. Choon invested approximately $250,000 in terms of drafting, filing, prosecuting and paying the associated maintenance fees and annuities related to these patents.

A Business is Born

Choon began trying to turn the invention claimed in his initial provisional patent application into a viable business at the end of 2010. One of his first steps was to learn more about the potential users of the Rainbow Loom. He conducted multiple study groups whereby kids would practice using prototypes in his home. While Choon had no background in marketing or sales, he was convinced that there would be sufficient demand for the Rainbow Loom. The product resonated with both genders and all ethnicities but was most warmly embraced by children between the ages of nine and twelve.

While the Rainbow Loom logged its initial sales—mostly word-of-mouth—in July of 2011, the product was not an instant hit. The product required the user to expend energy creating bracelets and accessories. The sophistication of the patterns possible to create with the Rainbow Loom intimidated many potential customers. A lot of pounding of the pavement was required to gain traction. Choon's lack of sales experience did not deter him. He tried to get the mass merchants such as Walmart, Sam's Club, Target, and Toys "R" Us to carry the Rainbow Loom but had no immediate success. He visited independent retailers, often with his daughters in tow. Many of these proprietors asked the Ng family to leave their stores. Choon was only able to convince a few of these mom-and-pop toy and gift stores to carry the product—and then only on consignment.

Choon, ever constrained by his limited resources, tried to sell the Rainbow Loom online. While he was able to upload videos on YouTube at no cost, resulting sales were sluggish. So, Choon's marketing tactics took a more guerilla-like turn. He went to shopping malls and handed out ready-made bracelets to shoppers, together with cards that contained the Rainbow Loom's website.

Choon's first big break on the sales front arose when Learning Express in Alpharetta, Georgia showed kids how to make bracelets with the Rainbow Loom. With rooms dedicated to parties where art projects were taught, Learning Express proved to be a great outlet for Choon's product. The store in Alpharetta quickly sold all of the looms it had on hand. This Learning Express store related its success with the Rainbow Loom to many other of that chain's franchisees.

Choon had more success on the social media front in 2012. This success was sparked when a young YouTuber named Angelynn began uploading videos of her Rainbow Loom creations to her popular OfficialTutorialsByA YouTube channel. Choon fueled the growing interest in the product by featuring some of the Rainbow Loom aficionados and their creations on the Rainbow Loom website. Often, these Rainbow Loom artists would place pictures of their Rainbow Loom designs on their own websites and then link back to the product's official website.

Scaling Production

How did Choon produce the Rainbow Looms? Initially, he created the designs for the loom and sourced the components from Dongguan, China. Shipping of the individual components—the loom, hooks, and rubber bands—was inexpensive because they could be packed with density. Assembly was a home-business affair: The components were delivered to the Ng home in Michigan, where final assembly and repackaging was completed by Choon, his wife and, intermittently, his daughters. This arrangement worked well enough until the end of 2012, when sales of the Rainbow Loom skyrocketed. From the end of 2012 to the end of 2013, sales surged 50% a month. In August of 2013, Choon entered into a one-and-a-half-year exclusive sales agreement with Michaels, the largest arts and crafts retail chain in the United States. Also, in 2013, Choon sold the product to Walmart stores under the Wonder Loom name. Choon began selling the Rainbow Loom in some of Target's stores in 2014 as well as related components through Hobby Lobby. Choon's crowning moment in 2014 occurred when the Rainbow Loom received four TOTY Awards, the most prestigious award in the toy industry.

To keep up with soaring demand, Choon outsourced all of the production (including the printing of the manual), assembly, and packaging to China by the end of 2012. Production problems naturally arose. Initially, the colors of the parts delivered did not match specifications. Some of the parts had sharp edges, a significant liability given how many times children's fingers would graze the looms and pins. Every now and then a foreign object would find its way into a Rainbow Loom box. Choon was able get these kinds of start-up snafus resolved relatively painlessly as he had experience dealing with suppliers at Nissan, and is a Mandarin speaker. But Choon did not leave anything to chance: He appointed his own quality control expert on the ground in China to inspect the products manufactured there.

Choon's initial manufacturer proved to be conscientious and quickly corrected the inevitable manufacturing hiccups. That initial manufacturer also made concerted efforts to scale its operations to meet the surging demand for the product. At peak production, Choon's dedicated manufacturing firm managed two factories, where a combined 2,500 employees were churning out Rainbow Looms. Choon and his manufacturer were continuing to work together at the time of my writing these pages.

This rapid expansion required capital that Choon didn't have. Choon applied for a line of credit with Comerica Bank. What happened with Choon's application? That bank only agreed to extend a $30,000 line of credit to Choon, hardly enough considering that filling one container of Rainbow Looms consumed $90,000 in capital. Fortunately, Choon's father and brother stepped forward and lent $250,000 to Choon's venture.

The Rainbow Loom Becomes Infested with Infringers

The Rainbow Loom was quite popular in 2013—and not just with customers, but also with infringers. Infringers were popping up everywhere. In 2013, Walmart.com was selling seven copycat versions of the Rainbow Loom and at least five times more infringing products were sold on both Amazon.com and eBay.com. When Michael's dispatched Choon to China to source more manufacturing capacity for its surging demand, Choon saw that some manufacturers producing on behalf of infringers had mountains of low-quality rubber bands piled up. A pandemic of infringement also broke out in shopping malls across the country in the form of kiosks selling knockoff Rainbow Looms. One New Jersey-based owner of dozens of shopping mall kiosks initially ordered Rainbow Looms directly from Choon but failed to remit payment—leaving Choon with a $50,000 outstanding invoice—when it found a source of much less expensive infringing alternatives.

The outbreak of infringement oversaturated the market, causing demand for Rainbow Looms to crash by the end of 2013. Choon wasn't the only one hurt by the sudden and dramatic reduction in demand—his dedicated manufacturer in China was flooded with excess inventory. Not comfortable with his loyal manufacturer being stuck with as much as $300,000 worth of inventory, Choon acquired the excess production and arranged for those units to be sold in Japan, Germany, Eastern Europe and Russia. In 2018, Choon was only selling five percent of the volume of Rainbow Looms that he was selling in 2013.

In addition to depriving Choon of volume, the infringers who sourced their products from China damaged the Rainbow Loom brand and the pricing of the product. The infringers seemed to be indifferent to product quality. The counterfeited looms were not inspected, did not bother with placing warning labels on the packaging, were rife with sharp edges, were manufactured with low-quality recycled plastics and even contained cancer-causing agents. In fact, the Assay Laboratory in Birmingham, UK determined that some charms (attachments to bracelets and necklaces woven on the looms) made by knockoff brands contained high levels of phthalates, a class of carcinogenic chemicals. Much of the reporting of the Assay Laboratory's study associated these carcinogenic chemicals with Rainbow Loom, even though the same laboratory determined that Rainbow Looms were free of any traces of cancer-causing agents. For instance, a related article posted by *Mother Jones* was titled, "Are Your Kids' Rainbow Bracelets Toxic?"[56] This combination of reckless manufacturing and guilt-by-association reporting must have deterred the purchase of at least tens of thousands of Rainbow Loom units.

> A somewhat similar story relates to the creator of a copyright. This Ohio-based app developer published a free-to-download app which was pirated and then illegally downloaded thousands of times. Not only was the developer of the pirated app depriving the creator of all of the ad revenues generated by the pirated app, but the legitimate developer of the free app was required to pay the invoices presented by the hosting service for the promotional videos generated by the pirated app.[58]

[56] https://www.motherjones.com/politics/2014/08/rainbow-loom-bracelets-phthalates-cancer-risk/

[57] https://www.ipwatchdog.com/2018/07/12/house-small-business-committee-holds-hearing-on-ip-in-digital-economy/id=99288/

Rather than repel retailers, such shoddy manufacturing attracted them—especially those of the here-today-gone-tomorrow variety. And once infringers got going, the only thing that could stop them was their own eroding profit margins. For a while, infringers and their confederate retailers were able to juice demand by slashing retail prices—in some situations to as little as $2.00 per unit. Such pulverized pricing forced Choon to reduce the price of Rainbow Looms from $15 to $11.99 a unit.

Many infringing products were sold to small time retailers, for which patent assertion was uneconomic for Choon. Online retailers often placed the burden of proof of infringement on Choon. For instance, in Choon's experience, Amazon usually refrained from removing allegedly infringing looms (or even disclosing the names and addresses of the alleged infringers) unless Choon first purchased the suspected products from that online retailer. When Choon complied, Amazon began its weeks-long investigations. In some cases, Amazon did remove infringing looms. Such removal did not always discourage infringers. Quite often, they would repost their infringing items under a different name.

By the end of 2013, Choon had had enough. He decided to put his patents to use by initiating lawsuits against 15 infringers. Most of the damages sought were directed towards recovering royalties from earlier sales as revenues from Rainbow Looms declined precipitously in 2014. Choon had some success with his efforts to collect damages for past infringement; settlements were reached with 13 small infringers. Some of these infringers got away with paying almost nothing as they threatened to file for bankruptcy protection. At the time of my researching Choon's story, these settlements only amounted to a fraction of the $5 million (and counting) in legal fees that Choon incurred in asserting his patents in the countries where he received patent protection.

Litigation against two large infringers—Tristar Products and Idea Village (whose CEO is the brother of A.J. Khubani, CEO of Telebrands)—was still pending five years after Choon filed patent infringement lawsuits against them. In the case against Idea Village, the defendant filed a petition for *inter partes review* with the Patent Trial and Appeal Board. Litigation was stayed during the time of the *inter partes review*, where Choon was pressured to give up some of his claims' scope.

The drawn-out lawsuits in the United States contrasts with the relative speed of corresponding litigation in Japan. Choon filed a lawsuit for patent damages against a Japanese infringer with the Tokyo District Court in 2014.

A very favorable judgment was rendered in Choon's favor three-and-a-half years later.[58] (However, the Japanese defendant appealed the Tokyo District Court's decision to the Tokyo Supreme Court and then Choon countersued. In 2018, the litigants negotiated a settlement that Choon considers to be very fair.)

Postscript

Choon is a relatively fortunate patentee. It is true that revenues from the Rainbow Loom have decreased by 95% since their 2013 highs. But not all of that revenue shortfall can be attributed to infringers: Much of the decline in the popularity of the Rainbow Loom is a function of the nature of the toy industry. I don't know how much money Choon made from the Rainbow Loom, but it must have been enough to finance roughly $5 million in net legal expenditures. Based on my discussions with Choon, his business continues to hum along and he stands a good chance of being awarded significant damages. Infringers have exited the market and his manufacturing and distribution channels seem to be well-oiled.

Still, Choon would have made much more money had infringers not pervaded the crafts market. A back of the envelope calculation suggests that the infringers deprived Choon of roughly 12 million units. This means that if Choon earned one dollar per unit, the infringers stole at least $17 million in lost profits and unnecessary legal fees.

And let's not forget that the infringers benefitted from a de-risked investment opportunity. They only latched on to the Rainbow Loom when its success was widely known. They didn't invest a dime or a moment pursuing patent protection. The infringers did not have to conduct study sessions. They did not have to pass out sample bracelets in shopping malls, which must have been demeaning to a former senior engineer. The infringers did not have to suffer the indignities of being asked to leave retail stores in the presence of their children. They did not have to evangelize a new product concept to discerning buyers at big-box retailers; Choon already paved the way to these vendors. The infringers took the fastest route to making money. These modern-day marauders infringed patents,

[58] While the decision was favorable to the patentee, my research indicates that it was rendered in almost twice the two-year timeframe such cases are said to normally require in Japan.

invaded shelf-space, slashed prices, burned the goodwill associated with the entire product category, placed their carcinogenic chemical-laden pirated products in the hands of unsuspecting children, took their liberties with the legal system, impregnated legitimate manufacturers with unwanted inventory, and walked away almost scot-free.

Patent Prosecution Purgatory

When New York City-based building contractor Shujen (Scott) Yu was in the process of renovating his apartment in 2006, he thought there must be a better way of installing kitchen sinks.

The Problem and the Invention

In those days, many sinks were self-rimming units. Sinks were either placed through pre-cut holes in countertops or were mounted from the underside of sink openings in the countertops. The sinks with the elevated flanges (lips) made it hard to swipe in food residue from the countertops. Sinks that were installed from below often resulted in chipping of the countertop material adjacent to the sink; for instance, as pots and pans banged against their edges when washing dishes. In either case, since the sinks seldom perfectly synched up with the countertops, mildew and germs accumulated in the gaps. Calking, which tends to crack and cry out for replacement, was needed to stabilize the positioning of the sinks relative to the countertops.

Scott asked quite a few plumbing supply wholesalers about obtaining a flush-mounted sink that would seamlessly integrate with the countertops; he wanted the countertops and sink lips to present one flat surface. No one knew of the existence of any such flush-mounted sinks. Most builders were skeptical in view of the engineering challenges associated with such a sink, especially when the issue of high-volume manufacturing arose. Sinks that were dropped into the holes featured elevated lips that relied on contact with the countertops to support their weight. Under-mounted sinks were held in place with adhesive bonds connecting the sinks' lips to the bottom surfaces of countertops.

In any event, Scott invented a solution that enabled sinks to reside at the same elevation as the adjacent countertops. This was accomplished by placing the sinks' flanges on top of mounting brackets, which could then be adjusted by turning screws in the mounting brackets to adjust the elevation of the sinks' flanges. Scott had to get the flanges to precisely hold the sinks in place in their flush-mounted positions. If the flanges were too big, the weight of the flanges would damage the bracketing system. If the flanges were too small, the system would deform over time. Scott's invention was described in a patent application originally filed on October 13, 2006 and what is now United States Patent No. 9,988,799.

Licensing Opportunities Lost Due to Prolonged Prosecution

Scott's journey to patent issuance proved to be a 4,253-day odyssey. I won't go into all of the details of the contentious patent prosecution process as they are available through the USPTO's PAIR site. Scott never wavered from his goal of securing patent protection for his invention. Years into his patenting campaign, his two initially sequentially retained patent lawyers suggested that Scott abandon his utility patent application and instead pursue a design patent. Nevertheless, Scott trudged ahead with his utility patent application. He and his lawyers responded to more than a dozen office actions issued by the same patent examiner over eleven-and-a-half years and participated in multiple examiner interviews. Scott invested well over $100,000 pursuing patent coverage.

In addition to his financial investment, Scott dedicated significant time to briefing his subsequent patent lawyers on the uniqueness of his invention and in responding to the examiner's rejections. (A total of three lawyers were retained over the course of the pendency of Scott's patent application.) Not only did Scott sustain large out-of-pocket costs and hemorrhage copious amounts of his valuable time, he suffered opportunity costs as well.

Approximately six years into the examination of his patent application, Scott was approached by Kohler Co., a global manufacturer of kitchen and bath products. A variety of potential business deals between Kohler and Mila International (Scott's company) were discussed over the course of some 15 meetings—some of which were attended by as many as 15 Kohler executives and engineers. The inability of Scott to obtain a patent on his flush-mount sink was one of the reasons that the Kohler discussions came to a halt. An unfortunate parallel episode was repeated shortly thereafter when American Standard sought to enter into a licensing agreement with Mila International; these negotiations came to naught when it became clear that Scott's patent application was going to remain in patent prosecution purgatory for the foreseeable future.

Many of the examiner's rejections consisted of her proclaiming that Scott's invention was nothing more than a larger flange. She neither produced relevant prior art depicting similar flanges nor took into consideration that Scott's invention was more complex than just a large flange.

To make a very long story short, on March 29, 2018, in less than two pages of analysis, the Patent Trial and Appeal Board held that the examiner erred in her citations of prior art when it reversed the examiner's rejection of all 20 claims that Scott pursued. By way of comparison, pendency at the USPTO was two-and-a-half times longer—and prosecution was five times as expensive—than the issuance of the same patent application in Canada.

Postscript

Scott told me he feels that his examiner's intransigent position was a function of her thinking that the case might go away if she issued enough rejections. After all, small investors have limited funds to respond to office actions. He told me that he felt the examiner demonstrated a lack of respect for small inventors. Instead of appreciating small inventors' time, efforts and initiatives, he feels that small inventors are nothing more than numbers to examiners.

It is true that the USPTO extended the term of the '799 patent by 604 days. But additional days of patent life do not trigger the resurrection of long-gone potential licensees. At least not in Scott's case. Rather, Scott's case demonstrated that justice delayed is justice denied. (Incidentally, inventor Nick Gross who you will meet later in this book, had a similar experience: It took Nick more than eight years to prosecute what eventually became U.S. Patent No. 8,924,558. Much of the examiner's rejections revolved around silly "and/or" language. As with Scott, the USPTO extended the term of Nick's '558 patent by 2,252 days but, by the time his patent issued, he lost all opportunity to license it.)

In a sense, Scott is very fortunate. At the time of the issuance of his '799 patent (and at the time of my writing these pages), he was still very active as a building contractor. A lot can happen over the course of a 10-year patent pendency, or even, let's say, a six-year excessive patent pendency. Inventors can pass away or become ill. They can retire or pivot their business away from the inventions claimed in their patents. Products can be leapfrogged by more compelling inventions and entire industries can become obsolete over such long periods of time.

Incidentally, Scott's 11.6-year odyssey through patent prosecution is not even close to the record for the longest patent examination conducted by the USPTO. Separately, a full 91 of inventor John Harvey's 300 continuation patent applications spent 17 years in prosecutorial purgatory. Mr. Harvey realized that this volume of patent applications strained the resources of the USPTO and took numerous steps to ease examiners' burdens. Apparently, the USPTO's resources were not terribly constrained: During just one two-year period, some 700 office actions were issued against the Harvey applications. Prosecution of these patents was replete with double patenting rejections, appeals, and suspensions of prosecution. One examiner reported his professionally diagnosed mental illness to his superiors, which resulted in his removal from his position and the withdrawal of all of the rejections he issued. Many of this examiner's office actions were declared *ultra vires* as he wrote about subject matter that was beyond the scope of the patent applications. This examiner's mental illness and *ultra vires* activity apparently escaped the attention of the supervisory examiners for years. In another situation, Gilbert Hyatt has been pursuing issuance of his patent applications for at least 43 years.[59]

[59] https://www.bloomberg.com/news/articles/2014-02-24/inventor-waits-43-years-for-another-chance-to-shock-tech

Retroactive Application of Patent Rules Decimates Patent Portfolio

By the mid-1990s, Peter Keller already had an illustrious career. He was a successful actuarial consultant who practiced before the Internal Revenue Service and signed government forms supporting the viability of pension plans covering the lives of many thousands of people. He bought into a broker-dealer and became a registered securities principal when he passed all required exams. Peter wasn't all business; he was a dedicated family man who adopted a Russian boy from a Moscow orphanage in 1992.

Peter was also a computer hobbyist and music collector whose inventive mojo hit its stride in the mid-1990s. Peter founded Advanced Audio Devices, LLC to produce consumer electronics in 1997. By July of 1997, with the three engineers Peter hired, AAD had working prototypes of its digital audio recorder, which featured a built-in hard drive that facilitated archiving music from degrading vinyl records and tapes and storing such music on CD-R media. This "plug-in-the-wall" device functioned as a "music jukebox" and required no computer literacy on the part of users.

Peter was ahead of the curve in terms of protecting AAD's inventions. Even before the first prototypes were developed, Peter began searching for patent lawyers to draft and prosecute patents covering the inventions brewing at AAD. He retained Trexler, Bushnell, Giangiorgi, Blackstone & Marr in Chicago. That firm filed Peter's first provisional patent application in July of 1997, one day before exhibiting AAD's digital audio recorder at the National Association of Music Merchants trade show in Nashville, Tennessee.[60]

AAD generated strong interest in its prototypes but orchestrating

[60] Trexler, Bushnell, Giangiorgi, Blackstone & Marr subsequently merged with Clark Hill.

manufacturing proved to be a challenge. In mid-1997, a La Grange, Illinois company produced prototype keypads ordered to AAD's specifications but at prohibitive cost. Peter then engaged a Chinese manufacturer to mass produce keypads but that firm could not meet AAD's requirements in terms of tensile strength, depression strength or internal and external dimensions. Consequently, by 1999, production boomeranged back to the U.S. Along the way, Peter learned that it is nearly impossible for start-up companies to compete with conglomerates in terms of manufacturing. Small companies lack both negotiating power with vendors and the capital to put the enormous machinery in place—both of which are necessary to achieve the economies of scale and low production costs that the large players enjoy.

Peter personally invested approximately $500,000 in prototype development and a similar amount in building AAD's patent portfolio in the late 1990s and early 2000s. These expenses nearly drove Peter to the poor house. In fact, he liquidated every asset that he and his family owned, including his principal residence. To survive the ensuing cash crunch, Peter incurred several hundred thousand dollars of mostly high interest debt.

While AAD was on life support, the Company did make some progress on the patent front: The first patent issued in 2001 and continuations filed in 2001 and 2003 were approved and issued. Receiving patent issuance was a source of great pride for Peter but those early patents did not (yet) pay the bills.

Peter conferred with the University of Chicago's New Venture Lab about his manufacturing predicament during 2001 and the first half of 2002. It was recommended that AAD relent on manufacturing and instead shift to a licensing model. When Peter heeded that advice, AAD's burgeoning patent portfolio became the bedrock of that emerging company. (Interestingly, as is the case with many innovators, Peter found himself in a bit of intellectual solitary confinement. Inventors are not positioned to receive the full benefit of conferring with consultants because they are limited in what they can disclose to their advisors. There is always a risk of misappropriation of proprietary information and ideas. Also, prematurely revealing inventions can imperil opportunities to patent those inventions.)

With his borrowing capacity tapped out and unable to raise funding from any of the 20 venture capital firms he approached, Peter turned to his friends and family for capital. Soliciting money from friends and family is always accompanied by the fear that failure to make them whole on their investments (if not rich) will result in the inventors' estrangement from those closest to them. (As a side note, in addition to being an innovator in consumer electronics, Peter demonstrated an acuity for financial innovation. Peter offered his friends and family the opportunity to invest half of the capital he needed in the first tranche [circa 2003]. These investors would have a call option on participating in the second tranche [circa 2005] at the valuation established in the first tranche.)

Concurrent with the first friends-and-family round, it appeared to Peter that quite a few large electronics manufacturers were helping themselves to the inventions claimed by AAD's patent portfolio. Not having a robust repertoire of patent licensing skills, Peter sought a law firm that could help recruit licensees through amicable negotiations (if possible) and via litigation (if necessary). He was inclined to expand Trexler's mandate to cover these services as Peter was pleased with that law firm's drafting and prosecution of his patents. Trexler was interested in expanding its representation of AAD but wanted Peter to have another law firm represent AAD in negotiating its contingency fee agreement with Trexler. This was a very above-board request on Trexler's part; AAD's law firm of record wanted to inoculate itself from later being accused of taking undue advantage of its long-standing client.

When seven law firms were asked to review the proposed AAD–Trexler contingency agreement, the funniest thing happened. They all believed AAD's patents were so strong and covered such potentially lucrative streams of infringing revenue that none of them wanted to see Trexler receiving bountiful contingency awards by asserting AAD's patents. (Remember, the 2003 timeframe was when iPods and MP3 players were becoming popular and appeared to be infringing AAD's evolving patent portfolio.) Since all seven of these law firms wanted to serve as AAD's patent counselors, they declined to provide opinions on the fairness of Trexler's proposed representation agreement. During the 18 months that Peter sought patent licensing and assertion representation, AAD was in a surreal state: Its patents were so strong that competition among law firms to represent AAD made it impossible to monetize AAD's patent portfolio. In any event, at long last, on August 4, 2003, AAD retained Niro, Scavone, Haller & Niro.

Challenges in Retaining Contingency Counsel

As we see from Peter's experience, retaining contingency counsel is more arduous than most people realize. Patentees seek lawyers who have subject matter expertise relevant to the patents-in-suit, sufficient resources to dedicate to litigation that can endure for a decade, and strong track records in winning large damages awards. Contingency lawyers want to make sure the patentees' patents claim the infringing activity, are strong enough to withstand invalidity challenges, and that the potential damages awards are high enough to justify the lawyers' time, resources, and efforts. (Incidentally, the America Invents Act discourages contingency representation as it prohibits joinder of multiple unrelated defendants in most circumstances.) While each side should thoroughly vet the other, the dating game can't take too long as players lose interest and key lawyers depart their firms.

Representation agreements between patentees and contingency lawyers are heavily negotiated. The following are among the issues that should be included in such negotiations:

- Which services are included in the representation agreement? Will the patent lawyer defend the patents in post-grant opposition proceedings such as *inter partes review*? (If not, how will the introduction of lawyers different from those litigating the case affect the patentee's chances of prevailing in the IPR proceedings?) What responsibilities will the patent law firm have, if any, to defend the patentee in the event the plaintiff is countersued?

- Which lawyers at the law firm will be involved in the case? The patentee prefers that senior partners remain involved as opposed to handing off the case to junior associates as a training exercise.

- Who is responsible for bearing which costs? And there are many costs to be borne—some of which include court filing fees, travel, expert witnesses, and jury selection experts. To what extent will the law firm contribute to paying fees required to respond to IPR attacks? What happens if the patentee loses the case and is required to pay the opponent's legal fees?

- Who has the right to determine when to settle the case? Under what circumstances can the law firm resign from the case? When can the patentee fire the law firm? If the patentee loses in the district court, can the law firm resign or be terminated when the case is appealed?

- How will the law firm be compensated if amicable resolution is reached between the plaintiff and defendant for terms other than a cash settlement? An example would be when the defendant acquires the plaintiff company.

Peter's search for a law firm to monetize AAD's patent portfolio quickly paid handsome dividends. AAD's licensing campaign commenced in 2004; by 2008, AAD had licensed its patents to most manufacturers of MP3 players as well as to producers of other merchandise covered by its patents. By 2013, AAD licensed three large cellular phone manufacturers whose products also provided digital audio player functionality. In total, AAD licensed its patents to more than 24 companies—including SanDisk and Alesis—and reached settlement agreements with several others.

About half of the firms that licensed AAD's patents entered into those agreements pursuant to amicable negotiations. No litigation was required in those cases, and litigation was not even threatened. Even in some situations where litigation was initiated, resolution was rapidly achieved. In one case, litigation was only on record for about 48 hours. Another license agreement was wrapped up in just a few hours after a senior executive employed by a European infringer met Peter in Chicago for lunch. (Admittedly, that lunch transpired after the same European company tangled with Peter's lawyers in an earlier case.)

In 2005, AAD filed a patent infringement suit against Apple which quickly settled out of court. That agreement arose after a high-powered Chicago litigation law firm spent six months reviewing AAD's patent portfolio and then recommended that its client settle with AAD. These nationally renowned patent lawyers apparently felt that AAD's patent portfolio was too well-constructed to litigate against. In most cases, when there was no alternative to invoking litigation, out-of-court settlements transpired rapidly. The success of AAD's licensing campaign is evidenced by the fact that AAD repatriated millions of dollars back to the United States from its many foreign licensees.

Despite AAD's success in cordially entering into so many licensing agreements, there were a few intransigent infringers. Left with no choice, AAD filed patent infringement suits against four large companies in the Northern Illinois district court; namely HTC, Amazon, and Kyocera on October 22, 2013, and Pantech on March 28, 2014. Unfortunately, this litigation commenced after the America Invents Act was implemented.

In July of 2014, one of the defendants, HTC, filed five *inter partes review* petitions with the newly created Patent Trial and Appeal Board. These petitions were instituted and carnage soon befell AAD's patent portfolio. Three Administrative Patent Judges presiding in the PTAB proceedings invalidated 80 of AAD's claims spread across just five patents in late December of 2015 and January of 2016. Within 30 days of each of these decisions, AAD filed requests for rehearing—all of which were denied on January 18, 2017. AAD appealed to the U.S. Court of Appeals for the Federal Circuit. All AAD received from its appeal was a one-word ruling, "Affirmed."

Newly-Created Body Destroys AAD's Patents

The America Invents Act (AIA) decimated AAD's licensing program. Since implementation of the AIA, no accused infringer has negotiated in good faith for a license on terms remotely comparable to those in the agreements AAD negotiated with more than 24 licensees prior to the AIA. Due to the PTAB demolishing its patent portfolio, AAD's revenue stream has virtually dried up. The $6 million (and counting) in legal expenses that AAD has incurred in its licensing, litigation, and IPR process to defend the validity of its issued patents have brought AAD close to extinction.

There are many facets of Peter's experience with the *inter partes review* process that are unfair. He was barred from submitting any expert testimony before the PTAB's decision to institute the five IPR proceedings. He was denied due process as there was no jury. The standard applied to constructing the claims in AAD's patents was the PTAB's "Broadest Reasonable Interpretation."[61] To justify its findings, the PTAB imputed claim elements and functionality not disclosed in the [cumulative] prior art cited, overlooked [dispositive] countervailing expert witness testimony, and assumed facts not in evidence. The PTAB ruled that some of AAD's patent claims were obvious—but apparently, they weren't obvious to much of the electronics industry that agreed to license those patents.

The most inequitable aspect of Peter's experience with the *inter partes review* process was that it was applied retroactively. The *inter partes review* process took effect on September 16, 2012. By that time, all but one of AAD's subject patents had issued. All of their related filing dates predated the implementation of *inter partes review.* And all of the subject patents claimed priority to the effective filing date of AAD's Provisional Application No. 60/051,999, which was on July 9, 1997.

The Patent Trial and Appeal Board Decimates AAD's Patent Portfolio

U.S. Patent	IPR	Appeal	Filing Date	Issue Date	Invalidated Claims
6,587,403	IPR2014-01154	17-1750	Aug. 17, 2000	Jul. 1, 2003	1, 3, 6, 7, 11, 12, 16, 22, 24, 27, 29, 30, 35, 36 ,37, 43, 45, 46, 47
7,289,393	IPR2014-01155	17-1748 (lead)	Jun. 30, 2003	Oct. 30, 2007	1, 3, 6, 7, 9, 11, 25, 30, 59, 77, 82, 85, 117, 118, 119, 120, 121, 122
7,817, 592	IPR2014-01156	17-1805	Nov. 7, 2006	Oct. 19, 2010	1, 2, 14, 20, 43, 44, 45, 46, 47
7,933,171	IPR2014-01157	17-1806	Aug. 12, 2010	Apr. 26, 2011	1, 2, 5, 6, 7, 14, 17, 20, 23, 26, 28, 37, 40, 42, 43, 45, 46, 47, 48
8,400,888	IPR2014-01158	17-1824	Apr. 25, 2011	Mar. 19, 2013	1, 2, 3, 4, 5, 6, 7, 8, 9, 10, 11, 12, 13, 14, 15

AAD filed a *writ of certiorari* with the U.S. Supreme Court on August 3, 2018. The issue that AAD raised was whether the invalidation of patents that had priority dates (as well as filing and issuance dates) earlier than

[61] Effective on November 13, 2018, the claims constructions standard for patents subject to IPR review is the Phillips standard which is used in U.S. courts and at the International Trade Commission.

the implementation of *inter partes review* proceedings can be invalidated by such proceedings without violating the Takings Clause in the Fifth Amendment to the Constitution. Unfortunately, we will not soon know the constitutionality of this issue because the Supreme Court declined to review Peter's case on October 9, 2018.

Peter followed the rules of the patenting game for more than 20 years. Then he was squashed by new rules applied retroactively. Peter invested his life savings in developing his inventions and in retaining highly reputable law firms to draft, prosecute, and enforce his patents. He responded to all office actions presented to him during years of rigorous examination. Peter disclosed sufficient detail in his patent filings so that people of ordinary skill in the art would understand the claims. He paid all required maintenance fees. He and his lawyers amicably entered into over two dozen licensing agreements with global electronics companies. Peter was willing to take the risk of having his patents invalidated in federal court when he initiated patent infringement suits against alleged infringers because he understood the rules of taking such action. Peter now feels betrayed by the government for depriving him of the assets he worked so hard to create and commercialize. The retroactive nature and the unfair process by which the government took those assets away from Peter is also a betrayal of the Constitution, whether or not the Supreme Court cares to consider the issue.

The Patent Trial and Appeal Board Plays Musical Chairs

Dr. Thomas Sawyer has had a distinguished career. Serving four American presidents have been among his crowning achievements. Three of these tours of service were as a Senior Advisor—for Presidents Nixon, Ford, and Reagan. The breadth and depth of Tom's imitable career is beyond the scope of this book. I will cut to the chase.

Tom served as Director of Digifonica International from May of 2007 until October of 2011. During this time, Digifonica was building a patent portfolio directed to the burgeoning and highly promising Voice-over-Internet-Protocol (VoIP) telecommunications market. Some of the VoIP technologies under development at Digifonica related to call routing, billing, and rating as well as lawful intercept and emergency assistance calling.

Digifonica was not merely a research facility or a patent holding company. Tests of the underlying technologies were being conducted from three switch sites in Vancouver, London and Norway. At one time, Digifonica had more than 20 engineers working on VoIP software design and implementation. As much as $8 million of engineering work was invested in developing the technologies covered by Digifonica's patent portfolio. The Company operated, supported, and maintained a VoIP platform for all of its customers and subscribers. Digifonica also operated a call center to manage subscriber related issues.

Voip-Pal Acquires Digifonica

When Voip-Pal acquired Digifonica in July of 2013, Digifonica's patent portfolio was comprised of one issued patent and four pending patent applications, all of which seemed close to receiving notices of allowances. Within in a few months of completing the Digifonica acquisition, Tom became the Chairman and CEO of Voip-Pal. Once at the helm, Tom had to return Voip-Pal's corporate affairs to order. There were lawsuits resulting from the previous management team's botched efforts to acquire telecommunications companies. Attention also had to be paid to the Securities and Exchange Commission: Voip-Pal's previous management team sold significant amounts of unlisted shares in an unsanctioned manner, which resulted in the suspension of Voip-Pal's shares trading electronically.

When Tom was not busy extinguishing the fires ignited by his predecessors, he spearheaded Voip-Pal's efforts to grow its patent portfolio. Under Tom's direction, Voip-Pal invested millions of dollars in legal fees related to patent drafting and prosecution. The fruits of those investments are now manifest in Voip-Pal's patent portfolio standing at roughly 20 patents.

In early 2014, Tom detected that more than 50 companies seemed to be infringing at least two of Voip-Pal's patents. Letters were sent to these alleged infringers in May of 2014, offering to enter into licensing negotiations. Initially, some of the alleged infringers maintained amicable discussions with Voip-Pal. However, this Kumbaya period was short-lived; none of the companies agreed to pay anything for licensing the patents they were using. (Thus, in retrospect, the amicable discussions could have simply been tactics to delay the payment of royalties on the part of the alleged infringers.)

Left with little choice, in early February of 2016, Voip-Pal filed lawsuits in the U.S. District Court in Las Vegas against Apple, AT&T, and Verizon. According to Voip-Pal's complaint, the asserted patents represented fundamental advances to Internet protocol communications—its patented technologies were especially relevant for the transmission of photographs, video, and mixed media. Voip-Pal alleged that Apple's iMessage and Wi-Fi calling features, both implemented on a wide range of Apple's products, infringed upon the patents-in-suit. In October of 2016, a similar suit in the same venue was filed against Twitter. The damages sought for the infringement believed to have been committed were, in aggregate, in excess of $7 billion.

How did Voip-Pal arrive at such an astronomical damages figure? With the help of a respected econometrics firm, the Voip-Pal team used a baseline consisting of 10 comparable recent major court decisions for damages relating to patent infringement. The weighted average of these damage awards/settlements as a percentage of profits derived from the underlying infringing device/services was 9.88%. The royalty rate sought by Voip-Pal was 1.25%, or an 87% discount to the comparable royalty rate of 9.88%. Applying the 1.25% royalty rate to the enormous volume of VoiP calls over many years resulted in the roughly $7 billion damages figure.

Alleged Infringers Retaliate by Moving to Invalidate Patents

Two of the defendants, and one of their proxies, named in the February 2016 Las Vegas lawsuit retaliated by filing a combined eight *inter partes review* petitions against two of Voip-Pal's patents—U.S. Patent Nos. 8,542,815 and 9,179,005. Both Apple and AT&T filed three *inter partes review* petitions against these patents on May 8, 2016, the day before the time limit to file *inter partes review* petitions was set to expire. Unified Patents, representing several large alleged infringers, filed an *inter partes review* petition against 14 claims of U.S. Patent No. 8,542,815 on May 24, 2016.

In June of 2016, Tom must have felt like he was forced to play a warped version of Russian Roulette. Instead of having an 87.5% chance of coming out of a round of Russian Roulette unharmed (providing there is only one bullet in an eight-round chamber), only about 26% of the challenged claims survived the institution of *inter partes review* at the end of 2016.[62] But Tom was forced to submit to not just one round of IPR challenges but eight individual attacks. And being a respondent to an IPR challenge was not a cost-free exercise; Tom estimated that each IPR challenge would cost Voip-Pal an average of $500,000.

The odds of Voip-Pal's two patents surviving the eight invalidity attacks being waged against them were overwhelming. Nevertheless, the '815 and the '005 patents not only survived, they emerged from repeated attacks unscathed. One of the IPRs put forth by Apple was not instituted; the same fate befell the IPR submitted by Unified Patents. None of the instituted IPRs were able to invalidate even one of the 143 claims listed in those two patents.

You might think this fact pattern is evidence of an open-and-shut case. Hardly. What transpired during the instituted IPR hearings must

[62] https://www.finnegan.com/en/insights/blogs/america-invents-act/special-report-ptab-ipr-stats-over-time-q4-2013-q3-2018.html

have made Tom feel that he was being suspended between Kafkaesque and Dantesque realities.

Let's Review What Happened During the IPR Proceedings

The PTAB agreed to institute multiple *inter partes reviews* against Voip-Pal's patents on November 16, 2016. The government tribunal agreed to consider the validity of all 12 claims petitioned relative to the '815 patent and all 23 claims petitioned relative to the '005 patent. Tom had his suspicions about the objectivity of all three Administrative Patent Judges initially assigned to review the *inter partes review* petitions seeking to invalidate so many claims. So, Tom filed a Freedom of Information Act request for information on the PTAB judges' personal, fiduciary, and financial interests in the petitioners, namely Apple, AT&T, Verizon, and Twitter. The response to Tom's FOIA request on the part of the USPTO was disappointing but not unusual: The USPTO withheld the requested information citing a FOIA exemption.

It turns out that Tom's suspicions were warranted. APJ Stacy Margolies represented Apple in a 2011 patent litigation case. APJ Barbara Benoit was a principal at Fish & Richardson, a law firm that represented Apple in patent litigation, including in a case before the PTAB. The third judge was Lynne Pettigrew who was employed by AT&T for eight years. Administrative Patent Judges Benoit and Pettigrew were among the APJs with the highest institution rates at 89% and 84%, respectively. APJ Pettigrew had a 97% cancellation rate.[63]

Tom, who had already been an octogenarian for several years, did not take being rebuffed by the USPTO or the prospect of being deprived of a fair tribunal quietly. He launched a letter-writing campaign and issued press releases. One of the themes of these letters was the inequity of APJs not being bound by statutes such as U.S. Code 28 USC Section 455 that require district court judges to recuse themselves when confronted with personal, fiduciary or financial conflicts. He stressed the importance of removing biased adjudicators from panels empowered to invalidate patents.

At least one of Tom's letters pointed out that then-USPTO Director Michelle Lee was a lead patent litigator at Google—another company which

---

[63] These figures came from an article published by the law firm of Ropes & Gray in September of 2015.

Voip-Pal alleged patent infringement—immediately before becoming the Director of the USPTO. Tom also requested that Director Lee be compelled to disclose her personal stock and options holdings in Google, invoking disclosure rules laid out by 28 U.S.C. §455. No such disclosures were made but Ms. Lee resigned as the Director of the USPTO a short time after the release of Tom's letter that brought her interests into question. In an October 23, 2017 letter to both David P. Ruschke (at the time, the Chief Judge for the PTAB) and Joseph Matal (then acting Director of the USPTO), Tom indicated that there might be cause for bringing Racketeering Influenced and Corruption Organizations Act (RICO) actions against the USPTO as well as individual PTAB administrators and judges.

These communications were well-crafted, well-argued, well-cited, and respectful. Tom sent his letters to President Donald Trump, Secretary of Commerce Wilbur Ross, Supreme Court Chief Justice John Roberts, Treasury Secretary Steven Mnuchin, and other high-ranking government officials. He only expected a response from someone at the USPTO but was disappointed by that agency's silence. Tom's efforts were complimented by IP Watchdog and other media sources publishing articles about the conflicts harbored by the APJs in the Voip-Pal IPR proceedings.

Letter-Writing Campaign Triggers Reaction

In June of 2017, in an apparent effort to disinfect its panels, the PTAB assigned a new panel to handle the IPR cases brought against Voip-Pal's '815 and '005 patents. It cannot be known to what extent Tom's public relations campaign, the IP Watchdog articles, or the PTAB's internal reviews are responsible for the replacement of all three APJs because the USPTO has been mute on this issue. The APJs holding court on the second panel were Josiah Cocks, Jennifer Meyer Chagnon, and John Hudalla. About five months later in November of 2017, this panel declared that Apple had failed to prove that the challenged patent claims were invalid.

Needless to say, Apple was not pleased that its efforts to invalidate Voip-Pal's patents failed. In early January of 2018, Apple moved to sanction Voip-Pal for the six allegedly *ex parte* letters that Tom dispatched from May through October of 2017. Basically, Apple argued that by disseminating his letters, Tom was trying to improperly influence the PTAB's review of the '815 and the '005 patents. In its January 18, 2018 response, Voip-Pal pointed out that Tom's six letters were not *ex parte* communications given that (1) they were sent from an individual shareholder (Tom) of the patentee who had no authority at Voip-Pal, (2) they were missives on the inequities of IPRs in general, (3) none of Tom's letters addressed the merits of the IPRs filed against the Voip-Pal patents, and (4) that Apple's request for relief was untimely and barred because it came after an adverse judgment, and Apple knew of Tom's letters before the PTAB ruled that the claims in question were not invalid.

No question about it, Apple knew of Tom's 2017 letters and press releases during the time its IPR petitions were being reviewed by APJs Margolies, Benoit, and Pettigrew. In fact, Apple became aware of Tom's May 1, 2017 letter just a week later on May 8, 2017 and knew about Tom's October 23, 2017 letter on November 1, 2017. Apple took no action to mitigate any alleged prejudice relative to Tom's May 1, 2017 letter for seven months and refrained from taking any measures until six weeks after learning of Tom's October 23, 2017 letter. In both cases, Apple only took action after it lost its IPR petition on the merits by final judgment. Apple's own counselor stated, "No actions were taken [by Apple] or the board with respect to that letter [the May 1, 2017 letter]. We [Apple] didn't take any action in response to that [the May 1, 2017] letter because we had no reason to believe that it had any impact."[64]

In the midst of all of this drama, Knobbe Martens, the law firm representing Voip-Pal in its litigation against the alleged infringers withdrew from the case. (I will let the reader draw his own conclusions as to who 'may have' leaned on Knobbe Martens. I can't say who 'may have' made a persuasive phone call to Knobbe Martens. It could have been anybody, right? Maybe it was a company that threatened to cease directing any business to that law firm unless it dropped its representation of Voip-Pal.) Losing Knobbe Martens' representation was a blow to Voip-Pal as the patentee was quite pleased with the law firm's work. Of course, Voip-Pal had to scramble to replace its patent litigators and was disadvantaged in that quest as patentees are stigmatized when their counselors terminate their representation.

[64] https://docs.wixstatic.com/ugd/768c4e_9dfffa216b8c4a1cb54ac7ecf1c7894f.pdf

Apple's Motion for Sanctions

Back to the PTAB. On August 22, 2018, the PTAB removed the panel of APJs that had been adjudicating the Apple v. Voip-Pal IPR. This was the second time that the panel of APJs had been completely replaced in the proceedings that Apple initiated to invalidate certain claims of two of Voip-Pal's patents. The new APJs were PTAB heavy-hitters: Deputy Chief APJ Scott Boalick and Vice Chief APJs Jacqueline Bonilla and Michael Tierney. The only issue remaining for these elite APJs to render a ruling on was Apple's motion for sanctions relating to Tom's letters.

I am not aware of another instance where the entire panel of APJs has been replaced twice in the same proceeding. Who knows why such panels were replaced two times during Apple's attempt to invalidate Voip-Pal's patents? Maybe the panel that upheld all of Voip-Pal's claims was not sufficiently accommodating towards Apple?

> The optics of the PTAB replacing a panel to include APJ Michael Tierney in a case involving Apple raises concerns because APJ Tierney has overwhelmingly sided with Apple. According to data collected by Lex Machina in mid-2018, never once has a final decision involving both Apple and APJ Tierney ever led to a finding that all claims remained valid. Also, APJ Tierney sat on the *inter partes review* proceedings filed by Apple against VirnetX. As discussed below, that was the panel where Apple was able to skirt the statute of limitations for filing an *inter partes review.*[66]

Also, Apple's motion for sanctions in the context of IPR proceedings is highly unusual, especially on the grounds that a shareholder of a patentee wrote letters to government officials. (I thought that, in a democracy, private citizens were allowed to communicate with government officials.) Perhaps, Apple's motion for sanctions was just a stalling tactic used to try to starve Voip-Pal into submission. Apple may have calculated that Voip-Pal would soon exhaust its limited resources and would be unable to continue its legal battles against that company and other alleged infringers.

---

[65] http://www.ipwatchdog.com/2018/09/09/ptab-brass-ipr-apple-motion-for-sanctions/id=100813/

On December 21, 2018, the PTAB rendered its decision with respect to Apple's motion for sanctions. The Panel denied Apple's request for judgment invalidating the '815 and '005 patents and denied Apple's request for entirely new IPR proceedings. However, the PTAB granted Apple's request for a new panel as a sanction against Voip-Pal for what the PTAB deemed were improper *ex parte* communications. The validity of Voip-Pal's patents has been upheld and that is a relief for Voip-Pal and Tom. But the PTAB stated that it would appoint an entirely new panel to consider any request for rehearing from Apple if such a request is made. Who knows who might sit on that panel and where their sentiments may lie?

In the meantime, the patent litigation that gave rise to the *inter partes review* proceedings continues to grind on. Recent to the time of my writing these pages, that case has been moved from Las Vegas to California.

Postscript

The PTAB's consideration of Apple's motion for sanction also gives rise for concern—and not only for the reasons expounded upon above. As we will see in the two stories below, the PTAB is very liberal in terms of it allowing petitioners to move to invalidate patents through its tribunal but hostile to patentees who make similar motions in efforts to demonstrate the validity of their patents.

Let's look at a situation in which the PTAB was very accommodative in allowing goalposts to be moved in the furtherance of patent invalidation. In both 2010 and 2014, Apple was served with patent infringement complaints in lawsuits filed by VirnetX. Apple requested to institute an IPR trial to challenge the validity of VirnetX's U.S. Patent No. 6,502,135, but did so after the statute of limitations ran its course. To its credit, the PTAB initially denied Apple's request to institute in late 2013 and then again in February of 2014.

However, on April 14, 2015, Mangrove Partners, a hedge fund, filed a petition for IPR against the '135 patent. Apple locked onto the Mangrove IPR petition. In January of 2016, Apple was successful in having its petition for IPR review of the claims in VirnetX's '135 patent joined to Mangrove's IPR. At the end of the IPR process, Apple was able to knock out patents that were proven to be valid and infringed in four trials and four CAFC appeals during ten years of litigation, and for which more than $1 billion in damages resulting from patent infringement were previously awarded.

During its litigation with VirnetX, U.S. District Judge Robert Schroeder essentially deemed Apple to be an irredeemable and unrepentant infringer. VirnetX moved for the court to enhance its damages award against Apple by 100% in light of willful infringement. Indeed, Judge Schroeder found that the evidence "clearly supports a finding that Apple attempted to conceal its infringement, and this factor weighs in favor of enhancement." Over half of the factors from the Federal Circuit's 1992 precedential decision in Read Corp. v. Portec Inc. governing enhanced damages were in VirnetX's favor; none were in Apple's favor. Nonetheless, on August 30, 2018, Judge Schroeder denied VirnetX's motion for enhanced damages. Judge Schroeder was not persuaded that enhancement of the verdict would lead to the deterrence of future infringing conduct.

Now let's review a situation in which the PTAB has obstructed a patentee from defending its interests in that tribunal. In September of 2017, Allergan assigned patents related to its RESTASIS drug to the Saint Regis Mohawk Tribe. As beneficiaries of sovereign immunity protections, Native American tribes (and their patents) were (supposed to be) shielded from government tribunals such as the PTAB. The Allergan transaction caused quite a political backlash. For instance, Senator Claire McCaskill (D-MO) introduced a bill to abrogate Native American tribal sovereign immunity in all IPR proceedings. The Saint Regis Mohawk Tribe was concerned that such political sentiments could unfairly influence the PTAB in its consideration of challenges to its patents in that forum. The Native Americans were rightfully concerned that the PTAB could stack its panels, ensuring that it would receive the outcome that that body wanted. In fact, the PTAB stated that it had the authority to expand panels where trials touch on issues of great importance. To the Native Americans' dismay, the PTAB forbade Saint Regis from filing any additional papers related to their motion to dismiss the PTAB's ability to render rulings on the validity of the tribe's patents. However, the PTAB's November 2017 invitation for *amicus curiae* briefs relating to the Allergan-Saint Regis case resulted in the submission of numerous arguments adverse to the Native Americans' maintaining their sovereignty vis-à-vis PTAB.

Do Companies Really License Invalid Patents?

Ted Tsao, who immigrated to the United States from China in 1981, is a prolific inventor. He has accumulated more than 40 patents since he began innovating in 1987. Many of these inventions relate to cloud computing, which includes information sharing, IT operation as well as video and storage on-demand.

Ted is also a frugal inventor. He pursued research into video-on-demand technology on a moonlight basis from 1999 until he founded STT WebOS in 2002. As an inquisitive engineer with a limited budget, he drafted and prosecuted many of his patents himself, avoiding paying patent attorneys somewhere in the neighborhood of $50,000 per patent.

Ted's inventions inarguably eased the use of computers. How so? Earlier in the web computing era, it was difficult to manage and share files by using web browsers. These browsers were often blocked due to the low speed of the Internet and the problems that existed with web protocols such as HTTP. Ted solved all of these problems and shared his solutions with the world when he disclosed these inventions in his published patent applications.

Overview of Ted Tsao's Inventions

So, how did Ted render it easier to manage files? A brief review of four of Ted's inventions follows:

- Years ago, when Yahoo was a dominant web browser, many people managed their electronic files via the Yahoo Briefcase. By today's standards, the Yahoo Briefcase was primitive. Users could not copy-and-paste or cut-and-move their files between folders because all of the folders were presented in one flat level. It was like trying to organize your dishes while being restrained to the counterspace next to your sink. Ted's solution to this unwieldy organizational problem was covered in his 9,280,547 patent which has priority date of July 2004 and issued on March 8, 2016. The '547 patent introduced hierarchical lists in memory to mirror the actual structure resource. Such mirrored hierarchical lists are sent to the end-user's device, thus reducing the data load on the Internet. With Ted's invention, you would be able to more quickly organize your dishes by using multiple shelves in many cabinets with less risk of breakage.

- Once a file is disseminated through the Internet, nothing can be done to stop its circulation, correct? That was the case before Ted figured out how to use dynamic workspace technology and metadata deletion to withdraw (or un-post) messages, files, and folders from the Internet. Prior to Ted's related 8,396,891 patent, users who wanted to cease sharing files with certain people would have to delete said files which prevented them from sharing those files with other authorized recipients. If creators wanted to share the files with authorized recipients, the files would have to be painstakingly recreated.

- Ted's 8,713,442 patent shares similarities with the '891 patent. With the virtual presentation features claimed by the '442 patent, files or folders do not need to be physically transferred to servers for sharing; removing this physical transference tremendously reduces the data load on networks.

- Years ago, it was common for web browsers to become blocked when users submitted requests via browsers to access and download content on the Internet. Users were required to wait for the first task being performed by the browser to finish before the second task would begin to be processed from the same web user interface. In 2002, it took about 25 minutes to transfer a four-gigabit video across the web. Ted's invention unblocked browsers by introducing control management systems as described in his 8,799,473 patent which has priority date of August 2002.

Licensing Negotiations Leads to Patent Invalidation

In the 2004 and 2005 timeframe, Ted believed that Yahoo could benefit from embracing his inventions. (Note that the patents discussed above have priority dates as early as August 6, 2002.) While Ted maintained licensing discussions with two senior managers at Yahoo, he was unable to persuade Yahoo to replace its Briefcase remote access online server with his new web folder system. Yahoo declined to license any of Ted's patents but, as we will shortly see, that did not mean that Yahoo was uninterested in practicing the covered inventions.

Rather than wallowing in self-pity, Ted moved forward. The four patents discussed above, together with the remainder of his patent portfolio, was licensed to a very large Silicon Valley technology company for a seven-figure lump sum payment in 2016. Before pulling the trigger on that transaction, this technology behemoth conducted extensive due diligence on Ted's patents for nearly one year. In formulating a value for Ted's patents, the licensee's in-house patent analysts and patent lawyers were complemented by outside counsellors and consultants. The licensee was not the only party interested in paying a seven-figure sum for rights to practice Ted's patents. In 2016, Ted was approached by at least six very large technology companies that were interested in taking somewhat similar licenses on Ted's patent portfolio.

By 2016, Ted's suspicions of Yahoo's infringement crescendoed. When it became clear that Yahoo would not enter into licensing discussions or agree to a very reasonable settlement proffered by his lawyers, Ted filed suit against Yahoo for patent infringement in the District Court in San Jose, California. This suit backfired in a barbarous fashion. That court invalidated all four patents-in-suit on September 1, 2017 without going through claims construction in Markman hearings. (Claims construction proceedings are important because it is at this stage in patent litigation where each word in the claims is defined. Without claims construction, the litigants really do not know what they are arguing about.)

Rather than trouble with technicalities that would have arisen in a claims construction proceeding, the judge invalidated the patents-in-suit by holding that they were ineligible due to their covering abstract ideas. For instance, the judge essentially held that the multi-tasking feature associated with unblocking browsers (covered by the '473 patent) was no more novel than a person multi-tasking by tying his shoe, chewing gum and listening to songs through an iPod while tripping on LSD.

Further, it seems to me that the District Court ignored the 2016 Enfish LLC v. Microsoft Corp. decision which held that improvements in the way computers operate are patent eligible: Ted's inventions improved computer functionalities by solving specific problems relating to bandwidth constraints, managing folders, and sharing information. Ted appealed this decision at the Court of Appeals for the Federal Circuit in November of 2017. In a one-word decision ("Affirmed") on July 17, 2018, that court upheld the district court's invalidation of all four of Ted's patents-in-suit.

Postscript

What were the consequences of Yahoo causing Ted's four patents to be invalidated? For one thing, Ted's experience highlights how a judge's rush to invalidate patents contrasts with the scrutiny that at least seven teams of patent analysts and patent lawyers applied to the same patent portfolios. Due to judicial haste in destroying a patent portfolio, tremendous licensing opportunities were lost; none of the large companies with whom Ted was in discussions even replied to his overtures after his four patents were invalidated. Ted's unfortunate experience underscores the point that when one infringer invalidates patents, that infringer destroys the licensing agreements that the patentee has with all of its licensees and may have with potential licensees. The invalidation of four of Ted's patents cast a cloud—under which prospective licensees are reluctant to traverse—over the remainder of his patent portfolio.

Ted's story also illustrates the point that if a company steals an invention, that company will retain its ill-gotten market share even if a court finds that the infringer stole the invention in the first place. Thus, damages awards, if they exist and to the extent they are imposed, are just the price that infringers pay for the market share they have appropriated.

Crimes Against Patentee Declared in Nuremberg

Jon Capriola invented a way to insert light into modular toys in 2006. These LASER PEGS are assembled brick-by-brick, like Legos. In fact, LASER PEGS are compatible with Lego pieces. LASER PEGS illuminate their surroundings with Jon's patented invention and vibrant color combinations. This line of brain development toys enhances learning, boosts perception of spatial relations, stimulates abstract thinking, ratchets up problem-solving and math skills, and improves hand-eye coordination. These toys are still produced in many varieties such as action figures, insects, and miniature vehicles.

Jon was a visionary in more ways than one. On August 15, 2007, about two years before he began selling his LASER PEGS, Jon sought to protect his invention by filing a patent application with the USPTO. Having only raised $250,000 at that point, he had to economize his expenditures. When it came to retaining a patent lawyer, low fees were of crucial concern. He would soon realize that there is truth in the adage, "You get what you pay for." The resulting patent titled "Illuminating Toy Building Structures" issued on June 8, 2010 as U.S. Patent No. 7,731,558.

In April 2009, after three years of design trial-and-error and two years after filing for patent protection, Jon began selling LASER PEGS. Sales were strong right out of the gate. The line was available in major specialty retailers such as Hammacher Schlemmer as well as many independent toy stores and museum gift shops. In both 2010 and 2011, LASER PEGS received numerous awards and was featured on multiple national broadcasts (such as NBC's *Today*) as a "must-have" educational toy. Starting in 2011, Jon exhibited LASER PEGS at national and international trade fairs.

The Seduction and the Betrayal

The February 2011 New York Toy Fair proved to be a pivotal event for LASER PEGS, and for Jon. One of the attendees at that exhibition who visited the LASER PEGS booth was Mr. Larry Rosen. Later that evening, Mr. Rosen and his brother (Jeffrey) took Jon out for a fancy dinner in Manhattan. So fancy that the tab came to $3,000. The Rosen brothers got their money's worth by pummeling Jon for information about the LASER PEGS's sales levels, pricing plans, retail strategy, product line, intellectual property, and the like. Jon opened his kimono as he was led to believe that the Rosen brothers had $100 million to invest in toy enterprises and considered LASER PEGS to be an interesting candidate.

The next day at least three patent attorneys representing Mr. Rosen visited the LASER PEGS booth at the New York Toy Fair. Further volleys of questions relating to LASER PEGS's intellectual property were fired in Jon's direction. (Pictures of the inquisitive, if out-of-place, patent lawyers were snapped and included in a complaint filed against Mr. Rosen and his company, LaRose Industries.)

> Multiple sources told me they believe that large manufacturers scope out new products at exhibitions and copy them within six months. They are said to do so with the collusion or encouragement of retailers.

A few weeks later, Mr. Rosen paid a visit to Jon's office in Sarasota, Florida. Because Mr. Rosen represented himself as seriously weighing a substantial investment in Jon's company, Jon unveiled more information to Mr. Rosen. Such disclosures related to sales forecasts for LASER PEGS, foreign manufacturing capabilities, and sourcing. Jon did receive something from the discussions—a check for $650 when Mr. Rosen purchased a variety of LASER PEGS toys.

Discussions between the two men went cold after the Sarasota meeting. In late June of 2011, Mr. Rosen requested that all communications between them cease.

By this time, Mr. Rosen was hot on Jon's heels. On November 23, 2011, Mr. Rosen filed a patent application for "Construction toys; toy construction sets; toy construction blocks." At the February 2012 Spielwarenmesse

International Toy Fair in Nuremberg, Germany, LaRose Industries announced its plans to launch copycat LED-illuminated construction sets. While it took Jon three years to design his LASER PEGS, Mr. Rosen was able to produce a knockoff within 10 months of halting his investment discussions with Jon.

When he got wind of Mr. Rosen's declaration in Nuremberg, Jon requested that Mr. Rosen furnish samples of his toys, or at least related designs, so that Jon could determine if such products infringed his '558 patent. Mr. Rosen refused to comply with Jon's request. Further, LaRose exhibited its LITE BRIX knockoff toys at the February 2012 New York Trade Fair. However, LaRose did not publicly exhibit its illuminated construction sets. Rather, the LITE BRIX toys were displayed in a private viewing area where only potential mass retailers interested in issuing purchase orders could see them. This squirrely exhibition strategy prevented anyone associated with Jon from examining LaRose's LITE BRIX line of toys.

> Germany is very vigilant in terms of policing trademark and patent infringing products at exhibits in that country. At some of the largest trade shows in Germany, a trademark owner or an inventor who believes his intellectual property is being infringed by a product at that trade show may petition an on-premises judge. If the judge concurs that infringement is occurring, the judge can order the police to seize the infringing products and place them in a cage located on the exhibition floor. The culprits are subject to arrest, removal (with hands cuffed) from the trade fair, and fines.

Revenue Poured and Confusion Reigned

At the time of LaRose's Nuremberg declaration, LASER PEGS was selling like gangbusters through Costco. In one five-week stretch, the chain ordered 80,000 units. And these units were purchased by customers: Jon's sell-through rate at Costco was 98% in his first year, 99% in his second year, and 100% in his third year. LASER PEGS was selling very well through Target stores in the early 2010s; the product commanded seven linear feet of shelf space and generated an average of $50,000 a day in revenue.

And then came along Mr. Rosen's LITE BRIX which were placed right next to Jon's LASER PEGS in some of the largest retail chains. By September of 2012, with both LaRose and Jon's company marketing a popular product through many of the same sales channels, both revenues poured and confusion reigned. Social media sites featured posts of potential consumers of educational toys suggesting that there was a tight association between LITE BRIX and LASER PEGS. Jon believes this confusion inhibited sales of LASER PEGS because his products received better reviews; John told me that during this period, LASER PEGS received five stars on Amazon while LITE BRIX received one-and-a-half stars.

Once LaRose zoomed in on Target, Jon's sales were slashed by roughly 50%. Jon protested to Target that LaRose was infringing his '558 patent and that related patent infringement litigation was underway in the Middle District of Florida. The response by Target was along the lines of, "We don't know anything about patents. That's not our thing. Plus, since LaRose supplies us with so many products, we can't deprive that company of shelf space."

Walmart simply refused to carry LASER PEGS or even to take any units for a trial run. The situation with Toys "R" Us was seemingly more promising than Jon's experience with Walmart. LaRose had a strong beachhead at the toy chain, but Jon was eventually able to convince Toys "R" Us to sell LASER PEGS. Happy ending? Not quite. Jon only managed to distribute LASER PEGS through that struggling retailer in the last year of its existence. As a result, invoices for LASER PEGS went unpaid by Toys "R" Us.

> The demise of Toys "R" Us presents an often-overlooked problem with toy makers. Since the remaining toy retailers do not sell large volumes of toys year-round, they require the delivery of merchandise closer to Christmas. If the toys do not sell during this truncated window the toy makers will have to take back their products because the general merchandise retailers will not allocate much shelf-space to toys after the Christmas selling season.

Patent Litigation and Invalidation Interlude

From the outset of this saga, Jon was under the illusion that waiting for strong signals that his patent application would soon issue before putting his product on the market would insulate him from knockoff products. Remember, he filed his patent application in 2007 but introduced LASER PEGS to the market in 2009. The implementation of the Patent Trial and Appeal Board proved to be a rude awakening. In response to his initiation of patent infringement litigation against LaRose Industries and Mr. Larry Rosen on October 15, 2012, a petition to invalidate the claims associated with the '558 patent was filed with the PTAB. In July of 2014, the PTAB found all claims 1-27 of the '558 patent unpatentable and denied Jon's motion to amend. (It may be true that the '558 patent was weak. In fact, in my discussions with Jon, he mentioned that the '558 patent left a lot of his invention unclaimed. In any event, the inventor was ill-served by either his initial patent attorney, the patent examiner, or the Administrative Patent Judges serving on the PTAB, or some combination thereof.)

Given the short product life cycles in the toy industry, Jon believed he was better off investing in marketing LASER PEGS than continuing on the litigation front. During this episode, Jon considered filing a motion for an injunction against LaRose but could not afford the related bond. However, Jon wisely invested some of the revenue he generated from LASER PEGS; he hired an experienced patent lawyer to draft and prosecute a much stronger continuation-in-part. This patent incorporated more advanced features such as mobility, USB-to-USB connectivity, video, and audio into his line of LASER PEGS.

Big-Box Imbroglios

Selling to mass retailers was no slam-dunk. Every one of the few products that make it through the mass retailers' new vendor gauntlet must be submitted to a battery of tests. These tests include determining risks of chemical leakage, exposure to lead and phosphates, chocking, and a slew of other concerns. These tests typically take thirty to forty-five days and cost on the order of $4,400 per stock keeping unit per retailer. (Jon was selling some 36 SKUs to several chains.) These series of tests must be repeated by a testing firm, approved of by each retailer, upon every one-year anniversary the product is vended by a mass merchant.

Filling orders received from mass merchant customers is a gargantuan task. Jon needed two or three employees to manage each of his large retail accounts. These employees were required to understand their assigned retailer's robust interface. They were responsible for handling automated reorders, ensuring that the packaging was unique to each mass retailer, and collecting payments. Logistical requirements included packing the right products in the appropriate boxes and ensuring that labeling of those boxes met strict specifications. Consequences of failing to execute or delivering delinquently to the Costco account could include fines of as much as $10,000 a day. Of course, the toy business works on the consignment basis; toy producers like Jon are forced to either take back slow-moving merchandise or to sustain deep price markdowns.

In addition to forcing Jon to comply with their never ending and niggly demands, Jon's large retail customers did not remit payment for roughly eight months after being invoiced. So how does a vendor pay manufacturers to produce its products if it has not yet received payment for recently delivered products to big-box retailers? It has to obtain financing. Outside financing is critical in seasonal businesses, where vendors like Jon are pregnant with cash three months of the year but barren of cash for the remaining nine months. Demands for cash become even more acute when retailers place increasingly large orders with suppliers of popular products such as LASER PEGS.

From Inventor to Indentured Servitude

As soon as Jon received his initial orders from Target, he was approached by the Great White Shark Opportunity Fund, which was run by golfing legend Greg Norman and his partner, David Chessler. Savvy investors such as Mr. Chessler know that inventors/suppliers with large orders in hand are desperate. They can't walk away from huge orders that required enormous toil to obtain. New vendors like Jon can't ask their clients such as Target or Costco for financing as such requests will shake any fragile and fleeting confidence mass merchants have in their new vendors. In short, vendors with large orders and no means to finance the corresponding production will submit to any egregious terms imposed on them.

The Great White Shark Opportunity Fund agreed to provide the funding that Jon needed. But Jon soon realized that his toy business was clenched by that fund's powerful jaws. First, there was the $500,000 bonus that the fund demanded, payable upon Jon transferring control of his business. The sky-high monthly interest rate and aggressive compounding scheme imposed on the many millions of dollars provided by the line of credit received from Great White Shark resulted in Jon remitting monthly interest payments of between $160,000 and $180,000. Jon was basically sending his lenders a new Ferrari every month. In addition, he was required to keep at least $1 million of that credit line drawn at all times. All of this was legal as the Great White Shark entity that provided this line of credit was incorporated in Nevada, which has no usury laws.

A few other financial maneuvers were visited upon Jon. Shortly after engaging with the Great White Shark Opportunity Fund, Jon could not pay his outstanding $3 million debt to Bank of America. Neither could he find creditors to replace Bank of America when that bank declined to renew its loan. Mr. Chessler intervened when apprised of Jon's predicament. For a fee of $500,000 and the same monthly nose-bleed interest rates, Great White Shark replaced Bank of America's credit line to Jon's company. An entity affiliated with Mr. Chessler bought the debt that Jon racked up with Bank of America. Jon was also forced to enter into a stock purchase agreement with Great White Shark. Additionally, the Great White Shark Opportunity Fund required an additional sales bonus of $1.5 million if LASER PEGS sold its assets or if control was transferred to any third-party.

You might not think that a $2.0 million sales bonus going to Great White Shark was too onerous. You might think that if Jon sold his company for a handsome exit, paying his financer a $2.0 million sales bonus is within the realm of reason. However, this sales bonus effectively shackled Jon into indentured servitude; no one would want to acquire the LASER PEGS business if they would have to immediately fork over $2.0 million to a financer on top of the brokerage commission the fund stood to receive. Indeed, this sales bonus scared away the 149 private equity firms that Jon approached as potential acquirers.

While most of the private equity firms that took an interest in LASER PEGS were pleased that Jon had obtained patent coverage, they told him that they would be more comfortable if his continuation-in-part patent was validated. What was Jon to do? He could submit his continuation-in-part patent to post-grant review, but that would have cost at least $50,000. Remember, Jon was looking to raise money, not sink even more money into LASER PEGS. And what if Jon ended up invalidating his own patent along the way?

Unable to find a buyer and in breach of some of his covenants with the Great White Shark Opportunity Fund, Jon's business was taken from him. In November of 2015, Jon was terminated from the company he founded. Because he was terminated, Jon did not receive 49% of the proceeds of the sale of his business, which he stood to receive as long as he was an employee with the company at the time of its sale.

Conclusion

Not all of the misery that befalls inventors can be placed at the USPTO's doorstep. In any scenario, it is extremely difficult for a single product company to make money in the toy business. Jon admits that licensing LASER PEGS to a large manufacturer/distributor would have been the better business decision. Having fallen in with the Great White Shark Opportunity Fund, Jon may well have lost control of his company regardless of his patent situation.

However, having enforceable patents could have increased the odds of Jon's company remaining viable. LASER PEGS generated $45 million in revenue from 2009 to 2014. Jon believes that he lost $20 million in sales at the hands of LaRose's copycat products. If Jon was able to enforce his patent against infringers, his unit sales would likely have been at least 40% higher. The ability to exclude knockoff products would have given Jon more pricing power, and arguably, better terms from retailers. Higher sales could have yielded him more negotiating power against his supply chain partners. An enforceable patent may have delayed, or made unnecessary, Jon's encounters with ruthless financers. Or at least yielded him more leverage against cutthroat creditors. An enforceable patent would have increased Jon's chances of success. Or at least the financial flexibility to sell his company.

Duplicitous Delaying Tactics Damage Patentees

Some inventions are the product of serendipity. But it takes intelligence to realize when valuable inventions are randomly discovered. And hard work is required to commercialize such discoveries. All three of these factors are at play in Alan Stuart's invention of New Side.

In 2001, Alan was having a hard time scrubbing grill spatter off of his house's vinyl sidings. This former mechanic from the steel mills operated by Wheeling-Pittsburgh Steel decided to conduct a random experiment. He mixed all of the organic solvents he could find in his garage into a chemical cocktail. When he wiped this concoction on the siding of his house, he was shocked to find that the grease from his grill dissolved. Instead of dissolving the vinyl, Alan's formulation returned the siding to its original color and luster. Amazingly, the siding was rejuvenated; its great look endured for weeks, then months, and then years. Alan's invention was counter to common wisdom, which held that applying organic solvents to vinyl sidings would damage the vinyl.

Invention Sparks Interest

Alan applied for a patent in March of 2002 and then sought to license his technology to a variety of solvents companies. (His patent application issued less than two years later, as U.S. Patent No. 6,669,991, on December 30, 2003.) Zinsser took the most interest in licensing Alan's patent application. Zinsser was owned by RPM International, a leading manufacturer of high-performance coatings, sealants and specialty chemicals. After a non-disclosure agreement was put in place, negotiations revolving around Zinsser paying Alan a 3.5% royalty ensued. This royalty rate seemed equitable but an agreement could not be reached on the royalty base to which the 3.5% royalty rate would be applied. Zinsser wanted to pay 3.5%

of related net profits and—knowing that there is tremendous elasticity in the calculation of net profit—Alan insisted that revenues be used as the base for determining royalty remittances.

The resulting stalemate was punctuated with intermittent negotiations over the next two-and-a-half years. For instance, in December of 2003, Zinsser's Vice-President told Alan that if a licensing agreement could not be agreed upon by February 2004, Zinsser would "design around" Alan's patent and take the resulting product to the market.

Inventor Primes Multiple Sales Channels

Alan did not let this stalemate halt his efforts to commercialize his "New Side" solvent. First, he extensively tested New Side on automobiles, plastics, trims, vinyl sidings and conducted a variety of colorimeter tests. In 2003 and 2004, Alan began selling what has become several thousand gallons of New Side through four Pittsburgh-area retailers. Lowe's, the home improvement chain, was also interested in selling New Side but becoming a vendor to a big-box retailer requires massive commitment: Alan would have had to invest hundreds of thousands of dollars in delivery and distribution as well as establish and maintain an automated ordering system. Any hiccups in fulfilling orders to that mass merchant's exact specifications would have been subject to severe penalties.

In addition to generating interest from a big-box retailer, Alan thought outside of the box. He learned that home owner's insurers have millions of dollars in exposure to the damage that storms, hail, collision and fire cause to homes. When these events occur, the insurance companies are on the hook to re-side their customers' houses. And insurance regulations require that the color matches used to re-side the houses meet homeowners' satisfaction. To comply with related regulations and to achieve customer satisfaction, insurance companies typically re-side the entire house.

Alan believed that New Side would enable insurance companies to reduce the costs of arranging to re-side their customers' houses. With New Side, insurance companies would be relieved of re-siding entire houses while still achieving required color matches. Alan's plan was that when insurance carriers received claims involving vinyl siding, they could simply replace the damaged siding and treat the rest of the house with New Side, enabling the insurance company to reduce its costs by as much as 75%. So, back in 2003, Alan began speaking with some of the solvents companies whose products are used to re-side houses. As these discussions advanced, Alan supplied two of these companies, Alcoa and Owens Corning, with 20 gallons of New Side for testing purposes. No agreements were reached in the 2003 timeframe: Negotiations with Owens Corning were rounding third base but were ultimately derailed by that company's bankruptcy proceedings. (However, Alan tells me that similar negotiations resumed with insurers in 2018.)

Inventor Spots Infringers

Let's fast forward to 2014. One day, Alan saw an advertisement for "Wipe-New" when he was watching TV. Based on the chemicals listed on the Wipe-New packaging, Alan strongly believed that the chemical composition of the Wipe-New product infringed his '991 patent. Alan undertook a number of steps to test his hunch. The odor from Wipe-New seemed to parallel that of New-Side. So too did Wipe-New's manufacturing safety data sheets, which listed the incidence of each chemical used in the Wipe-New solvent. If any remaining doubt as to Wipe-New's infringement of the '991 patent existed, it was removed when the University of Akron reverse engineered Wipe-New.

Who manufactured and sold Wipe-New? Rust-Oleum, a subsidiary of RPM International, which acquired Zinsser in 2006. Alan's due diligence revealed that RPM set up an entity called Advanto in 2006 or 2007 to commercialize Wipe-New. A few years later, after Wipe New started generating traction, RPM moved Zinsser into its Rust-Oleum unit. Revenues soared seven-fold the first quarter that Rust-Oleum initiated sales of Wipe-New through mass merchants including Walmart, Target, Home Depot, Lowes and Dollar General.

Alan wanted equitable compensation for the use that RPM was making off of his patented invention. He was tempted to rekindle his discussions with RPM to avoid costly and prolonged litigation. However, a Pittsburgh law firm recommended that such overtures would not be requited. Thus began Alan's three-year journey to recruit a litigation law firm that would represent his patent infringement case on a contingency basis. In 2016, Kasowitz Benson Torres agreed to represent Alan. (Interestingly, Marc Kasowitz, the named partner in Kasowitz Benson Torres, has represented President Donald Trump since the early 2000s.)

Soon after the representation agreement with Kasowitz was in place, a complaint was filed against RPM with the District Court in Southern Ohio on September 23, 2016. Swift action was needed because Alan's patent will expire in March of 2022. Discovery obtained in the case in 2017 increased Alan's confidence that RPM's infringement will be crystalized during the trial. For instance, Dr. Eric Gerky, Director of Polymeric Science at University of Kentucky and the author of several books on solubility parameters, provided convincing depositions that demonstrated that Wipe-New infringes the '991 patent. To its credit, Walmart removed the infringing product from its shelves when Alan's lawsuit was brought to their attention.

Duplicitous Litigation Tactics and Disingenuous Settlement Offers

RPM has floated ideas for settling Alan's infringement claims during the course of the litigation. Given that Alan has invested in excess of $62,000, and the Kasowitz firm has dedicated more than $1 million worth of billable hours in the early stages of this case, Alan's side would be amenable to considering good faith settlement offers. The problem is that RPM's settlement offers seem disingenuous; they only arise in the aftermath of RPM losing a motion.

RPM has suggested that it might be amenable to paying Alan some royalties going forward but refuses to consider paying anything for its past infringement. When Alan requested that he be paid a guaranteed minimum royalty going forward, RPM refused on the grounds that financial information for accessing the viability of that request is lacking—even though RPM possessed related sales data from its years of selling Wipe-New. Also, having known that Alan's patent will expire in less than five years, RPM proposed entering into a 10-year distribution agreement with New Side. It seems that RPM's gambit is that if any contractual disputes were to arise after Alan's patent expires in March of 2022, Alan would have less leverage achieving relief over a contractual dispute.

Reaching an agreement could be profitable for Alan and RPM. Not only would the flood of litigation costs dry up but the two parties could approach revenue opportunities in a coordinated fashion. As mentioned, Alan reignited discussions with homeowner's insurance companies in 2018. Should these discussions result in agreements, they would stand a good chance of bearing fruit. Knowing that insurance companies support New

Side would likely stimulate retailers' interest in stocking Alan's product. Also, RPM launched Wipe-New Recolor in 2017. This RPM product engineered specifically for vinyl siding sells for $195 a quart, a massive premium compared to the $39.95 per gallon price tag that Alan placed on New Side.

Instead of working together to juice latent demand (which Alan is pursuing via the insurance companies) and to magnetize retailers up the pricing curve (which Wipe-New Recolor should help achieve), RPM insists on grinding through litigation pockmarked with its sophomoric settlement proposals. To wit: Instead of talking about paying Alan for turning insurance companies into demand generators for vinyl repair solvents, RPM suggested that it would be willing to promote Alan's image through related marketing initiatives.

RPM is also making good use of the delaying tactics that the America Invents Act affords infringers. Rust-Oleum waited 363 days after the service of Alan's complaint to file an *inter partes review* petition. In this post-grant procedure (filed by RPM two days before its one-year deadline), RPM is challenging two of the claims in the '991 patent by parsing the phrase "and/or" in relation to "restoring the 'color and/or luster' of surfaces such as vinyl." In any event, while this issue is being taken up with the Patent Trial and Appeal Board, litigation has been stayed in the district court in Ohio. The court did not hold RPM's delay in filing for an *inter partes review* petition against the defendant when it issued its stay even though RPM could have filed its petition much earlier in the litigation.

Postscript

Delaying tactics in patent litigation can be costly for patentees. Not only in terms of litigation but also in view of lost opportunities.

Alan only has a handful of years of patent life remaining. Patent litigation is exorbitantly expensive, time consuming, and emotionally draining. Few solo inventors have the time, money, or emotional bandwidth to pursue commercialization opportunities concurrent with patent litigation. This is a shame. Alan has been approached by a marketing company that would like to try to commercialize New Side. This company seeks a monthly retainer somewhere between $2,500 and $5,000. Assuming that this agent is legitimate and has a reasonable chance of achieving some success, an inventor like Alan might be well-served by engaging with this marketing company. After all, the costs of engaging with such a company are much less than pursuing litigation. The sad reality is that patent litigation suffocates commerce. Instead of putting superior products on the market and employing people up and down the supply chains, obstinate infringers reroute resources to the courtroom.

No Way to Treat a Veteran

If your image of a motorcycle rider is an older Caucasian man, inventor Richie Barnes would shatter that image. At the time of his initial patent filing, in November of 2000, Richie was a brawny young black man. He invariably wore tank tops, was bedecked with gold chains and sported dark sunglasses. So did his posse. But this muscular fellow who served as a nurse tech in the Air Force throughout Operation Desert Storm has a tender side: He owns and operates what South Carolina's ombudsman has twice deemed the number one assisted living facility in the Palmetto State.

Richie's sojourn with the patent system has its roots in 1998. That was the year he began riding motorcycles. Being a bit of a loner, Richie wanted to listen to music while riding his motorcycle but found that headphones were cumbersome. (It is legal for motorcycle riders to use headphones in South Carolina.) Up until the late 1990s, sports bikes did not have sufficient space for radios as these light vehicles are built for speed and agility.[66] That changed when Suzuki introduced its Hayabusa 1300 in November of 1999.

The sound system that Richie invented for sports bikes (initially the Hayabusa 1300) was ingenious. Its components were designed to reside discreetly within sports bikes' existing features. The front speakers are positioned in the front fairing, middle speakers are incorporated into the rearview mirrors, and the back speakers are placed on the cowling. Since the "Rich One" sound system is unobservable to passersby, there is little risk of them being stolen or vandalized. Richie told me it would be easier to steal the whole bike than just his speakers. Since components of the Rich One sound system are discretely placed, they do not alter the appearance of sports bikes.

With Richie's system, riders could listen uninterruptedly to crystal

[66] Sports bikes are a variety of motorcycles. They are powerful and have larger rear tires and minimal, sculpted bodies.

clear music through their Bluetooth-enabled helmets. The Rich One audio technology wicks out all of the considerable noise coming from the vehicle, traffic and wind. Richie's invention delivers a dynamic sound while consuming relatively little power, an important consideration given that sports bikes have relatively small batteries. In fact, a capacitor connected to the sports bike's battery is used to augment the battery for increased power; this increased power is necessary to amplify sounds.

Rich One is durable and designed to withstand friction. Marine radios and speakers are used to render Rich One immune to weather issues. But ruggedness should not be confused with weight. The components are of such light weight that they do not noticeably add to the bike's heft. Neither the aerodynamics nor performance characteristics of sports bikes are compromised when loaded with the Rich One sound system.

Richie's sound system is easy for motorcyclists to operate. All features such as song selection and volume can be controlled with the flick of a finger via a WiFi remote device. Bluetooth-enabled helmets facilitate voice activation. The sound system is compatible with all motorcycles and is easy to install in the aftermarket.

The Rich One Sound System Cranks Up Excitement

When the Rich One sound system debuted at the Bike 2000 gathering in Myrtle Beach, South Carolina, in 2000, near pandemonium broke out; the police had to contain the crowds converging on Richie's motorcycle. The website that Richie rigged up to solicit feedback on his invention crashed when nearly a million people visited the site within its first three weeks. Many of these visitors tried to place orders even though Richie wasn't selling his sound system. Back in the non-cyber world, quite a few motorcyclists offered Richie as much as $10,000 to install his sound system on their bikes. Richie never accepted such offers as he wanted to commercialize his invention in a more scalable fashion.

Back in the early 2000s, Richie didn't know much about patents. But with the torrential interest in his sound system pouring in, he knew he needed to protect his invention. Fortunately for Richie, he came in contact with Columbia, South Carolina-based Michael Mann of Nexsen Pruet, one of the top patent lawyers in the Southeast.

While Michael Mann saw great potential in Richie's sound system, he ran two searches to make sure there was no potentially invalidating prior art. When these prior art searches came back clean, Michael drafted the initial patent application himself (as opposed to delegating such duties to a junior lawyer) in just three weeks, much faster than the 90 days other lawyers said they would need to draft such a patent application. This patent application was broadly drafted in contemplation of future technologies; its claims cover technologies such as Bluetooth and music streaming. This application was filed with the United States Patent and Trademark Office on November 21, 2000.

It might seem that if multiple prior art searches detected no damaging prior art and intense consumer interest for the Rich One sound system served as indicia of novelty, Richie's patent application would be granted in quick order. This logic did not meet with reality in Richie's case. He received his patent—which was two continuations removed from his initial application—nearly 12 years later, on September 18, 2012, as U.S. Patent No. 8,270,640.

Malfunction at the Patent Office

Neither Richie nor Michael heard anything from the Patent Office for 18 months after the submission of the original parent patent application. According to my discussions with Richie, when inquiries were made regarding the status of the application about 18 months after filing, the USPTO claimed that the application was sent to the wrong art unit. After Richie and Michael woke up the USPTO, the application was then rerouted to the appropriate unit. Not wanting to suffer a repeat of such negligence, Richie and Michael dutifully called the examiner about every three months for the next few years to ascertain the disposition of his patent application. No office actions were issued during this time. Then, about four years later, in 2005, Richie was informed that the Patent Office again lost his patent application. At some point in this saga, Richie told me that he was prodded to refile his utility patent application as a design patent application because the examiner stated that nothing invented was disclosed on his initial patent application.[67]

[67] I was not able to confirm that Richie was prodded to refile his utility patent application as a design patent application. Richie's recollection of such a contorted patenting process may not be entirely technically accurate. For clarity, the 8,270,640 patent that issued to Richie on September 18, 2012, was a continuation of a continuation, the first of which was filed, as U.S. application Serial Number

A less well-tempered motorcyclist would have blown a gasket at the ill-treatment dished out by the USPTO. Nevertheless, Richie was understandably flabbergasted. The thought that his race could be responsible for his patent application being lost at the USPTO, and then twice placed at the back of the line entered Richie's mind.[68]

In any event, Richie persevered by filing another patent application. But this time he created Rich One Enterprises in hopes of making it appear that a corporation was behind the patent application. A few years later, in 2007, Richie began receiving rejections. These rejections seemed to be off-point as they referenced supposed prior art relating to bicycles (including those long-outdated specimens with giant front wheels and tiny rear wheels), airplanes, and wrestling. One highly cited piece of prior art was that of a box strapped to the gas tank of a motorcycle. Many of these inane prior art citations were used multiple times in the examiner's efforts to reject Richie's patent application.

09/721,184, on November 21, 2000. Both continuations have been abandoned. There were at least seven non-final office actions and three final office actions in Richie's patenting saga. The first office action on the initial continuation application arrived 40 months after that application was filed. After Michael filed a response, it was a little more than two months before the applicant received a response from the examiner. The third office action was received seven months after Michael responded to the second office action and Richie had to wait another five months after Michael replied to the third office action.

[68] Richie is not the only minority inventor to relate to me their suspicions that their race or country of origin could account for their mistreatment at the USPTO. For instance, I spoke with Mohamed El Gafi, an Egyptian-born inventor. Only one of Mr. El Gafi's 30 non-provisional patent applications issued. Nonetheless, I do not think that there is any evidence of discrimination at the USPTO. First, in Richie's case, it is highly unlikely that examiners even knew of Richie's race. Second, the mistreatment of inventors has been too pervasive to call attention to isolated instances of maltreatment. Third, many patent examiners are minorities or hail from foreign lands themselves. Fourth, in recent years, the USPTO has made special efforts to reach out to communities that have been underrepresented in terms of patent filings. And as for Mr. El Gafi, the one patent application of his that did issue on May 21, 2002 (6,391,080) was titled "Phosphate, phosphatic fertilizers manufacturing process." A fertilizer-related patent application listing an Egyptian national so recent to September 11, 2001, would have been a perfect application for a discriminating patent office to reject. (Fertilizer was heavily used in the Oklahoma City bombings that killed 168 people in April of 1995.)

When Michael complained to a supervisory examiner about the silliness of the prior art cited by the examiner, the supervisory examiner agreed that better prior art was available. When still more silly pieces of prior art were cited in rejections issued by the examiner, the supervisory examiner proclaimed that his superior believed that granting Richie's patent would have been an embarrassment to the USPTO. Thus, the Patent Office invented a rationale for rejecting patent applications (i.e., rejecting patent applications because of the embarrassment granting them may cause the USPTO) outside of what the law proscribes (namely, that patents be eligible, novel, and non-obvious). Also, the fact that the Rich One sound system generated tremendous interest among its target audience (such popularity being a secondary indicator of non-obviousness) was ignored by the patent examiner.[69]

As the prosecution of Richie's patent application limped along, patent life was slipping away. Legal fees were mounting, eventually reaching $68,000. Richie may have had to resort to selling his motorcycle to finance the prosecution of his patent had he not been able to raise $10,000 from eight investors. Commercial opportunities were impeded by the extended patent pendency. For example, Suzuki told Richie only to call once he received an issued patent. By the time the '640 patent issued, Richie's initial interlocutors at Suzuki were nowhere to be found.

While Michael continued to interface with the examiner, Richie sought the advice and assistance of minority business associations. He was also granted an audience with United States Representative James Enos "Jim" Clyburn, perhaps on account of Richie having been a classmate of Representative Clyburn's daughter. The combination of Michael's good lawyering and Representative Clyburn's intervention at the USPTO resulted in Richie's patent application issuing.

Conclusion

Richie served his country during a time of war. During this time, he became 100% disabled on account of major depression and chronic pain. Sadly, his government, at least in the form of the USPTO, did not serve him well.

---

69 Interestingly, even when the Patent Office is performing at its best, some window dressing still occurs. For instance, the patents deemed to be the x (e.g., tenth) million patents to issue are hand-selected, largely for their publicity value.

Also, Richie does not fit the depiction of a greedy patentee. Over roughly 18 years, he spent nearly $100,000 out-of-pocket on prosecution costs, fees to patent marketing companies and in attempts to monetize his patents directly. He is receptive to entering into friendly licensing arrangements and has even publicly vowed to donate a portion of such royalties to the following charities: Association for Women in Science, Society for Science and the Public, Heroes for the Homeless, Make A Wish Foundation and Shriners Hospitals.

Postscript

When the Patent Office causes delays in the allowance of a patent application, the number of days of delay are added to the life of the issued patent. In Richie's case, probably close to ten years of additional time would have been added to the life of his patent for unnecessary delays caused by the USPTO. If so much extra time were tacked on to his patent, it could have aroused the attention of the patent examiner's superiors. Thus, one reason that it took the Patent Office nearly 12 years to issue Richie's patent application is that the Patent Office wanted to mask its dilatoriness.

After so many years of prosecution, it was suggested to Michael that Richie's claims might be allowed if he (Michael) were to file a continuation application with a minor amendment. Michael complied and the application was promptly allowed. Thus, the examiner seemed willing to trade allowance of the patent application for the filing of a continuation application. The applicant's continuation application cleansed the thousands of extra days that the examiner would have had to add to the life of Richie's patent.

Much Will Be Taken From Those Who Have Given So Much

The New Testament states, "To whom much is given, much will be required."[70] Unfortunately, with the twisted state of the patent system today, that biblical construct has been changed to, "Much will be taken from those who have given so much." Let's meet Shane Chen, the founder of Inventist, a Washington-state invention factory.

Shane accomplished a lot since he immigrated to the United States from China in 1986. This lifelong tinkerer has been a successful inventor since 1998. Shane is listed as an inventor on 54 patents, mostly in the fields of water sports, skating, scooters, and cooking. While outdoors you may have come across Shane's Aquaskipper, Lunicycle, or Orbitwheels. Those who spend time cooking in their kitchens might be familiar with Shane's Leantisserie and Ultradrainer. Shane is also the inventor of several sleek, compact, and inexpensive personal vehicles such as the Solowheel, Iotatrax, Powerwing, and the Hovertrax (which is the original hoverboard). When I spoke with Shane, Inventist was about to launch its newest e-vehicle, the Hoverwheel.

Many of Shane's inventions encourage physical fitness by making exercise fun. His breakthroughs are also directed towards increasing mobility as well as offer the promise of alleviating traffic congestion and reducing pollution. Shane's innovations create jobs and are a boon to the retail channels that carry his inventions. Federal, state, and local governments benefit from the economic activity his inventions generate via their receipts of corresponding taxes. Inventors like Shane drive prosperity.

---

[70] Luke 12:47-49 Modern English Version of the New Testament of the Bible https://www.biblegateway.com/passage/?search=Luke%2012:47-49&version=MEV

Rampant Infringement

Shane has contributed mightily to the U.S. economy. But much has been taken from him. All 10 of the new products that Shane invented over the past decade have been knocked off. Seven of these inventions have been copied and sold worldwide. Some of Shane's most popular patent-protected products that have been infringed include the Powerwing (a three-wheeled scooter), the Solowheel (an electric one-wheeled vehicle), and his hoverboard, Hovertrax.

The Hovertrax is immensely popular—and for good reason. This self-balancing, two-wheeled hoverboard allows users to cruise at speeds of up to eight miles per hour for as much as 60 minutes of continuous use. The Hovertrax's anti-slip rubber traction platform keeps riders in perfect balance, even though maneuvering of the Hovertrax is foot-controlled. The ride is smooth and silent and the Hovertrax is compact enough to tuck under users' arms and to store in lockers.

Shane's Hovertrax has caught more than the attention of riders. It has also caught the attention of some 1,000 infringers in China. This 1,000 approximation is neither a typo nor hyperbole: In August of 2015, the Chinese government reported that 600 domestic companies were manufacturing unauthorized copies of the Hovertrax. These illegitimate attempts to clone the Hovertrax generated $4.6 billion in exports from China in 2015. Once neighboring Chinese manufacturers hear a cash register ring, a swarm of follow-on producers with requisite capabilities descend to replicate the product. (There is extreme concentration of the production of any particular product in China—one block may be dedicated to producing shoes while the next block is chock-full of tire manufacturers.) Thus, it should be no surprise that follow-on Chinese companies copied successive generations of the Hovertrax in the ensuing months and years. Scores of U.S. resellers have unlawfully and misleadingly marketed those knockoffs as genuine Hovertrax.

Impact of Knocking Off Knockoffs

It used to be that Chinese manufacturers who sought to copy products would buy one sample original product to study that unit's composition and structure. Now, Chinese knockoff factories are so proficient in emulating patented products that they often no longer need to purchase even one authentic product. This is especially true with the follow-on copycats; they just copy the first-generation knockoff products. The result is that it is becoming less common for patentees to sell even one unit of their original products to infringing manufacturers.

Another problem associated with rampant infringement for patentees is that the quality of the derivative knockoffs becomes increasingly compromised. Quality deteriorates, less attention is paid to safety, and inferior components (batteries in the case of hoverboards) are sourced. According to the Consumer Product Safety Commission, in 2016 there were at least 99 incident reports of the battery packs in self-balancing scooters/hoverboards overheating, sparking, smoking, catching fire, and/or exploding. Some of these mishaps resulted in burn injuries and property damage. However, none of these incidents were caused by Inventist's Hovertrax or the Hovertrax 2.0 which is manufactured by Razor, Inventist's exclusive licensee.

The economic impact of unbridled infringement on Inventist and Razor is severe. After learning about the dangerous malfunctions of infringing hoverboards, fewer parents will purchase any hoverboard. And, according to my discussions with Shane, infringers have captured at least 90% of the remaining hoverboard market. Thus, infringers shrink entire markets, deprive inventors and their authorized licensees of the vast majority of the remaining markets, and tarnish the brands and reputations of the legitimate inventors and licensees. Further, infringers are relieved of pesky issues that confront inventors; the former can deliver their knockoffs to the market much quicker than inventors since they are neither burdened with toiling in laboratories and workshops nor conducting a painfully prolonged series of trials and errors.

Recourse to Rampant Offshore Infringement

What recourse do Razor and Inventist have? Well, Shane told me that once upon a time, about 15 years ago, Chinese infringers could be sued in China to the reasonable satisfaction of foreign patentees. In fact, Shane successfully sued a Chinese infringer of his patent covering his Aquaskipper back in those days.

In 2013, Shane returned to his native China to try to sue several companies that were infringing his patent covering his Solowheel. The outcome was less favorable for Shane. A Chinese infringer paid him the equivalent of $150,000 for its misdeeds. However, Shane was pressured—by the judge who Shane believes was in turn pressured by the local government—to deem that amount as complete payment for a perpetual license to the named infringer. Shane was disappointed with this settlement for several reasons: For one thing, it cost Shane $100,000 in legal fees to receive the $150,000 settlement. Second, the infringer was given the green light to continue infringing at Shane's expense. Finally, the settlement provided the infringer with a veneer of legitimacy, producing an unholy precedent for budding infringers.

At least two Chinese judges had a hand in dissuading Shane from suing more recent infringers in China. These judges advised Shane to license his patents to Chinese manufacturers in order to preserve factory jobs. Even if there was no judicial bias or pressure, it would be impossible for Shane to sue 1,000 infringers in China. This is especially true given that infringing Chinese factories that are served with injunctions simply continue their illicit activities by reopening production facilities under different names.

There is hope for Shane and Razor. Back in 2016, Razor filed complaints against 35 alleged Chinese infringers with the International Trade Commission. Success with this tribunal is not assured. The alleged infringers have formed a joint defense and have lawyered up to the hilt. After waiting for a decision for 18 months, Shane and Razor learned that they lost the complaints case because a few misplaced words in Shane's 8,738,278 patent introduced the need for its reissuance. If the pending claims put forth by Razor and Shane are successful, Razor will be able to have infringing hoverboards impounded upon their arrival at U.S. ports. Such impounding would also prohibit the practice of U.S.-based web retailers marketing infringing products and then having related orders filled by Chinese manufacturers who send the infringing merchandise directly to the end customer.[71] (More about that in the story about Mighty Mugs, which follows.)

---

[71] On May 23, 2017, the Court of Appeals for the Federal Circuit affirmed a decision from the District Court for the Western District of Washington in which that court held that Amazon is not responsible for infringement when infringing products are sold via Amazon's online marketplace for third parties and its related "Fulfillment by Amazon" services. However, the district court stated that it was "troubled" by its own decision and its potential implications on patent infringement law in an era of ecommerce. The district court expressed concern that the law is

Despite Rampant Infringement, The Mighty (Mugs) Have Not Fallen

The Mighty Mug is another patent-protected product that has been the victim of unrestrained knockoffs. Maybe you have seen advertisements for the Mighty Mug or read about the product. What is unique about these thermos-size mugs is that they don't fall down. You can bump into them, hit them, push them, jostle them about, or shake the flat surface upon which they are resting. Nothing will topple Mighty Mugs. Thus, the risk of sedentary spills is eliminated. However, whenever the user wants to sip the contents of the Mighty Mug, he simply lifts the mug straight up from the surface.

How pervasive has infringement been of at least one of the four utility patents that cover the Mighty Mug? Online infringement alone has been so rampant that Jayme Smaldone, founder of the Mighty Mug, has employed Red Points, an artificial intelligence technology that detects infringers by crawling through e-commerce sites around the world. Within eight weeks of beginning to use Red Points' technology, Jayme detected more than 2,500 knockoffs of his Mighty Mugs.

A massively disproportionate amount of these copycat mugs originate in China. It is widely known that labor costs to pick and pack e-commerce orders in China are much less than in the United States. Some of the copycat Mighty Mugs on sites like AliExpress sell for half of the prices of authentic Mighty Mugs.

Shipping Costs Crush American Patentees

Chinese manufacturers have a major advantage in competing against U.S. manufacturers that is not commonly known. That advantage relates to

---

lagging behind the current technology in the marketplace. For patentees, the CAFC's affirmation presents one more enormous patent enforcement-free zone.

shipping costs. When Jayme ships one of his mugs to a customer located down the street from his Rahway, New Jersey warehouse, the postage cost is $6.30. How much does it cost Chinese infringers to ship a knockoff mug to a customer in the United States? As of the fall of 2018, just $1.30. While it costs Jayme at least $20 to ship four Mighty Mugs domestically (depending on their distance from Jayme's fulfillment center), a Chinese copycatter only spends $3.70 when shipping four infringing mugs. The 80% discount that Chinese infringers enjoy on their shipping costs relative to the expenses that American producers are required to bear will likely widen as parcel delivery costs are expected to rise in the United States.[72]

Wouldn't higher tariffs imposed on Chinese imports into the United States, favored by the Trump administration, help domestic manufacturers such as Jayme? Unfortunately, not. There is an $800 de minimis exemption to packages sent through the mail. When Jayme imports Mighty Mugs by the container load (which are valued in excess of $800), he has to pay whatever tariffs are on the books. However, Chinese infringers are exempt from paying any tariffs when they drop ship limited numbers of infringing mugs directly to any particular American customer.

Infringement of the Mighty Mug is not isolated to online retailers; infringing products have been sold through brick-and-mortar retailers as well. Back in 2013, Jayme began selling Mighty Mugs exclusively through Bed Bath & Beyond. This big-box retailer racked up roughly $25 million worth of Mighty Mug sales over the first four years. During this period of time, Jayme informed Bed Bath & Beyond that the Mighty Mug line was protected with patents. Also, during that same period of time, Telebrands contacted Jayme as that direct response retailer was interested in selling Mighty Mugs through its channels. Jayme conducted some due diligence

[72] However, at the time of my writing these pages, the prospect exists that the gulf between what American and Chinese shippers pay to have their parcels delivered to customers within the United States may not widen further, or could even contract. President Trump announced his administration's plans to withdraw from a 192-nation Postal Treaty, which allows poor and developing countries (among which China is included) to pay national postal services lower shipping rates than wealthier countries. Jay Timmons, president of the National Association of Manufacturers, said in a statement, "This outdated arrangement contributes significantly to the flood of counterfeit goods and dangerous drugs that enter the country from China."

on Telebrands and learned that that company was involved in hundreds of litigations. He respectfully declined Telebrands' overtures.

Within 18 months of rejecting a deal with Telebrands, Bed Bath & Beyond unceremoniously removed Mighty Mugs from all 1,200 of its stores. But their shelves did not remain bare; rather, they were stocked with knockoff mugs from Telebrands. Several months afterwards, Jayme paid a visit to his former buyer at Bed Bath & Beyond. The following approximates their dialog:

Jayme: "Our Mighty Mugs are selling very well through a variety of channels. Bed Bath & Beyond should resume its sales of our fall-resistant mugs."

Buyer: "Maybe you're right. The customer seems to be responding to those kinds of products."

Jayme: "What do you mean 'those kinds of products'?"

Buyer: "Telebrands has been selling similar mugs though our stores, and the product is very popular."

Jayme: "We patented the Mighty Mug line. Fall-resistant mugs with SmartGrip technology other than Mighty Mugs are infringing our patents. Telebrands' mugs are infringing our patents!"

Buyer: "Retailers can't be expected to be patent experts. We just don't have the resources to wade into patent issues. In any event, even if it is proven that infringing products are selling in our stores, our suppliers are responsible for indemnifying us."

> Retailers often prefer to buy infringing products from large manufacturers that agree to indemnify them in the event that patent litigation arises. In view of the larger manufacturers' reassuring balance sheets, lower manufacturing costs due to economies of scale, redundant supply chains, and integration with the retailers, cost-benefit analyses often favors buying from large infringers over small inventors.

Despite Bed Bath & Beyond never restocking Mighty Mugs, Jayme is a very fortunate patentee. Two factors have enabled him to restrain infringement of Mighty Mugs to manageable levels. First, Telebrands never unleashed its full wrath on Mighty Mugs. The New Jersey hawker of products via infomercials never figured out how to turn fall-resistant mugs into a money-making machine. Causing Jayme grief just wasn't worthwhile for Telebrands. A relatively amiable settlement was reached between the two companies whereby Telebrands was allowed to sell remaining units of its infringing mugs in return for Jayme agreeing to not sue Telebrands' retailers.

Second, Jayme has enjoyed success in having imports of infringing fall-resistant mugs impounded at American ports. Once he proved to the U.S. International Trade Commission that infringers were violating Section 337, he was able to obtain a general exclusion order which directs the U.S. Customs and Border Protection to exclude from entry all infringing articles regardless of source. While this general exclusion order fails to provide Jayme with any damages for the patent infringement that he sustained, it often proves to have sufficient weight in pressuring websites to remove infringing merchandise. Further, general exclusion orders are usually less expensive to obtain and can be secured more expeditiously than court orders. Jayme invested $150,000 over three years litigating against an infringer in China but has no verdict, damages, settlement, or injunction to show for his efforts. On the other hand, Jayme spent roughly $150,000 over only nine months to obtain a general exclusion order from the U.S. International Trade Commission.

Conclusion

Mighty Mugs has proven to be a successful consumer product. At the time of my writing these pages, approximately 3.7 million Mighty Mugs were sold, and when I spoke with Jayme, the product was selling in some 30 countries. The revenues Jayme generates from the Mighty Mug have enabled him to combat infringers on multiple fronts.

However, we should not make the mistake of deeming Jayme's success as justification for glossing over the damage that infringers inflict on patentees. Jayme spent $600,000 enforcing his patents over five years. We should remember that for every small company that can afford to invest $150,000 in securing a general exclusion order from the U.S. International

Trade Commission, many dozens cannot. In some cases, even when funds are available, it is illogical to pursue infringers. An example being when a patent-protected product that is being infringed has a shorter lifecycle than the time required to seek redress for patent infringement. Every day, Jayme spends his valuable time scouring the world of online commerce for infringers.

Given that Red Points identified as many as 2,500 infringers, the sales that Jayme lost to knockoffs over the first seven years of launching Mighty Mugs has to be absolutely staggering. Lost sales translate into less commerce for Mighty Mugs in the United States and fewer jobs for American workers. Reducing Jayme's order flow deprives his business of economies of scale, resulting in higher fulfillment costs. Infringers offering their copycat products at rock bottom prices depresses the prices that Jayme can charge his customers.

Postscript

The International Trade Commission has generally been the silver lining in the cloud hovering over patents. However, there is room for concern that the ITC is becoming a bit wobbly on protecting patentees from infringing products imported into the United States.

In a case brought by Qualcomm against Apple, the Administrative Law Judge found that Apple's iPhones—manufactured in China and containing Intel chips also made in China—infringed Qualcomm's patent (U.S. Patent No. 9,535,490, titled *Power Saving Techniques in Computing Devices)*. However, in November of 2018, Judge Thomas Pender refused to recommend that the ITC issue an exclusion order against Apple. Exclusion orders are the only relief patentees can hope to attain at the ITC as that body cannot impose monetary damages awards.

What was Judge Pender's reasoning for breaking with the precedent of issuing exclusion orders on infringing products? His reasoning was two-fold. First, judge Pender declared that blocking the infringing Apple imports would be against the "public interest." I am not sure how the public interest would be adversely affected if infringing iPhones were not allowed into the United States. If Apple's infringing iPhones were blocked entry at American ports, American consumers would still have quite a selection of handheld phones from other manufacturers as well as the iPhones that do not infringe Qualcomm's patents. In fact, in its exclusion order request, Qualcomm carved out those Apple devices that do not infringe Qualcomm's chips.

Second, Judge Pender held that Qualcomm is an "established and profitable" company and has the resources to pursue Apple for patent infringement. What did Judge Pender think Qualcomm was doing when it brought its case before the ITC? Does the esteemed jurist believe that "established and profitable companies" no longer deserve exclusion orders when infringement of their patents has been demonstrated? Did Judge Pender believe that the case before him was a David versus Goliath situation? If so, he was badly mistaken. As everyone (except, perhaps Judge Pender) knows, Apple is one of the most "established and profitable" companies in the world.

How Pervasive is Infringement on Amazon?

Many readers realize that online infringement is pervasive, but I bet few are aware of how pernicious counterfeiting on the Internet has become.

The Global Brand Counterfeiting Report projected that more than 25% of the $1.82 trillion in worldwide counterfeit sales in 2020 will hail from e-commerce. Gartner, the research firm, found that one-third of the brands offered for sale on Amazon by third-party merchants received at least one review by a customer reporting such products to be counterfeit. Also, nearly half of the 47 items purchased through five major web-retailers pursuant to a 2018 U.S. Government Accountability Office survey turned out to be knockoffs.

Let's consider what often happens to inventors when counterfeiters begin selling their knockoffs through Amazon.

The most obvious and immediate consequence of infringement is that the inventor loses sales to the copycatters. Inventors are deprived of their rightful revenues and since their production volumes take a hit, their production costs rise. Margins, already under pressure from Amazon, are further squeezed.

Customers become confused as categories are flooded with low-quality knockoffs. Their disappointment with receiving shoddy knockoffs is reflected in the low ratings and derogatory comments they mistakenly post about the legitimate products on Amazon's pages. However, posting reviews that point out that knockoff products are indeed illegitimate are routinely blocked by Amazon.

Amazon Facilitates Counterfeiting

In a sense, Amazon induces legitimate producers to facilitate the infringement of their own merchandise.

Customers have been conditioned to receive their orders within a day or two and e-merchants face consequences if their shipments are delayed. Related logistics can be complicated for small businesses. Many e-retailers find it more expedient to let Amazon handle order fulfillment. So far, so good.

The problem that arises is that Amazon commingles all of the products in any given product category as part of one stock keeping unit. It doesn't matter which Amazon storefront operator—legitimate producer or any copycatter—deposits its products at Amazon's warehouses; all such products are treated as being the same for fulfillment purposes. Suppose a customer in Maine orders a collapsible thermos from Amazon's main page featuring that stock keeping unit. Now suppose that the legitimate producer didn't deliver any of his collapsible thermoses to Amazon's warehouses in Maine but at least one infringer did. Since Amazon wants to fill the Mainer's order as quickly as possible it dispatches the infringing unit.

That Amazon assigns one page for every stock keeping unit (e.g., "collapsible thermoses") raises other problematic issues for legitimate sellers. The prices, shipping times, and customer reviews relative to all Amazon merchants selling that item are available on that page. Purveyors of counterfeit products can usually offer prices significantly below those of legitimate sellers because the former do not invest in research—nor do they secure regulatory approvals or intellectual property protections in the form of patents, trademarks, or copyrights. Knockoff artists save a fortune by producing shoddy merchandise. The discounted prices offered by copycatters elevates their listings among the other sellers and is a determinant as to whom Amazon assigns its Buy Box (where the critical "Buy Now" button is located).

In other words, Amazon awards the lower prices offered by counterfeiters with better visibility on its all-important product-specific page. Legitimate Amazon merchants lose sales from their less favorable product positioning. Because more shoddy products are sold, the entire category soon nosedives in terms of average customer reviews. What is the consequence of this? Since Amazon's algorithm favors higher-rated products, the entire stock keeping unit will start showing up less prominently. For instance, when a customer searches for "thermoses," collapsible thermoses will fall further below other types of thermoses listed on Amazon. Thus, the listings of legitimate sellers tumble as their category falls when search results are displayed, and as their offerings drop further relative to the illegitimate vendors within their product categories.

No Easy Remedies to Knockoffs

So, maybe when legitimate sellers are being shellacked from counterfeiters, they should boost their social media campaigns on other platforms to combat the bad reviews they are receiving on Amazon. This sounds like a logical countermove but poses its own challenges. One problem is that customers burned by copycatters often leave bad reviews for legitimate products on social media sites such as Facebook. Not only do legitimate sellers have an uphill battle in terms of countering these negative narratives, but the costs of doing so skyrocket. This is because sites like Facebook, which try to discourage ads by questionable advertisers, use sentiment when determining the auction prices for its ads. The poisoning of the well often causes the prices of corrective advertising to rise to levels that are simply unaffordable for legitimate online vendors.

Legitimate Amazon merchants can always send the e-commerce giant takedown notices when they spot knockoffs. But legitimate sellers usually have to undertake several steps to evoke a positive response from Amazon. Purchases of the phony products are typically required. Even paying pirates for their knockoffs is not always easy; many scammers can identify and block test sales to legitimate purveyors. Obtaining a test product from a scammer is just the beginning; the legitimate merchant must prove to Amazon that rival products are illegally produced and offered for sale on that site. Authorized merchants are often required to provide the identity of the sellers of fake products, but this is inherently difficult due to the scammers' sophisticated obfuscation. Legitimate Amazon merchants find that they can't even stop scammers from using the pictures that they (the legitimate sellers) post on primary product pages; Amazon sellers grant perpetual rights to all of the content they upload when they click through their merchant agreements with Amazon.

Taking on infringers who sell through Amazon invites retaliation. Scammers are often successful in provoking Amazon to deactivate the accounts of legitimate sellers by reporting that the legitimate sellers lack the authority to sell their merchandise. Scammers have a variety of tricks to induce Amazon to disrupt the operations of legitimate e-retailers. I call one of those dirty tricks "love bombing." Love bombing occurs when scammers hire someone to leave a flurry of glowing product reviews for legitimate sellers. Scammers know that Amazon's algorithms will detect such reviews as being fraudulent and then place legitimate sellers in penalty boxes.

Postscript

What can bona fide Amazon sellers do? They could take a more aggressive stance against Amazon; they could sue the juggernaut from Seattle. But what chance would any independent merchant have in prevailing in litigation against one of the world's best capitalized companies? And how would such merchant's listings and rankings on Amazon be impacted?

They can spend more money on lawyers to enforce their intellectual property rights. They can hire people to beseech their account representatives at Amazon to remove illegitimate products from that site. But these courses of action are expensive and distracting for small Internet merchants as they require the attention of the top people at small companies. They can place new QR-type codes on their products, but these technological fixes add to the costs of each product, making the legitimate retailers less price competitive against the scammers.

The ridiculousness of the situation is further illuminated when considering that the best remedy for legitimate e-commerce merchants to take to combat infringers might be to help their infringers produce higher quality knockoffs. At least this relatively inexpensive remedy would improve the rankings for—and traffic to—the affected product categories.

Post-Postscript

In fairness to Amazon, the Seattle-based e-tailer was testing an interesting program called Utility Patent Neutral Evaluation, designed to reduce the selling of patent-infringing products on its site in early 2019. Patentees that believe that an Amazon seller is selling infringing merchandise can make a $4,000 deposit. The two parties are then connected with a neutral third-party lawyer. If the alleged infringer fails to respond to the allegations leveled against it, its infringing products will be removed from Amazon and the patentee's $4,000 deposit will be returned. If the accused infringer wishes to contest its alleged infringement, it will also be required to deposit $4,000. The neutral lawyer reviews the evidence and makes a decision. The lawyer collects $4,000 from whichever side loses and the winner's deposit is refunded.

Patentee Busts Infringers But Comes Up Flat

Bragel International, founded by the Chen siblings from Taiwan, has been a leader in using silicon gels in medical devices, masks, and breast enhancement solutions since the late 1990s. In 1997, Bragel created the "Lia," a line of breast prosthesis products tailored for post-mastectomy patients. The Lia-Eternity introduced a real innovation to the breast prosthesis market—it is a self-adhesive prosthesis which attaches directly to the body. Two years later, in 1999, the Company launched a new product category led by its "Gel Bra," which are basically gel pads that are inserted into bra cups to enhance the appearance of breasts. This leak-resistant product was 30% lighter than the popular "Water Bra," which was widely known to leak.

In 2000, Bragel co-developed a medical device for breast augmentation called the "Brava Breast Enhancement and Shaping System." This product launched in mid-2001 but crashed in the wake of the heinous terrorist attacks of September 11, 2001. The Chen family proved to be very resourceful: Using the material accumulated to commercialize the Brava system, Bragel introduced its innovative "NuBra" in late 2002.

The NuBra, engineered by David Chen, is essentially two separate bra cups attached by a connector. This strapless and self-supportive bra features a specially formulated pressure-sensitive adhesive, which has been clinically tested to be safe and skin-friendly. Because the NuBra has neither straps nor rigid cups, the garment affords women comfort throughout the day as breast sizes slightly change. A woman can actually mix and match the cups to the connectors in the event that her breasts are not of identical size. NuBra has been heralded as practical, convenient, comfortable, versatile, and user-friendly.

NuBra's Commercial Success

Bragel filed for patent protection on its NuBra product on May 31, 2002. That application issued as U.S. Patent No. 6,758,720 on July 6, 2004. (As I write these pages, the NuBra is protected by six U.S. patents.) Corresponding patent applications were pursued around the world—with patent offices in Canada, Europe, India, Indonesia, Korea, Hong Kong, China, Japan, Taiwan, and Australia—at about the same time as the U.S. patent application was filed. Trademark applications were similarly pursued in close proximity to the time the patent applications were filed.

The NuBra initially encountered skepticism when it hit the market in early 2003. But once it was featured on QVC in Japan in the Spring of 2003, sales busted out all over the place. In its first year of production, 750,000 units were sold, yielding Bragel $23 million in revenue. A storm of positive publicity soon enveloped NuBra and women flooded all of the retail channels that were fortunate enough to stock the product. News of the NuBra traveled to the far corners of the world. The strongest markets at the time of NuBra's launch were in Asia, which accounted for about 75% of the NuBra's revenues. Demand was so strong that three shifts of production were required to keep the factories in Pomona, California humming 24 hours a day. By so quickly rebounding from the tragedy of September 11, Bragel proved that innovation often lies in the bosom of necessity.

Fast forward to 2017. Bragel sold 2.5 million units of the NuBra. You would think that the cup would continue to runneth over. Right? Unfortunately, not. Bragel's revenue line plunged 26% from $23 million in 2003 to $17 million in 2017. Further, the geographic distribution of this revenue shifted: Now, 80% of NuBra's revenues hail from the United States and Canada. What accounts for the NuBra's sagging sales? In a word, infringers.

In 2004, just one year after NuBra's launch, Chinese lingerie companies began infringing Bragel's patents. Infringement was largely contained in Asia for the first few years after NuBra's market debut. But in 2008, Chinese infringers began exporting to the United States. These knockoffs have been extremely difficult for Bragel to compete against as their prices are typically a quarter of those of authentic NuBras. Chinese lingerie manufacturers no longer have a monopoly on infringement as hundreds of illicit American companies (as well as producers from other parts of the world) have gotten into the knockoff game in recent years. (It should be noted that Bragel's

NuBra trademarks have also been promiscuously infringed.) As of late 2018, David Chen, President of Bragel, estimated that infringers claimed 90% of the worldwide market for strapless, backless bras.

Bragel Tries to Combat Infringement in China

What has Bragel done to combat the scourge of infringement? The Company certainly has not taken the infringement of its patents lying down. According to my discussions with David, his company sued 30 infringers, the majority in the U.S., over the last 10 years. At the time of my writing these pages, seven or eight litigations were ongoing.

One of Bragel's early patent enforcement actions took place in Guangdong, China, when Bragel sued Fu Li Kai in 2005. Bragel won this suit in the sense that the judge ruled that Fu Li Kai had infringed and that it must pay Bragel $45,000 in damages. However, when Bragel went to collect, David learned that the owner of Fu Li Kai transferred ownership of the infringing entity to his mother and then disappeared. Under Chinese law, Bragel could pursue the $45,000 in damages from the son, but he was nowhere to be found. In order to halt infringement at the infringing enterprise, Bragel would have to sue the mother, who would probably similarly transfer ownership to another relative and then disappear. David tells me that Fu Li Kai is now about 25 times as large as Bragel.

> The practice of changing a business's legal status to skirt charges of patent infringement is not confined to China. Francesca Kuglen, who you met earlier in this book, had a similar situation happen when she was running her first company, Jontee Accessories. Jontee had sales representatives marketing its accessories in many geographical markets but not in Boston. Instead, a small company was authorized to sell Jontee's goods from two stands in Boston malls.
>
> Francesca began to notice that sales of Jontee's products were rising consistently and notably in all markets except for Boston. She couldn't think of any reason for this anomaly so she hired an investigator. The agent learned that the Boston seller was indeed selling much more product than it reported to Jontee; this seller expanded its operations to about 20 stands

and three freestanding stores. But some of the merchandise it sold was unauthorized and contained features that infringed Francesca's patents. Francesca's efforts to amiably remedy the infringing sales did not bear fruit. Left with no alternative, Francesca initiated a patent infringement case against the Boston seller. Literally, on the court steps on the way to that trial, the Boston seller filed for bankruptcy protection. Francesca's patent infringement case was dismissed. Within a few days, the Boston seller resurrected its operations under a new legal name.

Hasn't the Chinese patent regime become more legitimate in recent years? Not in Bragel's experience. In 2014, Bragel brought a patent infringement suit against China's second largest lingerie maker, which was headquartered in Beijing. David thought he stood a good chance of prevailing in China's capital; after all, Beijing is no intellectual backwater. Unfortunately, he thought wrong. The opposing counsel warned David's counselor to drop the lawsuit or Bragel's Chinese patents would be invalidated. David thought this was a bluff and instructed his lawyers to fight on. Unfortunately, he thought wrong again. All six of Bragel's Chinese patents protecting NuBra in 2016 were invalidated in China's corollary to the *inter partes review* procedures. Bragel's paying all required annual patent maintenance fees, which were more expensive than those in the United States, did not help Bragel's case. Some suspect that Bragel's opponent paid off the Chinese Patent Office to render its invalidity rulings. These sources told me that they, "Do not want to go to China to try to prove that authorities in China's Patent Office accept bribes for invalidating opponents' patents because they might be disappeared."

I am familiar with a Chinese conglomerate that has designated only one employee to accept process of service; he always seems to be on vacation.

Waging patent infringement lawsuits did not remedy Bragel's counterfeit problem in China. Infringement in China was so bad that the only way Bragel could penetrate that market—and serve U.S. mass merchants that demand bargain basement prices—was to contract with a Chinese outsource manufacturer in 2005. Bragel's contract outsourcer produces the NuBra line at prices dramatically lower than can be found state-side. Production in China is according to Bragel's specifications and is subject to Bragel's quality control. Notwithstanding the Chinese operator's efficiency or Bragel's management of its supply chain, supporting an operation in China is inherently inefficient. Bragel ships required raw materials to its Chinese partner who then exports the final products back to the United States. David does not want to publicize which contract manufacturing concern Bragel is working with for fear of retribution on the part of infringers: There is no telling when aggressive tax assessors or fire safety inspectors will show up to shut down his partner's operation.

Bragel Tries to Combat Infringement Outside of China

In the mid- and late-2000s, the American lingerie market was crawling with hundreds of infringers of the NuBra. The sheer extent of the infringing community made unveiling counterfeiters' identities difficult. When they were identified, Bragel served dozens of small-scale infringers with cease-and-desist orders. Bragel sued these small-fry infringers in court and turned to the International Trade Commission, which has the power to impound infringing imports at America's ports. But with so many small-time infringers, it was hard to put a dent in the pervasive infringement of the NuBra.

Finally, in 2012, Bragel discovered the identity of one of the large importers of infringing NuBras. In 2013, Bragel demonstrated to the judge presiding in federal court in California that this East Coast-based importer was indeed infringing Bragel's '720 patent. A summary judgment was issued in Bragel's favor. The lawyers working for the East Coast importer must have been moonlighting archaeologists, because they unearthed a retail chain located in one of the Southern states that had been infringing the '720 patent in the 2006 timeframe. Bragel issued a cease-and-desist letter to the Southern retail chain around that time; subsequently, that chain agreed to stop selling infringing bras. But what actually happened was that this Southern retailer sold its inventory to the East Coast importer. It was the imparting of this litany of events—and the implication that Bragel tacitly approved of the continued selling of infringing bras, even though the Southern retailer agreed to cease selling such unauthorized intimate apparel—that caused the judge to overturn the summary judgment. Litigation was allowed to proceed.

In 2014, three days before the trial was scheduled to commence, the East Coast importer petitioned the Patent Trial and Appeal Board to invalidate Bragel's '720 patent. David panicked when he learned that, at the time, the PTAB was instituting some 90% of the petitions it received and was invalidating some 75% of the claims that it reviewed. Since David could not take the risk of his cornerstone U.S. patent being invalidated, he felt pressure to reach a settlement with the East Coast-based importer.

In 2017, he ended up settling for a pittance, about eight percent of the lower end of the range of damages his advisors expected he would receive at trial. The settlement figure, amounting to nearly nothing per infringing bra, was not even enough to cover a small fraction of Bragel's fees for outside legal representation. To add insult to injury, it was agreed that the East Coast infringer would be allowed to sell several hundreds of thousands of NuBra knockoffs that it reportedly had on hand over the two ensuing years. During discovery it was revealed that the East Coast importer was selling between one million and one-and-a-half million infringing NuBra units every year for the four or five years preceding the initiation of litigation.

At the end of 2018, the East Coast importer continued to infringe Bragel's '720 patent as that company claimed its sales mysteriously and precipitously dropped by 75%. David tells me he has a feeling that the infringer's sales of its NuBra knockoffs will last the East Coast infringer many more years. (Translation: The East Coast infringer is lying. Based on normalized sales results, it would have sold out of its inventory of residual infringing NuBra's in three or four months. That company is using the inventory it had on hand at the time of the settlement as an excuse to continue to infringe NuBra's patents by producing unauthorized garments.)

Bragel recounts a multitude of other frustrating experiences in terms of pursuing infringers. For example, there was a situation where infringing products were being sold from a web retailer that appeared to be registered to an office in Idaho. Bragel made contact with this operation's Los Angeles-based counselor. This lawyer stonewalled Bragel for about eight months before Bragel was told that the real operator of the entity in question was a Singaporean national. Of course, this individual could not be located. The opposing counsel withdrew from the case, causing Bragel to stop pursuing the matter.

In 2006, Bragel attempted to sue a large European lingerie importer.

This company was headquartered in the Netherlands, maintained a warehouse in Belgium, and served the German market. Bragel was issued patents in all of these countries and paid all required annuities. However, when Bragel sought to enter into discussions with the Dutch headquarters, it was advised to speak to the warehouse in Belgium. The Belgian managers indicated that they knew nothing about patents and sent them to seek redress in Germany. Seeking injunctions or damages from any of the affiliated parties proved to be an exercise in futility even though all of these activities occurred within a 10-mile radius. Bragel ceased trying to enforce its patents in these countries. As patents are emasculated, revenues become eviscerated: By 2018, Europe accounted for only one percent of Bragel's revenues.

Bragel continues to search for infringers. Once engaged in discussions with Bragel, the infringers often obfuscate the issue by arguing about claim construction, threatening to launch *inter partes review* petitions, demand to conduct extensive material testing, depose the inventors and seek to change venue. However, it must be said that many retailers selling infringing bras honestly do not realize that they are selling infringing bras or bras of inferior quality. To their credit, several retailers have replaced infringing bras with NuBras. But even reaching these amiable agreements requires expenditures of time and expense on Bragel's part.

Postscript

According to my discussions with management, Bragel invested between $300,000 and $400,000 in research and development before bringing the NuBra to market. The Company invested between $2.5 million and $3.0 million obtaining and maintaining its related patent portfolio. Bragel was spending as much as $2.0 million annually between 2012 and 2016 in its litigations designed to enforce the patents protecting the NuBra. (The Company's yearly patent litigation expenses have slowed to only about $200,000 since 2016.) From the time of the issuance of the NuBra patents, Bragel spent well over $15 million enforcing those patents. In other words, Bragel spent more than 37 times as much money enforcing its patents than it invested in the research needed to develop the inventions underlying those patents. All of these legal expenses were borne over the past 16 years, when Bragel's sales and profits were being consistently squeezed due to its infringers' pestiferous behavior.

David told me that he is losing faith in the patent system. He is shifting his budget from patents to public relations and marketing. A patent attorney familiar with the NuBra saga told me that he now advises young entrepreneurs to spend a discretionary $10,000 on marketing as opposed to patenting.

Patenting Money Goes Down the Drain

By the year 2000, Gene Luoma had accumulated plenty of practice trying to unclog his shower drains; his daughter did not like getting her long hair cut. Gene didn't have much success with the usual remedies—neither plungers, liquid drain chemicals nor bent coat hangers seemed to keep the Luoma family's shower drains working properly. He scoured the market for better solutions but finding an elixir proved elusive.

Tired of pouring money down the drain, Gene got inventive and resourceful. This enterprising mechanical engineer went into his garage and spotted a worn-out plastic sled hanging on the wall. He cut a 24-inch-long strip from the sled, narrow enough to fit down his shower drain. The barbs he cut out along both sides of the plastic strip were designed to grasp onto the hair and gunk found in shower drains and piping. Gene soon gave his invention a test drive. The strip slithered down his shower drain and when he pulled it out, a clump of his daughter's hair came with it.

The newly-created Zip-It drain cleaning tool proved to be simple to manufacture and use. This one-piece product is ready to use as soon as it drops out of injection molding machines. Using the tool requires nothing more than inserting the flexible strip into a drain and then removing it. Both actions are facilitated by a handle on one end which has an aperture for finger gripping and for hanging.

Zip-It Becomes a Hit

Searching for any prior inventions resembling the Zip-It failed to produce anything similar. So, Gene filed a patent application on December 11, 2000, and the related utility patent issued on August 17, 2004 with 12 claims. An application for a design patent was filed on February 9, 2000 and issued on January 2, 2001.

In the intervening years, Gene made significant strides in

commercializing his invention. He developed a prototype and established Luoma Enterprises whose mission was to commercialize Zip-It. Gene was able to sell tens of thousands of units within the first few weeks of securing Menards (a chain of home improvement centers located primarily in the Midwest) as a customer. But Gene wanted to expand Zip-It's footprint further. When Gene brought Zip-It to one of the largest big-box home supply companies, that company's plumbing buyer was impressed and intimated that the retailer would purchase thousands of units if they were available in large quantities. The snag was that most large retailers are reticent to purchase from single product companies.

With evidence of demand in hand, Gene entered into an exclusive patent license agreement with Cobra Products which is owned by publicly-traded MASCO Corporation on December 29, 2000. Presto! Once the ink was dry on that licensing agreement, Zip-It became available in some 30,000 stores across the United States.

Gene's Zip-It drain cleaners started selling like hotcakes in 2001. Generating 300,000 units of sales per month was not atypical. By 2011, many millions of units were sold through national retail chains such as Sears, Walmart, Home Depot, Lowe's, Ace Hardware, Walgreens and Rite Aid. The swelling sales were a function of Zip-It's novelty, effectiveness, ease of use, strong distribution and very reasonable retail pricing. The Internet is still strewn with rave reviews of Zip-It.

The resulting steady stream of royalties were not funds for frivolous spending for Gene. Rather, he relied on his royalties from Zip-It to combat Facioscapulohumeral Muscular Dystrophy—a terrible, progressive form of muscular dystrophy that not only afflicts Gene but also two of his children. The disease that has stricken the Luoma family requires adaptive equipment to keep them independent and ambulatory.

Things started heading south for Gene in 2010 when his exclusive licensee's plumbing sales representative, Doug Cohen, was dismissed from Cobra Products. Mr. Cohen soon became the president of G.T. Water. To his credit, Mr. Cohen did seek to license Zip-It from Cobra, but Cobra declined to sublicense Zip-It to G.T. Water. Gene's hands were tied; since he had an exclusive licensing agreement with Cobra, he couldn't execute a licensing agreement directly with G.T. Water or anyone else.

Infringement of Gene's 6,775,873 patent by G.T. Water soon ensued.

To its credit, Cobra initially defended Gene's patent by filing a patent infringement lawsuit against G.T. Water in July of 2011. However, when G.T. Water retaliated by filing for re-examination to invalidate the '873 patent's claims in September of 2011, Cobra became wobbly. Under Gene's licensing agreement, the exclusive licensee was committed to share the costs of defending the '873 patent equally with Gene. That commitment was not kept; Cobra elected not to participate in the defense of the '873 patent at the USPTO. Gene was forced to bear the total cost of those proceedings alone. Long and painful story short: Gene expended more than $250,000 over seven years before ultimately having 12 of the claims covering his Zip-It invalidated by the Patent Trial and Appeal Board in 2018. The 13th claim instituted before that tribunal (patent reissuance yielded Gene more claims) remained under invalidity attack at the PTAB in the beginning of 2019.

Postscript

What is at least equally as disturbing as the PTAB's wholesale revocation of the claims in Gene's patent is that Cobra began gearing up to produce and market knockoff Zip-It substitutes during the period of time in which re-examination was underway. At the time of my writing these pages, Cobra's Hair Drain Clog Remover and Snake Cleaning Tool is readily available to consumers. (It should be noted Cobra did not completely replace Gene's Zip-It with products that Gene believes are infringing his '873 patent. Rather, Cobra sells its infringing products alongside Zip-It. As of late 2018, Cobra was still remitting royalties to Gene based on its sales of Zip-It products.) Gene believes that the market is flooded with infringing products; some Chinese infringers make their products available through websites such as Alibaba and arrange for drop-shipping into the United States. Some infringers even have the gall to label their products Zip-It, a term for which Gene has secured trademark protection.

According to my discussions with Gene, infringing activity has already caused his royalty revenues to plunge as much as 80% from their peak. These reduced royalty payments make it harder for Gene's family to remain independent in light of their afflictions. The risk of the invalidation of all of Gene's patent claims threatens to completely eliminate Gene's royalties. In any event, Gene's '873 patent will expire in 2020.

Inventors bring the fire of invention while patent laws provide the environmental backdrop. The patent system can either provide the wind that enflames invention or it can extinguish the flame of invention by submerging patents in ill-conceived and unjust government tribunals. As we have seen from Gene's story and those of others, the patent system too often douses inventors' fire.

Inventor Builds A Better Raccoon Trap

Raccoons are cute. But don't be fooled by these beady-eyed bandits.

These wild animals leave damage and destruction in their wake. Raccoons devour cat food and bird feed. These sharp-clawed and sharp-toothed critters damage cornfields. Raccoons eat the high-protein food hunters leave for deer, so that their prey will be healthy and grow large antlers in time for prime hunting season. These rabies- and distemper-carrying mammals disfigure and stain decks. When they invade homes, raccoons tear up insulation surrounding pipes, rip insulation off of walls, and gnaw on wires. Raccoons are sufficiently fearsome to chase deer off of hunting reserves and kill chickens by chewing their heads off.

Raccoon traps have long been in existence, but many of them were rendered ineffective since they were susceptible to dogs, mice, and raccoons eating the bait and then escaping. A video of one raccoon turning a series of five Griz traps into a smorgasbord circulated on the Internet. Traps that enabled raccoons to maneuver their heads to their trapped feet were ineffective because raccoons will often bite off their feet in order to disentwine themselves from traps.

Traps of yesteryear would also frequently freeze in cold weather. How so? Raccoon trappers removed wet raccoons from the traps before resetting them. However, trappers were often not able to sufficiently clean out muddy traps after purging wet raccoons from the restraints. The residual mud would freeze, causing the restraint to freeze as well. This sequence of events allowed raccoons to eat the bait without consequence. Another problem with older traps freezing was that sometimes muddy raccoons could not be released, making it necessary to thaw out the raccoon before releasing its corpse and reusing the trap. Problems with ineffective raccoon traps were rampant.

Innovative Raccoon Traps

Carlis Stephens has dedicated much of his career to stopping raccoons in their tracks. He has been a raccoon trapper since he was 12-years-old. He even put himself through trade school—where he studied mechanics—by trapping raccoons.

Back in 2006, Carlis was determined to improve existing raccoon traps. In those days, raccoon traps were usually single-action, straight-trigger contraptions. That meant two things: First, single-action triggers were either pull triggers (that restrained the enticed animal when it caused the bait to be pulled upwards) or push triggers (which caused the restraints to grip the raccoons' paws when the raccoon stepped on the trigger). Second, straight triggers had narrow radii; animals were often able to sidestep the triggers en route to retrieving pelletized bait.

Carlis came up with a series of inventions that were incorporated into his line of Coon Dagger traps. His inventions included two-way, shaped triggers. Instead of capturing the animal with either push or pull triggers, Carlis invented dual (push-pull) triggers. Also, his ring-shaped triggers have broader radii compared to straight triggers. This activates more of the trigger's surface area when raccoons try to snatch bait out of cages.

Let's consider a few other points of differentiation between Carlis's traps and pre-existing traps. First, Carlis's raccoon traps are dog-proof; dogs simply cannot get their paws in the small opening of the Coon Dagger traps to activate the triggers. Since there was a risk of other traps ensnaring dogs, they had to be set in water where dogs were unlikely to set them off. However, since Carlis's traps are dog-proof, they can be placed on higher ground where the issue of drowning trapped raccoons is moot. Second, Carlis's traps are basically freeze-proof—they are much easier to clean out, and the restraints are on the outside of the housing.

Third, traditional traps featured U-shaped restraints that relied on tremendous spring pressure to restrain raccoons' paws. Carlis invented a diamond-shaped housing accompanied by a V-shaped restraining wire that wedges raccoons' paws on all four sides. Compared with older traps, Carlis's V-shaped restraining wire holds the trapped animal much firmer but with less spring pressure (or trauma) on their paws. Fourth, Carlis's traps were designed to be humane, at least in terms of preventing raccoons from chewing off their paws. Finally, the two-way triggers in the Coon Dagger traps can be set in safety mode.

Carlis's traps were no theoretical constructs. Carlis not only designed and manufactured the parts to assemble his traps, he also invested some $500,000 in producing the dyes necessary to make the parts. In total, Carlis invested roughly $750,000 in producing his Coon Dagger traps.

Destruction Through Drafting

With his invention reduced to practice, Carlis filed a non-provisional patent application on September 14, 2010, which later issued as U.S. Patent No. 8,484,886. The problem was that Carlis's Fargo, North Dakota-based patent lawyer dropped the ball. Repeatedly. The patent lawyer combined the V-shaped restraining wire and the exposed restraint in the same claim when those features should have been drafted as two independent claims. The lawyer did not claim the two-way shaped trigger which stopped the theft of bait, even though Carlis submitted notarized invention disclosures relative to this invention. Instead, the lawyer claimed the two-way *straight* trigger, which was prior art upon which Carlis's patent application was based. This two-way straight trigger later became the basis for the '642 patent (discussed below), which was issued to a competing raccoon trap-maker.

Carlis's traps accommodated interchangeable triggers. But the patent lawyer wrote claim 17 as "comprising...at least two interchangeable triggering assemblies..." This means that for a cage to infringe claim 17, it would have to have two triggering assemblies when the real invention was one triggering assembly. In other words, claim 17 gives a free pass to just about anyone who wanted to infringe since no other trap maker would see the need to include two interchangeable triggering assemblies in one trap.

Another avoidable mistake committed by Carlis's lawyer was that some prior art was not disclosed despite Carlis reporting such prior art to him. According to my discussions with Carlis, when his Fargo-based lawyer was asked why he did not disclose known pieces of prior art, the lawyer stated, "Doing so could have hurt Carlis's chances of receiving a patent."

Carlis pointed out these, and other drafting mistakes to his North Dakota-based lawyer. Despite his fee of more than $10,000, not all errors were corrected before the application issued. As a result, Carlis hired another lawyer who filed a better drafted application for a continuation patent on July 9, 2013. This application was issued on November 11, 2014, as U.S. Patent No. 8,881,447.

Raccoon Riches

The late 2000s and early 2010s were good for Carlis. Sales of his Coon Dagger raccoon traps were strong. Carlis had seven people producing as many as 900 traps each day, seven days a week. He was pulling in $30,000 to $40,000 at trade shows. Annual profits approximated $175,000 and were expected to surge another $100,000 once production went into full swing. At that time, Carlis wasn't much into banking: Cash was stashed in kitchen cabinets, in closets, under mattresses, and in drawers around the Stephens residence. The future looked so bright that Carlis convinced Linda, his wife, to retire from State Farm.

Not all of the visitors to Carlis's booths at trade shows were interested in purchasing Coon Dagger raccoon traps. In 2008, Neil P. Ziegmann of N.P.Z. Inc. showed up at the National Trappers Annual Convention in Mason City, Iowa, where Carlis had his traps available for sale. (During court proceedings, Mr. Ziegmann admitted as much. According to Carlis, "Mr. Ziegmann stated in litigation that he 'attends trade shows to find ideas to patent.'" A witness at trial reported that Mr. Ziegmann paid another trapper to demonstrate how to use the trap that Mr. Ziegmann claimed he invented.)

Shortly after the Mason City trade show in May of 2009, Mr. Ziegmann filed a provisional patent application for a two-way straight trigger trap. The invention claimed by this provisional patent application was essentially the prior art for Carlis's shaped trigger as described in his '886 patent. Mr. Ziegmann's so-called invention mirrored the trigger that Carlis displayed at the Mason City convention in 2008. This provisional patent application was issued to Mr. Ziegmann as U.S. Patent No. 8,230,642 on July 31, 2012. The claims contained in the '642 patent issued to Mr. Ziegmann were really the republication of prior art.

Suit, Countersuit

Mr. Ziegmann's '642 patent does not claim a two-way shaped trigger as Carlis's '447 patent does. But that didn't stop N.P.Z. from filing a patent infringement suit against Carlis in early 2012.

At about the same time, N.P.Z. began incorporating Carlis's push-pull, two-way trigger in its Z Traps. Subsequently, sales of N.P.Z.'s Z Traps were robust—N.P.Z. imported 383,000 foreign-produced traps in

2013 and reported that it sold 450,000 traps by 2014. Unlike Carlis, who produced his traps in Missouri where unit costs were more than $9.00, N.P.Z. arranged for the manufacturing of its traps offshore where costs per trap approximated $4.07. Resulting profits helped N.P.Z. fund its patent infringement suit against Carlis.

On multiple occasions in late 2014 and early 2015, Carlis notified N.P.Z. and other infringing merchants verbally and by email of their infringement of his '447 patent. (Carlis related to me that he even showed his '447 patent application to Mr. Ziegmann at the Fur Takers of America Annual Convention in Gilbert, Pennsylvania in June of 2013.) Carlis's informing the alleged infringers of their unauthorized use of his patent had no corrective effect on their behavior. Not only did their infringing activities continue unabated, but N.P.Z. amplified its misleading and false advertising campaigns. N.P.Z. filed suit against Carlis for patent infringement and resorted to falsely declaring that its Z Traps were covered by Mr. Ziegmann's '642 patent. In Carlis's recollection of the events, prior to November of 2014, Mr. Ziegmann was relating to people in the raccoon trapping business that Carlis's '447 patent application would not issue. Despite many knowing that the Coon Dagger traps were on the market (since 2010), some two years before the Z Traps (since 2012), some distributors were duped by this false marketing and misinformation. Those distributors and retailers that came to believe that Carlis was the infringer ceased selling Coon Dagger raccoon traps. It was against this backdrop that Carlis filed suit for patent infringement, unfair competition, and false advertising against N.P.Z. and a multitude of distributors on June 17, 2015, with the U.S. District Court in Eastern Missouri.

N.P.Z.'s patent infringement suit against Carlis and Carlis's suit to invalidate N.P.Z.'s '642 patent were both filed within one month of the other in the U.S. District Court in Eastern Missouri. It was Carlis's hope and expectation that these two lawsuits would be joined, but the judge separated them. Tremendous time and expenses would have been saved for the litigants and their witnesses if the cases were consolidated; the similarity in prior art and inventions would have made joining these cases logical.

Carlis Experiences Rotating Representation

How did Carlis fare in these separated litigations?

Let's first take a look at N.P.Z.'s suit against Carlis. Carlis needed to retain qualified counsel to mount his defense. He retained a Chicago-based law firm but paying their fees—which quickly approached $175,000—was a struggle. So, Carlis put a second mortgage on his house for $100,000 and mortgaged another piece of land that he owned for $40,000. He scrounged up another $35,000 by selling some of his vehicles and guns. Shortly after this fee was remitted, his law firm of record resigned from the matter.

At this point in time, Carlis found himself at the intersection of lacking legal representation and having only three months to respond to an *inter partes review* petition filed against his '447 patent. Having depleted the vast majority of his assets and in the midst of a downturn in the raccoon skin market, Carlis canvassed the country for a lawyer willing to represent him on a contingency basis. After a month of searching, he engaged David Duree, a lawyer based in St. Louis, Missouri.

With Mr. Duree's help, Carlis invalidated the first four claims listed on Mr. Ziegmann's '642 patent on grounds of both obviousness and anticipation. (Carlis may have been able to invalidate more of the '642 patent's claims had Mr. Ziegmann's attorney not caused the judge to believe that there was an agreement between the two men, whereby Carlis would be limited to attempting to invalidate just the first four claims listed in the '642 patent.) Remember, even if the claims in Mr. Ziegmann's '642 patent withstood the invalidity attempt, they still would not have claimed the two-way shaped triggers found on Carlis's Coon Dagger traps. In short, Carlis defeated N.P.Z.'s complaints accusing Carlis of infringing the '642 patent.

Litigation Drains Carlis Financially

The pyric victory left Carlis financially drained. The depletion of his financial resources was accelerated by N.P.Z. seizing on a variety of delaying tactics which further molasses-ized the slow-moving wheels of litigation. In one week during the litigation, N.P.Z. filed more than 40 motions. It took the court one year to rule on the first motion presented, and the case was stayed for about 18 months. The result is that litigation gobbled up valuable time and Carlis's money.

Carlis did have success defending his '447 patent from N.P.Z.'s efforts to invalidate it. N.P.Z. filed an *inter partes review* petition but the Patent Trial and Appeal Board refused to institute the case. As Carlis tells it, the PTAB reported that the patent examiner that initially reviewed his '447 patent application methodically considered, at the time of initial patent prosecution, all of the prior art presented in the *inter partes review* petition as well as many declarations from others in the raccoon trapping business. N.P.Z. did file a request for reconsideration of the institution of its *inter partes review* petition with an expanded panel. This request consumed another 18 months but was ultimately rejected. After issuing a 33-page precedential decision upholding Carlis's '447 patent, the judge lifted the stay in the case.

The Supreme Court's ruling in TC Heartland v. Kraft Foods Group Brands on May 22, 2017 further complicated Carlis's quest for justice. The Supreme Court's TC Heartland decision restricts corporations from filing lawsuits in their districts and instead requires lawsuits to take place in venues where alleged infringers have the home court advantage. The St. Louis judge ruled that Carlis's claims against his alleged infringers would have to be tried in eight different states. Such Balkanized litigation was impractical for Carlis due to the difficulties of recruiting local counsel in so many states as well as the time and expense of the anticipated litigations themselves. To their credit, many of the raccoon distributors and retailers that had infringed Carlis's '447 patent have recently agreed to halt their infringing activities.

Settlement is Reached

As a result of mediation that took place on August 27, 2018, N.P.Z. agreed to pay Carlis a token settlement. The puny royalty rate was applied to a royalty base of 100,000 infringing traps even though Mr. Ziegmann reported on a radio show called "Trapping Time" that N.P.Z. imported 383,000 traps just in the summer of 2013 and sold 450,000 (infringing) traps through 2014. Carlis plans to pay Mr. Duree a respectable portion of this settlement for his unflagging representation of his interests. It should be noted that Mr. Duree also suffered greatly during this ordeal; due to running a small law firm, he was not able to represent many other clients between 2015 and 2018. One of the catalysts for Carlis deciding to settle this litigation for far less than even the legal fees he sustained over the years was his being diagnosed with glioblastoma in August of 2017.

The infringement of his patents and Mr. Ziegmann's false and misleading statements about Carlis and his Coon Dagger traps battered Carlis's business. He was unable to have any injunctions imposed against his infringers. Carlis will not receive any damages beyond the settlement described above. There is no prospect that infringers will pay Carlis's attorneys' fees. There is no hope for Carlis receiving treble damages.

Mr. Ziegmann and N.P.Z. have prospered at Carlis's expense. In light of avoiding paying royalties and in view of N.P.Z. manufacturing its Z Traps in China, N.P.Z. has been selling its Z Traps for roughly 25% less than Carlis's Coon Dagger traps. While Carlis is struggling to keep his house, Mr. Ziegmann has reportedly been buying property and building new private residences.

Reflections from a Repartee with a Raccoon Raconteur

Throughout his travails with the patent system, Carlis has gained command of the patenting process. In his Warrenton, Missouri twang he is able to articulately, and in great detail, distinguish his inventions from prior art. He understands the utility of independent claims versus dependent claims. He can expertly recite the differences between examiner rejections based on anticipation versus obviousness. He knows how continuation patents work. He grasps quite a bit about inequitable conduct, office actions, summary motions, requests for continued examinations, *inter partes review* petitions, and declaratory judgments. Carlis's self-education into so many nuances of the U.S. patent system is extremely impressive. But his being forced to educate himself on arcane patent issues to such a degree is also a waste. Had Carlis been able to continue inventing instead of defending his patents, raccoons would wreak less damage, his business would be more vibrant, and he would employ more American workers. The country would have benefitted more from his ingenuity.

Carlis is clearly an irrepressible inventor. He was ill-served by his first patent lawyer. He was sued by his infringer. The same infringer tried to invalidate Carlis's patent by filing a petition for *inter partes review*. He was the victim of false and malicious misinformation. Carlis placed a second mortgage on his house, mortgaged his remaining plot of land, and sold vehicles and guns to pay a litigation law firm that resigned from the case shortly after receiving its $175,000 fee. He would have lost his house had his disability insurance not kicked in. At the time of my writing these pages, infringing traps were intermittently being sold on eBay and Amazon. The Supreme Court's TC Heartland decision made litigating against alleged infringers in a multitude of disparate states unaffordable and unviable.

Not long after Carlis's fleeting financial success as a raccoon trap-maker afforded him the ability to retire his wife, she was diagnosed with leukemia. In August of 2017, Carlis was diagnosed with glioblastoma, the same terminal disease that took the life of the late Senator John McCain. Carlis underwent two surgeries—one on August 6, 2017, and one on April 6, 2018—whose missions were to eradicate his brain tumor. Carlis suffered strokes during both procedures. The second stroke occurred when a laser, inserted into a hole drilled into his head, hit a live nerve. He has now lost most of the use of the left side of his body. But none of that is stopping Carlis.

Despite all of the adversity he has suffered, Carlis recently filed a new patent application unrelated to raccoon trapping. Carlis's new invention? In September of 2018, Carlis filed a patent application that claims an apparatus which eliminates all of the shock associated with driving a stake in the ground when hitting it with a sledge hammer. However, since Carlis's newest patent application is his fifth, he will have to pay higher filing fees as he no longer qualifies as a micro-entity filer.

I learned quite a bit from my many discussions with Carlis. And not just about raccoons, raccoon traps, and patents. I learned that inventorship is not relegated to the small part of the population whose names appear on patents. Ideas, initiative, and inventorship lie in every individual. The USPTO's patenting process as well as the laws and judicial decisions governing patents can either embolden inventorship or suppress it. I also learned from my interactions with Carlis that all segments of the economy, no matter how small or how remote, stand to benefit from innovations, even raccoon trapping.

Shoot First, Rationalize Later

Americans with disabilities are usually in need of financial assistance. Fortunately, there are government programs designed to provide these vulnerable citizens with financial support. Adults who become disabled before the age of 22 qualify for Social Security Disability Insurance (SSDI). And once they quality for SSDI they also are entitled to receive Medicare benefits. Receiving these tandem benefits can boost a disabled person's fortunes; failing to receive this package of financial assistance can lead to a precipitous plunge in the quality of life and medical options.

Whether a disabled adult receives the SSDI and Medicare benefits to which he is entitled hinges on one of his working parents retiring, becoming disabled or dying. Except in the case of death, that parent must register the disabled adult child when applying for his own Social Security retirement benefits.[73]

The social security regime befuddles most Americans. Thus, it is not surprising that there are a multitude of circumstances where a parent neglects to list a disabled adult child on his social security application. First, many people simply do not think of listing disabled adult children on their Social Security retirement paperwork. Maybe the child has been out-of-sight and out-of-mind—the disabled adult child may have been institutionalized for decades. It may also seem illogical to include a disabled adult child on a retirement application because that child may never have worked.

Second, the working parent may have divorced the custodial spouse and have lost contact with the disabled child many years earlier. In some divorce cases, the custodial parent may not have known of the non-custodial

[73] In the event the wage earner passes away, the responsibility for notifying the Social Security Administration falls on a family member or care provider who may not even be aware that the decedent was the parent of a disabled adult. Often, no one looks after the decedent's social security benefits.

parent's death; consequently, no application for the disabled adult child's SSDI benefit is filed. Third, the working parent may intentionally and fraudulently omit the disabled adult child; depriving this individual of his benefits results in the reallocation of benefits to other members of the household.

The costs of disabled adult children being deprived of their SSDI and Medicare benefits are far reaching. According to an Ohio State University study, 11.7% of qualified recipients fall through administrative cracks. These disabled adults have less income and fewer medical treatment options. As a result, they may have to move out of their communities or be placed on waiting lists for inclusion in preferable facilities. The provisioning of inappropriate treatment settings for disabled adults is often cited as grounds for the United States Justice Department filing lawsuits against the states. (Under the Americans with Disabilities Act, providing deficient treatment settings violates the civil rights and liberties of the disabled.) Additionally, overpaying for Medicaid coverage due to the lack of Medicare coverage is extremely costly for the federal and state governments.

Patenting a Solution to a Decades Old Problem

The professionals at the Social Security Administration, as well as disability attorneys, have been trying to solve the problem of SSDI benefits oversights since the inception of the SSDI program in 1956. Jeff Killian knows a great deal about these oversights as he served for many years as the Social Security Liaison between the Ohio Department of Developmental Disabilities and the Social Security Administration. In 2013, Jeff (who is the founder of Automated Benefit Solutions, LLC) invented a process for calking the administrative cracks through which disabled adult children fall.

On February 26, 2014, Jeff filed a provisional patent application outlining his solution for uncovering overlooked disabled adults who are entitled to benefits under SSDI. He filed his non-provisional patent application, which is numbered 14/450,042, with the United States Patent and Trademark Office on August 1, 2014.

Jeff's patent application covers three inventive concepts. The first concept is to identify which disabled adults have possibly been overlooked. This is accomplished by cross-referencing a particular state's Medicaid records (logging who is of advanced age, mentally ill or developmentally disabled) with those in the Medicaid population who are not receiving SSDI benefits. Jeff's invention removes those citizens who are 65 years of age and above from this population pool because they—as well as people with financial needs—qualify for Medicaid. The cross-referencing capability detailed in Jeff's patent application eliminates the need to investigate the 97% of the population that is not disabled. His process can function across of all fifty states.

The next challenge, or second inventive step, that Jeff's invention tackles is the issue of checking records of disabled adults without being burdened with obtaining consent from such individuals (or their caregivers) each time their records are inspected. How did Jeff legally and gingerly skirt the onus of obtaining consents? He realized that states have the authority to investigate Medicaid compliance and fraud since Medicaid is the payer of last resort. By fusing with the states' Medicaid investigative authority, Jeff's invention entails conducting audits and reviews of disabled adults' Medicaid records to determine if they should receive SSDI benefits. An additional benefit of Jeff's review of records is that parents or caregivers do not have to bring the disabled adult child (and his records) to a social security office to determine if benefits are available. Jeff's invention does all the pre-screening for the disabled person's entire lifetime. The prior art (or current procedure) is a "one and done" process that overlooks a triggering event for benefits if the timing of that one review is not conducted at the precise time of disability, retirement or death.

The third leg of Jeff's invention, or third inventive step, is an improvement over the current practice of monitoring disabled adults. Checking the status of a disabled person's SSDI eligibility—or summoning them to Social Security offices—is severely burdensome for the disabled individual as well as for his case workers. It is also cost prohibitive. Disability attorney's fees are capped at $6,000 for assisting their clients secure SSDI benefits. Scanning and verifying the disposition of disabled subjects too frequently causes disability attorneys to lose money and exhausts case workers. Instead, Jeff's invention calls for setting alerts that are activated when the working parents of disabled children retire, become disabled or pass away. Thus, Jeff's invention, which tracks the parent, not the disabled adult, eliminates the longstanding practice of bringing disabled adult children to the social security office where medical records are reviewed and applications for SSDI are presented. Schlepping a disabled adult child to a social security office is no easy task for a disabled or retiring parent or a caseworker. Worse still, as discussed above, not all parents file for SSDI benefits for their disabled adult children.

Killing Jeff Killian's Patent Application

Not only had no one ever designed a way to perform all three of the inventive steps disclosed in Jeff's patent application, no one ever performed any of these inventive steps. Moreover, no state even collects the information necessary to determine the identity of working parents of adult children. To demonstrate this point to his patent examiner, Jeff provided the patent office with a Social Security benefit application, a Social Security handbook and Medicaid applications from all 50 states.

When Jeff filed his patent application, he further documented the novelty and non-obviousness of his invention by submitting two independent third-party studies from researchers in the field of Social Security benefit administration. One of these researchers, Thomas Bush from Marquette University, had 35 years of experience. The other lead researcher, Barry Jamieson from Ohio State University, had 25 years of experience. Under the direction of the Ohio Colleges of Medicine, Government Resource Center, investigators from Ohio State University attempted to identify disabled adults who were overlooked by SSDI and Medicare. The researchers found it exceedingly difficult to identify who was overlooked. When they beckoned qualified subjects to come forward over a 24-month period, only 358 individuals presented themselves. In addition to a very small sample size, the Ohio researchers had to contend with obtaining consents and regularly scouring the state for individuals inappropriately deprived of SSDI benefits. In short, the Ohio researchers failed to make the current art work and discontinued their efforts after two years.

Along with his patent application, Jeff presented a mountain of evidence attesting to his novel and non-obvious invention. Nevertheless, in its July 27, 2016 first office action, the USPTO notified Jeff that his patent application was being rejected on the grounds that his process is an abstract idea that is "routine, well understood and conventional." The following are among the concerns one should have with the examiner's rejection of Jeff's patent application:

- Neither disabled adult children of Social Security claimants nor the SSDI benefits to which they are entitled are abstract. The needs they have and the consequences they suffer from falling outside of the purview of SSDI are real. So too is Jeff's three-pronged approach for detecting those disabled individuals who have been overlooked.

- The documentation that Jeff provided to the patent office along with his patent application attest that none of his patent claims have ever been performed by the Social Security Administration or disability attorneys. If no one else has done what Jeff describes in his claims, his process cannot be "routine, well understood or conventional." Further, Jeff's invention does not address routine processes but rather searches for disabled adults who have failed to be included in routine procedures. In other words, family members and professionals would necessarily have made oversights for Jeff's invention to kick-in.

- In supporting his decision to reject Jeff's patent application, the examiner cited court cases that have nothing to do with Jeff's field of technology. For instance, Alice Corp. v. CLS Bank International dealt with electronic escrow services for facilitating financial transactions while Electric Power Group, LLC v. Alstom S. A. addressed the eligibility of patents that cover simply analyzing data. Neither of these referenced inventions solved a known problem. Rather, a generic computer was slapped on an existing solution.

It seems that patent examiners have developed an allergic reaction to any patent applications that contain a whiff of software or business methods. Their rejections of such on grounds of their representing merely "abstract ideas that are routine, well understood and conventional" has reached epidemic proportions. Examiners cutting-and-pasting this trope in their rejections of patent applications have become such a reflexive response to any semblance of software or business methods inventions that examiners no longer bother with citing facts or evidence to support their contentions. Indeed, USPTO Director Iancu has extended the Berkheimer v. HP Inc. decision to patent examination. In this decision, the Federal Court held that the question of whether a claim element is "well-understood, routine, and conventional" under Alice is a question of fact and requires evidentiary support.

Since this initial rejection, Jeff has narrowed the scope of his patent application to emphasize that his invention searches for "overlooked" disabled adults who qualify for SSDI. Should his patent application issue with this revision, an infringer would have to serve an "overlooked" disabled adult child using the very "first ever" steps Jeff disclosed to the public as required by patent regulations.

While prosecution of Jeff's patent application trudges along, his prospects for commercializing his invention are dissipating; so too are the opportunities to assist disabled adults financially and treatment-wise. Shortly after the publication of his patent application, Jeff was approached by three Fortune 100 companies involved with Medicaid integration. They initially expressed an interest in building a national network to remedy the problems disclosed in Jeff's patent application. But it is virtually certain that Medicaid integrators will not invest tens of millions of dollars building out a national network if they lack patent protection. This is especially true when state governments award contracts. Without patent protection, changes in control of state legislatures could easily result in contracts being reassigned to other vendors. One large potential licensee of Jeff's pending patent reported that it executed a non-disclosure agreement with Jeff but, once it learned of the examiner's rejections, declined to return the NDA to him.

Postscript Regarding Patent Lawyers

I like patent lawyers. Some of my best friends and referral sources are patent lawyers. Some have been of invaluable help to me in writing this book. However, patent lawyers sometimes fail to see the forest for the trees. They become so engrossed in splitting legal hairs that they fail to see that those hairs belong to a severed head.

Patent lawyers may cite some statute or court decision to rationalize the examiner (at least initially) rejecting Jeff's patent application. (And maybe Jeff's patent application will issue; rejections of patent applications are to be expected during prosecution.) What those same patent lawyers may fail to realize is how ridiculous it is to deprive Jeff of his patent, especially when the solution claimed by that patent can save substantial tax dollars, improve quality of life and mitigate lawsuits. Jeff's unfortunate patent experience is even more ludicrous when considering that one branch of the federal government (the United States Patent and Trademark Office) is compromising the goals and objectives of two other branches of federal government (Social Security Administration and Centers for Medicare and Medicaid Services) with an analysis that is illogical and not factual.

Allow me to use very unintellectual prose to describe the folly of rejecting Jeff's patent application. "You have a problem that reduces the quality of life of millions of vulnerable people. You have an inventor who has a remedy for this problem and that remedy is not naturally occurring. If ain't nobody never solved that problem before, then the guy who solved the problem is entitled to patent his invention."

If the current patent regime does not support this simple notion, then it is the patent regime that is in need of change. The purpose of patent law is to incentivize and diffuse innovation, not to provide an intellectual romper room in which the cerebrally curious are invited to indulge in philosophy and etymology.

I would like to add another note regarding patent lawyers. There are instances where inventors are less than adequately served by their patent lawyers; sometimes patent lawyers simply do not understand the underlying technology well enough to draft related patent applications. In other cases, the blame belongs with the presumptive patentees; sometimes (typically large) companies negotiate such miserly rates with law firms that the patent lawyers cannot be expected to invest significant time in drafting and prosecuting related patent applications.

An Unbelievably High Price to Pay for A Million Dollars

Wayne Evans was born into poverty in the heart of the Great Depression in 1935. Soon enough he would be deprived of things much more valuable than material possessions. He was abandoned by his father when he was a child and he lost his stepfather and eldest brother in World War II.

As a precocious child, Wayne was fascinated with electronics, especially anything to do with radio communications. He pursued these interests with rigor as he became a young man. He studied electrical engineering at a trade school in Indiana and supported himself by working a midnight shift at a radio station. During his enlistment in the military, Wayne studied microwave communications and became a military instructor on that subject. He was honored with the Outstanding Instructor Award in 1957 and the military bestowed him with the Outstanding Soldier Award in 1959. After completing his military service, Wayne earned an electrical engineering degree with honors from Purdue University.

After graduating in 1965, he spent the first 13 years of his post-graduate career with RCA, which at the time was the world's leading consumer electronics company. At RCA, Wayne invented and obtained more than 10 patents on a number of groundbreaking innovations, including the first use of an integrated circuit in a consumer device, the first transistor in a color TV receiver, and the first prototype of a wristwatch wireless communicator.

Wayne had at least one disappointing experience with the USPTO during his tenure with RCA. Back in the 1960s, television reception wasn't great. Pictures were often fuzzy, screens were filled with squiggly lines, and sound was corrupted with static. To correct these kinds of problems, you had to walk over to the television and fiddle with the knobs and twiddle with the antennas. Once you took a step away from the TV, the problem often returned. Correcting poor reception was far from scientific and permanent.

Wayne knew there must be a more convenient and reliable way to correct these kinds of reception problems. His diagnosis was that the receptivity issues were caused by a big slope in television signals; there was too much frequency on one side and not enough frequency on the other side. Wayne determined that the solution for such lopsided signals was an amplifier that would greatly amplify the signal where it was weak and lightly amplify the signal where it was too strong. This discovery was reduced to a remote-controlled television reception modulation device.

On June 2, 1969, Wayne filed an application that was titled Automatic Fine-Tuning Circuitry. The examiner's reception to this patent application was worse than that of most owners of color television sets. The examiner basically accused Wayne of committing fraud upon the patent office when he held that his application addressed a nonexistent problem. Three days of discussions ensued, whereby Wayne tried to impress upon the examiner that virtually every owner of a television set was regularly confronted by the receptivity problems addressed in his patent application. Fortunately, this obtuse and obstinate patent examiner was replaced with another who immediately understood the novelty of Wayne's invention. Wayne's patent application issued on November 9, 1971 as U.S. Patent No. 3,619,492.

After 13 years with RCA, Wayne joined General Electric. His position at that conglomerate was eliminated four years later in 1981, when the country was plunged into a recession. Wayne would soon feel the pangs of losing the security, social stature, and compensation associated with being employed by a large company.

Whenever Wayne patented his inventions during his employment with RCA and GE, he had to assign them over to his employer. In return, he would receive a $100 bonus and a roast beef dinner. Some might say that such remuneration was exploitive to Wayne and his fellow inventors. I do not share these sentiments. I don't know the terms of Wayne's employment with these large companies but he must have received a respectable salary, health care coverage, stock grants, paid vacation, company-paid travel, and a slew of other benefits that employees of large companies take for granted. Being employed by these large companies also enabled Wayne the opportunity to use state-of-the-art research equipment and relieved him of the burden of paying the fees associated with filing and prosecuting his patent applications. He never had to pay for any of the research initiatives that failed to produce results. Also, Wayne knew how his inventions would be handled when he accepted employment at those companies; if he didn't like the terms, he didn't have to accept the job offers. Indeed, Wayne never regretted assigning his patents to companies that were affording him the ability to create comfort for his family.

On His Own

During the 34 years separating 1981 from 2015, Wayne's plight vacillated from scraping by to downright penury.

Shortly after being laid off from GE, Wayne was hired as a supervisory technician at Electronics Systems International, an energy management company. Much of his work at ESI consisted of supervising production lines. Dealing with minor production glitches and line workers' personal issues was much less intellectually stimulating than the research he had recently conducted at RCA and GE. This position also paid significantly less than what Wayne was earning at his previous places of employment. (This fact supports my argument that not much sympathy need be directed to Wayne regarding his receiving $100 bonuses and roast beef dinners when RCA and GE filed patent applications on his inventions.)

Before too long, ESI's management saw that Wayne was capable of much more; soon he was charged with developing smart thermostats. One of Wayne's inventions along these lines was an electronic thermostat that required no wiring and far less energy to operate compared to other thermostats in the market at the time. One of the unique features of this innovative thermostat was that it could be programmed to turn itself off when not in use.

In 1983, ESI filed a patent application in connection with the zero-power thermostat, as Wayne's novel thermostat was called. The lawyer who drafted the patent application claimed that the invention reduced power consumption by 20%. Wayne argued that the disclaiming phrase "up to" be placed between "by" and "20%." Wayne's advice went unheeded; the patent application was filed as the lawyer drafted it.

Shortly thereafter, the Department of Housing and Urban Development conducted tests which held that the energy savings afforded by the zero-power thermostats was 19.5%. The media picked up on the discrepancy between the 20% savings claimed in the patent application and the 19.5% energy reduction reported by HUD. As a result of the media relentlessly lambasting ESI for its so-called deceptive claims, that company's business dried up. As the nation was enveloped by building contractor scandals in the early 1980s, contractors and building owners avoided any products that were tainted by even a whiff of scandal like the plague. When ESI went bankrupt, Wayne lost the entire $25,000 he invested in ESI, money which he derived from his stock grants from RCA and GE. Wayne dreaded having to deliver the bad news to his wife, Annie.

A lesson to be learned is that a poorly drafted patent can lead to the demise of an entire company.

One Step Backwards, Many More Steps Backwards

Fortunately, Wayne saw the writing on ESI's wall before that company imploded. By the time that ESI folded, Wayne had already lined up a new endeavor. In 1984, he became an independent contractor for AT&T, which was rolling out emergency call dialers for homes. Homeowners that had the dialers installed were provided pendants that loosely resembled cell phones. When an emergency arose, the wearer could press a button on the pendant and a call would be placed through the dialer to a designated third-party. A synthetic voice would communicate appropriately chosen prerecorded messages to the recipients of those distressed calls. Wayne had to purchase these systems from AT&T and then hawk them door-to-door. When he made a sale, he would be required to install the system. This was a purely commission-driven venture. The remaining boxes of emergency call dialers that lie in the Evans' house today serve as reminders of this failed venture.

Wayne invested what was left of his modest savings and retirement funds in BioTronics, his next venture. BioTronics revolved around his patented invention called "All Code Receiver," a location tracking technology that loosely resembled an improvement to AT&T's call dialer systems. Under

Wayne's stewardship, BioTronics was successfully deployed in a 50-acre elder care campus in Naples, Florida. This location tracking technology was installed in each apartment and placed around the necks of every willing resident in the form of a pendant. The scanners positioned throughout the facility would send signals to nurses' stations, notifying them of the identity and location of elderly residents in need of emergency care. The work that BioTronic performed for the Naples installation was covered by a $2 million contract. Then the first Gulf War broke out. Concurrently, the banking crisis of the early 1990s erupted. Loans were being recalled and businesses were slashing capital investments. BioTronics' contract with the Naples facility was broken, causing BioTronics to become insolvent in 1991.

A few years later a company called Care Technology came along and took an interest in acquiring what was a barely revived version of BioTronics. One of the conditions that Care Technology placed on its acquisition of BioTronics was that Wayne would have to leave. Care Technology threatened to abandon its contemplated acquisition of BioTronics and the senior facilities it served if Wayne refused to leave or if he insisted on receiving any compensation, regardless of the sum or form of such compensation. While Wayne wanted some remuneration for the contribution he made to BioTronics, he didn't want to see his inventions vaporize or the seniors who relied on them deprived of their life-saving functionalities.

Wayne decided to walk away with nothing of any value. He resigned himself to allowing Care Technology to use his patents on a royalty-free basis. The only thing Wayne wanted to take with him was a stock certificate, simply as a memento. Care Technology threatened to sue Wayne unless he returned that stock certificate. When he refused, Care Technology's lawyers revoked the shares represented by that stock certificate. Wayne was again humiliated to have to relate this financial tragedy to Annie.

Wayne lost his entire investment in BioTronics. When he lost his house in the early 1990s, he and Annie had to move in with their daughter and two grandchildren for several months. The couple did whatever they could to bring in money. Annie took on two jobs. In what could have passed for a reenactment of scenes from the movie *House of Sand and Fog*, Wayne took on manual and menial work (such as plastering walls) while wearing business attire so that he would look presentable when discussing new ventures with business associates later in the day.

Things Begin to Stabilize

Wayne had to land better paying work. Fortunately, when he was with BioTronics, he became familiar with a company called Car Cop. This company was involved with enabling vehicle tracking via cellular towers. As part of his consultancy with Car Cop, Wayne worked with a South African company where he was in charge of converting vehicle tracking systems from an analog cellular system to a digital one. Within a few years of the Car Cop project coming to an end, Wayne became busy developing GPS systems to track school buses for a company called Bus Call. This consultancy project petered out within 18 months but did afford Wayne the opportunity to hone his expertise with GPS technology. Wayne's involvement with Car Cop and Bus Call were relatively positive experiences; he was paid something for his services, and since he no longer had any investment capital, he didn't lose anything when those two companies folded.

Wayne was never again fully employed once he completed his engagement with Bus Call in 1996. By holding down several technical jobs, Annie kept the couple afloat. In the late 1990s, Wayne spent quite a bit of time taking care of his mother—first at her senior living home in Florida and then at his home when he moved her to Atlanta. Wayne did inherit a bit of money when his mother passed away in November of 1999, but it took him—performing the duties of an executor—three years of legal maneuvering to claw away the money bequeathed to him and his sister from his step-siblings. Around this time, Wayne's health was deteriorating. In 2000, he injured his lower back. Shortly thereafter he suffered a mini-stroke. Then he fell backwards, cracked his head, and sustained a concussion. The money that Wayne inherited from his mother was far from sufficient to properly address his mounting medical setbacks.

The Beginnings of a Promising Patent

When he wasn't looking after his mother or serving as the executor of her estate, Wayne occupied himself by researching his ideas relating to location and positioning technologies. By this time, Wayne had decades of experience with such technologies. But his passion for coming up with advances in GPS technology was fueled by his concern for one of his nephews who was born deaf and mute. Wayne was particularly concerned about this young man as he approached driving age. What would happen if this deaf and mute driver found himself in a stressful situation such as an accident? He wouldn't be able to communicate with anyone. General Motors was working on a system that would allow drivers to interact with an operator if an emergency arose, but such "caller assist" technologies wouldn't help deaf or mute drivers. So Wayne, now in his sixties, invested about $50,000 researching technologies related to vehicle-tracking GPS. His fields of study included solid-state memory systems and prototype chips. He came up with four inventions that he believed were worth patenting but ended up filing three patent applications.

One of the patent applications was filed with the USPTO on June 12, 2000. To finance this and two other patenting efforts, Wayne loaded up his credit cards and asked the patent agent who was helping him to defer his fees. Just a little over a year later, on July 24, 2001, this patent application issued as U.S. Patent No. 6,266,617.

The patent application clearly stated, "In 1967, the Global Positioning System (GPS) became commercially available." So, what was novel about Wayne's patent? Well, his invention enabled automatic vehicle location, collision notification, and synthetic voice communication to selected recipients directly from the vehicle. Embedded in the invention was a latitudinal and longitudinal database with software capable of correlating GPS coordinates with street intersections. The invention obviated the need for a base-station operator to relay messages. It was specifically geared towards people who are physically impaired and who desire to communicate their present vehicle navigation position to third parties. Importantly, Wayne's invention was designed to allow third parties (such as first responders and highway safety researchers) to interrogate the system via a black box that could be connected to the vehicle via the port for cigarette lighters.

Wayne Attempts a Rebound

What did Wayne do after his '617 patent issued in July of 2001? Wayne was flat broke. How could he not be? He sold his stocks and liquidated his retirement funds in failed ventures. He maxed out his credit cards and deferred payments to his patent agent to develop his inventions and file his patent applications. He had no money to market his inventions at trade shows or to hire promoters. Whatever network of corporate executives he may have once maintained withered to the point of nonexistence. He knew nothing about creating websites or launching social media campaigns.

Wayne did what he could; he formulated a list of individuals and companies that might be interested in licensing his patents. His overtures to targeted companies that could best use his inventions were met with silence. Wayne turned his attention to raising capital. He created marketing materials and scheduled calls and meetings to pitch his prototypes and patents. He networked as aggressively as he could at inventor meetings and angel investor clubs. But time and time again, each group would bow out and leads would go cold. The frequency of Wayne having to deliver bad news to Annie never made the task any less dreadful.

Then, during the late summer of 2001, Wayne met an angel investor that was prepared to invest $500,000 in helping him commercialize his GPS-related inventions. Terms were agreed upon and a date was set for signing the investment agreements. On the appointed morning in mid-September of 2001, Wayne arrived at the designated conference room. CNN was quietly airing on the television set in the background. The agreements were placed on the conference table and pens were readied. As Wayne and his investor sat down to execute the agreements, the first plane struck the World Trade Center. Everyone in the room shifted their attention to the television. As the worst terrorist tragedy in history unfolded on the screen, Wayne's investor withdrew his intentions to help fund Wayne's commercialization efforts. Once again, Wayne would have to disappoint his loyal wife.

Once again, defeat seemed inevitable. What was even worse was watching hundreds of companies deploy his patented technology. It was painful to spend a decade witnessing so many companies prospering from the growing prevalence of his telematic inventions, including those that automatically recognize street intersections.

As Wayne approached his seventies in the early 2000s and then his mid-seventies in the late 2000s, he came to realize that no one was going to amicably pay him a cent for the use of his patents. If he was to see any money from his life's work, he would have to become much more aggressive. But how much of a threat could a near penniless septuagenarian in poor health pose to scores of the biggest companies in the world? Battling foes with endless budgets and ferocious lawyers seemed to be a recommendation for disaster.

A Knight in Shining Armor Emerges

And then one day in 2010, a young patent lawyer by the name of Gautham (Gau) Bodepudi gave Wayne a call.[74]

After some cordial chit-chat, Gau made Wayne an offer: IP Edge, Gau's newly founded company, would spearhead the monetization of his patents without Wayne having to invest a dime. Wayne would make himself available to address technical questions that would arise. IP Edge would do everything else—make contact with the alleged infringers, prepare claims charts and gather other evidence of use, negotiate with the infringers, and, if necessary, initiate patent infringement suits. Wayne would get a large and fair share of the monies recovered. All of this sounded great to Wayne but he was concerned about pegging his share of the recoveries to net proceeds. The tremendous work necessary to receive recoveries would trigger an eruption of costs. Wayne was rightfully fearful that he wouldn't see much money at the end of the day. (In my experience, one resolution to such an impasse is to base the patentee's recoveries on gross proceeds.) This issue was readily ironed out and Wayne and IP Edge arrived at a mutually beneficial agreement.

After all Wayne had been through, Gau must have seemed like a knight in shining armor to Wayne. Indeed, Gau proved to be a brilliant and persistent patent lawyer as well as a prince of a gentleman. However, back in 2010, Gau's armor was not as imposing as it may have seemed. As a result of a reduction in patent litigation, both Gau and Lillian Woung, his business partner, were recently laid-off patent attorneys when they formed IP Edge back in early 2010. Neither Gau nor Lillian had any money or experience in commercializing patents. In fact, Gau was upside down on his mortgage. He had to sell his house short and move in with his parents. No revenues hit IP Edge's books for its entire first year of operations.

But IP Edge was eager to make a splash in monetizing patents. To identify candidate patents worthy of their representation, the partners scanned patent databases for well-crafted patents whose technology was being infringed. They also limited their patent review to those patents owned by individual inventors, based on the theory that lone patent assignees would be much more amenable to monetizing their patents than

---

[74] Actually, this call was made by Gau's colleague, Sanjay Pant; I didn't want to complicate the storyline.

corporations. After suitable patents were screened, Gau went about trying to contact the inventors, a crucial step and more difficult than you might expect.

The Campaign to Monetize Wayne's Patents

Monetizing Wayne's patents wasn't easy. Wayne was opposed to becoming involved in litigation. He was nearing 80 years of age and his health was giving out. He didn't want to be deposed or called to serve as a witness in court.

Directly approaching infringers, no matter how gingerly, was highly risky. At a minimum, many large companies ignore demand letters and evidence of their infringement. Directly accusing a company of infringing runs the risk of those companies filing declaratory judgment actions. In these proceedings, the roles of the plaintiffs and defendants are largely reversed; the accused infringer can initiate the declaratory judgment in the court of his choosing at the time of his choosing. And once declaratory judgments are filed, the judge can quickly rule that the asserted patent is either not infringed or is invalid.

Gau took adhering to Wayne's wishes to avoid litigation to heart. He did everything he could to bring patent buyers, infringers, and potential licensees to the negotiating table. IP Edge created an extensive slide deck of marketing material illustrating the widespread market applicability of Wayne's patents. To whomever would listen, Gau and his team illustrated how Wayne's patents mapped to in-unit telematics, personal navigation devices, smartphones with GPS applications, docking stations, and other technology areas. IP Edge appealed to potential licensees and buyers all over North America and even as far away as Europe. Sadly, no group presented an offer to license or acquire Wayne's patents. Despite the risks of trying to reach licensing agreements amicably, at the end of two years IP-Edge had nothing to show for its exhaustive good-faith efforts.

If Wayne was to receive any money for his patents, Gau's extended hand would have to be placed inside of a boxing glove. Litigation, or the threat of litigation, would be needed to recover money from the infringers. Sometimes the only way to force an alleged infringer to review their possible use of patents is to present them with formal complaints. Wayne assigned his patents to NovelPoint Tracking, a new company that Gau formed. Then Gau hired at least three contingency-based patent litigators to approach the alleged infringers about paying for their past infringement and taking licenses for future use of the patents that Wayne created. From this point on, the patent litigators did most of the heavy lifting. Gau, and to a lesser extent Wayne, supported their efforts by producing evidence of infringement and patent validity.

The patent litigators working on a contingency basis took on massive risk. The small firms that joined forces with IP Edge and Wayne generated no fees and were exposed to fronting significant expenses related to the patent litigation. Patent litigation is a long-term affair and the negative cash flow can destroy a contingency patent litigator's practice. And unlike most other service providers, lawyers cannot withdraw from a client engagement so easily. Motions to withdraw from a case have to be presented to the court. These motions can be rejected, forcing the litigator to lose money and perhaps even become insolvent.

At Last, A Victory

The decision to take a tougher position—that is, to initiate litigation—bore fruit. After roughly seven decades of research into locationing technologies, 34 years of a series of business failures, 15 years from the time of his filing for his '617 patent, and five years of asserting patents in the '617 patent family, with Gau's help, Wayne finally got something. From what I can gather, the portion of the assertion efforts that Wayne received in 2015 was approximately $1 million. (Neither Wayne nor Gau would tell me exactly how much money Wayne received. I hope he received a full $1 million. I hope that Wayne was not rounding up his portion when speaking with me but I will assume that he received a round $1 million.)

When I spoke to Wayne, he gushed about the million dollars that I estimate he received. I am happy that he is happy with the $1 million. After all that he has endured over so many years, he deserves every penny of that $1 million. A million dollars was a fortune in the depths of the recession. But a million dollars just doesn't go that far these days. After paying taxes on his $1 million in income, he was able to restore his retirement accounts a bit and sleep a little easier. Wayne and Annie were delighted that they could help their son open a music store. They were also pleased that they were in a position to help their granddaughter buy a restaurant. (Unfortunately, both of these businesses have since closed their doors.)

The 85 infringers that accounted for what I am modeling as Wayne's

$1 million windfall didn't pay much. On average, they would have paid less than $11,800 each or about $840 a year since the '617 patent issued in 2001. Many of the infringers continue to use Wayne's patents but will not pay a dime more.

Vituperative Reaction to Wayne's Long Delayed Success

There were no parades for Wayne. No honorifics were bestowed upon him. He never received a key to his home city of Alpharetta, Georgia. He never became a celebrity. That is to be expected and, perhaps, as it should be. Wayne is grateful that his patent journey ended the way it did. He is appreciative of the fact that most small inventors never have anything resembling a happy ending.

Wayne never expressed a bit of bitterness in the hours that he spent relating his story to me. Gau was also extremely gentlemanly in his depiction of the events that transpired in connection with Wayne's story up to this point and beyond. I will take the story from here in a different tone.

As a result of his success, residual to that which he is deserving, Wayne's patents have been the subject of scathing attacks. Perhaps unbeknownst to Wayne, he has been lumped into a group that is commonly demonized as being patent trolls. Perhaps unbeknownst to both Wayne and Gau, as a millionaire, Wayne is now—or at least for a few fleeting moments was—a member of a segment of the population that many commentators and politicians as well as much of the populace has come to despise.

Wayne's Patent Declared the Stupidest

While Wayne gave the best he had to give for over half of a century, the Electronic Frontier Foundation wasted no time in disparaging his life's work. Even before Wayne received his $1 million, that organization deemed Wayne's 6,442,485 patent the "Stupidest Patent of the Month" in March of 2015.[75] The rapidity of the EFF's rebuke was a bit surprising given that it makes a practice of reserving its most rabid reproaches to patents that have been monetized. In the article deriding the '485 patent, the EFF writer contended that Wayne's patent "devolves into a wilderness of made-up

[75] The '485 patent is a divisional of the '617 patent.

words and technobabble. . ." and "includes fabricated phrases" that make understanding its meaning an exercise in "cross-reference and guesswork."

While everyone is entitled to their opinion about the quality and merits of a patent, few will conduct their own analysis of the '485 patent and its patent family. For now, we can consider the motivation and work that went into declaring that Wayne's '485 patent was the stupidest of the month. It is no secret that the Electronic Frontier Foundation detests patents. Mark Cuban, whose foaming-at-the-mouth fulminations against patents are discussed later in this book, funds the EFF's Stupidest Patent of the Month initiative to the tune of $500,000 a year. Railing against patents is what the EFF does. To keep sponsors' funds flowing, at least one patent a month must be skewered. Thus, it seems that the Stupidest Patent of the Month initiative has no more than a month to analyze the patent that it decides to crucify. Who knows how the EFF chooses the "Stupidest Patent of the Month?" For all I know, the patents chosen for the EFF's strafing runs could be selected by a random number generator.[76] But if the initiative truly screens many patents in its efforts to find the least meritorious, then less time would be available to study the selected patent. In fact, the article on the EFF's website disparaging Wayne's patent was published on March 31, 2015. This article contains a link to a complaint filed on March 27, 2015 on behalf of NovelPoint Tracking against Subway, the franchised eatery. Thus, EFF could have had as little as five days to determine that Wayne's patent was the stupidest one of them all.

The five to 31 days that the EFF spent screening for and reviewing Wayne's patent can be contrasted with the effort and scrutiny put forward by those who came to a conclusion different from that of the EFF. By

[76] Unlike at the USPTO, the EFF doesn't seem to have procedures in place to restrain the publication of articles that come to kooky conclusions. At the USPTO there are supervisory examiners and appeals processes. You might remember from earlier in Wayne's story that in the 1969 timeframe a patent examiner declared that Wayne was committing fraud on the USPTO by filing a patent that addressed a nonexistent problem even though millions of television set owners experienced such problems regularly. To the USPTO's credit, that examiner was replaced in short order. On the other hand, the further towards the sensationalism side of the truth-sensationalism spectrum that EFF's articles fall, the more ridicule is heaped on patents and the closer that group comes to its goal of dismantling the patent system. Indeed, Mr. Cuban said the patent system should be "blown up." (See: https://www.youtube.com/watch?v=qBH64zFew6k)

the time that Wayne drafted and filed his '485 patent application, he had had roughly 50 years of experience researching telematics and locationing technologies. The patent agent that helped Wayne draft this family of patent applications apparently thought they were sufficiently meritorious to accept the risks of deferred payment. The patent examiner that reviewed the related applications saw no reason not to grant those applications. IP Edge screened thousands of patents and Wayne's were one of the first four patent portfolios the newly created firm wished to represent on a contingency basis. IP Edge's confidence in its decision to represent Wayne's patents never dissipated over its five-year campaign to monetize them. At least three patent litigation law firms risked time and capital pressing for the enforcement of Wayne's patents on pure contingency. And despite having every means of invalidating Wayne's patents at their disposal, some 85 very large, very well-capitalized and very well-represented corporations ended up not invalidating even one of the claims associated with Wayne's patents.

Let's consider how easy it would have been for any one of these large companies to invalidate one of the stupidest patents ever. It wouldn't have taken much money on the part of one of the alleged infringers to exhaust NovelPoint's resources or those of its contingency lawyers. In other stories included in this book, we will see how delaying tactics can wear out even the toughest patentee plaintiffs. Take Richard X. Zawitz of Tangle Creations for instance. Richard is tough enough to have sold roughly 150 million units of product in the extremely cutthroat toy industry over several decades. The people that recommended I speak with Richard made it clear that "Richard is not to be f&*cked with." However, after spending $250,000 trying to enforce one of his patents, Richard threw in the towel.

NovelPoint's assertion efforts occurred during an era in which *inter partes review* procedures were in full-on mass execution mode; about 90% of the patents reviewed under that process had at least one of their claims invalidated. And just about every, if not every, one of the 85 infringers that NovelPoint's lawyers approached threatened to file an *inter partes review* challenge. One of the patent lawyers that I spoke with estimated that there was an approximately 90% chance of a finding of invalidity or non-infringement in patent litigation back in the early 2010s. To avoid succumbing to patent invalidation under *inter partes review* or in patent litigation, NovelPoint would have had to win every argument presented by every defendant every time. If one defendant invalidated one of the patents-in-suit, the cases against the other defendants would have crumbled. The odds of all of Wayne's claims remaining intact approached zero.

> **Wayne's Odds of Prevailing Would Have Been Lower Today** If NovelPoint's assertion efforts were carried out post the Supreme Court's May 2017 TC Heartland decision, its odds of prevailing would have been even slimmer. A judge in any friendly jurisdiction could rule to invalidate the patent-in-suit.

The Well-Worn Patent Troll Trope Gets Rolled Out Again

The EFF article designating the '485 patent as the stupidest patent in March of 2015 derided NovelPoint for its so-called nuisance suits; that is for agreeing to accept small settlements from alleged infringers. The aspersion is that 85 large companies believed that Wayne's patents were obviously without merit but whipped out their checkbooks and handed over something that I calculate to be on the order of $25,000 apiece to NovelPoint. The tired trope that EFF is peddling is that large companies can't be bothered with parasites like Wayne and Gau so they just pay these leaches to go away. Such has been the narrative revolving around patent monetization efforts since the early 2000s. This storyline has been so pervasively promoted that many members of Congress and the media have developed a Pavlovian response to hearing that a patentee is asserting its patent rights against infringers; the patentee is the parasite and the infringer is the victim.

The other way of looking at situations such as those described in Wayne's story is that patentees have no choice but to resort to retaining patent litigators, or at least to the threat of litigation. NovelPoint, which wasn't much more than a shoestring operation bound together by hope and hard work, didn't want to litigate. The odds of NovelPoint surviving, let alone prevailing, in prolonged legal fights against 85 well-heeled defendants would be extremely remote.

But what more could Wayne and Gau have done to receive some consideration for the '485 patent family on an amicable basis? Wayne tried for years to enter into friendly licensing agreements with companies that were using his patented inventions or who could benefit from doing so. Sadly, he found no takers. When he entered into an agreement with

Gau, Wayne expressly conditioned his collaboration with IP Edge on the avoidance of litigation. Again, infringers were respectfully approached but Gau's reasonable opening offers were unanimously rejected. The counterpoint to the patent troll narrative is that patentees are routinely reduced to accepting whatever crumbs they are lucky enough to get.

Among the cacophony of patent detractors are those who hold that enforcing patents is immoral. Non-manufacturing entities that own patents and seek some compensation from those who use them are labeled patent trolls, patent terrorists, or worse. (Mr. Cuban said that patentees who enforce their rights "are killing this country.") Wayne didn't manufacture products relating to his invention, so according to the patent foes, Wayne is an immoral patent troll.

Postscript

To put it mildly, I am bothered that detractors lump people like Wayne into a group they demonize for being parasites or patent trolls. I am bothered that people like Wayne are excoriated for their success, despite however long it was delayed or however diluted it may be relative to what is deserved. In the minds of too many, Wayne crossed the line—he became a millionaire.

The next time you hear politicians or media figures try to gin up class warfare, pay attention. You will hear them rant against "the fat cats who simply won the lottery of life and who should pay their fair share of taxes." As a function of his recoveries, Wayne is now included among those "millionaires and billionaires" too many politicians and media figures harangue us to hate. And how much of Wayne's $1 million recovery do redistributions think would be fair for him to pay in income taxes? At the time of my writing these pages, various members of Congress and those running for the highest office in the land advocate for a tax rate of as much as 70% on marginal income. Under such a proposal, instead of clearing a lump sum equal to roughly $840 per year per infringer, Wayne would only net the equivalent of $252 per year per infringer. Such confiscatory tax rates would reduce Wayne's net proceeds over the 15 years it took him to monetize his patents to the equivalent of $20,000 in annual payments.

Wayne was also fortunate that he didn't have children about to enter their university years when he received his $1 million payment in 2015. I know other inventors who have bled money year after year before finally receiving a long overdue settlement. The financial aid offices of the universities favored by their children only requested the parents' most recent tax returns. All hope for financial assistance was dashed once the settlement numbers popped out at the financial aid officers, despite the fact that these inventors have barely made any money over the previous decade or so. On a consolidated basis, some of these inventors lost money over the previous 10 years. In these cases, inventors must make heart-wrenching decisions—pay the tuitions and become insolvent, don't send their children to the universities of their choosing, or watch their children drown in student loans.

Examiner to Garage Door Inventor: Don't Let the Door Hit Your Ass on the Way Out

John Jella is a pioneer and innovator in the garage door industry, where he began his working life in 1972. By 1975, he formed his own garage door company, American Garage Door Services, in Denver. John started his second garage door company, Anozira Garage Doors, in Phoenix in 1982. Within a few years, Anoriza had expanded to Las Vegas and California and was generating revenues of some $40 million annually. In addition to being a successful installer of garage doors, John was already a prolific inventor as he had 10 garage-door-related patents to his name by the late 1990s. John was so successful in the garage door business that he was able to retire in 1996.

John had time to think while in retirement. He put this time to good use.

He pondered remedies to the deficiencies associated with traditional wood-based garage doors. Wooden garage doors just didn't hold up well. They rotted, warped, cracked, and splintered. Some wooden garage doors literally fell apart. Annual repainting and resealing was often required to prevent their demise. The upkeep of wooden garage doors was particularly important when listing a house for sale because they consume as much as 80% of the façade that homebuyers see when they approach a house. But even the best maintained traditional garage doors just do not look that attractive.

John began to realize that carriage-style garage doors would be popular with homeowners. Carriage garage doors often feature windows near their tops through which sunlight seeps. Carriage garage doors typically sport non-functional handles. These doors give the illusion of opening up like barn doors of yesteryear; in practice, they open up vertically at the push of a remote button.[77]

[77] To see pictures of carriage garage doors, and how their appearance contrasts with traditional garage doors, please visit www.firstudt.com.

Breakthrough Innovations in Garage Doors

The innovation that John came up with in 1998 was steel-based carriage-style garage doors. Steel garage doors hold up much better than wood-based doors. They require essentially no maintenance over their lives and can even be constructed to weigh less than wooden doors. Steel is typically on the order of 50% less expensive than wood due to manufacturing efficiencies that result from large-scale production runs. Steel is also preferable to other materials such as plastics and aluminum. Steel-based garage doors tolerate any climate or temperature whereas plastic garage doors warp, buckle, split, and crack once they heat up in excess of about 190 degrees Fahrenheit. Aluminum can be prohibitively expensive: At the time of my writing these pages, using aluminum instead of steel in garage doors can cause costs to spiral three-fold.

At the time of John's invention, about 90% of garage doors were made with 21-inch or 24-inch wood panels. John believed that three 28-inch (in height) steel panels that appeared to be wooden panels would look much more distinctive and carriage-esque than four 21-inch inch panels. Specifically, larger panels afforded larger windows in the top panels.

The engineering problem that confronted John was how to use 28-inch high steel panels that would open and close correctly without jumping the roller tracks. At the time of John's invention, four-, five-, and six-panel garage doors were standard. Garage doors operate on rollers that follow rails between a vertical orientation (when the door is closed) and a horizontal orientation (when the door is opened). The panels of the door must negotiate a tight 12-inch-radius curve as they change orientations. Four-, five-, and six-panel doors perform that maneuver reliably and six-panel doors traverse the narrow curve better than four-panel doors. It was widely believed throughout the garage door industry that a three-panel door with its 28-inch-wide panels could not reliably negotiate that curve. John's genius was figuring out how to make fewer large panel doors operate within a 12-inch radius. (A subsidiary engineering problem was that most industry players believed that steel garage door panels of any size would cause the mechanics of the roller tracks to malfunction.)

In his efforts to solve the engineering challenges, John conducted extensive research, performed hundreds of trials, and conferred with multiple press manufacturers. The innovative solution that John arrived at became the substance of two patent applications that he filed with the

United States Patent and Trademark Office in 2002. One covered the method of constructing the panels and the other covered the design of the carriage-style door.

John was convinced that his steel-based carriage-style doors would be a hit. So, in 1999, he founded 1st United Door. Within three years, 1st United Door was producing $20 million in annual revenue by serving customers in California, Arizona, Utah, and Colorado. Based on booming demand for its steel-based carriage garage doors, it seemed that 1st United Door was on its way to producing between $50 million to $60 million in annual turnover within a couple of years. Other garage door installation companies were so impressed with John's invention that, by 2006, seven of them licensed John's patent applications with the understanding that they would renew their licensing agreements as soon as John's pending applications issued.

Inventor's Bright Future Darkens

The future was looking bright for 1st United Door. And then, three things happened. The patent examiner repeatedly rejected John's patent applications, competitors wantonly infringed John's patent applications, and the imploding economy shredded demand for John's 28-inch-high steel-carriage garage door panels.

The immediate patent examiner, backed by his supervisory patent examiner, issued numerous rejections of John's method patent application based on grounds of obviousness. The examiner was unrelenting in holding that because there had been 28″ pieces of steel and because there had been carriage doors (on barns and the like), using 28″ sections of steel on retractable carriage-style garage doors constituted an obvious new product, underserving of patent protection. This persistent contention was put forth by the examiner despite widespread skepticism within the industry as to the ability to produce such garage doors, and in view of the fact that no one else produced the same kinds of garage doors. In fact, the seven competitors that became licensees filed sworn affidavits with the USPTO indicating that their disbelief turned to amazement when they saw John's 28″ doors maneuver the tight curves as the panels changed orientation.

Moreover, the examiner argued that John's invention was not commercially viable despite 1st United Door blowing the doors off in terms of generating revenue from installing such doors. The examiner's gross miscalculation of the commercial appeal of John's invention failed to take into consideration the fact that John closed multiple licensing agreements based on his patent applications.

John and Michael Mann (his patent attorney) respectfully responded to each office action issued against John's patent applications. John told me that at one interview with the patent examiners, Michael and himself, the examiners where dismissive and simply uninterested in the applicant's arguments as to why his patent application read on a nonobvious invention. The primary examiner was a young fellow who attended the meeting in running shoes and very casual attire. In other interactions, the supervisory examiner made no bones about his focus on his impending retirement. John was disappointed that he was not afforded with more deference, especially after traveling from Arizona (and paying his lawyer to travel from South Carolina) to Washington D.C. After having spent approximately $500,000 conducting the research behind his patent applications and in his efforts to secure issued patents, John believed that he was entitled to more than the examiners essentially saying, "Don't let the door hit your ass on the way out."

Actually, John's maltreatment at the hands of his patent examiners went beyond their demonstrating a lack of diligence and deference. Underhandedness was on display when the applicant lost an appeal due to the examiner cheating. As Michael tells it:

"The examiner invoked "common knowledge" to find the invention obvious rather than support his assertion of obviousness with proof. In his answer brief, to respond to my [Michael's] appeal brief that included an objection to the use of common knowledge, the examiner wrote this:

> "…it is not be [sic] unreasonable for the Examiner in an office action to have taken Official notice of facts by asserting that certain limitations in a claim are old and well-known expedients in the art without the support of documentary evidence providing the facts so noticed are of notorious character and serve only to fill in the gaps which might exist in the evidentiary showing made by the Examiner to support a particular ground of rejection."

The quoted text is a disingenuous distortion of section of 2144.03 of the Manual of Patent Examination Procedures, which actually stated this:

> "Furthermore, it might not be unreasonable for the examiner in a first office action to take official notice of facts by asserting that certain limitations in a dependent claim are old and well-known expedients in the art without the support of documentary evidence provided the facts so noticed are of notorious character and serve only to "fill in the gaps" which might exist in the evidentiary showing made by the examiner to support a particular ground of rejection."

The differences in the examiner's text—deletion of "first" from "first office action" and "dependent" from "dependent claim"—are telling and underscore that the examiner had announced his own, more liberal standard, and perhaps one not reviewed by the Office of Deputy Commissioner for Patent Examination Policy as all MPEP procedures must be. The appeal was from a *final* office action and the rejected claims were *independent* claims rather than dependent ones. So the examiner's use of "common knowledge" was not reasonable."

Further, the examiners, intentionally or otherwise, humiliated John by asking him for permission to use his patent applications as examples of what patent applications should not look like. After about four years of such disingenuous prosecution, John threw in the towel when he abandoned his patent application in 2006.

As a long-time thought leader in the garage door industry, John was used to other companies taking note of what innovations and improvements his companies were bringing to the market. However, he was amazed at the rampant infringement that took place during the contentious prosecution of his patent applications. The design, installation and mechanics of garage doors are transparent, making them ripe for infringement. John's patent applications never became enforceable because they were initially in prolonged prosecution and then abandoned. In light of pervasive infringement of John's patent applications and in view of their later abandonment, John's licensees discontinued their licenses.

Postscript

What are the consequences of John being deprived of patent protection for his steel-based carriage-style garage doors? Well, at about the time of his patent abandonment, 1st United Door employed 30 full-time installers. Now, that company has six installers on staff.

Patent protection would have enabled John to exclude competitors from offering infringing garage doors, and would have provided his company with a royalty stream that was already beginning to flow. The garage door industry is enormous. In recent years, there have been 1.2 million housing starts. Let's assume that the wholesale price of the materials that go into new garage doors is $400. Let's also assume that each new house has an average of one garage door and that there are no replacements of garage doors. Who knows how much of the potential market 1st United Door would have penetrated by itself or via its licensees or what average royalty rates its licensees would have remitted. But suppose that John's invention was deployed in three percent of the new homes constructed and its licensees paid royalty rates of three percent. That would mean that 1st United Doors has been deprived of some $432,000 each year for far more than a decade. That's no chump change.

Now, it is true that there may have been legitimate reasons why John's patent applications should not have been granted. There could have been prior art or another inventor may have been able to demonstrate that he was the initial inventor. However, these issues were never raised during the prosecution of the subject patent applications. Instead, the examiners clung to the notion that John should not receive patents because they believed it conceivable that another inventor could have invented the same invention (but didn't). They also ignored reality in holding that there was no indication that John's steel carriage-style garage doors would be commercially appealing. Instead of digging into the merits of John's patent application, the examiners turned to skullduggery and comported themselves unprofessionally.

It is also true that not all of the shrinkage in 1st United Door's business can be attributed to its being deprived of patent protection. The Phoenix housing market has certainly been volatile over the years. Having a highly compelling (patented) technology is not the only variable upon which commercial success turns. Maybe some of 1st United Door's competitors have other attractive features embedded in their garage doors. Maybe competing garage door installation companies have price points, financing options, referral programs, service, reputation and long-term contracts that account for their success. (It could also be the case that, on a relative basis,

1st United Door has not suffered at all; its business may have contracted less than that of its competitors.)

But what seems incontrovertible to me is that the examiners' unfair handling of John's patent applications is directly responsible for 1st United Door's loss of its licensees. The USPTO's delay in prosecuting John's patent applications resulted in his company's loss of revenue and market share from 2005 to 2007. When John abandoned his patent applications in 2006, there were four times as many housing starts in Phoenix as there were in 2018. A great many homeowners would have paid a premium for carriage-style garage doors, especially as doing so typically yields homeowners premiums when selling their homes.

Just as it is inappropriate to assign all of a business's misfortune to its patent problems, it is inappropriate to reflexively leap to the conclusion that there is never a multiplier to be applied to effectively utilizing an issued patent. In other words, John's loss is not limited to the contraction his company sustained or to the some $432,000 in annual royalties that he has been deprived of. At the time of abandoning his patent application, John had decades of experience running garage door businesses that generated tens of millions of dollars in annual revenues. He directly managed dozens of employees and expanded such businesses throughout much of the western United States. He had 10 issued patents to his credit and made enough money to retire a decade earlier. It seems to me that John could have parlayed the additional cash flow, which he rightly deserved, into even greater wealth for himself, his employees and homeowners. Nor will we ever know what other inventions this disheartened innovator could have brought to the market.

Patent Prosecution and Litigation Tricks from Netflix

Nick Gross has a highly suitable background for writing patents covering computer-related inventions. He earned a bachelor's degree in electrical engineering in 1983 from the California Institute of Technology. After a short stint in the technology arena, he became a patent attorney working for several law firms, including top-tier Wilson Sonsini. In the mid-2000s, Nick struck out on his own.

One of the first patent applications that Nick drafted as a solo patent practitioner was motivated by a mishap while delivering a PowerPoint presentation. During an important meeting one of the slides contained a typo: "Public" was spelled without the "l." This *faux paux* resulted in Nick devising a word-processing application that ensured that the words chosen match their intended contexts. The resulting patent (U.S. Patent No. 6,782,510) ended up being licensed to dozens of high-tech companies involved with content filtering.

An even more interesting story begins when Nick filed a patent application on February 2, 2004. This patent application covered a notification system for alerting users as to the availability of desired media content items. This invention is capable of automatically refreshing so that users are made aware of the status of their pre-selected items in real time. Nick recognized that his invention addressed a glaring problem with new online service providers—their members were disappointed with the lack of fresh content. This patent application spent more than four years under intense scrutiny from examiner Dennis Ruhl, whose allowance rate at the time reportedly approximated five percent. This patent application issued as U.S. Patent No. 7,389,243 on June 17, 2008.

Inventor Nick Engages with Netflix

A few years earlier, around the spring of 2006, a friend of Nick's introduced him to Netflix. The thinking was that Netflix ought to consider embracing the '243 patent because implementing it online would allow its subscribers to be constantly apprised of the availability of their preferred movies. By the time Nick made contact with Netflix he had built a portfolio of more than a dozen pending patent applications on inventions similar to what his '243 patent covered. These patents covered recommendation engines suitable for notifying which additional items customers might wish to consume based on their browsing, viewing, and purchasing history. Other patent applications claimed processes for notifying customers when their online carts or wish lists were in need of replenishment, to encourage engagement, and increase retention. Such notification technologies were a counterintuitive concept at the time, given that they encouraged customers to consume more product even though they were paying fixed monthly fees.

Through Nick's friend, Netflix expressed an interest in Nick's portfolio of patent applications but, curiously, Netflix was not at all inquisitive as to what the portfolio contained. Netflix declined an invitation to be shown what relevance the patent applications might have to their operations. Netflix simply requested that Nick state his offering price. The media company also insisted that Nick execute a standstill agreement that gave Netflix time to independently review the portfolio without fear that Nick would enforce his (presumptive) patents against the company during the time of the negotiations. Surprisingly, Nick's efforts to educate Netflix on the claims scope, possible infringement, and ongoing patent prosecution strategy were all rebuffed by Netflix. A few months later, after its initial review, Netflix offered Nick a $100,000 lump-sum payment for his portfolio, which consisted of roughly 15 patent applications. This puny price was summarily rejected. (Remember, these negotiations transpired in an era yet to feel the wrath of eBay v. MercExchange, Alice Corp. v. CLS International Bank, and the America Invents Act.)

Nick had good reason to believe that his portfolio was currently worth something in the ballpark of $1 million and would grow in value over the years as the applications turned into issued patents. He sought to be compensated largely when (and if) Netflix achieved objective, measurable, patent-oriented milestones. Thus, Nick countered with a graduated payment schedule whereby he would receive $250,000 upfront and more contingent consideration as the patent applications matured and achieved allowances, secured licensees, and/or were enforced against Netflix competitors. One component in Nick's counterproposal was that as each of the 15 applications in the patent family issued, Nick would receive a $50,000 payment. Under his proposed scheme, Netflix would only end up paying the full value of the portfolio (i.e., about $1 million) if the applications issued and offered the promise of being useful to Netflix.

Negotiations with Netflix Go Cold

At first Netflix rejected Nick's creative solution and silence ensued. Then, out of the blue, about four months later in August 2006, lawyers for Netflix indicated that Nick's tiered compensation schedule had merit and expressed an interest in revisiting it. At the conclusion of these new discussions, Netflix floated the idea of a tiered and contingent payment agreement along the lines Nick proposed but insisted on paying a smaller amount upfront. Netflix also insisted that it would have control over all aspects of the ongoing prosecution of the 15 patent applications, deciding which cases to keep and which ones to abandon.

Nick was concerned that if Netflix paid only a small upfront payment for his patent applications, the entertainment company could simply abandon his 15 patent applications, depriving him of potential licensing revenue. As a small protection, Nick proposed that Netflix commit that if the USPTO decided one of the applications contained patentable subject matter, Netflix would not be able to unilaterally abandon that case and deprive him of the bargained-for downstream remuneration. Nick sought some other minimal assurances. Case in point: If a deal were to be consummated on a graduated payment basis, Netflix would at least commit to notifying him if the video distributor were to abandon any of the 15 patent applications. It should be noted that even in this scenario, Nick would not have the ability to compel Netflix to continue the prosecution of applications that it deemed unworthy; he would only have the right to voice his opinion on the matters.

Netflix completely rejected these offers but indicated that it was still interested in acquiring Nick's patent portfolio outright. Given its behavior, Nick got the feeling that Netflix intended to obtain rights to his patent applications as inexpensively as possible for the sole purpose of euthanizing them. Such gambit would deprive any assignee of the ability to use them to sue the movie distributor for its practicing of the covered inventions. Consequently, Nick rejected this offer, but left the door open for several weeks for Netflix to reconsider. He never received a response.

On January 1, 2007, after some eight months of trying to negotiate with Netflix, Nick sent his erstwhile interlocutor a §154 Notice based on his contentions that Netflix was practicing the claims of his then pending '243 patent. (§154 Notices allow an inventor to inform an alleged infringer that the inventor intends to pursue damages for the period the patent was pending.) A month or two later, Netflix's outside lawyers responded by stating that Nick's patents were worthless in view of prior art that Netflix had developed. To substantiate its contentions, Netflix produced declarations and materials to that effect from its then Chief Product Officer, Neil D. Hunt. Netflix also demanded that Nick present what Netflix deemed to be its prior art to the USPTO so that the latter could pass judgment on Netflix's assertion.

Netflix Compels Inventor to Submit Forgeries to the USPTO

Nick was caught in a Catch-22 situation. Under his duty of disclosure to the USPTO, he was compelled to provide the patent office with any prior art that came to his attention; but he did not want to derail his allowed (but not yet issued) patent application. Erring on the side of caution, Nick examined what Netflix claimed to be its prior art. In doing so, Nick came to the conclusion that Netflix had forged its so-called "prior art" in such a way as to make it appear that Netflix was using the inventions prior to Nick's filing. To that end, Netflix produced emails showing that its recommendation engine was working as the '243 patent described well before Nick filed his '243 patent application. For example, Netflix produced an email that it reportedly sent to its customers in May of 2002, offering them to rent the movie "Spiderman" (sic) from its inventory. The red flag with this fabricated email was that the movie was not released on videocassette until November of that year. It was implausible that Netflix produced and dispatched an official email offer to (tens of) millions of real customers to rent a movie that could not possibly have existed in its inventory for some six months. There were other problems with this piece of purported prior art manufactured by Netflix, including the fact that it had noticeable typos. Such sloppiness would be uncharacteristic of a billion-dollar company engaging with many millions of its customers.

In addition, to counter Nick's claim that Netflix was infringing his patents, Mr. Hunt unequivocally claimed that Netflix stopped monitoring customer queues and notifying customers when their queues were empty back in 2003. In disproving such contentions, Nick had examples in hand of Netflix's system doing exactly that in 2007, precisely the time at which Mr. Hunt provided his declaration. Mr. Hunt's declarations were at best inaccurate and misleading, if not outright lies.

Nick contacted Netflix's patent counsel and apprised them that what was presented as prior art were really demonstrable forgeries. Instead of relenting, Netflix's lawyers became more entrenched in their position, insisting that the documentation was authentic. In light of their intransigence, Nick had little choice but to forward Netflix's forgeries to the USPTO even though such documents were clearly designed by Netflix to mislead the patent examiner. These submissions were accompanied by a letter from Nick explaining that he believed the documents were likely forgeries and inviting the USPTO to make its own independent assessment. A few months later the Patent Office agreed with Nick that the documents' authenticity was dubious and, on June 17, 2008, issued the '243 application over Netflix's supposed prior art.

Patent Infringement Suits Start Streaming

Shortly after the '243 patent issued, Nick sold the entire subject patent portfolio to Media Queue in September of 2008. Media Queue then filed patent infringement suits against Netflix and others in an Oklahoma Federal District Court in October of 2008. These cases were transferred to California in early 2009. Nick was never a party to these suits, but Netflix made his character a star witness in several of their pleadings. The media company besmirched his character and tried to discredit his stewardship of his patents. While Nick's reputation was sullied throughout the trial, Netflix was spared from admitting into evidence a 2009 letter penned by Mr. Hunt, its Chief Product Officer. This letter, which appears below, is an apology for Netflix's attempts to commit fraud on the Patent Office. The defendant cast Nick as "a disgruntled Netflix customer" even though he maintained his Netflix subscriptions as religiously as most customers from at least 2002.

In its papers to the California court, Netflix also misleadingly stated, "Once he (Nick) obtained his patent, the patentee then tried to sell his patent to Netflix. When he failed, he sold the patent to Media Queue, a nonpracticing entity created for the single purpose of the present lawsuit." This statement is riddled with revisionist history. The truth is that Netflix was much more proactive in seeking to acquire the patents than Nick was in trying to sell them; this is evidenced by his rejection of multiple offers after Netflix returned to the negotiating table in August of 2006. Given that it is highly unusual for a large company to give serious consideration to acquiring a portfolio consisting solely of patent applications, Netflix demonstrated a sustained campaign (albeit punctuated with strategically placed pauses) to take control of Nick's patent portfolio.

Further, Nick did not immediately seek to sell his patents to other buyers when his discussions with Netflix came to a halt in November of 2006. More than a month elapsed before Nick sent Netflix's in-house counsel an official notice under 35 USC §154 explaining why its system at that time was infringing several claims listed in the 15 pending applications in his portfolio. Nick offered to enter into amiable discussions with Netflix's counsel, but that offer was rejected. When Nick later decided to sell his portfolio in 2008, there were several interested parties. The ultimate acquirer was in no way affiliated with Nick and their transaction was at arms-length. Media Queue's acquisition of Nick's patent portfolio demonstrates that it was valuable even after having sustained Netflix's shenanigans to dismember and invalidate it.

Finally, Netflix offered a healthy sum of money for Nick's patent portfolio without ever receiving even one claim chart from Nick. This indicates that the video distribution company must have independently arrived at its own conclusion that it was likely infringing some of the claims in Nick's patent portfolio.

Unaffiliated Bankruptcy Freezes Patent Litigation

In a highly disputed hearing in late 2009, the Judge in Media Queue's actions against Netflix, Blockbuster, and a few other defendants ruled that the claims of the patents-in-suit did not cover the operation of the defendants' respective systems. This finding directly traversed the Patent Office's own independent assessment of the '243 claims during the prosecution of the patent. (Again, the reader can see the courts and the USPTO contradicting one another. The Patent Office granted Nick expedited review of his application based on the examiner's June 2005 determination that the claims in fact covered the monitoring of subscriber queues and notifications to subscribers of interesting content as practiced by the defendants.) Despite the loss, the judge agreed that Media Queue had done nothing wrong in bringing the case against the defendants and did not award any sanctions for Netflix based on the latter's insistence that Nick had somehow motivated or instigated the action against them in bad faith.

The evidence that it was Netflix, not Nick, that was consistently underhanded is overwhelming. Nevertheless, Netflix had the gall to put forth motions in the litigation to recover its legal fees from Media Queue based on Nick's supposed bad behavior.

Aside from the burdens associated with appealing any judicial decision, the continuing legal saga was not easily or quickly resolved. As mentioned, Media Queue initially filed complaints against several media companies other than Netflix. One of those companies was Blockbuster. Because the presiding judge consolidated the cases, Blockbuster's subsequent bankruptcy filing after Media Queue's appeal triggered the suspension of the patent litigation. As a result, Media Queue's case against Netflix dragged on for about 10 years before a settlement was apparently reached in 2017. While Netflix apologized to the Patent Office for brazenly casting forged documents as "prior art," the media company's executives never apologized to Nick for distorting and mischaracterizing the nature of his negotiations with Netflix.

> *May 15, 2009*
> *Commissioner of Patents*
> *P.O. Box 1450*
> *Alexandria, Virginia 22313-1450*
>
> *Commissioner:*
>
> *I am Chief Product Officer for Netflix, Inc. A declaration signed by me on March 16, 2007 (the "Declaration", Attachment 1 to this letter) was submitted during prosecution of a patent application, U.S. No. 101771,049, "Notification System and Method for Media Queue," which*

has since issued as United States Patent No. 7,389,243. This letter is to inform the Patent and Trademark Office ***that I have recently determined that certain information in the Declaration is incorrect.***

....

The Declaration erred, however, in stating that as early as December 16, 2002, a computer system that generated electronic messages to subscribers based on the compositions was placed in public use. The owner of the '243 patent has sued Netflix, alleging that Netflix infringes the '243 patent. ***As part of Netflix's preparation to defend the lawsuit, I have learned that the Declaration was inaccurate.*** *While Netflix utilized a computer system to send many different kinds of emails to subscribers for some time prior to December 16, 2002, my declaration should have reflected that the emails based on the compositions attached as Exhibits 1, 2 and 3* ***were sent to subscribers no later than March 2003*****.....**

I apologize for the inaccuracies in my Declaration and submit this letter to correct the record.

(signature)

Neil D. Hunt

Chief Product Officer
(emphasis added).

Postscript

Nick has suffered from other inequities at the USPTO. In one case he had a patent application pending for eight years while arguing about the use of the term "and/or." Also, he had to appeal his 13/551,454 patent application three times because the examiner refused to defend the merits of his rejections to the appeal panel. When Nick appealed the rejections, the examiner would rescind the most recent rejection and issue a new rejection. This repeated gambit was extremely expensive and time-consuming for

Nick. In the case of Nick's 12/858150 patent application, the examiner issued a §101 eligibility rejection after he lost on an appeal based on earlier §102 (novelty) and §103 (obvious) rejections. He ended up abandoning this patent application. Such experiences have caused Nick to believe that the USPTO is insulating the de facto monopolies that large companies enjoy by blocking competitive products that small inventors are ready to introduce to the market.

Transformative Invention Deemed to be Non-Inventive

Ari Rosenberg already had a dozen years of experience as a media advertising professional under his belt by August of 2000. Ari began his career as a media buyer at Young & Rubicam. Then he moved into advertising sales for *Newsweek*. His next stop was selling advertising for *Tennis* magazine.

Towards the late 1990s, Ari had a front row seat as ad dollars began migrating to digital ads placed on websites. The digital revolution must have made for exciting times for a young advertising executive. But not everything about this shift to Internet advertising was appealing. For instance, marketers would cancel their digital ad campaigns after a few weeks if initial ad performance did not meet their expectations. Poof. Up in smoke went advertising executives' credits towards quotas.

By the time Ari began working for Snowball (later acquired by IGN Entertainment) in 1999, he realized that banner ads did not always sync up with the corresponding site's visitors. Websites like IGN.com that appealed to young audiences with very little income would be flooded with ads from brokerage firms, for example. How would such website ad sales executives respond if their advertisers failed to receive sufficient clicks? They would authorize the display of massive amounts of bonus impressions for the very ads that failed to resonate with the sites' visitors, causing the ratio of clicks-to-impressions to continue its downward descent.

A Flash of Genius Strikes Inventor

Ari knew this was an untenable situation but couldn't put his finger on a solution. That is, not until one night in August of 2000. That night Ari was awoken by a flash of genius. His idea was to flip the prevailing wisdom of compensating unpopular advertisers with more impressions on its head. Ari decided that the most relevant ads should be rewarded with bonus impressions each time viewers clicked on related ads. This way, popular promoters would be rewarded with lower effective advertising rates. These contented advertisers would likely renew their campaigns, benefitting both the website owners and digital ad salesforces. Ari was so excited that as soon as he arrived at work the next morning, he called Tim Armstrong, Snowball's President of Advertising, and explained his idea.

Snowball's CEO greenlighted Ari trialing his IPC, which stands for impressions-per-connection, on the west coast. Ari wasted no time in evangelizing IPC. In October of 2000, he flew to New York City from his home in San Francisco and handed a booklet about IPC to Christina Elwell, Mr. Armstrong's right-hand woman, as well as to David Hirsh, another senior advertising executive at Snowball. Ari says at least 15 people at Snowball were aware of IPC, if not users of it.

Google Generates Billions of Dollars from Ari's Invention

Shortly after Ari began evangelizing IPC within Snowball, that company's senior ad salesforce began mutinying to Google. Mr. Armstrong was the first to depart for Google. Ms. Elwell and Mr. Hirsch soon followed. Ms. Elwell became Google's National Advertising Sales Manager and Mr. Hirsch became instrumental in launching and executing Google's advertising monetization strategy.

Soon after the arrival of Tim Armstrong, Google re-launched its ad sales system so that better performing ads were rewarded with lower rates. The press was quick to rave about the brilliance of Google's IPC-like digital ad strategy—the extent to which such glowing press coverage was a result of having been precipitated by Google is unknown. A then-24-year-old Googler by the name of Salar Kamangar who, as I understand it, never sold a digital ad in his life was coronated as being the genesis of the idea to launch a system that rewarded better ads with lower rates. Allow me to list a few examples of the media going gaga over Google's IPC-inspired ad platform:

> *BusinessWeek* wrote, "Google's auction methodology, invented internally and so important to its success, is far more innovative than auction experts once believed. While superficially similar to earlier types of auctions, it is a novel mechanism..."

MediaPost Blogs wrote this missive: "Google has made billions of dollars for many reasons. But the most important reason is that Google created a marketplace that rewards good advertising…when Google started rewarding marketers by reducing the price for "good ads" it created a virtuous circle; better ads, happier users, efficient pricing for marketers and more money for Google."

In his book entitled, *The Search: How Google and Its Rivals Rewrote the Rules of Business and Transformed Our Culture*, author John Battle, wrote, "In February 2002….Google incorporated the notion of an ad's popularity—the click-through rate into its overall ranking. The shift was simple, brilliant and extremely effective."

In the book, *I'm Feeling Lucky: The Confessions of Google Employee Number 59*, it was stated that, "Salar Kamangar experienced an epiphany…everyone would benefit. The user would see more relevant ads. The advertiser would get more clicks. Google would make more money…that one idea was worth billions and billions of dollars."

Steven Levy wrote in the pages of *In the Plex: How Google Thinks, Works, and Shapes Our Lives*, "The ad model that Veach and Kamanger created had yet another major innovation, but this one was exclusively Google's…The new system instituted financial incentives for better ads. It lowered the prices for effective ads."

As Google's star was rising, Snowball was losing altitude. Costs had to be reduced. Ari became a successful and handsomely remunerated national sales director, making him a candidate for termination. (Sales managers often boast histories of success in sales but they become removed from clients and revenues when they take on managerial roles. Thus, they are viewed as overhead.) In 2003, Snowball initially offered Ari a generous severance check in return for him surrendering his intellectual property. (Ari filed a non-provisional patent application that covered his IPC invention on April 30, 2001. At a cost of some $65,000 in attorney's fees alone, this patent application issued as U.S. Patent No. 7,089,195 on August 8, 2006.) Ari refused to relinquish his rights to his IPC patent application. Snowball didn't have much of a leg to stand on in seeking ownership of the IPC patent application as Ari was bound by no assignment agreements. His strong stance on this issue resulted in him retaining his patent application and in him receiving an even more generous severance payment compared to what was initially offered.

Ari kept busy after he left IGN, as Snowball came to be called. He taught online ad sales seminars all over the country. By 2007, and within a year of his '195 patent issuing, he entered into his first licensing agreement with Hallmark. The Kansas City greeting card company undertook months of due diligence, studying the invalidity risks associated with Ari's IPC patent. Then Hallmark agreed to pay him a 2.5% royalty rate for the online ad campaigns that it sold and that implemented the IPC method. In the 2013-2014 timeframe, Ari poured some $250,000 that he raised from family members into creating software that would automate the issuance of bonus impressions for popular ads. As of 2019, Ari counted the likes of Macy's, Monster, and MillerCoors as IPC advertisers. Not bad at all for a small company commercializing its innovative business model and technology. But nowhere near the ad search revenue that Google has generated, which in recent years has approached $100 billion.

Ari Sues Google for Patent Infringement

Ari suspected that Google was infringing his '195 patent application back in 2004. But he could not initiate patent infringement litigation until at least August of 2006, when the '195 patent issued. Ari did reach out to Google to discuss settling the issue but received no response. The lawyers that he was working with at the time advised him that it would be better to sue Google for patent infringement if he had at least two patents in his arsenal. Thus, began a $380,000 detour; his second patent application was filed in 2011 and issued in 2014. Then, Ari found himself traveling all over the country in his search for a contingency law firm to represent him.

> Many small patentees wishing to assert their patents have little choice but to retain contingency lawyers. And there are many advantages of doing so. However, there are also drawbacks. For instance, some patentees believe that their contingency lawyers lose focus as the litigation becomes extenuated. This can be

> attributable to some contingency patent law firms taking on too many contingency cases. Patentees often need to explain their technologies and patents to their lawyers time and again. Sometimes, counselors for patentees in damages suits simply render poor advice—such as having their clients obtain further patents at significant expense.

In December of 2015, Ari filed a patent infringement lawsuit against Google in the Southern District of New York. In early 2016, Google responded by filing a petition for review of the '195 patent under the PTAB's Covered Business Methods proceedings. One of the adjudicators on this tribunal was unexplainedly replaced with a peer who clearly was not prepared to render judgment. In fact, none of the CBM judges in this case really understood IPC; they were asking questions about applying IPC to print and outdoor ads. It even seemed like one of the judges was trying to demean Ari by asking questions such as those relating to Ari's undergraduate education. Ari lost the first round of the CBM proceedings, but quickly filed an appeal. In April of 2019, this appeal was lost when the Federal Circuit issued a Rule 36 decision—"affirmed." That one word invalidated both of Ari's patents—patents in which he invested more than $400,000 in legal fees. Ari's contingency lawyer decided to contain his exposure to Ari's case and resigned from representing IPC.

What Haunts Ari?

Ari did not take the Federal Circuit's Rule 36 affirmation well. He seemed depressed, if not despondent, when I called him shortly after this decision. Ari told me he felt like a failure and was too humiliated to look his family in the eye. His wife was concerned that he might have been harboring suicidal thoughts.

A back of the envelope calculation suggested that damages from Google's infringement could amount to between $9 billion and $12 billion. Imposing treble damages, not to mention interest penalties, on these numbers due to willful infringement could have brought his haul to at least $27 billion. (As discussed above, plenty of evidence indicates that Google knew of Ari's '195 patent. So too does the fact that the '195 patent was cited as prior art when Google was prosecuting one of its patents.) Of course, Ari should have been content with a settlement of even one percent of such figures. But he received nothing. Not one cent. And unlike PTAB petitioners, patentees like Ari never receive refunds of the fees that they pay to the USPTO.

> A settlement in the neighborhood of $270 million (one percent of $27 billion) would have approximated the charge that Google took when it gave Yahoo! 2.7 million shares of its stock in 2004 for its infringement of patents that Yahoo! acquired from Overture. Interestingly, Google reportedly realized an income tax benefit of between $100 million and $115 million related to this noncash charge of between $260 million and $290 million.

Postscript

Ari conceived a novel idea and went about patenting it according to the practices of the day. He was assigned a rigorous examiner who reportedly had an allowance rate in the single digits. He retained capable counsel, made his case to the examiner, argued office actions, participated in interviews, paid his fees, and achieved the issuance of two patents.

Ari played by the rules but Congress and the Supreme Court changed the rules of the game. Congress promulgated the America Invents Act which created the PTAB and the CBM. During these CBM proceedings, Google argued that Ari's '195 patent lacked an inventive step even though the media was bursting with stories that lavished praise on the inventiveness of Google's IPC-like advertising platform. Then, the Supreme Court clouded patent eligibility issues with its Alice decision.

Overseeing the Patent Office at this time was Michelle Lee, who immediately before becoming the USPTO Director, served as general counsel and head of patents and patent strategy at Google from 2003 to 2012. As discussed elsewhere in this book, Director Lee refused to disclose her personal stock and options holdings in Google. This is unfortunate as the independence of directors of the USPTO became especially important in the post-America Invents Act era. At least at the time of Director Lee running the USPTO, the agency's directors had tremendous influence over Administrative Patent Judges. APJs may have felt the need to issue decisions that aligned with their politically-appointed directors' proclivities. After all, directors had the power to hire and fire APJs. Directors had the authority to assign APJs for each panel and to convene expanded panels to re-decide cases when they were not in agreement with the decisions.[78]

I don't think it will be of any consolation to Ari, but he is not the only patentee who has a right to feel that the PTAB panels are stacked against inventors and in favor of Google. In September of 2012, Memphis-based B.E. Technology, L.L.C., filed a suit against Google in the Western District of Tennessee, alleging infringement of two of its patents. Unsurprisingly, Google petitioned to invalidate these patents when it filed for *inter partes review* proceedings at the PTAB. The same trio of APJs sat on both *inter partes review* panels. Who were these presiding APJs? They were Sally Medley, Lynne Pettigrew and Kalyan Deshpande. According to research conducted by Ropes & Gray, all three of these APJs were in the top 10 in terms of highest cancellation rates on some or all claims. Both APJs Medley and Deshpande had a 100% cancellation rate on some or all claims, and APJ Pettigrew had a 97% cancellation rate. B.E. Technology's patents did not survive their PTAB review.

---

[78] The USPTO is on record as having admitted that Director Michelle Lee stacked PTAB panels to ensure outcomes were to her liking. https://www.ipwatchdog.com/2017/11/13/ptab-targeted-advertising-patents-google-ad-revenue/id=90076/

The Plight of an Incandescent Inventor

Gene Dolgoff began his career in electronics as a six-year-old television repairman who charged a pretty penny for his service calls back in 1956. This precocious child soon became a prolific innovator.

The 3D television set that Gene made when he was 13-years-old awed patrons of the Brooklyn Museum where it was exhibited. By the time he was 14 -years-old, he was heavily involved in many facets of 3D technology and stereoscopic pictures. As a young man, Gene demonstrated a ravenous intellectual appetite. Before he set foot on a college campus, Gene:

- Created the first holography laboratory in New York;
- Developed an AM transmitter and established a radio station in his garage;
- Invented an ion-powered hovercraft;
- Designed a holographic invisibility cloaking device;
- Worked on 3D movies and polarized 3D glasses;
- Wrote a patent application on an electronic video projector;
- Invented the concept of matter holograms, an idea that was soon on display in *Star Trek*;
- Collaborated with another inventor to produce color videos on black-and-white televisions;

- Proposed a holographic model of the universe and the brain; and,
- Conceived the idea of using metal nanoparticles and induction heating to eradicate cancerous tumors.

Gene studied computer science, geometry, and astronomy at Columbia University. Then he matriculated at the City College of New York where he majored in physics, mathematics and electrical engineering. He also developed and taught a course in optics, lasers, and holography. Despite his indulgence in a boundless array of scientific quandaries, Gene was no square: During his college years, he worked with John Lennon on a holographic record cover, a 3D movie with Ringo Starr, and a laser-read record with the Grateful Dead.

Years later, Gene became a luminary in the burgeoning field of holography and the father of LCD projectors. While Gene's mind was perpetually racing ahead to produce the next cutting-edge invention, he never forgot his roots. At various points in his career, Gene found time to help his mother, an Auschwitz survivor, to try to recover money that his grandfather deposited in Swiss banks on the eve of the Holocaust. As I write these pages, Gene was busy running Holobeam Technologies, Inc., which is developing new techniques for using holograms to diagnose and treat diseases such as cancer.

There is much to learn from Gene's wealth of knowledge and coruscating intellect. We can also glean practical lessons from his career as an innovator and, by way of his experience, with the patent system.

A Luminary in Holography

In 1964, at the age of 14, Gene made his first hologram. By 1971, he devised the method for producing full-color holography on mass-scale. This was quite a feat for a 21 year-old, considering that only a handful of people were making holograms anywhere in the world in those days.

Let's discuss what Gene did at a high level. First, what is holography? In layman's terms, holography is the recording of interference patterns of energy. Holograms consist of clear features through which light passes and black features through which light cannot pass.

In the 1960s and early 1970s, holograms were processed on a piece of photographic emulsion film with photographic chemicals. The result was that holograms were made in a piecemeal fashion. Output was limited and the related costs were high. Encyclopedia Britannica, which wanted to put holograms in each volume of each of its successive series, learned the hard way that automating an inefficient process for making holograms was prohibitively expensive and impractical.

Gene engineered a process for producing full color holograms inexpensively, quickly and easily. (Unfortunately, describing his invention is not easy but what follows is Gene's explanation.) Gene's idea was to start with a photoresist emulsion to record the hologram. Once processed, the resulting hologram would have areas of different heights (instead of different densities) and would diffract light to produce the holographic images. This physical pattern could then be metal plated to make the pattern very strong and hard. This "master" hologram would be pressed against a thin sheet of plastic (like mylar or acetate) while being heated. The plastic would become soft and embossed; taking on the pattern from the master. The plastic would become part of the hologram as well. Once cooled (which happens quickly, using water cooling) the plastic hologram would be separated from the master and still retain the pattern. The plastic can come in long rolls, allowing many holograms to be embossed on the roll side-by-side. The plastic holograms are then coated with a release coat which dissolves with heat, which is then coated with a very thin layer of aluminum (by vacuum deposition), and then with a coating of heat-activated adhesive. Finally, the plastic hologram sandwich on the roll is placed against a credit card, or any other surface, where heat and pressure are applied. The heat melts the release coating, allowing the aluminum to be pulled away from the plastic roll, while still retaining its patterned shape, and the adhesive becomes activated, adhering the aluminum to the card. The reflective aluminum behaves just like the original hologram and reflects most of the light that hits it, producing a bright image.

Given the complexity, it is not surprising that the prototype for demonstrating the process to produce full color holograms on a large scale was not completed until 1979. It also took Gene quite a while to raise the money to reduce his invention to practice. Even considering the eight-year gap between conceiving of the invention and reducing it to practice, Gene was still way ahead of the pack. It wasn't until 1984 that the public was introduced to mass-produced holography when *National Geographic* ran a cover story on the subject called, "The Wonder of Holography."

Cash-Strapped Inventor Misses Massive Market

Around 1979, DuPont and American Banknote Corporation formed a joint-venture to produce currencies. I will explain the intersection of Gene and this joint-venture after I provide a brief backdrop.

Several years prior to 1979, DuPont introduced its Tyvek material, which are durable spunbonded olefin sheets that are stronger than paper and more cost-effective and versatile than fabrics. DuPont was in search of new markets for Tyvek and believed the material would be suitable to use in paper currencies. American Banknote was (and still is) a successful printer of financial documents and currencies. Before or during the time of its partnership with DuPont, American Banknote printed the currencies of Australia and Honduras. The DuPont-American Banknote partnership realized that it needed to ingrain its currencies with holograms to prevent counterfeiting. This partnership turned to John Caulfield in 1980, a world authority on holography. Dr. Caulfield was also the author of the *National Geographic* article mentioned above (which was circulated to millions of people) as well as 14 books, 41 book chapters, 252 refereed journal papers, and numerous popular articles.

Dr. Caulfield, a friend of Gene's since the late 1960s, told the DuPont-American Banknote executives that Gene had already invented a method for mass producing holograms in full color. Several executives from the joint-venture quickly requested a meeting with Gene. At the time of this meeting, Gene did not know much about patent law and, in any event, lacked the funds to file a patent application. He did, however, have DuPont sign a non-disclosure agreement before the meeting took place.

When the meeting with the DuPont and American Banknote executives transpired in the spring of 1980, Gene gave a tutorial to some of the engineers in attendance. The meeting included taking the executives on a tour of his laboratory, where some of Gene's sample holograms were observed by the executives. The meeting adjourned with DuPont agreeing to pay Gene to make some sample holograms. Gene delivered and was paid for such samples but the executives indicated that they had no further interest in collaborating with the young inventor.

By November 1982, Terrence Gallagher, one of the Banknote executives who toured Gene's laboratory and was exposed to the holographic samples, filed for patent protection on Gene's invention relating to the mass production of holograms. A related patent application issued as U.S. Patent

No. 4,728,377 on March 1, 1988 with American Banknote as the assignee. When learning of Mr. Gallagher's patent, Gene asked Mr. Gallagher why he would seek inventorship of something that he did not conceive. Mr. Gallagher responded by claiming that he had had the same idea before the spring 1980 meeting. This contention is hard to believe given that none of the executives seemed to know anything about producing holograms in volume at the time of their meeting with Gene. Filing patent applications that unfoundedly claim inventorship could be acts of inequitable conduct perpetrated on the USPTO.

When Gene and DuPont signed the non-disclosure agreement prior to the spring 1980 meeting, the Delaware-based conglomerate assured Gene that the NDA covered both DuPont and American Banknote due to DuPont's binding NDA with American Banknote. Thus, Gene believed Mr. Gallagher's filing of a patent application on an invention that Gene conceived and reduced to practice was a blatant violation of the NDA in place at that time. Needless to say, Gene was none too pleased when, around 1984, American Banknote began placing holograms on credit and debit cards issued by Mastercard and Visa; he believed that the enabling processes were purloined from him. At the time of my writing these pages, American Banknote continues to supply holograms used on Mastercard's and Visa's credit and debit cards.

Derivative NDA Proves to be Insufficient

While American Banknote—and by extension, DuPont—was raking in money from the holograms that Gene invented, he was struggling financially. While Gene was busy with a flurry of other projects, he didn't forget about his holograms or the violation of the related NDA. By the mid-1980s, he became concerned that the statute of limitations for initiating litigation for remedying the breach of contract (in the form of the NDA) would soon expire. So, in 1986, just before the clock on the statute of limitations struck midnight, Gene asked a real estate lawyer with whom he had some interaction to do him a favor by filing a lawsuit against DuPont and American Banknote; this suit was filed in New York federal court. True, a real estate lawyer may not have been the best choice for representation in a breach of contract case or in putting forth evidence of inequitable conduct at the USPTO. But Gene, like so many other inventors with limited budgets and time, allied with counsel that was accessible and willing to waive his fees.

In any case, about nine months after filing this breach of contract suit, the federal court declared that the lawsuit was filed in the wrong court. The federal court held that it lacked subject matter jurisdiction to hear the case and that the suit should have been filed in state court. (A federal court generally can only hear a civil suit if the case involves a "federal question" where the right arises from a federal law or the Constitution. Gene's case did not qualify for federal jurisdiction because the breaking of the NDA was a contractual breach governed by state law. The case could have been filed in federal court if jurisdictional "diversity of citizenship" was present, meaning the suit involved parties from other states. The parties named in the suit—Gene, DuPont and American Banknote—did not qualify as being citizens of different states as they all had a nexus to New York.)

What Gene did not know at the time of his initial lawsuit was that when a lawsuit is filed in the wrong court, the clock goes cold, meaning that the statute of limitations is extended by six months from the time of its dismissal. In 1987, Gene did not know that he had a six-month window for refiling his case in state court. In any event, a few years later, as his net worth was rising in lockstep with the ascendency of his LCD projectors, Gene hired more suitable lawyers to represent him at New York's Supreme Court's Appellate Division in Brooklyn. (Please see the related story about Gene and his LCD projectors below.)

In their 1990 appeal, Gene's legal team attempted to argue that the statute of limitations had not expired under the continuing breach theory. This legal argument asserts that every time a hologram is printed, the NDA is breached anew. Interesting theory. But the appeals court proved not to be a source of relief for Gene. That court held that the lawsuit was filed after the statute of limitations on breaking contracts ran its course. The appeals court also maintained that Gene did not have an NDA with American Banknote. The appeals court was correct on this point: Gene had an NDA with DuPont. DuPont signed an NDA with American Banknote. But there was no NDA between Gene and American Banknote. The joint-venture between DuPont and American Banknote was not deemed to be a remedy for this deficiency.

I can provide another example of a large company appropriating the intellectual property of a smaller company, despite the existence of an NDA between the two firms. Valkyrie Commissioning Services was a company that used robotically operated vehicles to execute subsea pipeline commissioning on the seafloor. VCS's newly introduced patent-pending method of gauging, filling, hydrostatic testing, dewatering, nitrogen packing, and drying was a worldwide game changer because it reduced the cost to perform those services in the deep-water by over 25%.

Two of the three largest subsea engineering companies—Oceaneering International and Sonsub International—were interested in entering into a joint-venture with VCS. Both of these potential partners signed NDAs with VCS. Concurrent with these discussions, VCS was in advanced negotiations with Shell Deepwater, which expressed an immediate need for VCS's robotically operated vehicles since it had 10 impending major deep-water projects for which VCS's technology was extremely well-suited. VCS shared the discussions it was having with Shell Deepwater with both Sonsub and Oceaneering under the protection of the NDAs. At the end of its evaluation for identifying the best joint-venture partner, VCS decided to align itself with Sonsub.

Oceaneering did not take its being passed over quietly. Rather it used its extensive relationship with Shell to convince that company to award Oceaneering its targeted projects. In return for Oceaneering agreeing to accept all patent infringement exposure (should it end up being sued by VCS), Shell agreed to pay for the engineering and build out of a technology that would parallel what VCS was patenting. Once this agreement was struck, Shell halted all communications with VCS.

Oceaneering infringed VCS's patented technology and violated its NDA with VCS. Moreover, Shell and Oceaneering pilfered the drawings, cartoons, descriptions, and performance specifications that VCS initially used in its brochures by placing such visuals in its own marketing materials. As a result, pursuant to two years of litigation followed by arbitration, Oceaneering agreed to license VCS's technology for its work with Shell and to pay VCS the $350,000 it incurred in legal costs.

Postscript

American Banknote has made enormous sums of money over several decades while commercializing the holograms that Gene invented. The extent to which DuPont profited from Gene's invention is unclear. But it can be said with certainty that Gene never made a dime from these inventions. Neither the patent system nor the broader legal system can be blamed for this tremendous missed opportunity; the rules were in place for inventors like Gene to monetize their inventions. In this case, the rules were not followed. Although he wrote an extensive disclosure on his holography process, Gene did not file related patent applications due to a lack of funds. The legal system provided a means of seeking redress for the breach of NDAs. However, Gene did not have an NDA in place with the breaching party. He also filed his complaint in the wrong court and did so delinquently.

Tragedies like Gene's occur frequently: Young inventors, bootstrapping entrepreneurs, new immigrants, less educated innovators, and busy executives often lack the money, knowledge, and time necessary to protect their inventions. Such are some of the risks associated with bringing inventions to market. What is truly unfortunate is that many innovators play by the rules only to have those rules changed in a manner that strips them of their legal protections covering their inventions. Such stories are provided throughout this book.

The Father of LCD Projectors

In the 1980s, home entertainment was limited. Cable was primitive. Satellites for use as an entertainment vehicle were non-existent. The Internet was, at best, a pipedream. Television was the unrivaled entertainment medium. Families that converged around their television sets of the day clamored for larger screens.

With his strong background in optics and liquid crystals, Gene thought he could develop a method for making larger television screens. Actually, he had a head start. Back in 1968, he designed an electronic video projector that was driven by light beams; these light beams were modulated by electro-optic materials passing through liquids or crystals. Quite a few experiments were conducted that entailed propagating acoustic waves through various liquids such as water, milk and gooey plastics. Eventually, in 1971, Gene came to the conclusion that liquid crystals would be the best substance for enabling televisions to project large-screen images with enhanced brightness. A further attraction of liquid crystals was that their relative low costs increased the likelihood that they would be embraced by television set manufacturers.

No Rush to the Patent Office

Some inventors rush to the Patent Office as soon as they believe they have come up with an invention. Not Gene. He put great thought into his patenting efforts.

Back in 1968, Gene didn't have much money, so he tried to write a patent application on electronic projectors himself. Before long, Gene realized that he needed a patent lawyer to at least review his drafted patent application. Gene was unacquainted with any patent attorneys but remembered that his college roommate's aunt worked in a building where patent lawyers practiced. So, Gene trudged into the Bronx and knocked on every door of this building until he came across Gerry Elman, a freshly-minted patent lawyer. (Gene and Gerry quickly bonded and their bond has endured the test of time—they continue to work closely on Gene's patent portfolio as of the time of my writing these pages.) With Gerry's input, Gene decided not to file a patent application in the late 1960s because he was unconvinced that his initially designed projector was practical.

Gene again resisted the inventor's impulse to seek patent protection in 1971, the year that he concluded that liquid crystals were the best medium through which light beams should traverse. Gerry impressed upon Gene that a common mistake that inventors make is filing patents that fail to accurately and thoroughly explain the invention. Thus, Gene refrained from filing a related patent application in the early 1970s because he wanted to more fully develop a prototype to be sure he could file a patent that accurately explained how the invention worked.

It wasn't until 1984 that Gene built a prototype of the world's first LCD projector. This time Gene was determined to patent and commercialize his invention. He filed his first patent application on December 31, 1987. A continuation-in-part of this patent application issued on April 30, 1991 with the title, "Active Matrix LCD Image Projection System."

Inventor Opens Up His Kimono

Gene believed that Japan's Seiko Epson would be the most logical partner for commercializing his LCD projection inventions. Selecting Seiko Epson as a partner was not a terribly difficult decision as no other company was producing LCDs. Contact with the Japanese electronics manufacturer was established and Gene invited executives from Seiko Epson to get a peek at his LCD projection invention in April of 1985. When the visiting executives arrived at Gene's New York laboratory, they were only privy to a private showing of his prototype. Nonetheless, the Japanese visitors snapped plenty of pictures and asked lots of questions. Because there was no NDA in place between Gene and Seiko Epson, he did not disclose proprietary insights to his Japanese visitors. At the conclusion of these cursory discussions, Seiko Epson notified Gene that the Japanese company was not interested in working with him.

Gene Wins $1 Million DARPA Award

Gene was undeterred. From 1984 to 1988, he privately demonstrated the prototype of his LCD projector to many potential investors from whom he was seeking capital infusions for Projectavision, his newly-founded company. Fortune smiled on Gene in 1988 when he was introduced to a senior partner at the Dreyfus Fund. This investment professional was so smitten with Gene's LCD projection technology that he wrote Gene a check for $100,000 on the spot. This check was handed over without the Dreyfus investor entering into any written agreement. Gene quickly parlayed this $100,000 investment into an additional $900,000 capital raise with the help of a penny-stock firm located on Long Island.

Shortly after this capital raise, in December of 1988, the U.S. Defense Department's Defense Advanced Research Projects Agency (DARPA) placed an article in hundreds of newspapers across the country. This brief article lamented that the United States lost a $15 billion opportunity as no American companies were manufacturing VCR players despite USA-based

AMPEX (arguably) producing the earliest permutation of a VCR player in 1956. The article stated that the Commerce Department was fearful of a repeat of American companies being shut out of a promising industry; this time the HDTV industry, which was projected to become a $250 billion opportunity. (By this time, Japanese companies were starting to roll-out HDTVs in, among other places, lobbies of Japanese office buildings.) The article concluded with DARPA offering a $1 million award to anyone who could come up with an HDTV system that worked better, but differently, than the Japanese versions.

Gene called DARPA as soon as he read the article. Once he tracked down the man in charge of the award, the inveterate inventor related to the DARPA man some of the advantages of his patent-pending invention. Gene's digital projection technology offered superior resolution compared to the analog technology used by Japanese manufacturers and could be connected to computers. Gene's LCD projection technology also escaped the screen size limitations common to cathode ray tubes used by almost every television manufacturer at that time.

The DARPA official was so excited that he summoned Gene to DARPA's headquarters in Washington DC the next day. At that meeting, DARPA requested detailed explanations about how Gene's technology functioned. Before divulging any technical details, Gene asked DARPA to sign an NDA. Initially, the agency refused to execute an NDA but ultimately relented as its thirst for keener insight into Gene's technology overwhelmed bureaucratic inertia. After listening to some technical details pertaining to his LCD projector, DARPA was sold. The officials asked Gene to write a proposal based on what he had already accomplished. When Gene won the $1 million DARPA award in 1989, he beat out 86 other proposals which were proffered by companies including AT&T, RCA, Westinghouse, Xerox, Sony, Philips, and Zenith as well as universities such as the Massachusetts Institute of Technology.

In 1989, advertising campaigns and magazine articles appeared describing the impending arrival of the world's first LCD projector, to be made by a joint venture between Epson and Kodak. The proposed product was essentially the same as Gene's early prototype. He filed suit against Epson and informed Kodak that Epson had stolen his technology. Gene's patent position was sufficiently strong to cause Epson and Kodak to quickly scrap their project, never introducing an infringing product.

Gene's LCD Technology Rockets Ahead

By the time 1990 rolled around, Projectavision went public on the NASDAQ and its shares were fast out of the gate. Its LCD projector technology was licensed to Matsushita, Panasonic, Samsung, and Radio Shack, among other firms. Projectavision also eventually subcontracted the manufacture of its own products which were sold in stores throughout the country. In 1993, Projectavision's market capitalization exceeded $200 million. Investors who held shares of Projectavision for the first five years after its initial public offering were rewarded with a 35-fold appreciation of their investments.

Gene was becoming wealthy. So too were other executives at Projectavision. Some of Gene's colleagues became stock jockeys; they didn't seem to care about anything but the price of Projectavision's shares. Several executives took to self-dealing and manipulating the company's shares. Gene blew the whistle on such malfeasance by informing the Securities and Exchange Commission and Projectavision's major investors. While the SEC declined to investigate the matter, the accused executives took action. They, together with several board members, banded together and retaliated by firing Gene in February of 1995.

Litigation Erupts at Projectavision

Gene counterattacked in the same year by filing suit against Projectavision and certain of its executives and board members; the ensuing litigation would cost him approximately $1 million in legal fees. Causes of action listed in Gene's initial compliant filed with the New York Supreme Court on April 7, 1995 included unjust enrichment, tortious conduct, breach of contract and self-dealing. In this litigation, Gene also requested receivership, which would require the appointment of an independent third-party (selected by the judge) to hold and prosecute the disputed patent rights while the suit proceeded.

The trial court upheld the sufficiency of Gene's complaint on all points but declined to appoint the requested receiver. However, that court took the fairly remarkable step of disqualifying Anderson Kill, Projectavision's counsel, from further work on the case because they also had been Gene's lawyers.

Gene's adversaries responded by filing their own lawsuit against

Gene and other executives with the United States District Court in New York's Southern District. The adversaries filed three complaints in this lawsuit, one of which accused Gene and other co-defendants of committing securities fraud based on their making allegedly false representations and omissions in filings with the Securities and Exchange Commission, and in Projectavision's press releases. All of the adversaries' complaints were dismissed on July 31, 1997.

The adversaries appealed the New York Supreme Court's decision refusing to dismiss Gene's case and the disqualification of their lawyers. The New York Appellate Division in Manhattan, consisting of a five-judge panel, unanimously upheld the lower court's decision and added receivership, which Gene had initially sought. This meant that his rights in the patents and patent applications would be protected by an independent lawyer at Projectavision's expense.

Projectavision found it difficult to sustain such defeats. That company lost its long-serving lawyers. Its litigation expenses were compounded by having to pay a receiver to look over its shoulders. Spooked by mounting expenses and the uncertainty of litigation, Projectavision's access to capital began to dry up. The company came to the conclusion that it was better off settling the suit.

While the exact terms of the settlement are subject to confidentiality, this award was much less than the millions of dollars that Gene sought. But it did result in rights to some of Gene's inventions reverting back to him. However, by the time the New York Supreme Court received such instructions from the appeals court, the judge presiding over the initial case passed away. The new judge appointed to preside over the matter took exception to the appeals court's decisions and ordered the litigants to negotiate a new settlement.

Through Gene's experience, we see how a judge can sidestep an appeals court's decision and force a prevailing patentee to relinquish much of what he won in litigation by negotiating a settlement with defeated antagonists. There are also situations where amicable negotiations are proceeding apace only to be derailed by a trigger-happy judge impatient to issue a decision against a patentee.

In January of 2017, the Federal Trade Commission issued an anti-trust complaint against Qualcomm. The FTC's motion for partial summary judgment sought the issuance of a ruling that would require Qualcomm to make licenses available to competing modem chip sellers. By mid-2018, discussions between the FTC and Qualcomm were proceeding smoothly. In fact, these parties notified Judge Lucy Koh of their serious settlement negotiations and jointly requested a delay in ruling on the FTC motion for partial summary judgment. In other words, the two parties were working out their disagreements on their own. However, the U.S. District Judge for the Northern District of California couldn't seem to let an opportunity to damage a patentee go to waste so she entered an order for the FTC's partial summary judgment against Qualcomm on November 6, 2018. Judge Koh ordered Qualcomm to renegotiate its contracts with smartphone manufacturers worldwide and to license patents based on stipulated chip prices. Qualcomm was also forced to submit to FTC monitoring for seven years, which to some extent, puts bureaucrats in charge of that company.

Naturally, Gene's adversaries made an opening offer in the new settlement discussions that was substantially less favorable to Gene than the already relatively paltry settlement arising out of the appeals court. At the end of the new settlement negotiations, the former Projectavision executives who arranged Gene's dismissal committed to pay him half a million dollars. In reality, they only paid Gene a quarter of a million dollars and retained some of the technology that he invented. Gene did manage, however, to retain some of his most coveted technology.

With Gene no longer at Projectavision's helm, it didn't take long for his opponents to drive Projectavision into the ground; in 2002 the Company filed for liquidation under Chapter 7 of the bankruptcy code. Projectavision's shareholders—founders, pension funds and retail investors alike—were completely wiped out.

Despite sustaining a financial body blow, Gene persevered. In April of 2002, he filed a continuation patent application titled, "High-Efficiency Display System Utilizing an Optical Element to Reshape Light with Color and Brightness Uniformity." This patent application, which claims an April

1994 priority date, issued as U.S. Patent No. 7,688,347 eight years later on March 30, 2010.

Patent Infringement Litigation Ignites

By 2014, Gene had reason to believe that roughly 100 companies were generating billions of dollars in revenues by infringing his '347 patent. Indeed, during the ensuing litigation against five alleged infringers, a patent damages firm calculated that Gene was owed approximately $1 billion in past and projected damages resulting from infringement. Recovering anything approaching $1 billion would require aggressive and tenacious litigation. Gene was wealthy in the early 1990s but such wealth dissipated over the years, requiring him to find a partner to finance his litigation efforts. He indeed secured a wealthy partner who recruited Susman Godfrey to represent Cascades Projection (the company formed by Gene and his investment partner) on a contingency basis. However, once *inter partes review* petitions were instituted against the '347 patent, Susman Godfrey resigned from the case. Cascades Projection scrambled anew to secure representation and litigation financing. After a battery of interviews with contingency-based patent litigation law firms and litigation financing firms, Cascades Projection selected Flachsbart & Greenspoon and the Mann Group.

On January 13, 2015, Cascades Projection initiated patent infringement suits in federal court in Los Angeles against the five largest companies selling projectors with Gene's technology. Included in these suits were Epson America and Sony Corporation. In these cases, only nine of the '347 patent's claims were asserted. In response to Gene's patent infringement suits, between May and September of 2015, these five defendants filed six petitions for *inter partes review* with the Patent Trial and Appeal Board.

Cascades Projection disclaimed three claims prior to the institution decision. Of the three instituted IPRs, one petition led to a settlement and two led to final written decisions by the PTAB that all of the asserted claims were unpatentable.

The PTAB relied on obviousness arguments to invalidate all of the Gene's asserted claims. With diagrams and scientific tutorials, Gene demonstrated that many of the references used to invalidate his claims simply could not be combined. The counselors representing the petitioners seemed clearly out of their league as they quoted definitions of complex engineering issues from dictionaries. Unfortunately, Gene's overwhelming intellectual firepower had no discernable impact on the PTAB judges. Their responses to most of the issues raised by the petitioners were, "…and this is persuasive to us." When Gene explained his technology, the PTAB judges typically responded by saying, "…and this is not persuasive to us."

Gene appealed the PTAB's invalidation of all of his asserted claims with the Court of Appeals for the Federal Circuit. At this proceeding, each side had fifteen minutes to make oral arguments. It was the impression of Gene and his attorney that the three judges had decided the case before the oral hearings began. In any event, by their own admission, the appeals court judges were overwhelmed by the complexity of the underlying technology. In fact, one Federal Circuit judge declared, "These are very technical terms….[Y]ou say one thing. Your friend says the other thing. I mean, you may be wrong for all I know. You may be right. I have no idea without expert testimony to distinguish between the two." Instead of seeking expert testimony, on March 13, 2018, the Court of Appeals for the Federal Circuit made short shrift of Gene's 50 years of related research by issuing a one-word affirmance of the PTAB's decision to invalidate all contested claims. Gene requested an *en banc* hearing at the CAFC but the majority of the twelve judges rejected Gene's petition. His efforts to have his case heard at the Supreme Court were forestalled by that court grating *writ of certiorari* to Oil States Energy Services, LLC v. Greene's Energy Group, LLC.

Postscript

In terms of his inventing, patenting and commercializing the LCD projector, Gene played by the rules. His patent applications were granted; in some cases, after eight years of examination. Licensing agreements were secured. Gene strove to protect shareholders from misrepresentations disseminated by other Projectavision executives. In return for his concern for the investing public, Gene was terminated from the company he founded. He won litigation at the state supreme court and appeals court levels and defeated litigation brought against him. Much of the money he devoted to securities litigation went down the drain when a New York Supreme Court judge forced him to negotiate a settlement with his defeated adversaries. Tremendous wealth was decimated when the same executives drove Projectavision into bankruptcy. Years later, when Gene tried to assert his patents against infringers generating billions of dollars from practicing his inventions, his patent claims were eviscerated by jurists who, by their own admission, had no understanding of the underlying technologies.

It is unfortunate that a man who has developed methods for manipulating light for the benefit of the world was unable to cause any adjudicating jurists to see the light in terms of upholding valid patents. Humanity will be worse off because those charged with enabling the enforcement of valid patents abdicate their duties. Such disregard for innovation and inventors will disincentivize the next generation of inventors and render the days a bit darker for us all.

Early-Stage Company Becomes a Victim of Economic Espionage

Diamonds are one of the hardest bulk materials found in nature. Diamonds are unmatched in their ability to diffuse heat, perform as a semiconductor, and create smaller and more powerful electronics. Due to their high resistance to scratching, synthetic diamonds have long promised to be an excellent material for smartphone displays.

Adam Khan began researching embedding diamonds in glass applications since he was a 19-year-old electrical engineering and physics student at the University of Illinois at Chicago. Adam's research into nanodiamonds continued at the Stanford Nanofabrication Facility and via collaboration with researchers at the U.S. Department of Energy's Argonne National Laboratory. One of the fruits of Adam's many years of research was a patented method for depositing a thin coating of tiny diamonds on materials such as glass.

In 2013, Adam formed Akhan Semiconductor to use proprietary low temperature diamond deposition technology in next generation diamond-based materials and devices. One manifestation of Akhan's technology is a nearly indestructible smartphone screen. Akhan's diamond glass, called Miraj, is 10-times more scratch-resistant and six-times stronger than Gorilla Glass which has long been the standard for smartphone displays. Reviewers reported that Miraj screens could be shoved into a pocket full of keys and coins and come out unscathed.

Huawei Becomes Interested in Diamond Glass

Miraj caught the attention of Huawei, the Chinese electronics giant, in late 2016. Angel Han, a Huawei engineer in San Diego, initiated contact with Akhan and expressed an interest in evaluating Miraj for suitability in Huawei's upcoming line of smartphones. The Huawei engineer pressured

Akhan into sending a sample of Miraj to her company's San Diego facilities by stating, "Vendor's capability to move fast and deliver is also crucial for us."

Akhan was both hopeful and skeptical. The potential of licensing the Miraj patents and technologies to a company that could place its diamond glass on tens of millions of smartphones was understandably appealing for the small research concern. But Akhan was concerned that Huawei may try to reverse engineer the Miraj samples that it requested. The material transfer agreement that both companies signed after intense negotiations covered all of Akhan's concerns. In order to deter reverse engineering, Akhan included language in the agreement that precluded Huawei from conducting tests that would cause damage to the Miraj samples. Huawei agreed to return the samples within 60 days. Knowing that its diamond coatings could potentially be used in laser weapons, Akhan required Huawei to comply with the International Traffic in Arms Regulations (ITAR), which govern the export of materials with defense applications.

With an executed agreement in place, Akhan sent two samples of its Miraj to Huawei's San Diego laboratories in February of 2017. Akhan pulled out all of the stops to ensure that these specimens would arrive in pristine condition. The four-inch square samples were wrapped in wax paper, tucked in a tray lined with a silicon gel, enclosed in a plastic case, blanketed by air bags, and sealed in a sturdy cardboard box.

Huawei Violates Material Transfer Agreement

Adam's earlier skepticism proved to be well placed when Huawei failed to return the samples in May of 2017. Emails to Ms. Han requesting the immediate return of the samples were ignored. When a delayed response arrived, Huawei reported that its "standard" tests were ongoing.

Akhan's samples were not returned until August of 2017, at least three months after the 60-day testing period concluded. Adam's nightmare scenario unfolded concurrent with his unpacking of the returned samples. The unscratchable Miraj samples were not just scratched; they were broken and three shards of diamond glass were missing. The missing shards proved that the damage did not occur during shipping; otherwise the shards would have remained in the box.

Akhan contacted Ms. Han about the broken and missing samples. Ms. Han responded by saying that she didn't know what happened to the Miraj samples because they had been in China. Ms. Han also confessed that the samples were shipped directly back to the Gurnee, Illinois company from China. Ms. Han seemed to be indifferent when told that diverting the samples to China was potentially a criminal violation of ITAR rules.

Akhan promptly alerted the Federal Bureau of Investigations about Huawei's apparent malfeasance. An investigation quickly commenced. Huawei clearly attempted to reverse engineer the Miraj glass by cutting through the sample to gauge the thickness of its diamond film. An FBI expert in forensic gemology concluded that Huawei blasted Akhan's Miraj glass with a 100-kilowatt laser, which was powerful enough to be used as a weapon. Huawei's representatives also admitted to breaking the contract with Akhan and, evidently, to violating U.S. export-control laws.

Huawei is a Repeat Intellectual Property Offender

Akhan Semiconductor is far from the only company to have its intellectual property expropriated by Huawei. Back in January of 2003, Cisco accused Huawei of copying its manuals (which buyers receive when they purchase routers) and software (which is visible when the routers operate). In its lawsuit, Cisco stated that, "Huawei made verbatim copies of whole portions of Cisco's user manuals." According to that lawsuit, the Shenzhen company's plagiarism was so extensive that Huawei inadvertently copied typos in the manual and bugs in Cisco's software. Former Huawei Human Resources Manager Chad Reynolds stated in a court filing that, "Huawei couldn't release its routers for shipment until it fixed a substantial number of the common Cisco bugs contained in the Huawei routers" for fear of revealing its unabashed copying.

Separately, David Barker coined the term "per user tilt" to describe his invention which entailed multiplying the number of signals from an antenna and tilting them to provide greater accuracy in communicating with mobile phones. Mr. Barker was the Chief Technology Officer of Quintel Technology, an Anglo-American developer of network antennas. He shared Quintel's per user tilt technology with Huawei in September of 2009, as negotiations relating to forming a partnership between the two companies were underway.

The partnership with Huawei never came to fruition. However, Huawei filed a patent application claiming per user tilt just one month after its executives met with Quintel. One of the documents used in this patent filing was still emblazoned with Quintel's name as well as the words "commercial in confidence."[79] The three-year court brawl only ended in 2018 when Quintel acquiesced to a legal settlement that was sealed with "a durable nondisclosure agreement."

[79] https://www.wsj.com/articles/huaweis-yearslong-rise-is-littered-with-accusations-of-theft-and-dubious-ethics-11558756858?mod=searchresults&page=1&pos=2

The Risks of Patent Reissuance

On a family drive from Chicago to Florida in the early 2000s, patent lawyer David Newman realized the importance of keeping his three young children entertained on long road trips. Fortunately for parents like David, electronic devices such as DVD players and iPads were becoming quite the rage at the time. But it was not yet *de rigueur* for each child to have his own electronic entertainment device. Not wanting his children to reenact battles from the Civil War over such a shared device on their drive to Florida, David conceptualized the Backrow Buddy. This mounting arm would host an electronic device such as an iPad or DVD player on a secure support surface, such as a seat back of a vehicle or in between the two front seats. Reducing the handling of such devices would lower the risk of damage from being dropped. Backrow Buddy would also allow all occupants of the backrows to view the screen and prevent the unit from being propelled across the car in case of rapid breaking or collision.

In his garage, David applied action to his idea. Initially, he drilled some holes in a piece of plywood, into which the rods of headrests could be inserted. He experimented with bungee cords to hold a DVD player to a plywood arm. Knowing that mass merchants appreciate density in their displays, David also tried a variety of hinges so that the Backrow Buddy could be folded. Many iterations were developed and accompanying drawings produced. David turned these drawings into a marketing piece which he distributed on the floor of a Chicago auto show.

David contracted with a Taiwanese manufacturer that developed an attractive prototype. With this beta Backrow Buddy in hand, David wasted no time calling in a favor from a friend who was a merchandise broker. This friend had three or four meetings with buyers for Walgreens but was unable to secure purchase orders from this national retail chain. In the midst of all of these efforts to bring his Backrow Buddy to the market, David filed a provisional patent application on September 17, 2003 and a non-provisional patent application on September 17, 2004. This patent application issued as U.S. Patent No. 7,111,814 on September 26, 2006.

Patent Lawyer Asserts His Patents

Beginning around 2009, David started seeing what he believed to be infringing mounting arms popping up in a variety of places. While David is a successful Chicago-based patent lawyer, he believed his case would appear more credible if he could demonstrate that other skilled patent lawyers thought enough of the strength of the '814 patent—and in the evidence of its infringement—to assert the '814 patent on a contingency basis. Early on in his assertion efforts, David retained two patent litigators to represent him in pursuing settlements or damages awards against alleged infringers.

These contingency fee patent lawyers achieved some degree of success. Pursuant to preparing and serving a complaint against Digital Innovations, that company remitted a $30,000 settlement to DVD Mount (David's company), in 2011 for its past infringement. Digital Innovations also identified other products reading on the '814 patent and agreed to pay David a two-percent royalty on future sales of such products. In my opinion, Digital Innovations behaved relatively respectfully. The only problem was that the mounting devices that Digital Innovations manufactured were directed to DVD players. With the introduction of the iPad by Apple in 2010, demand for DVD players collapsed a few years after the settlement, obliterating whatever royalty revenue expectations David may have had.

Between 2011 and 2015, DVD Mount asserted the '814 patent against about 30 infringers who were offering iPad mounts for automobiles. Due to David and one of his lawyers writing letters and emails, a few distributors agreed to cease selling infringing mounting arms. For instance, Ram Mount, Inc., had its law firm review the '814 patent. But instead of negotiating a license for sales going forward, Ram Mount agreed to stop selling its iPad/tablet computer mounting arms. David never knew the extent of Ram Mount's past sales but decided not to pursue enforcement of the '814 patent against Ram Mount for past damages. Separately, the other patent lawyer working on a contingency basis on DVD Mount's behalf brought in a $30,000 settlement in 2014 from AudioVox for that company's past infringement.

Inventor Believes Verifone Infringed His Patent

Around 2014, it came to David's attention that Verifone seemed to be infringing the '814 patent as it installed some 100,000 point-of-sale screens on mounting arms attached to the rods of headrests in taxicabs all over the country. David's efforts to initiate a dialog to reconcile the believed infringement were met with non-responsiveness.

David approached 10 contingency patent attorneys in his efforts to retain counsel to represent him in the Verifone matter. The potential damages caused by Verifone at that time were simply not large enough to attract contingency lawyers. They wanted to take on cases with at least $20 million in potential damages awards, and Verifone appeared to be causing something on the order of $10 million in royalty damages based on infringing sales at the time.

When David and his lawyers sent suspected infringers cease-and-desist letters, they sometimes received pieces of potentially invalidating prior art in return. Thus, David came to the conclusion that to strengthen his assertion efforts he would have to fortify the '814 patent. His choices were to demonstrate that the '814 patent was valid by putting it through the newly-created *inter partes review* process or by narrowing the claims in a reissue procedure at the USPTO. The *inter partes review* procedure was an unknown entity at the time, and at a cost of roughly $50,000, wasn't worth a roll of the dice for David.

So, off to reissuance David went. After paying the few thousand dollars in reissuance filing fees, he began narrowing the claims in the '814 patent. Early on in the process, David believed that Verifone was one of the most active and successful infringers. So, he narrowed the claims to better read on Verifone's infringement with its point-of-sale screens. During the five-year reissuance process, iPads became increasingly prevalent. But the more David narrowed the claims in the reissuance process, the more those claims moved away from covering the arm-mounted devices that cradled iPads and tablets. David never collected a dime from Verifone. (Interestingly, Verifone was later sold to an investor group led by Francisco Partners for $3.4 billion.) Due to the course that reissuance took, fewer of the devices that hold iPads or tablets are likely to infringe his '814 patent.

Conclusion

David was no patent troll. He made a valiant effort to produce and commercialize his invention. In the years immediately following the issuance of the '814 patent, a quick search on Amazon would have revealed hundreds of likely infringers. David was prepared to negotiate amicably with any of these firms. When silence followed his overtures, he was left with no choice but to assert his patent. These efforts only began after he recruited two other lawyers, both of whom agreed to represent David after independently coming to the conclusion that the '814 patent was valid and infringed.

David is actually a relatively fortunate patentee. Some sixteen years into his '814 patent saga, he is close to breaking even. It is true that he won two $30,000 settlements. But his contingency lawyers were paid $20,000 of that $60,000. The time that David devoted to pursuing the reissuance of the '814 patent alone represented at least $40,000 of his time.

The current patent environment is so disheartening that even highly talented patent lawyers are throwing up their hands. David decided to abandon the '814 patent as he could not justify paying the third maintenance fee.

Character Assassination and Patent Invalidation

The Asghari-Kamrani brothers emigrated from Iran to the west as teenagers. Kamran spent about a decade in the Netherlands, initially studying computer and software programming, and then working for private companies in the computer industry. Nader studied computer science at the Technical University of Vienna before programming professionally. In the late 1990s, Kamran and Nader left the comforts of Europe and moved to the United States to apply their software programming and computer architecture skills.

The brothers' emigration to the United States coincided with the Internet bursting onto the world's stage. People from the world over were flocking to the new medium. Kamran and Nader deduced that data and dollars would soon ricochet around the Internet. In the waning days of the last century, Internet activity was largely confined to reading static pages and viewing latently delivered videos. The Asghari-Kamrani brothers believed that the Internet would soon facilitate more important missions such as electronic communications, e-commerce, banking, security brokerage, and recruiting. They correctly surmised that the Internet would even become an enabler for telemedicine and a gateway for citizens to avail themselves of a variety of government services. One's credit scores, brokerage accounts, and job postings—not to mention national security—would soon stand at risk of being compromised by imposters.

Such opportunities afforded by the Internet would introduce risk. One user could maintain multiple virtual identities. The Persian programmers were also concerned that bad actors could expropriate the identities of others, depriving the rightful owners of their own identities. Today, this insidious cybercrime is known as identity theft.

The Importance of Online Authentication

Contemporary solutions for preventing the misappropriation of online identities were clearly inadequate. In the early days of the Internet, passwords were the default security mechanism used throughout the online world. The problem was that it wasn't too difficult for even novice hackers to infiltrate password-protected computers or online accounts. This was especially true at a time when so many users created easy-to-remember passwords that quite often were scribbled on sticky notes and then slapped on computers. The alternatives to passwords weren't that great either. Biometrics were not commercially available on a large scale and to the extent biometrics were available they were prohibitively expensive. Privacy fears abounded at the very notion of biometrics. Back in the olden days, there were apparatuses called smart cards and smart card drivers. (They really weren't that smart.) The regimen for using these archaic devices was that a business or government agency would send its customers a smart card and an accompanying device. These machines were difficult to configure even for professional computer programmers such as the Asghari-Kamrani brothers. Nor were they interoperable: A computer user would have to rig up one of these contraptions for each different business or government agency with which he interacted.

But what would be a better solution for preventing the hijacking of users' accounts and identities on the Internet? Whatever form the solution would take, it would have to (1) be nearly ubiquitous in the cyberworld, (2) be capable of handling massive numbers of verifications concurrently, (3) relieve end users of the necessity of having to install additional hardware, (4) be easy to use and manage, (5) be cost effective, and (6) have an extremely low error rate. Crafting such a solution would require an abundance of computer architect skills, capital, time, and hard work.

Kamran and Nader certainly had suitable academic training and work-related experience in data management and systems architecture. Nader had worked for large organizations such as hospital systems in Austria and Michigan, while Kamran was one of the top solution architects for the technology responsible for delivering the Affordable Care Act, more commonly known as ObamaCare.

Capital, however, was in short supply. The vulnerabilities associated with passwords and other cybersecurity measures in use in the early- to mid-2000s might seem obvious in hindsight. But during this time period, the Asghari-Kamrani brothers were unable to raise capital to take their patent pending authentication solution to the market because investors believed that passwords provided sufficient security. Rather than allowing the lack of external capital deter them from their mission, the entrepreneurial programmers redoubled their dedication to finding a solution for identity misappropriation online. Nader worked on producing a unique authentication solution between 50 and 60 hours each week for two years. Kamran dedicated at least 30 hours a week to the project.

Prior to patenting their invention, the Asghari-Kamrani brothers subjected their thesis—that an online authentication solution would be the way to go—to a battery of tests. Kamran and Nader performed a comprehensive market study and developed multiple authentication concepts. They selected the best concept and revised it many times by carefully evaluating market acceptance of alpha and beta versions. Part of their solution, later the subject of extensive patenting efforts, was that an institution could authenticate authorized users by sending them computer-generated codes through a medium such as email and text. Today, we all use such technologies when logging onto accounts or resetting passwords.

The Patenting Process Begins

After conceiving, refining and testing their online authentication technology, the brothers filed their first patent application on August 29, 2001. This patenting effort was to become part of an extended patent family.[80] As the brothers were strapped for cash, they drafted and began prosecuting this patent application themselves.

The patent review process, which cost Kamran and Nader tens of thousands of dollars, got off to a late start: It took the examiner about three-and-a-half years to produce his initial search results. The pace of examination didn't accelerate very much once patent review got underway. After almost seven years of examination, the patent application issued as U.S. Patent No. 7,356,837 on April 8, 2008. Who is to blame for this prolonged examination? Perhaps, the apportionment of blame can be approximated by using statistics from the USPTO: The Patent Office granted the '837 patent an additional 832 days of patent life due to USPTO delays while reducing patent life by 61 days due to applicant delays. Thus,

[80] At the time of my writing these pages, the Asghari-Kamrani's patent family consisted of nine issued patents and two pending patent applications.

roughly 93% of the prosecutorial delay was due to the USPTO while about 7% of the delay was due to Kamran and Nader.

As the prosecution of the '837 patent application got underway, examination became increasingly contentious. Thus, the brothers retained patent lawyers. In the later stages of the prosecution of the '837 patent family, at least one of these lawyers reportedly told the brothers that the Patent Office's intransigence seemed to be a ploy to drain Kamran and Nader financially. The brothers were further advised to accept the narrowing of the claims listed in the '837 patent application and to try to recover relinquished claims by filing continuation applications. Kamran and Nader complied with this advice. In response to the examiner's rejections, they canceled a broad swath of patent claims on September 24, 2007.

The brothers tried to recover lost claims by filing continuation applications to the '837 patent, an effort which has been ongoing for nearly 20 years. (The conclusion of the prosecution of the '837 patent family, at the time of my writing these pages, is indeterminable as one related patent application was filed in June of 2017, and another was filed in the summer of 2018.) This effort has been so extended, expensive, and daunting that there were several occasions when the patent lawyers advised the brothers to abandon their patenting efforts. They never wavered. They pursued child patents without financial support from the venture capital industry. The brothers could not rely on royalties from licensing their '837 parent patent; they did not even attempt to license that patent after it issued on account of its emaciated claims.

To preserve cash, the Asghari-Kamrani brothers drafted and prosecuted the first two children patents independently. However, they did retain patent counsel to draft and prosecute a grandchild patent (i.e., a continuation of a continuation patent). This patent effort claimed a priority date of August 29, 2001 and was filed on September 15, 2008. Titled "Centralized Identification and Authentication System and Method"—this patent application became U.S. Patent No. 8,266,432 on September 11, 2012. Thus, it took the brothers more than eleven years to secure most of the patent claims that they initially pursued. But the allowance of the '432 patent is far from the end of the story.

Infringement is Detected

As the winter of 2014 turned into the winter of 2015, it came to the brothers' attention that a U.S. Company—which will be referred to by the alias

"FinCo"—was likely infringing their '432 patent. Kamran and Nader notified FinCo of their suspicions by sending the supposed infringer a friendly letter. This correspondence identified the patent at issue and asked if FinCo was interested in discussing the potential licensing of the '432 patent or its wider patent family. Discussions transpired but FinCo expressed no interest in licensing the brothers' patents. Rather, FinCo let it be known that it was reserving the option to attempt to invalidate the '432 patent by filing petitions under *inter partes review* or covered business method procedures as set forth by the Patent Trial and Appeal Board.

Much of the talks between the brothers and FinCo revolved around the brothers signing a non-disclosure agreement drafted by FinCo. The backdrop of the proposed NDA was that the brothers were trying to estimate the extent of FinCo's alleged infringement. For instance, to estimate royalties, the brothers were trying to determine how many of FinCo's customers were availing themselves of FinCo's products in an infringing manner.

On the surface, it seemed understandable that FinCo would condition its disclosure of such information upon the brothers signing an NDA. Like many of its peers in the financial services sector, FinCo is heavily reliant on authentication technologies to serve its customers over the Internet. Fears arose on the part of FinCo's stakeholders that its critical technologies could be subject to injunctions or steep patent damages awards. In any event, FinCo dallied in executing its own NDA for several months.

A few days after signing the NDA, FinCo notified the brothers' lawyer that the financial institution was severing discussions with the inventors. Concurrent with this notification, in early September of 2015, FinCo filed an *inter partes review* petition against the '432 patent. It turns out that the reason FinCo stalled in executing its own NDA was that it was using the time to collect what it believed was prior art to try to invalidate the '432 patent during *inter partes review*. The brothers never received their quid pro quo for signing the NDA; FinCo refused to disclose the correct information relative to the extent to which it may have been infringing the '432 patent.

Litigation Explodes

FinCo may have thought that the brothers would buckle when confronted with the high risks of their patent being invalidated during challenges in government tribunals or by the prospect of having to pay exorbitant legal fees. If this is what FinCo thought, it thought wrong. Kamran and Nader were intrepid. Their failure to raise capital to any extent did not dissuade them from bootstrapping their litigation efforts. They scraped enough money together to engage a patent litigator. The brothers and their legal team assumed an offensive posture: On October 30, 2015, they brought suit against the alleged infringer in the District Court for the Eastern District of Virginia.

Based largely on a nearly two-hour hearing held on June 27, 2016, Judge Robert Doumar ruled that the claims in the '432 patent were invalid. This conclusion was handed down despite Judge Doumar acknowledging that, "there isn't any evidence that [the invention] was done before [the computer context]."

While admitting that the invention covered by the '432 patent was novel, the court seemed to be grasping for an excuse to invalidate it. Rather than putting forth any effort to uncover facts, the court allowed FinCo to present an imaginary story that had nothing to do with Internet security and authentication. The hypotheticality admitted into the court was about an in-store payment method that no institution has ever practiced before and that no institution will likely ever practice. Here is the story that FinCo was allowed to relate:

> Let's say that a company wants to buy a new chair. A local retailer will sell goods on credit to anyone who has an account at a local bank. By previous arrangement, when the company needs something from the retailer, an employee will go to the manager of the bank. The manager will, using a set of dice containing both letters and numbers, generate a random code. The manager writes down this code as well as an expiration time for the code and gives it to the employee. The employee then goes to the retailer. The retailer calls the bank manager and confirms that the code is correct and still valid. The code confirmed, the retailer knows that the individual is an employee of a company that has an account at the bank. The retailer gives the employee a chair.

As if this concocted story did not require sufficient suspension of disbelief, the court ad-libbed by presenting its own imaginary story:

> If this seems a rather involved way to purchase a chair, imagine instead that an intelligence service has a source within a foreign country. Periodically the source conveys a packet of information to a courier sent by the intelligence service. Although the same courier is never used twice, it is important that the source confirm the identity of the courier. By previous arrangement, whenever a courier goes to pick up the packet, the courier first visits the source's handler, who works at an embassy in the foreign country. The handler gives the courier a time-sensitive code. The courier then goes to the source and tells the source the code. The source relays the code back to the handler who confirms its validity and thus the identity of the courier. The packet is then handed over.

Allegations of Inequitable Conduct

The decision invalidating the '432 patent was rendered on July 5, 2016 on grounds of its claims being abstract. No definition of what "abstract" meant was ever provided. Further, this decision was rendered with prejudice, meaning that the brothers were barred from filing a lawsuit on the same issue at a later date. To add to their injury, FinCo delayed Kamran and Nader's ability to appeal the decision by one year when it filed inequitable conduct suits against both brothers and all of their prior patent lawyers. Judge Doumar even entangled the litigation lawyer representing the brothers into defendants in the inequitable conduct case because, during the initial trial, he filled out a form to correct a minor patent priority issue.

Besides delaying an appeals court trial by a year, the inequitable conduct charges shifted the focus of the litigation from patent infringement to the commission of crimes, in the form of inequitable conduct, allegedly perpetrated upon the Patent Office by the Asghari-Kamrani brothers. Knowing that Judge Doumar was a long-time criminal judge, FinCo used the inequitable conduct case as a platform to imply that the brothers were criminals, or worse. FinCo went far beyond the usual name calling, such as referring to Kamran and Nader as trolls. FinCo seemed to have calculated that portraying the Asghari-Kamrani brothers as foreign agents from a hostile country during the inequitable conduct case would resonate with Judge Doumar. During an inequitable conduct-related deposition, FinCo accentuated the fact that it caters to U.S. military personnel while prompting the brothers to disclose their Iranian origins. During this deposition, FinCo posed questions to the brothers such as, "Which country do you come from?" and "You know that FinCo serves the U.S. military, correct?" Other questions that FinCo posed were designed to insinuate that the root of their litigation funding was somehow linked to Iran, an enemy of the United States.

Questions such as these were dripping in irony given that the authentication technology developed by the brothers can enhance America's national security. FinCo also stated that it intended to drain the brothers financially by moving to invalidate their entire patent portfolio. After months of discovery and many depositions, FinCo still had not presented a shred of evidence to justify their aggression or to support their allegations of inequitable conduct committed by the brothers or their counselors. Yet, Judge Doumar allowed the trial to proceed. In the midst of the trial, when it seemed to Kamran and Nader that such lines of questioning were influencing Judge Doumar and that FinCo's scorched-earth tactics were reducing their ability to defend their patent portfolios, the brothers filed a motion seeking Judge Doumar's recusal. This motion was rejected. In any event, when the inequitable conduct cases drew to a close in the spring of 2017, no decisions for inequitable conduct were found in any of the suits filed by FinCo.

The result of the brothers losing their infringement suit and FinCo losing its inequitable conduct complaint triggered a flurry of appeals to the Court of Appeals for the Federal Circuit. The brothers appealed the district court's invalidation of their '432 patent, and FinCo appealed the decision against its failing to demonstrate that the attorneys working on behalf of Kamran and Nader committed acts of inequitable conduct. These two appeals were coincided by an appeal of two invalidity challenges under the covered business methods program (discussed below). To top it off, FinCo filed motions to have the brothers pay their attorney's fees.

A Corollary with Real Estate

I realize that this story might be a bit technical for those readers who are not familiar with patents. So, allow to me summarize Kamran's and Nader's story with a corollary with real estate.

The Asghari-Kamrani brothers worked hard and saved money for years. They rigorously researched real estate investment opportunities for months and months. Finally, they identified a large plot of land outside the city that they believed could one day be very valuable. They hired lawyers to make sure the acquisition of this land was in compliance with all applicable laws. Kamran and Nader did not immediately develop this real estate but they paid all of the required property taxes since the day they bought the property.

A few years later, the brothers decide to take a drive to take a look at their land. They were surprised to see a thriving shopping center attracting throngs of shoppers at the site.

Kamran and Nader contacted the owners of the shopping center to discuss rents for past and future use of their land. The owners of the shopping center responded by turning to the county's records office and the courts to invalidate the brothers' title to their land. It is alleged that the Asghari-Kamrani brothers acquired their land through fraud but no evidence to support such contentions was ever produced. To increase their leverage in possible settlement talks, the owners of the shopping center moved to invalidate all of the land titles that the brothers accumulated throughout the state. After spending a fortune in legal fees, the brothers demonstrated that no such fraud was ever perpetrated in any of their real estate deals. But damage to their reputations had already been done; the media's coverage of the dispute was replete with labeling the brothers as "land trolls."

After more legal fees were expended by both sides, the shopping center succeeded in invalidating the brothers' title to the land underneath the shopping center. Their title wasn't defeated based on the presentation or review of facts or evidence. Rather, the title was deemed to be invalid when the owners of the shopping center and the judge engaged in a free-association exercise based on hypotheticals, which were further distorted by the introduction of increasingly disconnected intellectual detours.

Half of the money saved by not paying the Asghari-Kamrani brothers their back rents was handed out as bonuses to the executives responsible for invalidating the brothers' title. While these executives celebrated their victory with champagne and caviar, a group of their tenants also convened a meeting. Their only agenda item was how to revoke whatever rights the shopping center was using to justify collecting its rents. The title-revoking precedent set by the shopping center may prove to be the demise of its business.

Erroneous Institution Leads to Claims Invalidation

While FinCo and the Asghari-Kamrani brothers kept the Eastern District Court of Virginia busy, there was considerable activity happening concurrently at the PTAB. The *inter partes review* petition that FinCo filed against the '432 patent was denied institution in February of 2016. FinCo did not relent in its crusade to destroy the '432 patent; in May of 2016, that company filed two Covered Business Methods (CBM) petitions against the '432 patent.

Kamran and Nader believe that the CBM proceedings were erroneously instituted because the CBM program was designed to review claims for data processing or other operations used in the practicing, administering, and managing of financial products or services. The CBM program was expressly not established to review claims covering technological inventions. The brothers' position was since neither the '432 patent's specifications nor claims covered financial activities, that patent should not be subject to scrutiny under the CBM program. The administrative patent judges serving on the CBM panel stretched the truth by saying that the claims in the '432 patent cover "funds transfers," "accessing bank account," and "payments," but none of those terms are used in either the specification or the claims contained in that patent. The Asghari-Kamrani brothers tried to remove their '432 patent from the jaws of the CBM panel by putting forward cases (such as the Federal Circuit's decision in SecureAxcess) which proved the brothers' point. They also described the financial hardship that they would bear if they had to defend the patent's validity while under review by the CBM program. These arguments did not sway the CBM panel.

The PTAB instituted repeated CBM challenges against patents owned by another company, Trading Technology International. These patents cover various graphical user interfaces, which are not business methods as graphical user interfaces present a technological solution to a technological problem. In fact, these same TTI innovations have been patented in Europe where there is an absolute prohibition against business methods patents.

Further, the administrative patent judges that served on the panel that heard the CBM petitions were different from those appointed to consider the petition for *inter partes review*. Since the *inter partes review* petition was not instituted, the selection of new administrative patent judges led the brothers to think that the USPTO was selecting adjudicators that were more inclined to invalidate the '432 patent. Unsurprisingly, the PTAB not only instituted two CBM panels but, on August 15, 2017, invalidated all of the challenged claims.

Back to the Appeals Court

All of the appeals—the invalidation of the '432 patent, the decisions from the inequitable conduct cases, and the Patent Trial and Appeal Board's decision with respect to the two covered business methods matters—were consolidated shortly after they reached the Court of Appeals for the Federal Circuit.

The decisions that the Court of Appeals for the Federal Circuit handed down on September 11, 2018 were devastating for Kamran and Nader. The appeals court issued two Rule 36 decisions. One affirmed the district court's decision holding that all of the claims listed in the '432 patent were invalid on account of their covering ineligible subject matter. The brothers' request for an *en banc* hearing was denied. The other affirmation upheld the district court's finding no inequitable conduct on the part of the brothers or any of the patent attorneys that served them over the years. But the appeals of the covered business method invalidity challenges were deemed to be moot. It was also decided that the brothers would not have to pay FinCo's legal fees.

What was even more heart-breaking to the Asghari-Kamrani brothers was the CAFC's short-shrift treatment. The facts were not sought. None of the claims at issue were analyzed. And the CAFC offered no explanation for its one-word ("Affirmed") decision. To the extent that any rationale could have factored into the CAFC's decision, it could only have come from the district court tenuously tethering its own tangential tale to the defendant's imaginary story. Such random reasoning could doom any patent.

Kamran and Nader Asghari-Kamrani told me that they detected a distinct change in the posture of examiners after the America Invents Act was signed into law by President Obama on September 16, 2011. In the Asghari-Kamrani brothers' experience, the examiners became more antagonistic once the AIA was promulgated. For instance, the brothers' examiner would repeatedly reject their patent applications on the grounds of their being abstract, but never explained what constitutes "abstract." Multiple examiner interviews were required so that the brothers could discern what the examiner found troubling.

Another sleight-of-hand that the Asghari-Kamrani brothers shared with me occurred in connection with the examination of their 15,639,020 patent application, which was filed pursuant to the Prioritization Patent Examination Program on June 30, 2017. Up until April of 2018, the examiner repeatedly rejected many of the claims sought based on §101 eligibility issues. Once the Berkheimer memo (which requires examiners to provide more rationale and/or support for patent rejections) was issued on April 24, 2018, the examiner shifted the thrust of his objections to §103 obviousness grounds.

Inter Partes Review and Witchcraft

Let's say your doctor, Dr. Elder, spent $250,000 getting his medical education from a fine medical school and has been practicing medicine with distinction for 40 years. Then, some young doctor, Dr. Young, just out of medical school learns that the seasoned doctor has built a lucrative practice. Dr. Young could work hard for 40 years and hope to build up a practice as successful as Dr. Elder's. But why bother? Why not just knock out the seasoned doctor via administrative proceedings? So, Dr. Young decides to file a motion in favor of revoking Dr. Elder's license with the medical boards. Dr. Young's lawyer points out that when Dr. Elder went to medical school, he did not take courses in acupuncture or faith-healing—familiarity of which is now a requirement for licensure. Dr. Elder responds by saying that he would gladly take classes in acupuncture and faith-healing if that would enable him to maintain his license to practice medicine. But this petition is struck down. On top of that, one of the members of the medical panel says that even if Dr. Elder were to take courses in acupuncture and faith-healing, he would still lose his license because the doctor never studied or ever indicated his willingness to learn the teachings of witchcraft. I don't see much difference between this scenario and the goings on during *inter partes review* proceedings.

Postscript

The Asghari-Kamrani brothers wouldn't disclose how much money they invested in patent prosecution, defending their patents in a variety of procedures at the PTAB and in patent litigation. But the cumulative figure must be in the millions of dollars. The brothers have yet to see one dime in revenue for their efforts and they may never earn anything approaching a reasonable return on their patenting efforts. What is certain is that the nearly 20 years (and counting) that Kamran and Nader dedicated to developing and enforcing their patent portfolio directed to online authentication can never be recovered. Another thing is certain: The consequences of patent invalidation—whether on the grounds of their being abstract, or otherwise—are not abstract.

Inventors like Kamran and Nader often spend more of their lives developing their patent portfolios than raising their children. The Asghari-Kamrani brothers had no children when they embarked on their patenting journey. Kamran now has two children and Nader has three. Some of these young adults are now on their way to college.

For a small subset of the community of independent inventors, money is no object. But for the vast majority of independent inventors, there just isn't enough money to pursue the development of their innovations while meeting familial obligations. Money is always lacking and financial concerns are a source of constant angst. I did not delve into Kamran's or Nader's personal lives to any extent, but they mentioned that their tenacious pursuit of patents required enormous sacrifices on the part of their families. And not just temporary or sporadic sacrifices but, in the case of their children, deprivations all throughout their formative years.

Many struggling inventors who are also parents are confronted with a zero-sum dilemma. They are haunted daily by the fear that the more money they invest in their patent portfolios, the more they are stunting their children's development. Should an inventor spend $20,000 on a court motion or enroll their family in a better health insurance program? Should an independent inventor register for a conference that costs $3,000 and could help him identify a potential licensee, or should he use that money to send his children to summer camp? Should an independent inventor authorize a damages expert to work another hour or buy his children new shoes? Should an independent inventor travel to an examiner interview or hire a math tutor for his kid struggling with geometry? Is it worthwhile for an inventor to file another provisional patent application if paying that fee requires his children to forgo guitar lessons for six months? Questions such as these were not abstract to Kamran and Nader. Nader told me that his children never flew on an airplane and that he could not afford to send his daughter to the university of her choice.

You may think that the Asghari-Kamrani brothers are undeserving of sympathy. Perhaps their '837 patent family simply consisted of lousy patents. If this was the case, then the Patent Office was correct to rigorously challenge those patent applications over long periods of time. But this does not seem to be the case. In fact, the brothers immediately notified the USPTO when the '432 patent was invalidated by the district court in Eastern Virginia. They even furnished the USPTO with Judge Doumar's decision. Was this notification proof that Kamran and Nader were gluttons for punishment? No. They took this action because they wanted the examiners to consider the same §101 patent eligibility issues that Judge Doumar found to be abstract during their review of pending and future patent applications from the '837 patent family. The patent application under examination at the time Kamran and Nader notified the Patent Office ended up issuing as did four later related applications from the same patent family. While every patent application is unique, the fact that the Patent Office repeatedly granted patent family applications indicates that the examiners disagreed with the district court's finding of invalidity on grounds of the '837 patent family being abstract. As further evidence that the '432 patent was not invalid, FinCo's *inter partes review* petition filed against the '432 patent was denied institution in February of 2016.

You might reserve your sympathy for Kamran and Nader because they could have mitigated their financial hemorrhaging at any time during their patenting journey by ceasing their patenting efforts. That is true. But when justice is repeatedly denied, it is not the seeker of justice that is deserving of rebuke. Rather, it is those who routinely withhold justice that should be condemned.

When the Asghari-Kamrani brothers left Iran for Europe they were seeking to acquire technical skills. And this they did. When they departed Europe for the United States, they were in search of a large market, an entrepreneurial ecosystem, and reasonable laws consistently applied. The United States indeed offers the world's largest single market where the entrepreneurial spirit is still very much alive. However, the nation's patent laws have become incomprehensible, contradictory, and unfair.

To my knowledge, the immigrant inventors have complied with all applicable American laws—including those related to immigration, taxation, and the conducting of business—for more than 20 years. Kamran and Nader expended enormous time, energy, and money trying to navigate the patenting process and complying with the procedures governing patent litigation. Their tenacity was a function of their conviction in the inherent equitableness of the American patent system. Sadly, their reasonable expectations have repeatedly and unequivocally been dashed.

It took the brothers more than eleven years to secure most of the patent claims that they initially pursued. When the brothers sought relief for infringement, their patent was invalidated based on hypothetical yarns spun by opponents, which were then embellished by the presiding judge. Their patent was subject to two covered business methods invalidity challenges, a forum that appears to be legally inappropriate for such efforts. During litigation, Kamran, Nader and most of the lawyers that represented them were charged with perpetrating fraud on the Patent Office. During depositions it was insinuated that the brothers were proxies of a state sponsor of terror. Their appeals trial was delayed by one year. In upholding the lower court's finding that the '432 patent was invalid with a one-word verdict, the appeals court put a nail in the coffin of the brothers' '432 patent.

As we have seen time and again in these pages, the rewards for conducting one's patenting efforts within the law are, at best, illusory. A more apt analogy is that dipping one's toe in the business of patents is like stepping into a minefield covered by snakes. On the other hand, patent challengers have carte blanche in their efforts to invalidate patents. In these pages we have seen that those who commit inequitable conduct while trying to invalidate patents (Netflix) get away scot-free. We have seen that patent infringement is so rampant that patentees (Mighty Mug) have little choice but to use artificial intelligence to identify thousands of infringing products online. We have seen that infringers are now so skilled in manufacturing counterfeit products (the Hovertrax) that patentees no longer can sell even one product to infringers (for purposes of them learning how to copy originals). We have seen infringers making counterfeit products laden with cancer causing carcinogens and then the patentee (Choon Ng) suffering the consequences. And on. And on.

Waterboarded by the Patent System

During the 2002 timeframe, Glen Duff and his wife, Diane, bought a boat and joined a Williamsburg, Virginia water skiing club. The Duffs, with their four daughters, often took their fellow congregants from the Williamsburg Community Chapel out for boating excursions on the James River. Glen tried to teach the more adventuresome members how to water ski and wakeboard. (If you don't know what wakeboarding is, picture water surfing while being towed by a motorboat). Many participants found the balancing act difficult and spent more time wading in the water than surfing on the water.

Glen wanted to develop surfboards that would enable even those with limited strength and athleticism to pull themselves up out of the water and into a standing position while being towed behind a motorboat. From 2008 to 2013, Glen and his team spent five years researching and designing their new ZUP Board concept. The fruits of their labors offered ease of use, maneuverability and improved stability; with the ZUP Board, surfers of all skill levels could enjoy the water sport. Glen and his team developed prototypes, conducted safety testing, began working with manufacturers, and consulted with industry experts to devise marketing and retail strategies.

Inventions Arise Out of Years of Research

With the ZUP Board, newcomers to watersports can begin their rides by lying down on the board. When they feel comfortable, they can reach for, and hold onto, the side handles. Then they can position their feet into the foot straps from a kneeling position. When kneeling, the rider can reach and grab onto the double-handled tow rope, which is called the "DoubleZUP" Tow Handle. Since only one of the pair of tow handles is attached to the tow hook on the front of the board, the rider can grasp the handle unattached to the tow hook, which ensures that he will not pinch his fingers. Further, the DoubleZUP handles are highly floatable and their bright colors enable dismounted surfers to easily spot them. ZUP Boards can also be outfitted to include rails and fins on the bottom portion of the boards; the resulting planar orientation relative to the surface of the body of water enhances stability and maneuverability of the board.

What were the inventions imbedded into the ZUP Board? Well, the ZUP Board features a patented tow hook on the middle front of the board, enabling a tow handle and rope to attach the waterboard to boats for easy pulls. Perhaps more important innovations include placing two side-by-side handles on the front of the riding board and side-by-side foot bindings on the middle of the ZUP board. The foot bindings are patented multifunctional straps—they serve as elbow pads when riders begin by laying down, kneepads when riding on one's knees, and as foot straps when users stand on their feet.

Glen filed a provisional patent application on December 2, 2008 and a non-provisional patent application one year later on December 2, 2009. Less than three years after that, on October 23, 2012, this application issued as U.S. Patent No. 8,292,681. The '681 patent contains 12 claims, with claim number one covering the apparatus and claim number nine covering the method for using the ZUP Board. This patent combined three elements that were found in other patents, but in a way that people in the industry for as long as 40 years never thought of combining them. These three elements—two side handles, a tow hook in the middle, and the two side-by-side foot straps—in combination created a product and a system that enables a water surfer to pull himself up out of the water and get into a full standing position with minimal upper body strength.

The ZUP Board Hits the Stores

Glen's team introduced the ZUP Board at the Surf Expo, a world-renowned trade show for the water sports industry, in September of 2012, approximately one month before the '681 patent issued. The product showed promise and sparked interest with the largest retailers in the world. ZUP received its first order, worth many hundreds of thousands of dollars, from Overton's (a watersports superstore) in 2013. A few weeks later, representatives of Overton's said they'd never had any product sell so well. This was quite a compliment considering the ZUP Board's relatively high price and Overton's 37-year history. The ZUP Board also caught the attention of Keith Parten, owner of Nash Manufacturing. With a lineage dating back more than five decades, Nash Manufacturing is a leading designer and manufacturer of water skis, knee boards, wake boards, and other similar sporting equipment.

Mr. Parten expressed an interest in manufacturing the ZUP Board in the fall of 2013. Glen provided Mr. Parten a sample ZUP Board so that Nash could formulate a manufacturing quote even though Mr. Parten refused to sign a confidentiality agreement. After receiving the sample ZUP Board, Mr. Parten told Glen that Nash would "never do this item." Nevertheless, a little more than a month later, Mr. Parten was back and expressed an interest in discussing the production and distribution of the ZUP Board. This time, Glen insisted that Mr. Parten sign a non-disclosure agreement, which Mr. Parten did on February 5, 2014.

Once an executed confidentiality agreement was in place, Glen imparted quite a bit of valuable information to Mr. Parten. This information related to ZUP's costs of production, vendors, marketing strategies, agreements with retailers, and new design concepts, including those modeled with proprietary 3D computer design technology. Nash also elicited information from ZUP in connection with vulnerabilities associated with some of the claims in the '681 patent as well as ZUP's patent enforcement strategies.

The cascading flow of information from ZUP to Nash Manufacturing was insufficient to cause Mr. Parten to enter into any kind of manufacturing, distribution, or licensing agreement with Glen. However, in May of 2014, Nash introduced its Versa Board to the market.

Infringers Enter the Market

What suggests that Nash's Versa Board was infringing Glen's '681 patent? Well, the Versa Boards largely resembled and functioned like ZUP Boards. They do, however, have several holes on their top surfaces. These holes are positioned at the same places where the foot bindings and handles are placed on the ZUP Board. Versa Boards are sold with handles and foot bindings that can be affixed to the holes. It is true that Nash instructs users to use these holes in four approved configurations. Rather than teaching customers to use the Versa Board with the same combination of three elements taught by the '681 patent, Versa Board-approved configurations are designed to isolate the elements engaged by the user. For instance, one approved use of the Versa Board calls for authorizing users to only attach the foot bindings to the board in a side-by-side, horizontal configuration, allowing the user to water ski. It is also true that Nash instructs users of its Versa Board to refrain from leaving the handles attached while standing up on the board. This obviously disingenuous, winking, instruction makes it appear as if Nash does not wish to infringe Glen's patent. The reality is that once in the water, users will never go back to the boat to grab a screwdriver each time they wish to change their riding position.

Mr. Parten did not immediately crash into the "all-in-one" segment of the wakeboard industry. (By an "all-in-one" board, I mean a board that encapsulates the riding styles of kneeboards, water skis, wakeboards, and wake surf boards.) Rather, he waited and observed the uptake of the ZUP Board for about a year. When it became clear that the ZUP Board resonated with the watersports community, Mr. Parten pounced. Nash Manufacturing unleashed its more than fifty years of manufacturing experience and relationships with retailers to become the prevailing purveyor of "all-in-one" waterboards, a newly coined term for a product category claimed by both ZUP and Nash Manufacturing.

Nash Manufacturing exhibited its Versa Board at the Surf Expo in Orlando, Florida, in September of 2014. A buyer at Overton's informed Glen that Nash's Versa Board looked eerily similar to the ZUP Board. Glen approached Mr. Parten at the Surf Expo and conveyed his belief that Nash's Versa Board was infringing his '681 patent. More technically, the Versa Board induced users to infringe claims numbers one and nine of the '681 patent or contributed to them doing so. It was likely that many Versa Board users would leave the handles attached when they stood up and rode the board with their feet placed side-by-side.

According to my discussions with Glen, Mr. Parten's response to Glen informing him of the Versa Board's suspected infringement of the '681 patent was along the lines of, "Get over it. Everyone infringes in the watersports industry. Besides, you can't afford to sue us."

Infringers Benefit from Low Cost Production

Nash Manufacturing, which has a reputation for selling its watersports equipment for below minimum advertised prices, upheld its reputation in this regard. When Glen was selling ZUP Boards for $319, Nash was selling similar boards for $199. Nash was able to sell its Versa Boards at low prices, in part, because it assembled them with inexpensive immigrant labor at its own factory close to the U.S.-Mexican border while ZUP outsourced production to an Ohio-based roto-molding manufacturer. Further, most of Nash's manufacturing investments had already been expended, whereas ZUP was faced with manufacturing ramp-up expenses of approximately $500,000. With these divergent manufacturing realities, it is no wonder that within three months Nash Manufacturing was outselling the ZUP Board to the same large retail chains that ZUP coveted. Within a year of securing its first order from Overton's, that retailer diverted its wakeboard business to Nash Manufacturing. Further, Nash Manufacturing found it much easier to sell one additional product to its mass market accounts such as Bass Pro Shops than was the case for ZUP, which had to navigate rigorous vendor qualification gauntlets for each of the retailers it targeted.

The consequences of ZUP having to compete against Nash's aggressive pricing reverberated beyond the two companies. Glen was forced to shift ZUP's manufacturing from Ohio to China. Numerous factory workers in the Buckeye state must have lost their jobs as a result, given that producing thousands of boards is highly labor-intensive. What can be said with certainty is that moving manufacturing from Ohio to China was disruptive to ZUP's business—in part, due to communications challenges. Even when designers, tooling professionals, and manufacturing people speak the same mother tongue, they don't necessarily speak the same vernacular. When you add in two distinct languages, multiple dialects, choppy Skype and Facetime calls, and miscommunication with interpreters of varying qualifications, communications breakdowns are not far behind. Glen was required to invest heavily in quality control and product inspections. Nevertheless, production delays inevitably abounded.

One manifestation of the communications problems between ZUP and its Chinese contractor arose when Glen realized that his manufacturer subcontracted out the work of filling the ZUP Boards with foam to a firm located in what can be described as a "hole in the wall, far off of the beaten track in China." The shoddy jig produced by this subcontractor failed to keep the boards secured when the boards were filled with foam. As a result, the boards did not hold the correct shape and Glen had to scramble to replace this subcontractor. All told, it took two years for ZUP to achieve a complete production shift to China.

There are benefits of manufacturing in China, but not when it comes to shipping manufactured products to the United States. First, it is impractical for Glen or his colleagues at ZUP to inspect every board produced in China. Second, when ZUP ships its ZUP Boards from China it must pay 30% of the cost of its shipment at the time its products are ordered; typically, the balance must be remitted when the boards are placed in the containers at Chinese ports. Remitting these payments months in advance of receiving the products at ZUP's warehouse strains ZUP's cash flow. This stress becomes especially acute as ZUP's business is seasonal; there simply isn't much cash on hand for ZUP to pay shippers as it goes into its busy season.

Nash's promotion of its Versa Boards resulted in that company taking sales away from ZUP and depressed ZUP Boards' pricing power. The related revenue erosion was accompanied by the ratcheting up of Glen's manufacturing and logistical headaches. Mr. Parten's stance on his alleged infringement never became any more conciliatory. And then came all of the distraction, trauma, and expense associated with patent litigation.

Litigation Commences

When Glen was contending with revenue shrinkage and manufacturing woes, he knew he would have to gear up for litigation. Actually, several years before in 2013, ZUP purchased patent enforcement insurance from Lloyds of London. The thinking behind buying such insurance was to demonstrate ZUP's resolve in battling infringers. The reality was a bit different: In return for paying the lowest possible premiums, ZUP faced the steepest deductible. Since the $100,000 deductible was too rich for the ZUP team to stomach, Glen searched far and wide for a law firm to represent his company on a contingency basis. (Glen also dropped his patent enforcement insurance coverage.) About 10 of the 18 law firms that he approached were interested in representing ZUP on at least a partial contingency basis. Being squeezed for cash, ZUP entered into representation agreements with the two law firms that agreed to take on the ZUP case on a 100% contingency basis.

After retaining these two law firms, ZUP brought a suit against Nash Manufacturing in the District Court for Eastern Virginia on March 1, 2016. It didn't take long for this district court to destroy Glen's patent. In its January 13, 2017 decision, the district court invalidated claims one and nine of the '681 patent on the basis of those claims being obvious.

Decision on Obvious Grounds is Anything But Obvious

What's wrong with this decision? For one thing, the presiding judge admitted that he didn't know anything about patents. The judge also explained that he felt comfortable invalidating two of the '681 patent's claims because he was confident that Glen would appeal to the Court of Appeals for the Federal Circuit where three patent savvy judges awaited. (Indeed, Glen did appeal this decision to the Court of Appeals for the Federal Circuit in February of 2018.)

The second reason that the invalidation of two of the claims in Glen's patent was troubling relates to obvious standards. To hold a patent obvious, a court must support its decision with "clear and convincing" evidence that "one of ordinary skill" (in this case) in water recreation arts would have studied the prior art and come up with the claimed invention himself. The district court that invalidated ZUP's two '681 claims failed to meet this standard. As to this point, ZUP introduced evidence that Nash spent some 50 years in the industry patenting various products but failed to develop a product (before copying the ZUP Board) that allowed even the most athletically challenged waterboarder to arise from the water and to assume a standing position. Instead, this court used the '681 patent as its guide and combed the prior art looking for the elements contained in the ZUP patent.

The judge could have applied secondary tests to determine if the invalidated claims were obvious. These tests would have required the court to analyze what happened in the marketplace after the '681 patent was made public. Appropriate questions to raise along these lines could have included, "Did others copy the patented invention?" and "Did the patent address a 'long-felt need'?" If the answers to either of these questions was "yes," then these secondary considerations provide the court with objective proof that the patent is not obvious. Let's consider the first question presented above. This issue seems to be open and shut: ZUP introduced evidence demonstrating that Nash's Versa Board copied the patented features that were made a part of the ZUP Board. The answer to the second subsidiary question also seems clear: The representative from Overton's said that the ZUP Board sold better than any other product that that chain sold in its 37-year history. Further, watersports enthusiasts must have had a long-felt need for the "all-in-one" type product as demand was strong for both the ZUP Board and the Versa Board.

In issuing a finding that the '681 patent was obvious, the district court simply rejected ZUP's evidence to the contrary. It also ignored the fact that Nash was unable to present evidence demonstrating that the invention could have been produced by people skilled in the art at hand. Further, the district court granted Nash's summary judgment with respect to non-infringement of one of the two independent claims contained in the '681 patent.

The Shark Tank Interlude

In between the district court's decision and the decision from the Court of Appeals for the Federal Circuit, the ZUP team appeared on *Shark Tank* on January 14, 2018. In response to a question about ZUP's patent profile from Lori Greiner, one of the sharks, Glen's partner Scott Parks disclosed that [two claims in] the '681 patent had been invalidated. After this disclosure, none of the sharks expressed any interest in investing in ZUP.

Some might speculate that Mr. Parten may have leaked the fact that two of the claims in the '681 patent were invalidated to the sharks. This theory would continue by holding Mr. Parten responsible for the sharks refraining from investing in ZUP. I haven't seen any evidence to corroborate this thesis and therefore cannot ascribe credence to it. The '681 patent and its surrounding litigation is a matter of public record. The sharks may have conducted their own research with respect to ZUP's patent situation, or someone from the ZUP team could have let slip the disposition of ZUP's patent. Even if the '681 patent had not been invalidated, ZUP would not necessarily have received an acceptable offer from the sharks; unanimous decisions not to invest in candidate companies are frequent on *Shark Tank*. Also, ZUP's proposed valuation, $300,000 for 10% of the Company, was rich relative to other companies that have participated on that reality-TV show.

However, the '681 patent was invalidated by a judge who admitted to having limited knowledge about patents. Thus, a travesty of justice would have been visited upon ZUP if its patent invalidation was the reason that investors decided against investing in ZUP. Such a miscarriage of justice would have been magnified by ZUP being rebuffed in front of *Shark Tank's* six million viewers.

What is peculiar about *Shark Tank's* interest in ZUP's patent position is that the sharks are not known for their respect for patents. In fact, patentholders who attempt to monetize their patents have been viciously attacked by the sharks.

Scott Jordan, the CEO of Technology Enabled Clothing (TEC), appeared in a March 2012 broadcast of *Shark Tank*. TEC was the assignee of at least one patent that covered placing special pockets to hold electronic devices in apparel. The patent covered placing passageways in the garments so that wires, inter alia, could be better managed as part of Personalized Area Networks. (Does Scott's invention sound obvious? Later in this book, when we read about Tesia Thomas, we will see that there is quite a bit of room for innovation in clothing, even in zippers.) During the show, Scott discussed the strength of the patent(s) controlled by TEC. He also explained that his company's business model consisted of licensing out those patents to a variety of established clothing manufacturers. At the time Shark Tank aired, TEC had already secured at least 10 reputable licensees including Under Armour and North Face.

Mark Cuban, one of the sharks, went ballistic upon hearing that Scott had the audacity to license his patents. He mercilessly excoriated Scott for charging royalties to licensees that wanted to make use of his patented inventions. Among the invectives spewed by Mr. Cuban in Scott's direction were, "People like Scott are killing this country with their dumb-ass patents.... He (Scott) is so full of crap....Scott's patent is horrible, horrible, horrible, horrible." In a subsequent podcast, Mr. Cuban stated that his goal of lacerating Scott was to precipitate him to cry on national television.[82]

Interestingly, Mr. Cuban did not exhibit any moral qualms about acquiring a 7.4% stake in Vringo in April 2012, just two months after berating Scott. Vringo's most valuable asset was a patent infringement case—other than this litigation, Vringo only had a visual ringtone app and unimpressive revenues.

---

[81] https://www.scottevest.com/about/shark-tank.shtml and https://www.legalteamusa.net/shark-tank-scottevest-controversy-leads-to-dropping-of-clause/

Ten months later, in February of 2013, Mr. Cuban reported to the Securities and Exchange Commission that he increased the number of Vringo shares he owned, from 1.03 million to 1.13 million.

Justice Takes a Detour at the Appellate Court

About seven months after appearing on *Shark Tank*, Glen had his day at the Court of Appeals for the Federal Circuit. The CAFC held that the district court's hindsight obviousness analysis was improper. (You may remember that the district court went hunting for prior art and then postulated that anyone skilled in the art would have composed those disparate pieces of prior art into the claims described in the '681 patent.) In any event, Glen's appeal was unsuccessful. On July 25, 2018, in a two-to-one decision, the CAFC affirmed the district court's holding that claims one and nine are invalid as obvious and did not find it necessary to reach the infringement question.

What was the problem with this decision? The majority opinion declined to apply federal circuit law requiring evidence of a skilled artisan's motivation to combine. Worse, however, the federal circuit declined to apply the Apple v. Samsung case in ZUP's favor. In that case, Apple showed that Samsung had been trying to invent a touchscreen locking mechanism for its phone, but failed. Apple showed that Samsung copied Apple's patented mechanism. The federal circuit held that Apple's evidence showed the Apple patent was not obvious. Of course, these are the very facts that ZUP introduced to the district court and the federal circuit. Again, the majority simply rejected ZUP's evidence and denied ZUP a trial.

At the time of my writing these pages, ZUP was in the process of petitioning the Supreme Court to review its case. One sign of hope for ZUP is that the Supreme Court reviews cases where the lower court has declined to apply Supreme Court precedent, such as Graham v. John Deere Co. of Kansas City, which stresses the prominent role of secondary considerations in the obviousness analysis.

Postscript

Glen must feel waterboarded by the patent system. His business has been kneecapped by a blatant and flagrant infringer. In the midst of ZUP losing retail accounts and being forced to slash prices, he had to move production from Ohio to China. He derived no value from purchasing patent enforcement insurance. Glen has been on the receiving end of the courts' knee-jerk reaction to invalidate patent claims. Glen and his team were deflated and humiliated on national television when the issue of his patent having been invalidated arose but no one illuminated the district court's misapplication of justice when it came to its decision.

Despite its contingency lawyers carrying most of the weight of the ongoing litigation, maintaining the validity and enforceability of ZUP's patents has been a major distraction for Glen and his team. He spent weeks scrubbing through two years of emails, and discovery took place during ZUP's busy season. In early 2019, Glen was still spending between five and 10 hours a week on patent issues. Such time could have been better spent by selling ZUP's products or continuing its work on the innovation front. At the time of ZUP's appearance on *Shark Tank*, ZUP had 10 patent pending applications on file—a few of the underlying new technologies related to skateboard concepts, a stand-up paddleboard, and accessories for life jackets.

Infringer Walks Away with Disproportionate Share of the Market

Richard X. Zawitz has been hugely successful in the ephemeral toy industry for nearly four decades. Through his businesses, he sold or gave away approximately 150 million toys through channels ranging from independent toy stores to Walmart and from New York's Museum of Modern Art to McDonalds (through its Happy Meals). Richard conceived and developed Tangle Jr., the original line of fidget toys promoted by Tangle Creations. Tangles, which are miniature works of art, offer therapeutic benefit as they are used as stress relievers. These twistable serpentine toys are worn around the wrist. Tangles can be bent into all sorts of shapes and are available in a variety of colors and forms including smooth, groovy, metallic, furry, and harry.

Richard has long had to protect his inventions and brands against infringers around the world. Back in the 1980s, Richard combatted pirates and even his own Hong Kong-based manufacturers who backdoored his inventions. (Backdooring occurs when authorized manufacturers produce in excess of what a licensor authorizes; proceeds resulting from sales of excess production are illegitimately pocketed by the rogue manufacturers.) He obtained injunctions from authorities in Hong Kong and hired the police to raid the offending factories. Not only were unauthorized products seized but so too were the tools and molds necessary to produce such products. Decades ago, when Richard detected that Taiwanese counterfeiters were attempting to export their knockoffs to the United States, he arranged to have U.S. Customs seize containers of unlawful products. Impounding infringing merchandise at U.S. ports deterred those copycats from attempting to infringe Richard's intellectual property ever again.

While a combination of patents, trademarks, and copyrights afforded Richard the ability to protect his inventions back in the 1980s, his ability to secure and enforce patent rights has been severely curtailed more recently. Every year, Richard detects approximately 50 counterfeit Tangles on websites such as Amazon and Alibaba. In Richard's experience, while e-commerce sites such as these are largely responsive to patentees' take-down notices, infringers almost invariably pop right back up under new banners.

Richard Invents the Night Ball Line

In the early 2000s, Richard began working on a new invention—a line of LED sports balls that now includes footballs, soccer balls, basketballs, softballs, and baseball bats. The LED technology Richard used in Night Balls is preferable to glow-in-the-dark technology; that technology consists of adding a phosphorescent powder to resin, requires illumination by an incandescent light, and lasts a very short time. With Night Balls, customers can play a variety of sports in the dark of night since these balls illuminate when in motion.

The first self-illuminated ball that Richard pursued was a football. It wasn't easy to tackle the engineering behind embedding electronics in a ball without affecting the football's performance. After approximately six years of sporadic research and an investment of at least $100,000, Richard perfected his invention. Placing a light-weight pulse module inside of the balls enabled the footballs to spiral normally. These pulse modules also eliminated the need to connect wires in the Night Balls, which would have added additional expense and complexity. Night Footballs were designed with an innovative and open exterior. Rather than producing a solid ball encapsulated with a skin, the Night Football is composed of a variety of matrix-like plastic exoskeleton parts that fit together. The result is that no air is trapped in Night Footballs.

Once Richard finished his development of the Night Football at the end of 2007, he tried to patent his invention. Specifically, he wanted to protect the physical construction of the bounceable ball, the structure of the matrix football, and its airless cavities. As Richard tells the story, he pursued obtaining a related utility patent for several years but was constantly rebuffed by the patent examiner. A few years after spending considerable money on the utility patent application and with no sign of such application granting in the near-term, he abandoned his application. Fortunately, Richard did secure a design patent on the exoskeletal structure of his Night Football, which issued as U.S. Patent No. D576,235 on September 2, 2008.

The Night Ball Becomes a Hit

It took Richard a few years to bring the Night Football to the market as he had other, more pressing business priorities and limited capital. But once Richard put the capital in place and ensured that manufacturing worked smoothly, sales took off as soon as consumers learned of the product. The Night Football was selling through retailers such as Dick's and Big 5 like hotcakes. Sales reached approximately $400,000 in 2013, $800,000 in 2014, and $1.2 million in 2015. Beginning in 2016, these buoyant sales figures and respectable $20 price points attracted an infringer by the name of Jamie O'Rourke who arranged to have Magic Time (a Hong Kong company) produce the infringing products.

This infringer began distributing its knockoff Night Footballs through chains such as Target and Walmart for prices as low as $10. The combination of wide distribution and slashed prices effectively destroyed the viability of Richard's Night Footballs. In addition to losing the product line, Richard was compelled to purchase the excess inventory of Night Footballs from his Asian manufacturer. (Richard, not his manufacturer, sustained the risks and consequences of infringement. Manufacturers receive 50% of the value of the products they produce at the time of accepting an order; they receive the remaining 50% of the value when the products are shipped. Promoters who stick their manufacturers with inventory will never be able to work with those manufacturers again.) To move this inventory, Richard had to work out snap deals with closeout companies. Having no leverage in such negotiations, he ended up selling such inventory at pennies on the dollar. The closeout companies immediately resold the inventory to companies like Five Below. With the Night Footballs selling at retail for as little as $5 it was guaranteed that his legacy accounts would cease carrying the product.

When Richard was about to begin asserting his design patent against his infringers, he was approached by an older, independent patent lawyer who told Richard that he was highly confident that he (the veteran lawyer) would be able to have the infringer cease the infringing activity and remit back royalties to him. Richard decided to give the lone patent lawyer a chance and diverted this work away from his long-standing, established law firm. One tact that the seasoned lawyer took was to try to win damages based on violations of the Night Football's trade dress. This effort failed because the Night Football was only on the market for about two years; Richard said that to win on trade dress, the product needs to be on the market for at least five years. In any event, the older lawyer was unsuccessful in halting infringement or in recovering damages. After a few years, Richard was out about $250,000 in legal fees. He decided to pull the plug and terminated his engagement with the older lawyer.

At the end of the saga, Richard reached a settlement with the infringer. Richard declined to disclose the terms of this agreement to me. However, based on my research, it seems that the infringer now controls the selling of Night Footballs to mass market retailers while Richard's original Nightballs only seem to be available through specialty retailers and the Tangle Creations website. Thus, the infringers avoided the expenses and risks associated with developing the Night Footballs and walked away with a disproportionate share of the market that Richard developed.

Postscript

Richard told me that he relies more on copyrights and trademarks (rather than patents) to protect his inventions. He said, "If you don't have the money to enforce patents, they are worthless." He also told me that, "Whoever has more money will win in patent litigation." Some have said that if a patentee doesn't have $3 million in cash to enforce his patent against infringers his patent is worth zero dollars. Others have said that if there are less than $10 million worth of damages to pursue the patent is worthless because contingency lawyers will not want to represent cases where potential damages fall below this threshold.[82] With these truisms in mind, is it any wonder that large companies feel that they have carte blanche to infringe?

[82] There is a caveat to the statement about not being able to attract contingency lawyers to represent patent assertion efforts where potential damages appear to be less than $10 million. Since patent litigation is such a lengthy process, damages relating to infringement could surpass the $10 million mark several years into the litigation; thus, making the case worthwhile for contingency lawyers.

Intimidating Inventors with Fraudulent Cease-and-Desist Letters

Zippers are a serious business. You are probably wearing at least one right now. Every year, the largest manufacturer of zippers produces enough of them to wrap around the earth 50 times. Compromising (but often calculated) fashion mishaps are not the biggest risk associated with malfunctioning zippers: The lives of fire fighters, military personnel and astronauts can be imperiled if zippers are not working properly.

Despite the ubiquity and importance of zippers, there hasn't been a breakthrough in zipper technology since 1851 when the first zipper tape was born. Sure, incremental improvements were applied to zippers over the years. First there were tooth fasteners with slider devices and then there were tooth fasteners without sliders. Then the invention of plastic led to zip tracks, plastic coil zippers and plain plastic toothed zippers. A variety of coatings have been applied to zippers and YKK, the largest zipper maker, has 20 shades of black zippers in its color library. But at the end of the day, zippers are still comprised of tiny, individual interlocking parts. Zippers are better than buttons at joining two fabric halves but they aren't made to seal separate fabrics together.

The first real revolution in zipper-like technology in more than 160 years was sparked in 2016 when Tesia Thomas's pet rabbit damaged the zipper on her laptop case. The destruction of this zipper made it evident to Tesia that zippers are not repairable and are often the weakest point of any garment, purse or carrying case. She realized that the time for new zipper technology had arrived.

What kind of closing apparatus did Tesia invent? She created a zipper that seals as well as joins by enabling two interlocking U-shaped channels to slip together. The U-shaped metal clips are covered by flexible material and create what Tesia has tested to be an air and water-tight seal. In addition, based on independent testing, Tesia believes her invention is fully functional, more than twice as strong as regular zippers, offers excellent tensile strength, and will cost the same to produce as regular zippers when manufacturing reaches high volumes.

With one published patent application and several non-published patent applications at the time of my writing these pages, Tesia is in the early stages of her patenting journey. Nonetheless, this inventor is already confronting serious challenges. Tesia has already experienced elitism in the awarding of federally-funded grants and has been on the receiving end of a competitor's foul play.

Gerrymandering the Granting Process

At the time of inventing her unique closure, Tesia was a very young inventor. She had no formal degrees from institutions of higher learning. What she does have is a multitude of companies interested in licensing and using her patent-pending invention. Investors have also approached Zipr Shift, Tesia's company, about funding the commercialization of her invention.

So, what's the problem? Tesia's potential defense, space, and aerospace customers expect her zippers to undergo a rigorous battery of testing. To close a deal with one of these companies, more than 10,000 hours would have to be devoted to air tightness testing, water tightness testing, materials testing, durability testing, strength testing and related tooling. The costs would amount to hundreds of thousands of dollars. As is the case with so many inventors, Tesia's inventions are not yet throwing off cash. What money she can get her hands on goes towards patent drafting, filing and prosecution.

Tesia did apply for the SBIR A 16-062 grant issued by the United States Army to develop gear to protect service personnel from chemicals and biologics in February of 2016. So too did a competitor. This rival company is a spin-off from a world-renowned university and is said to be staffed by a stable of researchers with impressive degrees. This rival, which I will identify with the alias Gamma Grip Corporation, was awarded the multi-million-dollar grant.

What irks Tesia the most about her project having been passed over? The stated reason was that her company was too small; not that her technology was inadequate. The granting authorities both insulted Tesia's intelligence and demonstrated arrogance. Soon after awarding the grant to Gamma Grip, the granting authorities wanted samples of

Zipr Shift's patent-pending closure technology—unaccompanied by any confidentiality agreement—so that they could bring Tesia's research and development in-house.

Fraudulent Cease-and-Desist Letters

Gamma Grip not only won the SBIR A 16-062 grant that Tesia pursued but also secured multiple research awards from the likes of the National Science Foundation, the U.S. Defense Department, NASA, and the Pennsylvania NanoMaterials Commercialization Center. Despite winning many millions of dollars in government funding over roughly a decade, Tesia's research indicates that it is unlikely that Gamma Grip sold anything to the military or government.

Gamma Grip's webpage dedicated to "Applications" lists seven industries that could be served by its products. In all seven of these applications, Gamma Grip's product descriptions are couched in the applications that Gamma Grip's products *can* address, not which applications their products *are* addressing. The contact page of Tesia's real rival's website invites those who have adhesive, gripping, or fastening challenges to email its engineers. No mention is made about placing orders for products despite that company having been in business since 2009.

Tesia has written that Gamma Grip received multiple grants for the same research proposals and that doing so is a violation of the False Claims Act. Despite Tesia conducting rigorous research into the issue, Gamma Grip has not been proven guilty of bilking grant money from the government. Maybe Gamma Grip's business model is based on developing custom solutions for clients rather than selling manufactured solutions. Maybe you think Tesia is a bit tempestuous. Maybe you think Gamma Grip is innocent until proven guilty. Fair enough. But let's look at how Gamma Grip responded to Tesia publishing her assertions about her rival violating the False Claims Act.

In September of 2017, Gamma Grip sent Tesia a cease-and-desist letter, asking her to halt defamation of that company. It seems to me that this was within Gamma Grip's right. However, this cease-and-desist letter was written by the president of Gamma Grip on that company's letterhead. Throughout the letter the president of Gamma Grip referenced a large law-firm that it purportedly retained. Suspiciously, there was no mention of any specific lawyer at the large law firm representing its interests. After receiving the cease-and-desist letter, Tesia tried to contact both Gamma Grip and the referenced law firm. She was unable to elicit a response from either target despite her repeated phone calls, twittering and direct messaging. Given that there was no response from the law firm, it seems that the law firm neither reviewed the cease-and-desist letter nor represented Gamma Grip.

Postscript

Tesia feels that government granting authorities place too much weight on the pedigree of the applicants rather than the merits of the underlying technologies. She believes that capital goes to the companies that are skilled in writing grant proposals, not necessarily those who have the best business cases or are best positioned to meet customer demand. Even at the early stages of commercializing and patenting her invention, she is afraid that her presumptive patents will be at tremendous risk of being whimsically invalidated. Tesia has written, "The patent office only invalidates the patents that threaten the status quo, while patents of market leaders are left intact."

Licensee Seeks to Destroy Licensor

Beginning in 2011, Apple licensed patents covering state-of-the-art modems from Qualcomm for use in its iPhones. Apple's annual iPhone revenues soared from about $45 billion in 2011—when Apple incorporated Qualcomm's modems into its iPhones—to $160 billion in 2018.

Apple profited from its relationship with Qualcomm but wanted to cease paying for the use of Qualcomm's patented technologies. Apple set the stage to extricate itself from its Qualcomm relationship long ago. Apple locked Qualcomm into contracts that required the San Diego company to continue supplying its modems to Apple even if it didn't receive royalty payments from Apple's contract manufacturers. Then, Apple dropped the hammer on Qualcomm in 2017: It effectively severed royalty payments to Qualcomm by notifying its contractors that it would halt reimbursing them for the royalties they remitted to Qualcomm.

Apple documents indicate that Apple was aware of the risks of executing such an aggressive policy against Qualcomm. One Apple document stated, "Apple will be at risk for infringement, tortious interference and full royalties (plus any interest, penalties, etc.)." However, these risks seemed to be acceptable for a company with $1 trillion in market capitalization and $245 billion in cash. The risk-reward equation was different for Qualcomm. The prospect of losing all of Apple's business—a real possibility given Apple's billion-dollar lawsuit against its supplier—caused Qualcomm's stock to crash.

More mendaciously, Apple conspired to destroy Qualcomm. According to documents that surfaced during patent litigation between the two companies, Apple discussed ways to "Plot and Pressure...to...hurt Qualcomm financially" and to "Put Qualcomm's licensing model at risk."

Apple Claims Industry Monopolized by Worthless Technology

Apple had been planning to "provoke a patent fight" with Qualcomm as early as 2014. However, the Cupertino-based company decided to wait until after the end of 2016, when Qualcomm was expected to pay Apple billions of dollars as part of a business cooperation agreement. In the meantime, Apple began working with Intel to "apply commercial pressure to Qualcomm."

Apple brought two charges against the wireless pioneer in the billion-dollar lawsuit that it filed against Qualcomm in early 2017. The first charge was that Qualcomm's technology was "worthless." (It has even been written that Apple pressured its suppliers to lie about Qualcomm's modem quality and pricing.[83]) This charge was contradicted by a multitude of glowing reviews of Qualcomm's technology by Apple officials: Many Apple engineers considered Qualcomm's technology unparalleled. According to a March 2015 email, Apple's Vice President of Hardware, Johny Srouji, wrote of Qualcomm's technology, "Engineering wise, they have been the best." A memo from an Apple accountant stated, "Qualcomm is widely considered the owner of the strongest patent portfolio for essential and relevant patents on wireless standards." Another Apple memo described Qualcomm as having a "unique patent share" and "significant holdings."[84]

The other Apple allegation was that Qualcomm used its monopolization of the chip market to gouge its customers for wireless modems. This allegation was refuted by Apple's internal documents in which Apple declared that it entered into its patent licensing agreement with Qualcomm "based on Qualcomm's established and relatively transparent actual monetary collection of patent licenses."

But Apple tried to make it appear as though Qualcomm was price gouging. For instance, Apple orchestrated a strategy of creating low-ball precedential royalty rates by executing agreements with the likes of Ericsson and Huawei. What proof is there that these agreements were entered into for such purposes? One of Apple's internal documents detailed

---

[83] https://ipcloseup.com/2019/04/29/apple-conspired-to-discredit-qualcomms-inventions-even-though-it-believed-they-were-the-best/

[84] These memos were presented by Qualcomm during its trial with Apple, from which a negotiated settlement resulted in April of 2018. Source: https://beta.washingtonpost.com/technology/2019/04/19/apple-said-qualcomms-tech-was-no-good-private-communications-it-was-best/?outputType=amp

that company's efforts to "create evidence" by licensing other less expensive patents to make Qualcomm's patents appear expensive.

Apple also sponsored research that grossly exaggerated the licensing fees that smartphone handset manufacturers pay for their use of standard essential patents. Famed academicians Mark Lemley and Carl Shapiro, both funded by Apple, claimed that the total 3G royalty stack is somewhere north of 20% or as high as 30% of the price of a phone.[85] Lawyers from one of the law firms most active in defending Apple concluded that standard essential royalties are potentially $121 to $124 for smartphones.[86] However, Apple's Chief Operating Officer stated that Apple pays $7.50 in standard essential royalties to Qualcomm. (This statement can be found in Judge Lucy Koh's Finding of Fact and Conclusions of Law issued in May of 2019 in connection with litigation between the Federal Trade Commission and Qualcomm.) This Apple executive, Jeff Williams, also stated that Qualcomm charges Apple more than everybody else put together. Thus, according to Apple's testimony, licensors receive less than $15, or royalties of no more than 1.88%, when Apple sells iPhones for $800.[87] These numbers are dramatically less than the $121 per unit and 20% royalty rates that Apple's boosters have estimated inventors who collectively contribute to standard essential patents receive.

Apple not only used the more than 80 lawsuits that arose with Qualcomm as a means of inflicting pain on that company, but also as a means of reshaping the patent laws for which it has an aversion. For instance, part of the Apple document entitled "Qualcomm Royalty Reduction" discussed plans to "reshape FRAND"—the royalty setting framework for standard setting bodies. Apple's sworn depositions and testimonies throughout its disputes with Qualcomm were presented to judges, juries, lawmakers, and regulators such as the Federal Trade Commission (which accused Qualcomm of antitrust violations in California Federal Court). Given the tremendous amount of contradictory evidence that has surfaced, one has

---

[85] In their paper entitled Patent Holdup and Royalty Stacking, Professors Lemley and Shapiro clearly state in the first footnote to that article that, "We are grateful to Apple...for funding the research reported in this Article."

[86] https://www.linkedin.com/pulse/sep-royalty-stacking-myth-apple-calls-its-own-bluff-david-l-cohen/

[87] https://www.ftc.gov/system/files/documents/cases/qualcomm_findings_of_fact_and_conclusions_of_law.pdf

to wonder the extent to which Apple was engaging in presenting bad faith arguments to jurists and government officials around the world.

Settlement is Reached

Apple and Qualcomm formally settled their legal disputes on April 16, 2019. This settlement appears equitable to Qualcomm. According to some reports, based on the settlement's six-year licensing agreement as well as a multi-year supply agreement, Qualcomm stands to generate $9 per handset, which is as much as $6 billion in revenues, or $2 per share in earnings.[88] Apple also agreed to pay an undisclosed lump sum of money to Qualcomm.

Apple respected and relied on Qualcomm's chips for years on end. But that did not restrain Apple from investing many tens of millions of dollars in litigation all over the world in a multi-year campaign to cause the demise of a $100 billion company. Even with Qualcomm's tremendous resources, Apple's campaign still damaged both Qualcomm and many of its employees. The San Diego chip maker was forced to lay off 1,500 employees during the course of its litigation with Apple. The loss of many hundreds of engineers represents a tremendous reduction in intellectual capital for Qualcomm. Many of the Qualcomm alumni were hired by Intel. Now that Intel has retreated from its efforts to produce chips that compete with those from Qualcomm, many of these former Qualcomm engineers are again unemployed.

Postscript

I have no qualms with Apple working with Intel to "apply commercial pressure to Qualcomm." Apple has the right to find multiple suppliers for the components it requires. Nor do I take issue with Apple attempting to design its own chips which would obviate the need for Qualcomm's chips. The publication of patents is designed to help inventors learn current art so that even better art can be developed. However, Apple stepped over the line when it presented corrupted financial data in its litigations against Qualcomm.

---

88 https://ipcloseup.com/2019/04/29/apple-conspired-to-discredit-qualcomms-inventions-even-though-it-believed-they-were-the-best/

Inventor Encounters a Gut-Wrenching Ordeal with Sears

Dan Brown is a seasoned inventor with almost 40 patents to his name, many of which are in the fields of polyurethane, plastics and foam technologies. Dan opened his own product design consultancy outside of Chicago in 1999. He enjoyed the freedom to innovate and appreciated the flexibility associated with being his own boss. But Dan soon learned that running his own shop had its confinements.

Like most proprietors of small professional services firms, Dan spent as much time selling his services as plying his craft. He was also bound by secrecy agreements with his clients: When the products he designed won awards, Dan was required to keep mum. Sure, Dan could show potential clients that he was listed as an inventor on patents corresponding to the hot products he developed for earlier clients, but patents have a way of causing the eyes of creative people to glaze over. It would have been much easier for Dan to excite prospective clients by allowing them to view the products he created rather than the related patents.

Inventor Craves an Invention of His Own

Within a few years of running his own consultancy, Dan wanted to direct his skills towards solving problems faced by tens of millions of people. He also wanted to develop a product that he, rather than his clients, would own—a tangible product that he could use to woo future clients to his design consultancy. Dan got his flash of inspiration when he saw his son struggle to remove bolts on a lawnmower with a pair of pliers in the summer of 2002. Dan's skills were well-suited to develop a tool to remove nuts and bolts with the comfort of pliers and the tautness of a wrench.

Most people start off using pliers to remove nuts and bolts because they like the ease of adjustability and gripping afforded by pliers. The problem is that pliers grip on the corners of the nuts and bolts; the friction applied destroys the corners, making it impossible to remove the nuts and bolts with pliers or wrenches.

Dan devoted much of the next three years to developing what he would call the Bionic Wrench. Dan does not bemoan the efforts he expended as such initiatives were underway in tandem with his other projects. But he crafted scores of prototypes and invested hundreds of hours at his workman's bench optimizing the Bionic Wrench.

How does Dan's Bionic Wrench work? Sort of like a pliers-wrench hybrid. The Bionic Wrench adjusts like pliers but performs like a wrench. The tool grips and engages all six flats found on nuts and bolts simultaneously; as the user squeezes, the Bionic Wrench's self-energizing grip directs the force to the flats, not to the corners. The tool's circle of metal prongs, which were inspired by the aperture in a single-lens reflex camera, descend evenly to lock onto almost any nut or bolt.

Inventor Achieves Product Lift-Off

Having witnessed his father lose his factory job due to foreign competition, Dan was resolved to produce the Bionic Wrench in the United States. Thus, he developed a fully domestic supply chain. Knowing that the Bionic Wrench would compete with tools produced in low-wage labor markets outside of the United States, Dan took great pains to make sure the components could be assembled cost-effectively at Penn United Technologies, the Pennsylvania contract manufacturing company he selected. Over the years, the Illinoian would be cajoled to offshore production of the Bionic Wrench in order to slash prices and to provide some cushion against the aggressive stance that large retailers are prone to take against their smaller vendors.

> What are some of the aggressive policies that big-box retailers take against their vendors? Many mass merchants expect their suppliers to operate on a consignment basis. They also demand that suppliers guarantee certain levels of sales in return for the retailers' promises to run defined promotional campaigns. The problem is that the large retailers sometimes fail to run the promotions that they promise. The result is that

sales fail to meet their targets and the vendors are required to take back their merchandise. Some mega-retailers simply pocket co-op advertising monies. Separately, vendors feel that big-box retailers overreach when they take deductions for supposed infractions in the way their merchandise is packed and delivered.

In other instances, vendors agree to fund the promotion of their wares through their retail partners. For instance, LoggerHead Tools (Dan's company) agreed to pay to promote its Bionic Wrench at Sears. However, Sears diverted LoggerHead's funds to promote its own competing Craftsman products. Another common provision in agreements with large retailers requires vendors to compensate the retailers for the profits they lose due to stockouts of the vendors' products. Of course, vendors that sell multiple products to a large retailer have reason to refrain from enforcing any of their patents against such key retailers; the retailers are likely to effect retribution by ceasing to stock any of the merchandise produced by a patent-asserting vendor.

Dan would eventually spend north of $500,000 obtaining and maintaining patents (some of which were issued in European countries, Japan and South Korea), trademarks and copyrights related to the Bionic Wrench. To raise funds for procuring such intellectual property and starting up the commercialization of the Bionic Wrench, Dan cashed in his retirement funds, put a second mortgage on his house and drained his savings accounts. He filed his first patent application on January 23, 2004, which became U.S. Patent No. 6,889,579 on May 10, 2005. His second patent relating to the Bionic Wrench was filed with the USPTO on April 11, 2005, and issued as U.S. Patent No. 7,992,470 on August 9, 2011.

Dan launched LoggerHead Tools in 2005 with the purpose of commercializing the Bionic Wrench. The year 2005 turned out to be a barn burner for the newly-formed company. In May of 2005, just days after his first patent issued, LoggerHead Tools exhibited the Bionic Wrench from a small booth in a corner of the basement at the National Hardware Show in Las Vegas. (Having never participated in this show, LoggerHead Tools was relegated to the bowels of the exhibition.) On the first evening of that show, the Bionic Wrench won the Product of the Year Award and the Editor's Choice Award from Popular Mechanics. The next morning throngs of people congregated around the Bionic Wrench exhibit. (It turns out that the awards the Bionic Wrench received in 2005 were the first of many: Within a few short years, Dan's innovative tool won some 10 international awards.)

> Many patentees are under the impression that marking their products as "Patent Pending" acts as kryptonite against infringers. However, "Patent Pending" markings do not always repel infringers; injunctions cannot be obtained based on such markings and the threat of litigation often seems remote to infringers.

Despite having contracted with a manufacturing company and having primed the supply chain, there wasn't sufficient time to deliver the Bionic Wrench to the big-box retailers in 2005. But LoggerHead arranged to distribute the tool through Amazon, and a variety of smaller retailers by the fourth quarter of that year. The Bionic Wrench racked up over $10,000 in sales within the first few minutes of its airing on QVC. In 2006, the company started selling the Bionic Wrench through Canadian Tire north of the border. Within three years of hitting the market, the Bionic Wrench generated some $20 million in retail sales.

Sales of the Bionic Wrench Crater and Then Rebound

Everything was going great for this young company until the economy started circling the drain in 2007. The economic crisis hurt sales of the Bionic Wrench as retailers slammed the brakes on orders. LoggerHead's banks pulled the company's line of credit in the midst of the economic meltdown even though it never missed a payment. Some of the suppliers that LoggerHead relied on went into bankruptcy. Not only was the supply chain that Dan worked so hard to construct disrupted but many of the custom tools and molds that he provided to bankrupt suppliers were trapped behind the locked doors of these insolvent businesses. Fortunately, some suppliers accepted delayed payment and Dan's brother lent LoggerHead enough money to meet payroll. Dan stopped paying himself a salary so that he could refrain from firing any of his employees despite there being no economic reason for keeping them onboard.

In any event, Dan persevered. In 2009, Sears agreed to run a test sale of 15,000 Bionic Wrenches. The innovative tool quickly sold out, causing Sears to order 75,000 Bionic Wrenches in 2010. LoggerHead entered into a vendor agreement with Sears whereby terms relating to product specifications, packaging regimens and payment procedures were fully delineated. Issues such as required units and delivery schedules were conveyed from Sears to LoggerHead throughout the year. Grateful for its relationship with Sears, LoggerHead decided not to sell its wrench to Sears's most competitive rivals such as Home Depot and Lowe's. However, the Bionic Wrench was sold to other retailers including Costco, Amazon, Ace Hardware, True Value, and Menards.

Sales of the Bionic Wrench continued to accelerate. In 2011, Sears sold all 300,000 wrenches it had in inventory two weeks before Christmas. Thus, the Bionic Wrench was deemed the most successful and profitable product in Sears's hand tools category that Christmas season. Dan had every reason to believe that 2012 would be the best year yet for selling the Bionic Wrench through Sears. However, notwithstanding the high volumes of wrenches that were sold, Dan wasn't making much money. One reason was that LoggerHead spent about $500,000 on a media purchase to air a television commercial it produced promoting the Bionic Wrench. (Interestingly, Sears required LoggerHead to allow the retailer to make the related media purchases; the discounted rates that Sears received when it bought the air time were not credited back to LoggerHead. Also, when Sears ran out of Bionic Wrenches it shifted some of the funds that LoggerHead contributed to the media purchase to airing commercials for Sears's Craftsman products.)

The upward trajectory of the revenues generated from Sears selling the Bionic Wrench reversed course in 2012. The first troubling sign was that Sears began marketing the Bionic Wrench as a loss leader; prices plunged as did LoggerHead's turnover per unit. Sears benefited—the Bionic Wrench was bringing in droves of customers who were buying a great deal of additional merchandise from the retailer. But, as you will see, much more ominous developments began to unfold.

Sears Slams Brakes on LoggerHead and Steps on Gas with Apex Tools

Sears provided LoggerHead with verbal and written representations that it would purchase at least 300,000 units of the Bionic Wrench in 2012. Additionally, Sears's employees repeatedly told LoggerHead that it would enter into a written supply agreement for 2012. Despite not having obtained an executed purchase order, LoggerHead demonstrated good faith towards its retail partner by taking the necessary measures to ramp up production to meet Sears's forecast. This action was prudent on LoggerHead's part as it simply takes time to produce large volumes of units. Without such forward-thinking, bottlenecks can arise: Some components have long lead times, at least for procuring them at prices approximating reasonableness.[89] Then, on June 20, 2012, tragedy struck. Sears slashed its order by about 99%, to just 2,971 units. No explanations were provided and Dan's email inquiries were left unanswered.

The consequences of losing so much business were devastating for LoggerHead and its partners throughout the supply chain. LoggerHead was stuck with some $500,000 in inventory, much of which had to be discounted. Penn United Technologies alone laid off 31 workers. The number of workers terminated elsewhere in the Bionic Wrench supply chain is not known.

It turns out that Sears was using its radio silence to shield its orchestrating with Apex Tools to stock its shelves with the Max Axess Locking Wrench, a product that highly resembled the Bionic Wrench and was later deemed to infringe LoggerHead's patents. Apex Tools, one of the world's largest manufacturers of tools, arranged for its Max Axess Locking Wrench to be produced in China. The infringing tool retailed under Sears's Craftsman brand for less than half of the price of the Bionic Wrench when it was introduced to the market in September of 2012.

A fan of the Bionic Wrench tipped Dan off about the infringing Max Axess Locking Wrench in November of 2012. Dan immediately scrambled to find a law firm that would be willing to represent LoggerHead on a contingency basis. This was no easy feat as some contingency lawyers are most interested in scoring quick settlements and district courts apply tremendous pressure on patent litigants to settle. Wealthy defendant corporations seize on these dynamics. They proffer settlement proposals that include insultingly low-ball cash payments in return for ongoing royalty-free licenses to all of the plaintiff's intellectual property that the defendant needs. Long story short, Dan was fortunate to retain the law firm of Skiermont Derby. With that firm's help, LoggerHead didn't miss a beat. Dan's company sued Sears and

[89] In litigation, Sears would claim that LoggerHead should not have proceeded with the production of its Bionic Wrench, and thus no liability was to be assigned to Sears, because no firm contract was in place.

Apex Tools in the Northern District of Illinois for patent infringement and other claims such a fraud and trade dress violations in November of 2012.

Apex Tools became the primary defendant when Sears exercised its indemnification provisions in its contract with Apex Tools. One of the first actions taken by Apex Tools was to sue LoggerHead for defamation. Dan had the foresight to bind Skiermont Derby to defend LoggerHead in such suits. Consequently, the defamation suit was quickly thrown out. Other parts of the litigation process were much more painstaking. For instance, Dan was subject to double depositions—both Sears and Apex Tools hired lawyers that drilled Dan in depositions. The LoggerHead CEO found himself spending tons of time fulfilling document discovery requests. During at least one deposition, opposing counsel tried to make Dan read from one specific word of a contract to another specific word in the contract; Dan refused to comply since doing so would have taken the agreement out of context.

During one of Dan's depositions, the lawyer representing Sears asked him to read a sentence out of the Sears UTC (Universal Terms and Conditions) statement that is a boiler plate part of the Supply Agreement. The broader sentence that Dan was instructed to recite reads: "A commitment to purchase Merchandise shall arise only at such time as Company issues a Purchase Order or enters into a separate Vendor Agreement for specific quantities of Merchandise and Company's obligation to purchase Merchandise shall be limited to such quantities." The lawyer directed Dan to read on camera only the following part of the sentence: "A commitment to purchase Merchandise shall arise only at such time as Company issues a Purchase Order."

Dan argued that reading this cherry-picked portion of the sentence would portray a warped version of reality as LoggerHead and Sears were working under the "separate Vendor Agreement for specific quantities" part of that sentence. The lawyer wanted to capture Dan on video saying that an order only existed if there was a "Purchase Order" which contradicts how LoggerHead's business with Sears had been conducted. LoggerHead operated under the separate Vendor Agreement part of that sentence. Realizing that the Sears lawyer was trying to ensnare him in self-impeachment before the jury, Dan refused to recite the selected portion of the sentence.

However, no amount of Apex Tools's subterfuge was able to mask the fact, as evidenced by the jury's decision, that Apex Tools's infringement of two of LoggerHead's patents was premeditated. Sears stalled placing orders for the Bionic Wrench with LoggerHead while it was busy coordinating the delivery of the Max Axess Locking Wrench with Apex Tools. Both defendants knew about the LoggerHead patents. They analyzed the Bionic Wrench and referred to their infringing wrench as the "Bionic 2.0" and "Bionic Replacement." They predicted that the Max Axess Locking Wrench would likely "evoke a response from LoggerHead, Brown Patent 6,889,579, because the product is so close to their Bionic Wrench."

Further, Apex Tools's general counsel recommended that his company "get a formal opinion letter from outside counsel stating that the final design does not infringe…[as] insurance against a claim of willful infringement." This formal opinion letter was just window dressing—the general counsel did not wait for the opinion to manufacture the knock-off. Rather, he instructed the development team: "Do not slow down or hold anything up that you are doing."

Judge Reverses Jury Verdict

In May of 2017, after four-and-a-half years of litigation and nearly two weeks of trial, a federal jury rendered a verdict. The unanimous verdict found that two of LoggerHead's patents were valid and willfully infringed.[90] The damages award amounted to nearly $6 million, with another some $800,000 assessed for related interest charges.

[90] The finding of willful infringement came despite Apex Tools having moved for summary judgment on willfulness under law that was abrogated by the Supreme Court after Apex Tools filed its brief. LoggerHead opposed on that basis and Apex Tools introduced a new theory on reply. LoggerHead was never able to respond to Apex Tools's new theory for summary judgment and the court applied a higher burden of proof compared to what was required under prevailing Supreme Court law.

Nevertheless, a massive injustice was about to be visited upon Dan. For more than seven months, the district court did not enter the jury's verdict or decide the post-trial motions, which included LoggerHead's motion for enhanced damages based on each defendant's egregious and willful infringement. Then, pursuant to an appeal by Sears and Apex Tools, on December 22, 2017, the last business day before Christmas, District Court Judge Pallmeyer, on her own motion, ruled the case a mistrial on the grounds that certain terms used in the patent claims were construed incorrectly. Judge Pallmeyer ordered that a new trial proceed with her new, improper, and untested claim construction. A final order of non-infringement in favor of Sears and Apex was entered.

LoggerHead was shocked to receive this New Trial Order ("NTO"), since neither Sears nor Apex Tools requested a new trial on infringement, and because the order itself was filled with errors. For instance, the NTO impermissibly adopted Sears's version of the facts at trial by siding with Sears's technical expert, even though the jury had indisputably made findings of fact and found for LoggerHead.

LoggerHead timely appealed on August 17, 2018. As I write these pages, LoggerHead awaits its opportunity to make oral arguments before the judges at the Federal Circuit Court of Appeals.

Dan's case of a judge whimsically riding roughshod over a patentee's rights is not unique. Let's consider what happened to Evolutionary Intelligence LLC. This company was issued two patents relating to automating mobile search results. When Evolutionary Intelligence learned that technology titans such as Twitter, Groupon, Sprint, Facebook and Apple were infringing these patents, it filed patent infringement lawsuits in the Eastern District of Texas. The defendants successfully petitioned to move the case to the Northern District of California. But before the case got underway the defendants filed eight requests for *inter partes reviews* at the Patent Trial and Appeal Board. Evolutionary Intelligence successfully defended all of the *inter partes review* proceedings, including an instituted trial, without a single revision to any of its claims. This victory came at a price tag estimated in excess of $1 million.

When the case returned to the California District Court, the court granted the defendants' motion to dismiss the case. In doing so, the California District Court acted as a backstop for slaying the few patents that escape their demise at the PTAB death panel. The court failed to consider any of the underlying facts as found by the PTAB; instead, the court accepted the defendants' characterizations that the patent claims were abstract under 35 U.S.C. §101.

Conclusion

The inordinate amount of time that Dan spent in this litigation will never be returned to him. As I write these pages, no one knows if LoggerHead will receive damages relating to Sears and Apex Tools infringing its patents. Even if it wins and receives treble damages for willful infringement, LoggerHead will not receive more than $20 million. A good portion of any such award will be rightfully shared with Skiermont Derby. But during the nearly seven years that this litigation has been raging, Apex Tools made out alright. It was acquired by Bain Capital for $1.6 billion in 2013.

LoggerHead has the right to pursue Sears for the other causes (e.g., fraud and tortious interference) listed in its initial complaint, but there isn't much point given that Sears filed for bankruptcy protection in October of 2018. As other retailers have come to be aware of LoggerHead's litigation over the years, they have been wary to partner with that company. However, in fairness, LoggerHead did benefit from the publicity arising from its litigation to a limited extent.

GoPro Delivers a Body Blow to Small Inventor

GoPro represents itself as a company that takes social responsibility very seriously. The company that enables sports enthusiasts to film their activities in immersive and exciting ways deploys more than 4,500 words on its website to articulate its dedication to maintaining its pristine ethical hygiene. GoPro rhapsodizes about its supply chain code of conduct as well as its positions on human and labor rights, safety and health, and environmental responsibility.

Here is the San Mateo, California company's statement on intellectual property: "Supplier must commit to respect intellectual property rights, and transfer of technology and know-how is to be done in a manner that protects intellectual property rights." In the third paragraph of the related webpage, GoPro maintains that since its internal compliance team is so well-versed in its corporate code governing social responsibility, "GoPro currently does not need third parties to conduct verifications [of its ethical code]."

But is GoPro's ethical behavior, at least in terms of its commitment to protecting intellectual property rights, really beyond review? Let's consider how Michael Kintner fared in light of GoPro's self-declared irreproachable respect for intellectual property rights.

Inventor Gives Birth to a Successful Company in His Garage

Michael Kintner has been honing his hardware and software designing skills since the late 1980s. Over the ensuing three decades, he also accumulated a vast knowledge of photography and videography. In 2012, Michael melded these disciplines together when he created the first multi-camera rigs; each of his rigs restrain several action cameras in specific arrays. The technology that he created stitches together the images captured by each camera to create 360-degree composite images of the scenes of interest. These breakthroughs were memorialized in a provisional patent application that he filed on November 5, 2012. A corresponding non-provisional patent application was filed on November 5, 2013 and was issued as U.S. Patent No. 9,152,019 on October 6, 2015. The title of this patent is "360-degree camera mount and related photographic and video system."

In 2013, Michael founded 360Heros in his garage in Olean, New York. 360Heros developed and produced high-definition 360-degree video and virtual reality content that enabled users to experience live, real-world activities taking place from around the globe. By connecting their Oculus devices with 360Heros' video hosting centers—or by logging onto Facebook or YouTube—users could simulate scuba diving with sharks, parachuting out of airplanes and spacewalking above the Earth. 360Heros was inducted into the 2015 *Guinness Book of World Records* for shooting the first fully spherical HD 360° video on top of Mount Everest. 360Heros' technology enabled even the most mobility-challenged as well as financially-confined people to enjoy a wide array of unique experiences from the comfort of their couches, or even from wheelchairs.

Within a few years, 360Heros became a successful company. Approximately 10,000 content producers from at least 23 countries were filming with rigs produced by 360Heros. Clients of 360Heros included the Department of Defense, the NAVY, NASA, Paramount Studios, MythBusters, and Stanford University. Many customers made repeat purchases of Michael's rigs; returns were rare. In the middle of the 2010s, 360Heros was chalking up annual growth rates of 50%. At its peak, Michael's company employed eight people and retained another eight contractors. Since its inception, 360Heros sold $7.3 million in camera gear and generated approximately $500,000 in content-related revenue.

Industry Giant Awakes

Michael decided that he needed to protect the 360Heros' brand; thus, he filed a related trademark application with the United States Patent and Trademark Office on May 22, 2013. This trademark application was published for opposition on March 25, 2014. Just a few days before the 30-day window to oppose closed, GoPro filed a petition for an extension of time to oppose the 360Hero trademark application. GoPro initiated a formal opposition proceeding on July 21, 2014. As Michael tells it, GoPro sent him an email stating, "We believe this mark [360Hero] infringes on our HERO mark." GoPro also stated, "while we have been willing to allow you to use the 360Heros product name, we did not at any time agree that you could register 360HEROS as a trademark." GoPro encouraged Michael to abandon his trademark application when it imparted these words via email: "*The simple fact is that you do not need a trademark registration in order to operate your business.*"

Based on GoPro's statements, Michael agreed in good faith to abandon his trademark application on August 14, 2014. 360Heros continued to conduct business under the 360Hero name for the next 20 months. During this time, Michael developed more than 12 different virtual reality 2D and 3D 360-degree video rigs, which contributed to 360Heros becoming the largest virtual reality company in the world in terms of rigs sold. GoPro also worked hard after dissuading Michael from pursuing his 360Hero trademark registration. Within 10 months it released multiple products—including the GoPro Odyssey, Kolor Abyss, and GoPro Omni—that infringed on other of 360Heros' patents and trademarks.

From 360Heros' point of view, GoPro's launch of the Kolor Abyss was particularly galling; much of the $30 million that GoPro paid to acquire Kolor was attributable to 360Heros' intellectual property. How so? Back in 2012 360Heros began discussions for joint-collaboration with French-based Kolor. Once a non-disclosure agreement between 360Heros and Kolor was put in place, Michael shared a great deal of confidential and proprietary information with the French company relating to hardware drawings, patent applications, camera gear and underwater rigs. Also, 360Heros secured a U.S. trademark on "360Abyss" on September 27, 2016. When Kolor began marketing technology it misappropriated from 360Heros under the Kolor Abyss brand, there wasn't much Michael could do. He didn't trademark 360Abyss in France and could not afford the monetary outlays or distractions associated with pursuing breach of contract claims against Kolor in France. But when GoPro acquired Kolor in 2015, the San Mateo company soon began infringing both 360Heros' '019 patent and the 360Abyss trademark when it introduced its Kolor Abyss products in the United States. However, Michael's initial reaction was to refrain from provoking the industry behemoth.

GoPro Files Baseless Infringement Lawsuit

Despite its pervasive infringement, in early 2016, GoPro pressured Michael to cease using the 360Hero name altogether. To demonstrate its resolve in litigating against 360Heros, GoPro showed Michael evidence of its having filed a trademark infringement suit against 360Heros and threatened to serve Michael with notice of such suit unless he rebranded his rigs within 90 days. Michael succumbed to GoPro's pressure: In April of 2016, he rebranded his company (and product) from 360Heros to 360Rize. This rebranding exercise immediately caused 360Heros' website traffic, sales and income to nosedive. Many loyal customers believed that 360Heros folded. Moreover, Michael's accommodative stance was not reciprocated. Far from it. A day or two after he changed the name of his company, GoPro sued 360Heros for past trademark infringement as well as for copyright infringement in federal court in California. (In August of 2016, 360Heros countersued GoPro in federal court in Delaware for infringement of its '019 patent and of its 360Abyss trademark.)

GoPro's charge relative to its trademark complaint was that the "Heros" in the "360Heros" name misled some customers into believing that 360Heros and GoPro were affiliated. This seems like a spurious charge to me. 360Heros sold its 360° virtual reality rigs to virtual reality production companies; these sophisticated buyers could easily distinguish 360Heros' rigs from GoPro's cameras.

Not only was there no confusion about the identities and independence of both GoPro and 360Heros, but 360Heros proved to be a strong generator of GoPro's camera sales. Over $30 million worth of GoPro's cameras have been used in rigs that 360Heros produced since its inception. In fact, some of 360Heros' rigs are specifically designed to harness GoPro cameras. (Some of the rigs produced by 360Heros were not designed to solely accommodate GoPro cameras. Perhaps, GoPro intended to squash 360Heros because some of its rigs were suitable for rival cameras from the likes of YI Technology, Garmin and Kodak.) In addition, Michael believes that GoPro generated an additional $14 million from the sales of its infringing rigs which were introduced to the market in 2015. To provide some perspective of the magnitude of such infringement, the $14 million in sales that GoPro generated from its alleged infringement of 360Heros' rigs is essentially twice as much as 360Heros' rig revenues from 2012 to the middle of 2019.

Let's recap for a moment. GoPro strong-armed Michael into abandoning his 360Hero trademark application. Then, GoPro threatened to sue Michael's company for trademark infringement unless he rebranded his products and company. As soon as Michael acceded to GoPro's demands, the industry giant sued 360Heros (the company that generated at least $30 million worth of sales of GoPro's cameras) for trademark and copyright infringement.

But wait. We are just scratching the surface of GoPro's duplicity.

The craziest thing is that GoPro never registered the "HERO" trademark (at least not in the United States) that it used to bully Michael and 360Heros. I conducted a trademark search on the United States Patent and Trademark Office's website and could not find any evidence of the USPTO assigning a "HERO" trademark to GoPro. Michael confirmed that GoPro did not register the "HERO" trademark at the time it initiated trademark infringement litigation against 360Heros; rather, GoPro's complaints were solely based on what it believed were common law rights to the "HERO" mark.[91]

GoPro Unleashes Litigation Fury

One might think that GoPro would appreciate the $30 million in sales that 360Heros generated on its behalf. Logic might hold that in view of its self-professed ethical unassailability, GoPro would cease selling infringing rigs once 360Heros put it on notice; 360Heros put GoPro on notice when it filed its countersuit in California in April of 2016. One might believe that, if GoPro doubted the accuracy or veracity of the complaints filed by

---

[91] In the summer of 2019, GoPro's website stated that it owned the "HERO" and "Be a HERO" trademarks. Again, I could find no evidence of GoPro registering such trademarks. GoPro did file a trademark application on "GoPro Be a HERO" but that trademark application was abandoned on February 20, 2014. I sent GoPro emails asking for registration numbers of the trademarks it declared that it owns but, as of the time of my writing these pages, have not received a response. In any event, GoPro sued 360Hero because it professed to believe that 360Hero would cause confusion with its common law rights in its HERO mark. Purporting to own trademarks in which it only has common law rights may fall within the strict definition of owning trademarks (and therefore be legally permissible) but it is a practice (only undertaken by GoPro, as far as I can tell) that publicly-traded companies should avoid because it is misleading to investors.

360Heros, GoPro would make some effort to enter into an amiable dialog to resolve the dispute. One might believe that GoPro would exhibit some mercy towards Michael in view of his having abandoned his trademark application as well as having rebranded his company and products—all based on GoPro misrepresenting its registration of a "HERO" trademark.

Quite the opposite was the case. GoPro did everything it could to use trademark and copyright litigation as tools to discredit and bankrupt Michael's company as well as to obtain the free use of 360Heros' patents. (Michael told me that his lawyers reviewed documents from GoPro stating that its intention was to drive 360Heros out of business.) During the California litigation, GoPro made numerous efforts to prevent the admissibility of documents favorable to 360Heros; one such document was a signed GoPro book from its staff, indicating how much they loved 360Heros' work.

GoPro directed a tsunami of services of process, depositions and court motions towards 360Heros. To maximize Michael's personal pain, legal papers were served on holidays, his birthday and the birthdays of his family members. To maximize 360Heros' financial pain, papers were served immediately before multiple crucial tradeshows. In some cases, responding to these court papers was so onerous that Michael had to withdraw from the shows that must have cost as much as $15,000 when taking into account lost deposits and the expenses associated with the development of exhibits. GoPro deposed large numbers of experts in attempts to invalidate the '019 patent and to drain 360Heros financially. As was its prerogative, GoPro filed for declaratory judgment of non-infringement of 360Heros' '019 patent in the Northern District of California in April of 2016.[92]

GoPro's litigation against 360Heros took some pretty bizarre turns.[93]

---

[92] This claim, and 360Heros' subsequent counterclaim for infringement of the '019 patent, also in the Northern District of California, was dismissed without prejudice on November 14, 2017 because that court found that Michael did not assign the '019 patent to 360Heros until October 2016. Dismissal on such grounds seems unjust to me: Michael assigned the '019 Patent to 360Heros in October of 2016, nearly a year before 360Heros filed the original complaint in the present lawsuit.

[93] One bizarre (and tragic) event tangentially related to this story is that one of GoPro's outside lawyers, Jim Gilliland of Kirkpatrick Townsend, was shot dead on his front porch in July of 2017. To my knowledge, there are no known motives or suspects.

For instance, before litigation got underway, one of GoPro's dealers—a Rochester, New York company called RU4 Scuba—furnished 360Heros with images showing how 360Heros' rigs accommodated GoPro cameras. Why? Because RU4 Scuba wanted to be the conduit through which 360Heros would purchase more GoPro cameras. Indeed, 360Heros had purchased about $600,000 worth of GoPro cameras through RU4 Scuba. Even though 360Heros generated sales of GoPro cameras from its website, GoPro accused 360Heros of misappropriating the copyrighted images that RU4 Scuba furnished to 360Heros. GoPro even pressured RU4 Scuba and one other distributor to sign a letter attesting to their having never given 360Heros permission to use their images. Tellingly, despite enormous pressure from GoPro, both channel partners refused to sign the illicit document.

What makes GoPro's allegations of 360Heros misappropriating copyrighted images even more interesting is that GoPro's lawyers discovered details about the Rochester dealer conveying images to 360Heros under Michael's "Attorney Eyes Only" deposition. The terms of such depositions hold that GoPro should never have known what transpired during Michael's deposition, only its lawyers. It doesn't seem to me that there are that many dots to connect: GoPro's lawyers must have violated the "Attorney Eyes Only" terms of the deposition. But the judge seemed to believe that GoPro's coming into possession of such intimate details relating to the conveyance of the images in question was just a matter of happenstance as he refused to sanction GoPro or its attorneys.

Separately, during the patent and trademark litigation in 2018, GoPro referenced two Skype calls that took place between Michael and Alexandre Jenny, founder of Kolor, in 2014. GoPro claimed that since Michael did not mention that 360Heros was using the 360Abyss name during these Skype calls, Kolor had the right to use that name. Michael holds that he did mention his company's use of the 360Abyss name during these Skype sessions. (Michael filed a U.S. trademark application on 360Abyss on November 24, 2014.) Eight months after these Skype calls took place, Kolor began using the Kolor Abyss name. In the 2018 litigation, GoPro argued that Michael altered documents demonstrating his mentioning 360Heros' use of the 360Abyss name during the 2014 Skype calls with Kolor's founder.

However, citing a French privacy law, Michael was not allowed to review evidence that Kolor presented to the court regarding his alleged altering of records of the Skype sessions. Nonetheless, Judge Susan Illston sanctioned

Michael for lying to the court; he was ordered to pay for GoPro's expert witness that opined on the authenticity of the related Skype transcripts. It seems that GoPro's bigger strategy with introducing these two Skype calls into the litigation and with its motions for sanctioning 360Heros was to discredit Michael throughout the balance of the litigation.

Michael Mortgages Everything

As litigation heated up, 360Heros' fortunes continued to plummet. Michael's attention was diverted from running his business to extricating his company from the legal minefield that GoPro was sowing. Michael ceased retaining independent contractors and downsized his employee count. (As I write these pages, 360Heros is staffed solely by Michael and one other employee.)

No longer able to rely on whatever cash flow his business had been generating, Michael took to building up the war chest he needed to combat GoPro. He poured his life savings of $289,000 into his litigation efforts and placed two mortgages on his house. (I asked Michael about the profitability of 360Heros but he declined to comment on this sensitive issue. But he did state that 360Heros generated at least $7.3 million in revenue. Given that his life savings stood at $289,000, 360Heros couldn't have been very profitable—maybe not profitable at all.) He also took out massive loans; some $500,000 in Small Business Administration Loans and roughly another $150,000 in lines of credit. Realizing that GoPro was killing his cash cows, Michael directed some of these proceeds towards developing a new camera called the 360Penguin. Third, Michael retained SpencePC to represent 360Heros on a contingency basis. Fourth, Michael was fortunate that, at least in the beginning, 360Heros' general liability insurance carrier bankrolled much of its initial litigation costs.

GoPro Moves to Shut Off 360Heros' Air Supply

GoPro made significant efforts to asphyxiate 360Heros. One example of GoPro trying to cut off 360Heros' financing involves the relationship between 360Heros and its insurance carrier, Mainstreet America Assurance. Mainstreet was initially extremely supportive of 360Heros' litigation efforts; it defended 360Heros to the tune of nearly $3 million. Michael related to me that he understood that there was no limit on 360Heros' business liability insurance. However, according to my discussions with Michael, GoPro contacted Mainstreet and leaned on that insurer to cease defending 360Heros. This pressure tactic proved to be effective; Michael lost his suit against Mainstreet for unlawfully withdrawing from its prior agreement with 360Heros. As a result, Michael is on the hook to pay his attorney a remaining balance of $250,000.

After Mainstreet ceased covering 360Heros' litigation costs, GoPro lost in claims construction hearings, where it was trying to establish that it was not infringing claims included in the '019 patent. Shortly thereafter, GoPro attempted to get the patent dismissed from the California case even though GoPro initially added the patent to the case. Michael believes that GoPro's sole purpose in executing this gambit was to force him to defend the '019 patent again at a later date without Mainstream's support.

It is true that GoPro and 360Heros reached a settlement in May of 2018 relating to 360Heros' alleged infringement of GoPro's common law, but non-registered, "HERO" trademark. GoPro also agreed to cease using 360Heros' 360Abyss trademark but, as of at least the summer of 2019, continued to infringe that mark—again claiming common law rights to the word "Abyss." GoPro also agreed to pay 360Heros $10,000 as part of the settlement but wanted that payment conditioned on receiving a royalty-free license to the '019 patent. 360Heros refused to acquiesce to the condition of GoPro's ongoing use of its '019 patent. Shortly thereafter, GoPro dutifully mailed a $10,000 check to 360Rise. But a day or two later, GoPro stopped payment on that check, causing Michael's company to bear hundreds of dollars in insufficient funds fees.

The San Mateo company also made concerted efforts to create a wedge between 360Heros and SpencePC, the Olean, New York company's contingency patent lawyers. GoPro took numerous steps to increase SpencePC's costs to a point where that firm would not be able to recover its investments in representing 360Heros. According to GoPro documents reviewed by 360Heros' lawyers, GoPro calculated that its strategy of running up litigation costs would pressure SpencePC to resign from the case.[94] One manifestation of this strategy arose when GoPro filed motions

---

[94] Here is a direct quote from one of GoPro's attorneys: "Even if 360Heros is not paying attorneys' fees in the Delaware litigation, it will soon have to incur and pay costs, including for among other things, experts and discovery. Likewise, to the extent that Spence PC has been retained on contingency, it will be unlikely to recover on its investment in the case."

to move the trial from Delaware to California—where the jury would likely lean towards the San Mateo-based company.

PTAB Institutes Delinquent Inter Partes Review Petition

GoPro, as was its right, attempted to invalidate 360Heros' '019 patent by filing a petition for *inter partes review* in September of 2018. The fact that GoPro filed its petition for *inter partes review* in September of 2018 instead of when the first countersuit was filed in April of 2016 supports the contention that GoPro was calculating to grind Michael down over a long period of time. If another one of GoPro's ulterior motives of filing its *inter partes review* petition was to exhaust Michael's funds and to cause SpencePC to remove itself from representing 360Heros in those proceedings, it achieved those goals. Shortly after forking over his last $30,000 to his lawyers to begin representing 360Heros in the PTAB proceedings, SpencePC withdrew its representation of 360Heros before that tribunal. (Fortunately for Michael, SpencePC continues to represent 360Heros in other parts of the litigation. Also, Josh Malone of Bunch O' Balloons fame provided financial assistance to 360Heros in its PTAB proceedings and the John Marshall Law Clinic expressed an interest in representing 360Heros pro bono.)

What was particularly disturbing with GoPro's *inter partes review* filing was that the PTAB agreed to institute the petition even though it was filed delinquently. Remember that this petition was filed in September of 2018, about 13 months after GoPro's time to file the IPR expired in August of 2017. (The governing statute clearly precludes institution of an IPR more than one year after "a party receives notice through official delivery of a complaint in a civil action, irrespective of subsequent events." Thus, the time bar was set in August of 2016, when 360Heros countersued GoPro for patent infringement in California. Shortly before I went to press, the panel that sets precedent for PTAB decided that the one-year window to file an *inter partes review* petition begins when an infringement complaint is filed, even if the plaintiff lacked standing or the complaint has other defects.)

When GoPro filed its *inter partes review* petition, it challenged six of the 24 claims in the '019 patent. GoPro was able to freeze its litigation with 360Heros in Delaware in June of 2019 when, citing its initial IPR proceeding, it won a six month stay. Michael is concerned that GoPro purposely challenged only 25% of the claims in September of 2018 so that it will have the opportunity to further delay the litigation. Because each

IPR proceeding takes one year (or possibly as long as 18 months if good cause is demonstrated), IPR petitions provide GoPro the opportunity to seek additional stays in its litigation against 360Heros, and costs Michael $450,000, win or lose.

Conclusion

When I spoke with Michael in the summer of 2019, he and 360Heros were in a state of limbo. It really didn't matter what inventions he developed or how many customers 360Heros attracted. If GoPro is able to invalidate critical claims in the '019 patent during *inter partes review*, 360Heros will be dead in the water. Even if 360Heros prevails in its *inter partes review* proceedings, unless that company receives additional help funding its litigation, there is a good chance that 360Heros will have to close its doors. I can understand how even the most driven entrepreneur and inventor would lose his desire to pursue his business interests as ruinous patent invalidity attempts and litigation hang over his head. Even if the challenged claims in the '019 patent are upheld and 360Heros wins its Delaware case against GoPro—for patent infringement and infringement of the 360Abyss trademark—it will be extremely difficult for 360Heros to regain its momentum.

360Heros is far from the only company that has alleged that GoPro infringed its intellectual property. C&A Marketing, which had exclusive rights to Polaroid's Cube action camera, sued GoPro over the similarities of GoPro's Session product in late 2015. Contour sued GoPro for patent infringement related to its remote viewfinder feature, which wirelessly connects cameras to smartphones so that users can see what is being recorded. Also, despite entering into a co-promotional agreement with Dinkum Systems in the spring of 2012, Dinkum felt compelled to sue GoPro for patent infringement: GoPro's Jaws Flex Clamp, a flexible, ball-jointed camera mount, allegedly infringed the patents covering Dinkum's ActionPod.

Further, 360Heros is not the only company to have been subjected to GoPro's warped enforcement of its intellectual property: In March of 2013, GoPro issued a Digital Millennium Copyright Act takedown notice to website DigitalRev.com, which had posted a comparative review of GoPro and Sony action cameras. GoPro claimed that the use of a GoPro trademark in DigitalRev.com's comparative review was a copyright violation. The DMCA notice was heavy-handed. Under the DMCA, offenders' Internet providers are required to shut down access to offending websites within 24 hours, no questions asked, unless the URL is taken down. In any event, GoPro's notice was retracted 10 days later, citing "erroneous enforcement."

GoPro has clearly made life miserable for a number of inventors and even its own dealers and distributors. GoPro has also made life miserable for (possibly tens of) thousands of its own shareholders. When GoPro began its opposition to Michael's 360Hero trademark application on July 21, 2014, its stock closed at $41.98. As I write these pages, GoPro shares are trading at $5.46. That company lost gobs of money in 2016, 2017, and 2018. Perhaps if GoPro was more focused on bringing its own innovations to the market instead of litigating against inventors, its shareholders would not have suffered such dramatic losses.

Postscript

Each reader has the right to their opinion as to who, GoPro or Michael, acted more ethically. (Professor Cherkoff, who you met in Part I of this book, believes that GoPro acted more ethically.) If you base one's ethical position solely on self-characterization, GoPro wins hands down. That company uses 4,500 words to bloviate about its ethics on its website whereas I couldn't find anything about 360Rize's ethical standards on its website. But if you deem one's character as a function of how one behaves, rather than how one says he behaves, you might come to a different conclusion.

In my opinion, companies should be judged on their actions not on the feel-good, politically correct applause lines they disingenuously purvey. Entrepreneurs and inventors should be judged on the products they bring to the market and the wealth they create rather than the extent to which they embrace ethical exhortations. One metric by which one's ethics can be judged is how one satisfies his financial obligations. GoPro stopped payment on its $10,000 settlement check, causing it to bounce. This below-the-belt tactic was designed to further humiliate and demoralize a company whose registered intellectual property it infringed and which was the recipient of litigation based on an unregistered trademark. In contrast, despite 360Heros hanging on by a thread after having been reduced to a skeletal version of its former might, Michael is still current on his small business loans, credit lines and multiple mortgage payments.

As a further postscript, Michael mentioned that his daughters have ideas for inventions but are discouraged from developing them after witnessing how their father has been abused by the current patent system. The USPTO has some well-intentioned initiatives to help more women become patentees. (In my opinion, discrimination is discrimination is discrimination. The USPTO should not, in any way, be in the business of finagling the allocation of patents to any particular group of inventors.) The USPTO would encourage more women—and men as well as people of every gender identity and ethnicity—to become patentees if the patent regime became more equitable to all inventors.

Acknowledgments

If you have made it this far, you probably realized that I do not confine my thinking or writing to the narrow confines of political correctness. Some of the content in this book could be perceived as controversial. Thus, I will do the injustice of depriving the many people that were of immense assistance to me in researching and writing Plight of the Patentee the credit they deserve in an effort to shield them from any unwanted attention.

I would like to thank my father, Dr. Lawrence Wanetick, for reading my manuscript and giving me such important feedback. My father challenged many of my thoughts and pointed out the sections of the book that could be written in a clearer manner.

My editor Nikki was instrumental in all aspects of editing and producing Plight of the Patentee. Nikki proved invaluable in editing the manuscript and shielded me from the gritty mechanics associated with publishing this book.

Most importantly, I must thank my wife, Neomi, for allowing me to pursue this project. I know my preoccupation with Plight of the Patentee made the last twenty months or so difficult for Neomi. She has always been supportive of my pursuing my passions and has had to take on more of the family workload in my absence. I must also tell my children (Daniel, Zoe and Zachary) how much I missed them when this project took me away from them. I am very pleased to see them turning into young adults.

About the Author

David Wanetick has valued thousands of patents for Fortune 100 companies, start-ups, university technology transfer offices, national laboratories, and institutional investors. David is a Managing Director at a boutique investment bank, where he is active in capital raises as well as facilitating acquisitions. He developed and runs the Certified Patent Valuation Analyst designation. He is the author of seven books including Solution Nation: One Nation is Disproportionately Responding to the World's Most Intractable Problems; The Strategic Negotiator: A Manual for Negotiating at the Elite Level; and, Business Model Validation: What Makes Business Models Work.

www.ingramcontent.com/pod-product-compliance
Lightning Source LLC
LaVergne TN
LVHW102226300926
849160LV00005B/34